Cambridge Studies in Social and Emotional Development

General Editor: Martin L. Hoffman

Advisory Board: Nicholas Blurton Jones, Robert N. Emde, Willard W. Hartup, Robert A. Hinde, Lois W. Hoffman, Carroll E. Izard, Jerome Kagan, Franz J. Monks, Paul Mussen, Ross D. Parke, and Michael Rutter

Children in time and place

Each generation of American children across the tumultuous twentieth century has come of age in a very different world. How do major historical events – such as war or the depression – influence children's development? *Children in Time and Place* brings together social historians and developmentalists to explore the implications of a changing society for children's growth and life chances. Transitions provide a central theme, from historical transitions to the social transitions of children and their developmental experience.

This book has two stories to tell – one about children growing up and coming of age in various times and places and another about how collaboration worked across the disciplines of history and psychology. *Children in Time and Place* begins with studies that link historical and life transitions in children's lives, with an emphasis on wartime experience. It turns to studies of historical variation in the effect of life transitions, from the onset of sexual experience in girls' lives to the transition to fatherhood in boys', and it concludes by introducing the reader to the collaborative efforts involved in the workshop that led to the volume.

Children in time and place

Developmental and historical insights

Edited by

GLEN H. ELDER, JR.
University of North Carolina at Chapel Hill

JOHN MODELL
Carnegie Mellon University

ROSS D. PARKE
University of California at Riverside

CAMBRIDGE
UNIVERSITY PRESS

Published by the Press Syndicate of the University of Cambridge
The Pitt Building, Trumpington Street, Cambridge CB2 IRP
40 West 20th Street, New York, NY 10011-4211, USA
10 Stamford Road, Oakleigh, Melbourne 3166, Australia

© Cambridge University Press 1993

First published 1993
First paperback edition 1994

Printed in the United States of America

Library of Congress Cataloging-in-Publication Data is available.

A catolog record for this book is available from the British Library.

ISBN 0-521-41784-8 hardback
ISBN 0-521-47801-4 paperback

Contents

Preface

This volume represents the culmination of a long journey that began in the fall of 1983 with a working group on child development at the Social Science Research Council (SSRC). The group proposed a view of children and child development that extends across the life span and the settings of a rapidly changing world. At the time, contemporary studies of children were beginning to show more appreciation for a life-span view of child development, but little progress had been achieved in studying children in historical time. The senior editor of the current volume proposed a project that would bring developmental studies and social history together in the study of children. This book is a result of that venture.

The study of children in historical time and place identifies an important and neglected perspective in the ecology of human development. Psychologists assess the nature of the social world in terms of the child or individual. They ask, What social influences are relevant to specific developmental processes, such as children's thinking or perceiving, and to developmental outcomes, such as achievement or aggression? By comparison, historians, sociologists, and anthropologists are more likely to view the social environment as a research problem in its own right. From this perspective, they would trace the behavioral influences of a specific time and perhaps place, such as the impact of the Great Depression on a small community, to the experiences of children within particular families and neighborhoods. Their inquiry begins with the larger social context and its implications for children. The research venture resulting in this book was guided primarily by this social-historical perspective.

Other differences between social history and developmental psychology are worth noting. For example, historians try to evoke a sense of human experience in a changing world for a broad audience, and they do so with attention to the particularities of historical time and place. They focus, as a matter of course, on those characteristics of a social context that might promote distinctive patterns of development among the inhabitants. On the other hand, drawing from the biological and social sciences, developmental psychologists seek to advance theory and knowledge about the developmental process in general, with aspirations for the discovery of invariant processes and principles. Though aware of these points of difference, we had good reason to believe that the historical thinking on families and children could and would promote more sophisticated studies of children's social world than have been observed to date. Moreover, a newly emerging perspective on the life course provided a way to achieve this end by linking social history to children's experience.

Our objectives here concern the substance of the journey and its outcomes as well as the collaboration process of the research enterprise itself. Empirical results from our cross-disciplinary collaborations were discussed and worked out over 6 years (1984–90) through research meetings, long-distance communications, and conferences. Our final products were anything but easy or straightforward to achieve. In part, this situation reflects the lack of prior intellectual exchange between the fields. Developmental psychology and social history may both have been actively engaged in studies of children, but we found them very nearly as far apart on collaboration as any two fields could be in the social sciences (though, fortunately, not in opposition on key paradigmatic points). For the most part, professional contact between history and the interdisciplinary field of child development was nonexistent at the time of our initial proposal.

Our first step toward a cross-disciplinary project involved a planning session at the Social Science Research Council in New York City on January 17, 1984. Co-chaired by two developmentalists, Glen H. Elder, Jr., and Ross D. Parke, the group also included three social historians, John Modell and Peter N. Stearns from Carnegie Mellon University and William Tuttle, Jr., of the University of Kansas, and a staff person, Lonnie Sherrod, a developmental psychologist and now Vice President for Research at the W. T. Grant Foundation. Following a lengthy exchange of views concerning fruitful means of interaction between the two fields, a plan for action emerged that included cross-disciplinary exchanges on key topics to be followed by a conference. The central theme of the conference, which was held at the SSRC in October 1985, concerned the major social changes of the twentieth century and their effects on children's development and lives. In lieu of delivering formal papers, the participants discussed research topics involving major historical events and developmental processes as well as a more collaborative agenda requiring both developmentalists and historians to work on the same project.

Consistent with this objective, the entire group met 2 years later (October 1987) at the Belmont Center, Oak Ridge, Maryland, with prepared papers based on their cross-disciplinary collaboration. Out of this working group came the substance of the chapters in this volume, the final stage of a lengthy and challenging research program. We believe that knowledge of this collaborative process is essential for a complete understanding of the results we achieved and report. With this in mind, we present our empirical chapters in Parts II and III and then take the reader through the collaborative process itself in Part IV. Some readers may wish to alter this sequence by turning first to our description of the research enterprise in Part IV.

We are pleased to bring the fruits of our labors to this volume. We trust that developmentalists and historians will take other steps in the collaborative study of children and their lives across time and place.

Glen H. Elder, Jr.
John Modell
Ross D. Parke

Acknowledgments

In this collaborative project of many years duration, our trail of indebtedness and gratitude is long indeed. The initial idea became a possibility when colleagues from the Social Science Research Council (SSRC) Committee on Life-Course Perspectives on Human Development and its Subcommittee on Child Development in Life-Span Perspective voted to approve a planning meeting in January 1984. The Foundation for Child Development generously provided funds for this venture and for a multidisciplinary conference held in October 1985 at SSRC headquarters in New York. Viviana Zelizer, Carl Kaestle, and Orville G. Brim, Jr., made valuable contributions to this session. The first editor is indebted to the National Institutes of Mental Health for a research scientist award that provided time for this project. We could not have managed the logistics of this organizational stage without the superb staff assistance of Lonnie Sherrod at SSRC. Even after official SSRC sponsorship ended, Lonnie's counsel proved to be critical in the development of this venture. We are delighted that he is carrying on this vital leadership role in multidisciplinary efforts at the W. T. Grant Foundation in the role of vice president in charge of research.

At the New York meeting, we made plans for the next phase of cross-disciplinary projects and a conference in which to discuss the resulting manuscripts. We were on our own in securing funds for this part of the operation and turned to the Interdisciplinary Studies Committee of the Society for Research in Child Development and the National Endowment for the Humanities. Fortunately, these agencies generously approved our proposal, thereby enabling us to reassemble the teams of historians and developmentalists at the Belmont estate outside Baltimore for an intensive conference. Frances Horowitz sent us notes and commentary that were very helpful in the conference, and she, Michael Lamb, and Arnold Sameroff gave yeoman service as discussants. We are grateful for all of this support and for the special hospitality of the Belmont Conference Center.

An undertaking of this sort involves a wide range of skills, from organizational to clerical to editorial. We relied on the expert clerical work of Tanya Rogers at Carnegie Mellon University and Julie Locascio at the Carolina Population Center, University of North Carolina at Chapel Hill, and on the superb editorial assistance of Lynn Igoe at the center. Doris Helbig and Laurie Leadbetter of the center's library were of invaluable assistance in the final push of getting the copyedited manuscript back to the press. At Cambridge University Press, we have been blessed with a nurturing editorial team led by Julia Hough. She made this project feasible and rewarding.

Last but not least, we want to salute our collaborators, who maintained their faith in this project as we moved toward and into uncharted territory. To encourage more work of this kind, we dedicate the book and our share of the proceeds from its sales to the mission of the Interdisciplinary Studies Committee of the Society for Research in Child Development.

Contributors

Joan Jacobs Brumberg
Department of Human Development and
  Family Studies
College of Human Ecology
Cornell University
Ithaca, NY

Emily Cahan
Division of Continuing Education
Harvard University
Cambridge, MA

Robert B. Cairns
Department of Psychology
University of North Carolina at Chapel
  Hill
Chapel Hill, NC

Glen H. Elder, Jr.
Department of Sociology and Carolina
  Population Center
University of North Carolina at Chapel
  Hill
Chapel Hill, NC

Tamara K. Hareven
Department of Individual and Family
  Studies
University of Delaware
Newark, DE

William Kessen
Department of Psychology
Yale University
New Haven, CT

Jay Mechling
American Studies Program
University of California
Davis, CA

John Modell
Department of History
Carnegie Mellon University
Pittsburgh, PA

Ross D. Parke
Department of Psychology
University of California at Riverside
Riverside, CA

Steven Schlossman
Department of History
Carnegie Mellon University
Pittsburgh, PA

Robert S. Siegler
Department of Psychology
Carnegie Mellon University
Pittsburgh, PA

Peter N. Stearns
Department of History
Carnegie Mellon University
Pittsburgh, PA

Ruth Striegel-Moore
Department of Psychology
Wesleyan University
Middletown, CT

Brian Sutton-Smith
Department of Folklore and Mythology
Graduate School of Education
University of Pennsylvania
Philadelphia, PA

William M. Tuttle, Jr.
Department of History
University of Kansas
Lawrence, KS

Sheldon H. White
Department of Psychology
Harvard University
Cambridge, MA

Michael Zuckerman
Department of History
University of Pennsylvania
Philadelphia, PA

Part I

A proposal

1　Studying children in a changing world

Glen H. Elder, Jr., John Modell, and Ross D. Parke

> Developmental researchers have been carrying on a clandestine affair with
> Clio . . . the muse of history. . . . It is time we embraced her as a legitimate
> partner in our creative scientific efforts.
> > Urie Bronfenbrenner and Anne Crouter (1983, p. 394)

Across the twentieth century each generation of American children has come of
age in a different world of realities. The differences are typically expressed
through the experiences of families and the lives of parents, as when migration
from farm to city placed children in social worlds unimagined by their parents.
The Great Depression made families and children materially insecure; then, mass
mobilization in World War II removed fathers from countless households over a
period of years. Prosperity in postwar America meant that children of the depression had moved in one lifetime "from scarcity to abundance, from sacrifice to
the freedoms made possible by prosperity" (Elder, 1974, p. 296). Such changes
add proper caution to generalizations from one historical era to another and
underscore the need to bring historical insights to the developmental study of
children. The developmental significance of this link stems from a widely recognized connection between children's lives and their ever-changing world.·

The question of how to achieve studies that are informed by both historical and
developmental insights prompted this volume and its research project during the
1980s. We gave this matter a good deal of thought at the time. One approach
would be to educate developmentalists in the theory and practice of historical
work, thereby producing something akin to an interdisciplinary perspective within the investigator's mind. As illustrated by the study *Children of the Great
Depression* (Elder, 1974), the joining of historical and developmental insights
and expertise avoids the collaborative problems of multidisciplinary teams. This
fusion, however, is perhaps more readily achieved during graduate or postgradu-
ate studies than during a well-established career.

An alternative regime would be to provide training in developmental or psychological science for historians, a design commonplace among the practitioners

3

of psychohistory. Runyan (1988) has written a primer for such education. As he puts it (p. 43), "A psychologically informed history is crucial for addressing" important issues of historiography, including the relation between human agency and social constraints, the psychological process of groups and their members, and the persistence of behavior patterns.

In contrast to these models, we chose the approach of a multidisciplinary team, comprised of social historians and developmentalists, who would be invited to form collaborative research units. The rationale for this decision has much to do with the multidisciplinary philosophy of the Social Science Research Council (SSRC) in New York. Each of us came to this joint venture with prior experience on SSRC committees. As members of the SSRC Subcommittee on Child Development in Life-Span Perspective, Ross D. Parke (a developmental psychologist with an ecological perspective) and Glen H. Elder, Jr. (a sociological developmentalist with roots in social history) are advocates of what Kreppner and Lerner (1989, p. 2) call the "contextualization of human development." John Modell, a social historian with sociological and demographic training, served on the Social Indicators Committee of the SSRC and has a long record of multidisciplinary collaborations that share the contextual objective.

In our own way, we are participating in the emergence of a life-course perspective that has brought greater attention to temporal and contextual distinctions in the study of families, of children, and of human development generally. In concept, the *life course* refers to the age-graded life patterns that are embedded in social institutions and subject to historical change. These patterns are defined by *trajectories,* which extend across much of the life course, such as family and work, and by *transitions,* or short-term changes, such as leaving home for school, getting a full-time job, and marrying. Family transitions invariably place the life course in a broader matrix of kinship relationships, one that extends beyond the boundaries of the immediate family to in-laws and grandparents.

We found the concept of transition useful in thinking about the relationship between children's lives and their social world and in working up an agenda for the history-developmental group. Transitions occur in the course of social change and in lives, and in many cases the two are intimately related, as when mass unemployment in the 1930s was experienced as job loss by individuals. Likewise, the mobilization of military personnel in wartime is encountered by individuals through induction into the armed services. Historical and life transitions are "disturbances of habit," to use W. I. Thomas's colorful phrase (1909, pp. 13–26), and thus they represent strategic opportunities for understanding the link between lives and times. Examples appear throughout the empirical studies in this volume.

At our initial meeting on the project, both the social historians and the developmental psychologists were already actively engaged in studies of children, but we found them to be as isolated from each other as scholars in any two fields in the social sciences could be. There are many explanations for this separation, though we are convinced that the lack of contact owes more to the nature of academia in America and to the formal structure of inquiry in the two fields than to the substantive concerns of the fields or to their modes of inquiry. The roots of child development are in individual psychology, the biological sciences, and experimental psychology (social or otherwise), whereas social history draws its internal structure, goals, and critical standards from its mother discipline and many of its methods from sociology, demography, and anthropology. Historians aim to evoke a sense of the human experience in the course of social change for a broad audience; psychologists seek to advance theory and knowledge of generalizable developmental processes. Despite and even because of their differences, we were and are persuaded that the two fields need to share each other's sensibilities in studying children.

For developmental studies of children, the uses of history extend from increased sensitivity to the contexts of behavior – historical or not – to the actual incorporation of a historical perspective in the approach itself. The importance of historical insights is most vividly shown by those studies that have neglected them and by contextual variations more generally. In the sections that follow, we cite prominent examples of such neglect. We then survey those applications of historical analysis that paved the way for projects like this one by establishing key features of a life-course perspective. We close by reviewing the contents of this volume around the theme of multidisciplinary collaboration.

Children out of context

The pioneering longitudinal studies of American children were launched in 1928 and 1931, at a time when psychologists frequently studied children out of context. Three longitudinal studies at the University of California at Berkeley (Eichorn, Clausen, Haan, Honzik, & Mussen, 1981) were initiated by staff of the old Institute of Child Welfare (now the Institute of Human Development): the Berkeley Growth Study and the Berkeley Guidance Study, both with birth years 1928–29, and the Oakland Growth Study, with birth years 1920–21. All three birth cohorts (people born at the same time) have been followed up to their later years across a period of dramatic social change. However, this larger world did not inform the original conceptual models of these projects.

Children in the Berkeley and Oakland cohorts grew up in the Great Depression and experienced the mobilization of World War II, but neither of these historical periods was perceived as relevant to developmental issues at the time. Nevertheless, the investigators collected some information on the larger environment, and, years later, these data provided the basis for empirical studies of the impact of depression hard times and wartime experience on lives (Elder, 1974, 1979, 1981). This work is continuing, tracing the long-term influences of these times to the later years.

A similar story of the study of child development out of context is told by the records of the Lewis Terman sample of gifted Californians born mainly between 1904 and 1917 (Oden, 1968; Terman, 1925). Selected as exceptional children (IQ above 135) from schools in the survey, study members were first questioned with their parents in 1922 and then again in 1928. Other follow-ups occurred about 5 years apart up to the mid-1980s. Over 900 men and women completed forms in 1982. A large number of the men had finished school and started careers in the Great Depression, and nearly half had entered the armed forces during World War II. Depression and war thus defined their collective life for a continuous period of 15 years. Even so, the Terman study almost succeeded in not collecting any systematic information on the sample's depression experiences, and it paid very little attention to the home front and overseas experiences of wartime Americans.

Blindness to social history and context was not restricted to psychologists. Indeed, prominent sociologists, specialists in contextual sensitivity, were equally blind to social-historical realities. Consider August Hollingshead's *Elmtown's Youth* (1949), a study of social class and life chances in the social world of adolescence in a small midwestern community, circa 1941–42. When Hollingshead and his research team arrived in Elmtown, the community had just begun to recover from nearly 10 years of hardship in the Great Depression. It was a time of concern for one's life chances – the chances lost and perhaps regained in the depression and the chances threatened by the military requirements of a global war. National statistics on the birth cohort of 1923–24 suggest that 8 out of every 10 Elmtown boys who had graduated from or left high school by 1941 were in uniform by the end of the war. Young women entered the work force in large numbers, especially in war-related industries. Instead of relating these developments to the life experience of Elmtown's youth, Hollingshead focused on the social structure of the town and its consequences for adolescents from the upper middle class to the lowest economic stratum of society.

Elmtown's Youth offers a vivid portrait of adolescent social stratification and documents the control functions of age and class in adolescent behavior. It gives four themes special attention: (1) the social ambiguity and status contradictions of the adolescent life stage, a poorly defined no-man's-land; (2) competition and conflict among youth-training institutions; (3) age segregation as a social control mechanism; and (4) class variation in the transition to adult status.

Fieldwork in Elmtown disclosed few widely shared concepts in the community regarding the lower or upper boundaries of adolescence, other than the span of years encompassed by secondary school and the assumption of adult roles. This definition of adolescent boundaries varied markedly between social strata.

Middle-class youth remained in school much longer than youth from lower social strata. With earlier school leaving, employment, and marriage, boys and girls from the lower classes followed an accelerated route to adult status.

Hollingshead found Elmtown to have an elaborate system of age segregation, which sought to ensure "proper" development by separating youth from the adult world of their parents. Anticipating concerns that became prominent in the 1950s and 1960s, Hollingshead (p. 108) cites the essentially self-defeating character of a system that turns young people toward themselves and away from the realities of adult life: "By trying to keep the maturing child ignorant of this world of conflict and contradictions, adults think they are keeping him 'pure.'"

His eyes on Elmtown in 1941–42, Hollingshead did not take into account the Great Depression experience of his subjects, the consequences of which might include a father's unemployment and a severe income loss, in turn leading to adverse changes in family roles and increased family tensions. Income loss among men during the worst years of the depression increased their irritability and general explosiveness, which in turn made family relationships less stable and supportive (Elder, Caspi, & Van Nguyen, 1986). Marital discord also increased, along with arbitrary and often punitive parental behavior. The depression hit the working class especially hard. All of these changes had major implications for Hollingshead's thesis regarding social classes and family behavior.

Nearly 80% of American men with birth dates in the early 1920s were called to serve in World War II. Young women of the same age were drawn quickly into the work force of war industries, along with their mothers in many cases. Despite such developments and the activities of home front mobilization, the Second World War is not even mentioned in *Elmtown's Youth*. When combined with its omission of the depression decade, the study's disregard of the war could well mean that Hollingshead failed to appraise the most powerful determinants of the life opportunities of Elmtown's youth. Elmtown is described as if the war had never occurred, as if no fathers and older brothers were being called to serve. It is a community without propaganda and the pressures of home front mobilization – a community in the timeless realm of abstract sociological theory.

Following World War II, the increasing size and specialization of public schools tended to shift the relative contributions to socialization from family to school and peers. This presumed transfer of control over socialization set the stage for James Coleman's *The Adolescent Society* (1961), a study of teenagers that shares some of the limitations of Hollingshead's research. Looking at students from 10 high schools in the Chicago area, Coleman found that a sizeable percentage of adolescents were more reluctant to break with a friend than to receive parental or teacher disapproval; that student leaders in the liberated climate of large high schools were more inclined than were followers to side with peers (against the perceived wishes of parents) on issues involving social participation and club membership; that students placed greater emphasis on popularity, social leadership, and athletics than on academic excellence; and that the anti-intellectual climate of youth groups generally discouraged intellectual accomplishment. The overall impression is one of stronger peer influence than parental influence and cultural cleavage between the adolescent and adult communities.

The data that support these conclusions came from questionnaires that the teens completed. Parent interviews were not available to offer an alternative or differing view. Indeed, very little is learned about the parents and their life history, though various dates and events suggest that a majority were born between 1910 and 1925, the birth category that provided the largest proportion of men for the armed forces in the Second World War. Had Coleman been sensitive to factors that distinguished his particular adolescent sample in 1957 from neighboring birth cohorts, younger and older, he would probably have discussed this fact.

Most of the students in *The Adolescent Society* were born in the early 1940s and thus were exposed in large numbers to the deprivations caused by father absence and to the stress of family readjustment on the father's return. Though socially accepted, the temporary absence of fathers (3 or more years) markedly altered family relations, placing mothers in a dominant, instrumental role and establishing fertile conditions for conflict when the returning veteran attempted to resume his former family roles (Hill, 1949). Especially relevant to Coleman's generational theme are Stolz and colleagues' (1954) empirical observations that sons born during the war experienced more stressful relations with fathers who served in the military than did those born after the war to veterans. Even several years after the fathers' return to their families, their relations with their war-born sons were characterized by greater emotional distance and strain.

Our purpose in taking a brief look at some pioneering studies that neglected the contexts of children and adolescents is to suggest the potential benefit of research that brings historical insights to the study of children in time and place. From the Berkeley studies to the Coleman project, research largely ignored historical times in lives. However, social historians have begun to study children, and we turn now to examples of work that have contributed to a life-course perspective on studies of children.

Historical studies and the life course

The emergence of a new social history in the 1960s, emphasizing the lives of common people and families, represents a move toward historical perspectives on children and their development. In conjunction with their use of personal and cultural documents, the new social historians draw upon records of the population, such as census forms, marriage and death certificates, and residential directories, to depict lives and human experiences (Hareven, 1982; Modell, 1989). Of complementary significance is the convergence of two lines of research in a view of the life course. One line of research, pursued by sociologists and psychologists, investigates the course of lives and family patterns over time. The other, more sociological, mode of inquiry studies social change, from macroscopic trends to cyclical events and microscopic processes. Their convergence reflects an expanding and more profound appreciation of the link between changing lives and a changing society. Social-historical and life-course work have enlarged current knowledge of children and their development. Both traditions place children in context and provide a contextual perspective frequently lacking in research on child development.

History, life course, and children

The historical study of childhood has come a long way from when it was only of interest to antiquarians. Much of the credit for moving the field into a new realm of scholarship goes to Philippe Ariès's *Centuries of Children* (1962) and its pioneering statement on the mutability of childhood.

In his seminal 1950 volume, *Childhood and Society,* Erik Erikson proposed a developmental model of psychosocial stages that influenced John Demos's path-breaking study of family life in seventeenth-century Massachusetts, *A Little Commonwealth* (1970; see also 1971). Developmental insights from psychology enabled Demos to portray the children of Plymouth as actors in the family. Early or primitive versions of Freudian psychology and theory remain a common view of development in social history. However, the extraordinary richness of historical scholarship on childhood and children does not appear in Erikson's or Demos's accounts of social life.

We have learned much about the worlds of children in the past through studies of nineteenth-century rural and urban youth (Kett, 1977), juvenile delinquency and the juvenile court (Brumberg, 1982; Hawes, 1971; Schlossman, 1977), the growth of public schooling and its age grading (Kaestle, 1973), the evolution of the high school, long-term economic change in the functions and value of children (Zelizer, 1985), the changing meaning of age and age differences (Chudacoff, 1989), and the cultural meaning of physique in different historical times (Brumberg, 1988). Community studies have traced some of these interconnected changes across the life course of the young.

Michael Katz's study of Hamilton, Ontario (1975), graphically documents the community's transformation, between 1850 and 1870, from a small commercial city to an industrial-commercial center with double the population. Prior to industrialization, teenage boys and girls lived and worked as members of a household other than that of their parents in roles such as domestic servants and apprentices in trades. Katz and Davey (1978) refer to this stage of semiautonomy as the "lost phase" of the life course; it was replaced during industrialization by more prolonged residence in the parental home.

With extension of their family residence, the prevalence of "idle" youth – those who were neither in school nor employed – declined. This change reflected increasing educational and economic opportunities. In 1851 nearly half of Hamilton's children aged 11 to 15 and one-fourth of those aged 16 to 20 were neither enrolled in school nor working. This pool of youth was greatly reduced by rising school enrollment during the first decade of educational expansion and by the impact of the increased job opportunities that followed in a diversified and enlarged economy. Among children aged 13 to 16 who were living at home, *school and work* recruited a larger proportion of boys in 1871 than in 1851; for girls, school attendance accounted for the major change in their status.

Rapid change thus rearranged the timing and sequence of events in the transition to adult status. But industrialization had other consequences as well. With the workplace separated from the domestic unit and urban schools largely staffed by female teachers, prolonged family residence and education placed male youth in a socialization environment managed by women. This environment was too sheltered, some believed, from male influence and real-world discipline. The resulting climate of "masculine anxiety" converged with the perceived dangers of idle, unruly youth in the lower classes and acted as a stimulus to middle-class support for adult-led organizations – boys clubs, the YMCA, and the Boy Scouts.

The Hamilton study is thus instructive in two respects. It shows (1) how sociohistorical changes are reflected in the way different cohorts age, and (2) how the characteristics of different cohorts may bring about this change. First, we see that industrialization is accompanied by alterations over time in age-appropriate norms and in practices of role allocation. The configuration of residential, educational, and work transitions after industrialization gave the adolescent a distinctly different experience than was possible before industrialization. Second, we see that problems often ensued in the allocation of roles and in the proper socialization of individuals for these new roles. Indeed, the characteristics of cohorts after industrialization brought about new institutional forms, such as adult-sponsored youth organizations, that have continued to shape the experiences of subsequent cohorts.

A sense of historical depth notwithstanding, the Hamilton study, which relies on demographic snapshots that describe the patterning of one segment of the life span at different times and places, cannot offer a precise explanation of such change and its developmental effects. Sequential strategies involving successions of longitudinal data are required to examine the interplay between historical change and life patterns.

The life-course perspective

A way of doing historical studies of children in past time emerged in the form of a life-course framework during the 1960s (Featherman, 1983; Riley, Johnson, & Foner, 1972). Especially in periods of rapid change, a serious study of lives must attend to issues of time, process, and context (Elder, 1978, 1980); that is, to the temporality of people's lives, the process by which lives change in a changing society, and the setting in which people live. The life-course framework brings these elements together for programmatic study.

The perspective is temporal and contextual in that it locates people and family members in history through their birth years and in the life course through the social meanings of age. The life course is structured by variations in the timing, duration, and order of events, as are in passage to adulthood (Modell, Furstenberg, & Hershberg, 1976). This age differentiation is expressed over the life span in expectations, options, and choices that shape life stages and transitions. Life-course change takes place over a relatively long span of time, as implied by the concept of trajectory, and also over a short time span, as in the experience of life transitions.

Any exploration of the life course requires a general understanding of development. Central to this field of study is a focus on the processes by which development occurs. Multiple intersecting processes, including biological, social, cognitive, and affective factors, are assumed to influence the course of development. Significant advances have been made in our understanding of the operation of these processes as they independently contribute to developmental outcomes, such as cognitive changes that alter approaches to problem solving and information processing. In sympathy with the life-course and historical perspectives, child developmentalists are increasingly receptive to the interactive view of developmental domains and to the concept of *multiple* processes for the explanation of developmental change.

Recognition of the interplay among different processes has, in part, been stimulated by evidence that social-contextual factors have an important impact on the operation of nonsocial processes. A revival of interest in Vygotskyian theory (Rogoff, 1990), which emphasizes the social-contextual determinants of cognitive development, along with the invitations of social ecologists such as Bronfenbrenner (1979) have spurred developmentalists to place development in a more context-sensitive framework. Finally, the expansion of developmental research to embrace naturalistic contexts as important settings along with laboratory-based analyses has made the views of child developmentalists and life-course theorists more compatible.

In recent years, the traditional assumption that developmental processes are universally applicable is being questioned (Rogoff, 1990; Valsiner, 1987); instead, an appreciation of how processes in fact may operate differently in different cultures and in different historical periods has emerged. Together these shifts have made it possible for a fruitful dialogue to emerge among child developmentalists, life-course scholars, and historians.

Norman Ryder's (1965) thoughtful essay, "The Cohort as a Concept in the Study of Social Change," proposes the notion of cohort life patterns as a way of thinking about historical change. With its "life-stage principle," the essay illuminates the interplay of social change and cohort trajectories: the impact of a historical event on the life pattern of a cohort reflects the stage at which the change was experienced. Differences in age or life stage tell us something about the adaptive resources, options, and meanings that become potential elements in linking social change to life outcomes.

From their rudimentary stage in the 1960s to the present, perspectives on the life course and its dynamics represent an orientation that defines a context for empirical inquiry. They identify relevant problem foci and variables, and they structure the generation of evidence and hypotheses. The bearing of research on theory is equally important – the active role of longitudinal studies in shaping perspectives on the life course. Concerning this influence in general, Robert Merton (1968, pp. 162–168) refers to unexpected findings and the discovery of new data that exert pressure for new theories.

Longitudinal studies begun in the 1960s were instrumental in developing notions about the life course, especially by producing knowledge about lives over time periods that have to be taken into account to understand changes in developing individuals. A useful example of this point is the Michigan Panel Study of Income Dynamics (PSID; Duncan & Morgan, 1985), launched in 1968 as an annual longitudinal study of Americans. One of the beliefs that prompted this study was that poverty was self-perpetuating. People enter poverty through misfortune, the inheritance of an attitude of dependency from parents, or some other circumstance; they seldom manage to become self-supporting. The longitudinal design of the PSID enabled analysts to determine whether such views correspond with reality. Are poverty and welfare dependency passed on from one generation to another?

Contrary to prevailing beliefs at the time, only a very small fraction of the sample members who actually experienced poverty did so beyond a year or more (Duncan, 1984). However, two-thirds of the persistently poor households were headed by women, often with young children. Minority children were most likely to experience poor living conditions. Using panel data, Hofferth (1985a, p. 95) found that about four of five black children (born 1975–79) will not be living with both natural parents by age 17. For white children the figure is two of five.

With the increasing availability of longitudinal samples, analysts found they could address life-course issues that generally eluded the grasp of the historian of childhood, such as the diverse pathways individuals take from childhood to young adult years and middle age. We know, for example, that not all problem children become problem adults, but the challenge is to account for this apparent discontinuity. What happens to change the future of problem youth?

A study of predominantly black teenage mothers in Baltimore in the 1960s addressed this challenging question by reinterviewing a group of former teenage mothers after 17 years, when their children were approaching adolescence (Furstenberg, Brooks-Gunn, & Morgan, 1987). Under what conditions, the researchers asked, are the legacies of teenage motherhood most likely to persist? Under what conditions are such young mothers able to change the course of their lives? Contrary to the usual predictions, a disadvantaged life course was not a certain outcome among the former teenage mothers. The explanation has much to do with the occurrence, timing, and sequencing of events in the mothers' lives subsequent to childbirth. This study, although not written from a social-historical perspective, was especially aware of the changing demographic and institutional contexts in which these young women lived, an awareness that makes the work more specific and more generally useful.

The most powerful escape route from a disadvantaged life involved education. The adolescent mothers who completed high school were half as likely to be receiving public assistance as those who had dropped out. A second component of success involved the young mothers' ability to prevent additional childbearing. A third important route to a better life involved a stable marriage and independence from the family of origin. However, none of these escape routes completely eliminated the handicap of having given birth as a teenager.

Today we find that historical studies of children and families frequently employ a life-course perspective (Hareven, 1978, 1982, 1987; Modell, 1989; Vinovskis, 1988), and that life-course specialists are increasingly using the materials, knowledge, and insights of historians in their studies of children's lives and subsequent life course (Elder, 1980; Featherman, Spenner, & Tsunematsu, 1988; Kertzer & Hogan, 1989; Moen, 1989). This application extends beyond using history to define the setting of a developmental study to actual incorporation of a historical perspective in the analytic model.

To understand the imprint of historical change on the lives of children and adolescents, we must first trace its effects to the family. If developmental change qualifies as one of the more subtle and important consequences of social change, as we have reason to believe, then its understanding requires knowledge of the process by which these modes of change are linked, a process that involves family relationships. This process is illustrated by the Social Change Project (Elder, 1974, 1981), a longitudinal program of research launched in the 1960s to study the interplay between the Great Depression and children's life experiences, as mediated by the family.

Children of the Great Depression: The interaction of history and ontogeny

The influence of a historical event on the life course depends on the stage at which an individual experiences the change. Consider two families in 1930: family A has two children born around 1920, and family B has two children born between 1928 and 1930. On the basis of the life-stage principle, we would expect the meaning of economic hardship in the Great Depression to differ significantly for the two sets of children. The older children, at 9 to 16 years old during the height of the depression, were too young to leave school and face a dismal employment situation but too old to be highly dependent on the family. By comparison, the younger children, 1 to 8 years old, were at the ages when they would be most dependent on their families in the midst of the economic crisis and thus were at the greatest risk of impaired development and life opportunities.

In addition to these differences, the historical experience of offspring in these two families may have varied according to the ages of the parents. The parents of family A were much older than those in family B. Because an economic decline makes a difference in families through the lives of parents, this age difference has powerful implications for children. The family is thus a meeting ground for members of different cohorts, a meeting ground for interdependent lives. Because each person's actions are a part of the social context of other members, any change in a member's life constitutes a change in the lives and context of other members. In view of this interdependence, we should think of the interaction between historical time and lifetime as a function of changes in the life courses of multiple family members.

Within a longitudinal perspective, Elder and his colleagues (1974, 1979) have examined the sociohistorical context of two cohorts who lived through the Great Depression: the Oakland Growth sample (birth dates 1920–21) and the Berkeley Guidance sample (birth dates 1928–29). With predepression birth dates that differ by about 8 years, these cohorts seem to share historical conditions from the 1920s to the 1940s, but close examination of Table 1.1 shows noteworthy variations in developmental stage at points during which these cohorts encountered stressful times and prosperity, economic depressions and wars.

The 167 members of the Oakland cohort were children during the prosperous 1920s, a time of unparalleled economic growth in California and especially in the

Table 1.1. *Age of Oakland and Berkeley cohort members by historical events*

Date	Event	Age of cohort members	
		Oakland	Berkeley
1880–1900	Birth years of OGS parents		
1890–1910	Birth years of BGS parents		
1920–21		Birth	
1921–22	Depression		
1923	Great Berkeley Fire	2–3	
1923–29	General economic boom, growth of "debt pattern" way of life, cultural change in sexual mores	1–9	
1928–29			Birth
1929–30	Onset of Great Depression	9–10	1–2
1932–33	Depth of Great Depression	11–13	3–5
1933–36	Partial recovery, increasing cost of living, labor strikes	12–16	4–8
1937–38	Economic slump	16–18	8–10
1939–40	Incipient stage of wartime mobilization	18–20	10–12
1941–43	Major growth of war industries (shipyards, munitions plants, etc.) and military forces	20–23	12–15
1945	End of World War II	24–25	16–17
1946–49	Postwar economic growth	25–29	17–21
1950–53	Korean War and the McCarthy era	30–33	22–25
1954–59	Civil rights era begins	34–39	26–31
1960–73	Civil rights mobilization, urban civil strife, Vietnam War	40–53	32–45
1974–	End of affluent age in postwar America: energy crisis, rising inflation	54–	46–

San Francisco Bay region. Thus, they entered the Great Depression after a relatively secure phase of early development. Later, they avoided the scars of joblessness after high school by virtue of wartime mobilization. By contrast, the 214 members of the Berkeley cohort experienced the vulnerable years of early childhood during hard times and the pressures of adolescence during the unsettled though prosperous years of World War II. Wartime pressures extended the depression hardship for the Berkeley cohort compared with the Oakland cohort. Some Berkeley members endured economic hardship up to their departure from the family in the mid-1940s.

Variation in income loss serves as the point of departure for examining the effects of economic change on Oakland and Berkeley study members and their families. In Oakland, two deprivational groups within the middle and working class of 1929 were identified according to income loss (1929–33) relative to decline in cost of living (about 25% over this period). Families suffered asset losses with some frequency only when economic loss exceeded 40% of 1929 income. Therefore, deprived families were defined in terms of income losses above 35%; all other families were categorized as nondeprived. This division proved equally appropriate for the Berkeley sample.

From the early 1930s to the end of the decade, three modes of change distinguished deprived families in Oakland and Berkeley from relatively nondeprived families: changes in family economy, changes in family relationships, and changes in the level of social and psychological stress. In both cohorts, Oakland and Berkeley, income loss sharply increased indebtedness, as savings diminished; curtailment and postponement of expenditures; replacement of funds for services and goods with family labor; and reliance on the earnings of women and older children. Changes in family relationships stemmed from fathers' loss of earnings, and withdrawal from family roles and from family adaptations in economic support. The economic loss increased the relative power and emotional significance of mother vis-à-vis father for boys as well as for girls. Finally, economic deprivation heightened parental irritability, the likelihood of marital conflicts, arbitrary and inconsistent discipline of children, and the risk of fathers' behavioral impairment through heavy drinking, demoralization, and health disabilities, raising the level of stress in the family.

The most adverse effects of the Great Depression appear among the younger Berkeley males, and we focus on them for purposes of illustration. Compared with the nondeprived, young men from hard-pressed families in Oakland entered adulthood with a more crystallized idea of their occupational goals and, despite some handicaps in their formal education, managed to end up at mid-life with a slightly higher occupational rank. These men not only valued work, they were also more inclined than the nondeprived to consider children the most important aspects of marriage and to emphasize family activity, the responsibilities of parenthood, and the value of dependability in children.

By comparison, the Berkeley boys experienced the depression crisis when they were more dependent on family nurturance and more vulnerable to family instability, emotional strain, and family conflict (Rutter, 1979). Family hardship came early in their lives and entailed a more prolonged deprivation experience, from the economic trough to the war years and departure from home. Consequently, the Berkeley boys from deprived homes were less likely to be hopeful, self-directed, and confident about their future than were youth who were spared such hardship. However, between adolescence and mid-life, deprived men achieved notable developmental gains in self-esteem and assertiveness, though not sufficient to erase completely the inadequacies of the early years.

The vulnerability of the younger Berkeley boys is in keeping with other findings showing that family stressors are most pathogenic for males in early childhood (e.g., Rutter & Madge, 1976). But why did the older Oakland boys fare so well in their transition to adolescence and young adulthood? Part of the answer centers on their family roles in economically deprived circumstances. The older Oakland boys were more likely to assume jobs outside the home to aid their financially troubled families. Family change of this sort enhanced their social and family independence and reduced their exposure to conflict and turmoil in the home.

In looking for a more complete explanation, however, Elder and colleagues turned to entry into higher education, the stabilizing significance of marriage, and military service. Higher education provided new opportunities, marriage offered emotional support, and military service pulled men out of deprivational experiences. Of these, military service proved to be the most powerful force in turning lives around (see chapter 4).

In sum, although economic deprivation produced similar changes in the family environment of both cohorts (division of labor, altered family relationships, and social strains), its developmental effects varied in ways that conform to differences in life stage relative to historical events. Historical conditions are variable at points in time and in how they are experienced by individuals of different ages. By encountering such events at different points in their lives, Oakland and Berkeley men have different stories to tell about their childhood, adolescence, and adulthood. It is the particular sequence of prosperity, depression, and war – their variable timing in the life course and their variable meanings in the family – that distinguishes the developmental histories of the two cohorts.

Transitions in children's lives: The intersection of historical and developmental insights

The depression experience of Americans had much to do with historical transitions and their personal significance, from the initial loss of family income and well-being as the economy plummeted to the survival adjustments of families in response to events of continuing misfortune. From the perspective of the individual family and child, historical transitions often become personal transitions, thereby exemplifying a notable type of intersection for history and biography. As concept and theory, transitions represent a central theme for most studies in this volume on children in time and place.

Part II is organized around the relation between historical and life transitions. We begin with specific interactions between history and life patterns, the interplay between war mobilization and the experience of children and older youth. Full-scale mobilization in World War II transformed the life experience of children by changing their proximal worlds of family, neighborhood, school, and local community. William M. Tuttle, Jr., in chapter 2 examines this change and its developmental implications. The Second World War also pulled young men out of their niches of deprivation and limited experience and opened up for them an array of experiences that broadened their perspectives and life chances. Just how this change was experienced by young American men in two communities is explored in chapter 3 by Glen H. Elder, Jr., and Tamara K. Hareven. In both chapters, the family represents one of the bridges between the Great Depression, war mobilization, and postwar opportunity. Part II concludes with a long view of transitions or change. In chapter 4 John Modell and Robert S. Siegler address questions regarding differences between children across historical time. Have American children become more or less different from each other over the past century as society has evolved into a more complex social system? Some changes, such as the growth of universal public schooling and the decline of immigration, suggest increasing social homogeneity. Other trends demonstrate a more complex, diverse social world. Modell and Siegler also ask whether people today follow more differentiated paths as they age. Are older people more different from each other than younger children are?

In Part III we view life transitions and their developmental effects as a partial function of historical time or setting. Instead of exploring the interplay of historical and life transitions at a specific point in history, we ask whether and how the consequences of particular transitions vary across historical time. One way that consequences have changed is through cultural change that alters the meaning of particular behavior or attributes. Steven Schlossman and Robert B. Cairns in chapter 5 show that the boundaries between conventional and delinquent behavior have shifted for American girls over the past half century. Entry into sexual activity no longer defines a transition from conventional to delinquent behavior for teenage girls as it once did. The culture has changed and so has the meaning of this behavior. In chapter 6, Joan Jacobs Brumberg and Ruth Striegel-Moore link the contemporary prevalence of anorexia nervosa to emerging cultural standards of female beauty. Ross D. Parke and Peter N. Stearns in chapter 7 claim that cultural expectations have much to do with presumptions regarding the changing nature of fatherhood.

Some life transitions involve little change in social status, as when children become a year older, whereas others place children in new social roles and social worlds. Examples of the latter transitions include the first day of school, entry into high school, and the decision to join the armed forces. These transitions are structured in part by expectations governing the timing of events in the usual life course.

Other life changes are shaped by the imperatives of historical change. Hardship imperatives for children in the 1930s were frequently expressed in households that became more labor intensive. Instead of purchasing services (e.g., haircuts) and goods (e.g., children's clothes), family members had to produce more of these services and goods with their own labor. In this new world, young children had valued roles to play; they could contribute to the family through an expanded range of chores and community tasks.

The social imperatives of new situations vary greatly, but they address in common the requirements of life in the particular situation, as already noted in the case of children in Great Depression families. According to life-course theory, the effect of any imperative depends on what children and their families bring to the new situation. Situational change tends to accentuate prior dispositions or inclinations.

Vulnerable children are at risk of exhibiting problem behavior when they experience stressful change. In the Berkeley Guidance Study, Macfarlane, Allen, and Honzik (1954, p. 174) found that the emergence of problem behaviors tended to occur at points of notable role change. The problem behaviors generally "coincide[d] with the ages at which children are called upon to make major adjustments in their school life, the year of kindergarten entrance, the last year of elementary school, and the year of entrance to junior high school." Though not mentioned, presumably some children managed to rise to the challenge in these transitions and even acquired greater competence as a result.

Such accomplishments as caring for children or the elderly may come from disadvantaged youth who have shown little evidence of this kind of competence. John E. Anderson (1960) found the prediction of later adjustment to be least accurate for children who were poorly adjusted at an early age. His Minnesota longitudinal study began with children between the ages of 9 and 17 who were followed up some 5 to 7 years later. In reference to the adolescents who were having difficulties in their home and school environments at the beginning of the study, Anderson was surprised to find in the follow-up that a large number were doing quite well in meeting their obligations and responsibilities. "Putting them on their own brought out qualities which had not appeared to the same degree in their earlier school and home experience" (p. 68). Just how such qualities were brought out is unclear, but the observation confirms a well-known fact, that most problem children do not become problem adults.

The life-course perspective brings to mind other conceptual distinctions that provide some insight into children's life transitions. These include the extent to which children experience multiple life changes at the same time, as in the case of a divorce that is soon followed by residential change and a substantial decline in family income. Concurrent changes are more difficult for children to manage or surmount than is a single change (Simmons & Blyth, 1987). A second distinction involves the interlocking nature of parental and child life changes. Change in the lives of parents is one major route by which broad historical changes alter the lives of children. Conversely, children's life changes, whether through their physical impairment, pregnancy, or military service, have powerful effects on the experience of parents.

A third distinction concerns the temporality of life transitions, their timing and order or sequence. As the Great Depression study makes clear, the age of children at the point of change determines the behavioral impact of the change. Younger children are more vulnerable to family stresses than are older children. Particular sequences of life changes may tell us something about the stressfulness of change in the family, such as when children are born before parents are economically independent and mature.

An early effort to put the concept of life transitions to work in a historical study occurred in an Essex County, Massachusetts, project under the direction of Tamara Hareven (1978), a social historian. In the mid-1970s, Hareven organized a workshop of historians and sociologists to do a life-cycle study of Essex County residents in the 1880s.

Using a common source of social data, the participants developed ways of examining key life transitions, such as entry into adulthood, mid-life, and old age. Over the course of five workshop meetings, the group shifted from research on stages of the life cycle to research on the timing of social transitions, a change that brought issues of dynamics and context more fully into the enterprise. Unlike the current project, the Essex County study involved historians in an empirical study of life-course transitions, usually as solo investigators of specific topics. For their part, the sociologists provided theoretical and methodological guidance to the collective enterprise; with only one exception, workshop members did not actually collaborate in joint research and writing.

Overview

The project represented by this volume is based on a model of multi-disciplinary exchange and collaboration between developmentalists and historians. Collaborative teams emerged from exchanges within the group itself, and each team pursued different sets of empirical data – a strategy that produced diverse lines of inquiry. We end up not with a general portrait of people at one historical time and place, like the Essex County study does, but with a picture of children and youth at different historical times and places.

All experimental ventures tend to raise more questions than they answer, and this project is no exception. A good many of the questions about our venture relate to the process of collaboration, and we have taken pains to convey as much of the flavor of this process as we can in the chapters of Part IV. Readers who would like to travel this road *before* taking up the empirical studies should turn at this point to Part IV. The collaborative journey outlined there offers many lessons that illuminate the work we completed. In chapter 8, we detail the evolution of the investigative teams; in chapter 9, we explore in theory the study of children in past time; and we step back to listen to the reflections of psychologist William

Kessen and historian Michael Zuckerman, who participated in our final work-shop, in chapter 10. Chapter 11 presents our commentary on their reflections and on what we consider to be promising agenda for future studies of children in time and place.

Our cross-disciplinary collaboration resembled the experience that many of our students had when they studied abroad during their undergraduate and gradu-ate years. We encountered different preferences, understandings, and concepts, just as they had. Although the boundaries between history and developmental science may be more subtle than linguistic or cultural boundaries, they proved to be a substantial challenge. Through our collaboration the underlying premises of our respective disciplines were made explicit for pondering and debate. We ourselves became actors in a developmental process. As always, compromises were made along the way. We mention them in the appropriate chapters and talk freely about the collaborative journey, its pluses and minuses. This venture is a beginning, not an ending, and thus we seek to lay bare the issues we faced.

As developmentalists and historians, we came to this project with an apprecia-tion for a lesson that the noted playwright Arthur Miller (Martin, 1978) drew from his personal experience in the 1930s. Claiming that he did not "read many books in those days" (p. 177), Miller refers to the depression as his "book." The "economic crisis and political imperatives" of the period had "twisted, torn, eroded, and marked everything and everyone" (p. 181). Out of this experience, he had learned an ecological truth, that "you can't understand anything unless you understand its relations to its context" (pp. 178–179). We share Miller's perspective and have sought in this collective venture to link the contextual richness of historical analysis with a processual understanding of human devel-opment in studies of children in time and place. Efforts of this kind are neces-sarily work underway, and we think of this volume as a first report from the field.

Part II

Historical and life transitions

In Part II, we begin our exploration of how developmentalists and historians together can increase our appreciation of changes across the life span. The essays in this section take either of two approaches. On one hand, a macroanalytic, long-term view of human development across the century guides the study of how individuals have changed over time. On the other hand, a microanalytic view is provided by examining the impact on development of specific historical events in this century – namely, the Great Depression and World War II. Both approaches share a commitment to life-course analysis but choose different time frames for their work. Although they use different strategies to achieve their goals, each essay provides a model of how collaborative effort can advance the common goal of understanding children and their development across time. For example, history provides dramatic natural experiments that permit evaluation of the impact of important psychological processes; events such as the Great Depression and World War II offer opportunities to evaluate our theories of social and personality development.

In his thoughtful essay (chapter 2) on home front children during World War II, historian William M. Tuttle, Jr., reminds us that contexts of development must take into account events children are denied as well as those they experience over the developmental course. Reduced familial contact resulting from paternal absence, as well as from maternal absence because of employment outside the home, provides just as dramatic an impact on children's development as the formative role played by increased contact with relatives or possibly with other children (a consequence of the use of day-care during this period). Tuttle shows how psychological studies can aid in illuminating the impact of some of these events.

At the same time, Tuttle reminds us that historical analyses are context sensitive and time sensitive, and he underscores the importance of recognizing that the same event, such as family disruption through father absence, may have a different impact when the experience is embedded in a wartime rather than in a peacetime context. One of our tasks is to determine the differing impact of events

23

under different historical conditions. By selecting historical eras that offer opportunities to examine similar types of psychologically relevant changes, we can begin to understand the interplay between processes of development and historically defined contexts. Some processes may, in fact, be robust enough to be evident and to operate similarly across a span of historical periods. Other processes may be more sensitive to the peculiarities of particular sets of historical circumstances.

In chapter 3, Glen H. Elder, Jr., and Tamara K. Hareven continue the exploration of the role of specific historical changes on development not just in childhood, but into adulthood as well. One of the major themes of their essay is the profound role that later life events can play in modifying the impact of earlier childhood experiences. As noted in chapter 1, the life-course view assumes that developmental change occurs over the entire life course. This important corrective to a more traditional psychological view of the primacy of early experience in shaping later development is well illustrated by Elder and Hareven.

In spite of the adversity that children and adolescents experienced as a consequence of the Great Depression, the economic, social, and educational opportunities offered by the mobilization efforts of World War II went a long way toward permitting young men and women to overcome their earlier childhood experiences. The advent of the massive mobilization effort surrounding the war radically altered the life-course trajectories for these young people, dramatically underscoring the degree of plasticity that can occur across development.

Timing of experience is important. The cohort of men who were ready in terms of age to take advantage of the opportunity to serve in the military benefited more than did the cohort of either their older or their younger peers. Clearly, stage of development interacts with historical events; the same set of events may have divergent effects on individuals who are at different ages and stages of development.

A recurring question in charting the impact of historical events on the developmental trajectories of children and adults concerns the degree of generalizability across particular contexts in which the events are embedded. The central issue is whether observed processes or relationships are invariant across time and place. With this in mind, the Elder–Hareven essay makes a contribution through its comparison of the impact of the depression and later of World War II on development within two different communities.

In both sites – Berkeley, California, and Manchester, New Hampshire – the life-enhancing role of military service was evident, thus increasing our confidence in the developmental principle that later events can play an important role in altering the life course of individuals. At the same time, the comparison underscores the importance of context, for the extent of reversal of the depression's impact by the war-related experiences and this reversal's effect on subsequent careers varied by context. Whereas the Berkeley men succeeded in moving beyond their social-class origins, the Manchester men could only maintain the social position of their parents.

The interaction of historical time and place needs to be considered in our attempts to explain the influence of prior historical events on development. The Berkeley–Manchester comparison provides some initial insights concerning the boundaries that may constrain the extent to which later events will yield changes in developmental outcomes. Earlier events and different contexts may impose limits on the degree of plasticity in the system across development. Stability and restraint always need to be considered in our search for developmental patterns. Change is possible at a variety of points in development, but pressures to maintain and carry forward prior experiences are always present as constraining conditions on the amount of deviation from earlier trajectories. Discovery of the rules governing the balance between stability and change and of the role that prior experience and contexts play in this delicate interplay of opposing developmental forces is a major problem for historians and developmentalists.

In their own ambitious undertaking, in chapter 4, historian John Modell and psychologist Robert S. Siegler tackle a central issue in modern democratic theory, namely, decreasing the diversity between individuals in our society. Their essay places in sharp relief the characteristically different approaches taken by the developmentalist and the historian in seeking to understand the factors that promote homogeneity and heterogeneity among members of a population. Developmentalists focus on mechanisms that operate within the individual or between the individual and the environment. In contrast, historians rarely focus on individuals; instead, they view the institutional level of analysis as the most productive vehicle for achieving understanding. Modell and Siegler develop a "demographic" approach that permits the integration of both of these disciplinary strategies: aggregate characteristics of a population that are the sum of *individual* development trajectories are in turn related to larger shifts in the environments of the developing individuals across historical eras.

Although their central illustrations use IQ and height – easily measured and available characteristics – Modell and Siegler's analysis has more general implications of interest to historians and developmentalists. Their analysis suggests the need to distinguish between shifts in level across time and changes in variability. As they show, although overall levels of IQ or height may, in fact, rise across time, the variability, or degree of difference, between individuals may remain relatively unaltered. These findings have very different implications for our social policies as well as for our views on development. From a policy standpoint, it is clear that our most heroic efforts often do little to reduce discrepancies across groups; at the same time, raising levels of competence, even relatively, may remain a worthy goal of policy. From a developmental viewpoint, the findings may serve as a reminder that the concept of relative standing, as well as absolute level, needs to be more consistently integrated into our theories of development.

What are the implications for our sense of well-being, for example, if our level rises but our relative distance from our peers persists? It is clear that a renewed focus on the implications of continuing inequalities for developmental outcomes is needed as well as continued efforts to determine ways of achieving the elusive goal of reducing variance across individuals. Finally, the essay by Modell and Siegler underscores the limits of our efforts to produce change in developmental outcomes through planned interventions. Although plasticity is evident, the forces that promote continuity and stability remain present as correctives or counteractants to our efforts to produce change.

**America's home front children
in World War II**

William M. Tuttle, Jr.

The war I grew up with was World War II, and you think about what
happened to children then

Maurice Sendak (Rothstein, 1988, p. C-19)

An excellent way to approach any topic involving children is through the imagination – with a fairy tale. One of the most fascinating books published in 1988
was *Dear Mili*, a tale written in 1816 by Wilhelm Grimm. Its surfacing made
front-page news when it was discovered in 1983. "After more than 150 years,"
the *New York Times* reported, "Hansel and Gretel, Snow-White, Rum-
pelstiltskin, and Cinderella will be joined by another Grimm fairy-tale character"
(McDowell, 1983).

"There was once a widow," the tale begins – a widow who had a little house
and garden and one little daughter, "a dear, good little girl, who was always
obedient and said her prayers before going to bed and in the morning when she
got up" (Grimm, 1988). But a horrible war threatens, and Mili's mother sends
her daughter into the forest to save her. Mili's guardian angel guides her to the
hut of a kindly old man who gives her shelter. She repays his kindness by serving
him for what she thinks are three days. Actually, 30 years pass. When she finally
leaves to be reunited with her aged and heartbroken mother, the old man reveals
himself to be St. Joseph and hands her a rosebud. "Never fear," he says. "When
this rose blooms, you will be with me again" (Grimm, 1988).

When mother and daughter reunite, Mili's mother exclaims, "Ah, dear child,
God has granted my last wish, to see you once again before I die."

"All evening they sat happily together," the story says. "Then they went to
bed calmly and cheerfully, and next morning the neighbors found them dead.
They had fallen happily asleep, and between them lay St. Joseph's rose in full
bloom" (Grimm, 1988).

Dear Mili is a tale of children of war. It deals with war's consequences:
separation, life, death. On its publication, the book was a sensation. Part of the
reason for the fanfare was that its illustrator was Maurice Sendak, whose books

include *Where the Wild Things Are*, *Outside over There*, and an earlier collaboration with Wilhelm Grimm, *The Juniper Tree*.

Sendak has talked about the book *Dear Mili*:

If you can reduce it to one aspect . . . you think of children and wartime, and what
children have suffered in wartime. . . . [T]he war I grew up with was World War II, and
you think about what happened to children then, what happened to children who were my
own age; what happened to them, and not to me, because they lived over there, and I lived
over here. When I had my bar mitzvah, they were dead. And yet they should have had
their bar mitzvahs just like me. Why was I having one, and why were they not? (Rothstein, 1988, p. C-19)

Sendak contends that subjects such as war, separation, and death are

all the concerns of children. . . . I know children think about these things. Some people
say they don't, that if you put these things in children's minds, it'll frighten them. But that
so underestimates the seriousness of children, and what they think about . . . : Where do I
come from? Where do I go to? How does it happen? How does it feel? (Rothstein, 1988,
pp. C-19, C-24)

In this chapter, I examine the experiences of America's home front children
during the Second World War. First, I lay out some of the historical facts about
the rapidly changing social landscape of the American home front. Second, I
consider the developmental results – or at least the implications or possible
results – of these home front events in the lives of America's girls and boys. I
ponder the developmental significance not only at the time these events occurred
but also later on, in the years following the end of the Second World War, as
these children progressed through the life course and became adolescents, young
adults, adults, and now middle-aged Americans. Finally, I make a plea for
collaborative approaches between historians and developmentalists. Such collaboration would be of obvious benefit to historians, and it should enhance the study
of human development as well.

Children in historical context

In recent years, some psychologists have lamented what they have
called the "progressive fragmentation of our field . . . that is, looking more and
more at less and less" (Bronfenbrenner, Kessel, Kessen, & White, 1986, p.
1219). These critics believe that their discipline has generally failed to take
serious account of the outside world in which children develop because that
world – in its economic, social, cultural, and political realities – is simply too
overwhelming to contemplate, let alone quantify. Some also contend that most
members of their discipline suffer from a belief that if a phenomenon cannot be
counted, or quantified, it literally does not count, or even matter.

Bronfenbrenner, for one, has criticized the study of human development, particularly after infancy, for becoming "the study of variables, not the study of systems, organisms, or live things living" (Bronfenbrenner et al., 1986, p. 1220). Emanating from this narrow perspective, he says, has been "the almost pointed avoidance among developmental researchers across the decades of speaking to the question, What do we mean by human development?" (p. 1220). In a discussion published in 1986, four distinguished psychologists, including Bronfenbrenner, bemoaned this fragmentation. Another of the authors, William Kessen of Yale University, expressed his belief that

the fractionalization or modularization of developmental psychology represents . . . primarily a loss of nerve. One tries to get the research domain that is small enough and in which there are few enough competitors that one can live without raging anxiety. But that, you see, runs against the notion of . . . the community of scholars. It's perfectly all right for people to till their own gardens, but once in a while they are going to have to talk over the back fence. (Bronfenbrenner et al., 1986, pp. 1223–1224)

Scholars should seize every opportunity to talk over the back fence. Perhaps they could do so with the Second World War as their subject. What were America's girls and boys doing on the home front? Many of America's children backed the war effort by pulling their wagons up and down neighborhood streets collecting scrap rubber, tin cans, and old newspapers. Going door to door, these young patriots sold War Bonds and distributed government pamphlets about civil defense, price controls, and rationing. Among the most active participants on the home front were the Boy Scouts, Campfire Girls, and Girl Scouts.

The home front experiences of these boys and girls were often highly emotional, fueled by government propaganda and popular culture. The federal government provided propaganda through the Office of War Information. Schoolchildren recited the Pledge of Allegiance every morning, and their call for "liberty and justice for all" was heartfelt. The nation's leaders proclaimed this to be a "people's war," a battle for democracy against dictatorship and brutality. And the ideology imparted in the public schools was usually very much in accord with these lofty ideals: democracy, respect for individual differences, and cooperation in the pursuit of common goals.

America's children enthusiastically enlisted their energies for the duration. Some believed they were living on the front lines; these boys and girls feared that the next air raid siren might signal not another drill, but the real thing. Even more provocative to many youngsters were the emotional war messages they received over radio, through pictorial magazines such as *Life*, and from comic books, advertisements, feature-length films, animated cartoons, and newsreels.

Many children spent their Saturday afternoons at the movie theater watching war films such as *God Is My Co-Pilot* and *Back to Bataan* as well as serials featuring Superman, Spy Smasher, and Captain America, who were usually at work smashing subversive plots by enemy agents. Other boys and girls took advantage of the "kiddie cartoon special" to see three hours of cartoons in which Donald Duck, Bugs Bunny, and Mighty Mouse made fools of the Germans and the Japanese. The Japanese were invariably depicted as leering, bespectacled subhumans; in movie dialogue they were sneered at as "monkeys" and "slant-eyed rats."

In addition, every weekday afternoon from 4:00 until 6:00, children sat next to their radios to listen to "Hop Harrigan," "Dick Tracy," or "Captain Midnight." Again, the topic usually was spies on the home front. Many of these youngsters then spent the remaining hours before bedtime engrossed in the latest war stories in Action or True Comics.

But these children's lives were touched in other ways as well, particularly by the social changes unleashed by the war. Adults worried about the postwar consequences of these wartime developments. America's home front parents joined the child-welfare experts in expressing concern that rapid social change was demoralizing the family, thus diminishing children's prospects for happiness and individual fulfillment. "America may be on the way toward creating another lost generation," moaned a writer in the *Woman's Home Companion,* in April 1944. "We run the risk by paying too little attention to the welfare of our war babies – the helpless creatures being born into a topsy-turvy world" (Toombs, 1944, p. 32). Toombs was not alone in fearing that the United States might win the war against the Axis powers, but lose the important battle for the physical and emotional health and welfare of America's children (Packard, 1945).

What, in fact, were the events and processes, the losses and gains, the dreams and fears, that affected American children's lives during the Second World War? Probably the best way for a historian to answer this question is to examine American families' home front experiences during these years. One change is immediately apparent: wartime prosperity, which stimulated marriage and baby booms. But the war also separated many fathers from their families, and it stimulated women's employment, thus contributing to the ranks of latchkey children.

Tamara K. Hareven (1971), a social historian, has written that family historians begin with the assumption that "the key to an understanding of the interaction between personal development and social change lies in the family" (p. 400). From this perspective, the study of "children in wartime" is, first of all, a study of "families in wartime." Or as James Bossard (1944) a sociologist of the family, explained: "So comprehensive and fundamental are the changes wrought by war, and so closely is the family interrelated with the larger society, that there is perhaps no aspect of family life unaffected by war" (p. 33). This situation was particularly true during the Second World War, which brought such immense economic, social, and cultural change to the United States that historians have called it a watershed in American history (Nash, 1985; Norton et al., 1986; Sosna, 1982).

It was not the family alone, however, that mediated the influence of wartime on children's lives. As the girls and boys began to grow up and move into settings outside the family, other institutions and people became increasingly important as mediators – namely, the neighborhood, school, church, peers, popular culture, and the workplace. Thus the historian, in assessing influences on childhood, must adopt an age-specific perspective on childhood development. And since social historians and developmentalists alike endorse the need to study the institutions mediating between society and the developing child, this shared perspective suggests possibilities for interdisciplinary research.

The sociologist Glen H. Elder, Jr., presents conceptual approaches to such collaboration: "The imprint of history is one of the most neglected facts in [human] development. Lives are shaped by the settings in which they are lived and by the timing of encounters with historical forces" (Elder, 1981, p. 3), whether depression or prosperity, peace or war. In addition to the family and kin system, the neighborhood, and the school, other obvious variables include those of gender, race, socioeconomic class, ethnicity, religion, and region. In varying configurations, these elements function to shape children's lives, and, of course, considering the seemingly endless configurations possible, they do so differentially. By the same token, the timing of children's encounters with historical change is crucial in explaining individual development. Using this perspective, scholars can begin to explain why children's development during the joblessness of the Great Depression was distinguishable from that experienced by America's home front children during the full employment of the Second World War, or by the "baby boomers" during the generally prosperous 1950s and 1960s (Elder & Caspi, 1990).

The life course is an example of "the timing of encounters with historical forces" (Elder, 1981, p. 3) – only in this case the timing refers to the child's age at the time of the encounter. As Elder (1978) defines it, the life course refers to

pathways through the age differentiated life span, to social patterns in the timing, duration, spacing, and order of events; the timing of an event may be as consequential for life experience as whether the event occurs and the degree or type of change. (p. 21)

Was the child in infancy when a historical event occurred or in early childhood, play age, or school age? An example from the Second World War is father absence, an experience that doubtless had a differential impact depending on whether the child was 1, 3, 6, or 10 at the time that the father embarked for military service. Children's other encounters with change on the wartime home front – for example, encounters resulting from a family's migration, a mother's employment, or a child's exposure to the widespread and intense mobilization propaganda that filled the airways and movie screens – similarly had variable effects depending on the child's age and state of development at the time. Age – defined, for example, as level of understanding – thus was instrumental in determining the life-span consequences that these historical events and personal experiences had as the child entered adolescence and adulthood (Elder, 1981).[1]

A cohort in World War II

The cohort on which I focus is America's children during the Second World War – that is, the boys and girls born between about 1933 and 1945 who were children during the war and still preadolescents when the war ended. According to the sociologist Norman B. Ryder, "A cohort may be defined as the aggregate of individuals (within some population definition) who experienced the same event within the same time interval" (1965, p. 845). The home front children thus comprise a cohort. (A generation, on the other hand, is usually thought of as comprising a longer period of about 30 years; see Mannheim, 1952, pp. 276–322.)

To complicate the matter, two distinct "intragroup cohorts" were born during the years from 1933 to 1945. Between 1933 and 1939 there was a dearth of babies, between 1940 and 1945 a surfeit of newborn. The first cohort was born into an economy – and mentality – of scarcity; the second emerged during a period of full employment and victory. Considering the contrast between childhood in the 1930s and in the 1940s, America's home front children seem to be split not only into two intragroup cohorts but also between two generations (Elder, 1981).

The Second World War is a complex phenomenon, and for this reason it is a useful subject. Historians can benefit from the example of demographers, who use events such as wars as "natural experiments" for nomothetic reasons. Among the social phenomena that the Second World War engendered, and that deeply affected the home front children's lives, are those in the list that follows. These phenomena are ordered in the "natural" chronological and causal sequence in which they would most likely have occurred in children's lives between 1940 and 1945.

1. Wartime migration of families and children
2. Family formation, noting particularly the increases in marriages and births between 1940 and 1945
3. War separations and the rearrangement of family roles:
    a. father absence
    b. working mothers and latchkey children
    c. reliance on extended families
    d. "war-born children" arriving while their fathers were overseas
4. Wartime governmental policies regarding children:
    a. Emergency Maternal and Infant Care program
    b. Servicemen's Dependents Allowances

     c. Lanham Act to aid "war-boom communities" by providing funds for schools, child-care centers, police and fire protection, and so forth

5. Children's health during wartime, featuring both epidemics (e.g., polio, scarlet fever, and meningitis) and dramatic decreases in infant mortality because of governmental policies bolstered by wartime prosperity

6. Children's home front participation in wartime:
     a. activities of the Boy Scouts, Girl Scouts, and other children in scrap collection drives, campaigns to sell war stamps and bonds, and so on
     b. education and children's political socialization, affecting ideology, morale, values, and attitudes during the war and afterwards during the life course
     c. similarly, effects on attitudes and values during this period of war-intensified popular culture, emanating particularly from
        (1) films and newsreels
        (2) radio
        (3) animated cartoons and comic books
        (4) advertising

7. War's psychological and emotional effects, including fears of air raids, heightened concerns about death and dying, anxieties stemming from a strong sense of danger accompanied by feelings of defenselessness

8. War's effect on professional child-rearing advice and, presumably, on child-rearing practices

9. Difficult readjustments for all family members, adults and children alike, on the return of fathers and older brothers from military service and mothers from wartime jobs

A final item is also significant, but it necessarily occupies a separate category: the different experiences of children of color during the Second World War – for example, Japanese-American children interned in war relocation camps, black children caught in the 1943 race riots, Hispanic children of migratory farm workers, and native-American children, who suffered the nation's worst poverty. Other special perspectives were held by refugee children, Jewish children, and the children of pacifists.

The first two items on the list – migration and family formation – are interesting because they clearly show the causal relationship that existed between economic and social change, on the one hand, and peoples' behavior and life choices, on the other.

Migration

The importance of wartime migration begins with its sheer size. In March 1945, about 15 million civilians were living in counties different from the ones in which they had lived on December 7, 1941. Added to that number, of course, was the military migration; by the end of the war, almost 16.4 million men and women had served in the armed forces. The wartime migration between 1941 and 1945 thus far exceeded 30 million people, involving one of every four Americans (see Clague, 1945, pp. 66–67; Hauser, 1942, p. 314).

The largest wartime population shift was from the farms to the metropolitan areas. The rural population of Oklahoma, Kansas, and other plains states, for example, decreased by about one-fourth between 1941 and 1945. Large numbers of rural blacks from the South and whites from Appalachia moved to cities in the North and West. Not only was the rural population declining, but it was the younger people and their families who were leaving the farms, many of them never to return. For one thing, these young men and women were at an age to make lifetime career decisions. As demographer Conrad Taeuber pointed out at the end of the war, "Two-thirds of the young [farm] men who had been between 20 and 25 years of age in 1940 had migrated or entered the armed forces by 1945" (1946, p. 239). Migration from the farm included large numbers of children because entire families were on the move. "Family groups," Taeuber explained,

were fairly mobile when children were young, less so when the children had reached adolescence. This age pattern of childhood migration is consistent with the fact that the proportion of migrants [during the Second World War] reached its peak in the group aged 25–29, declining regularly in the older age groups. (p. 239)

Family formation

Many other couples, once they found employment, decided to marry and have children. The wartime upsurge in marriages and births stands in such stark contrast to the history of family formation during the 1930s that we have here an excellent opportunity to compare a bust-and-boom cycle producing a very different-sized cohort in the 1930s as compared with that of the 1940s and 1950s. During the massive unemployment of the Great Depression, many American women and men had reluctantly set aside their dreams of starting families, sadly acknowledging that they would have to wait until economic well-being returned. Reflecting the economic depression as well as people's uncertainty about the future, the marriage rate plummeted for ten years beginning in 1929. In 1939, however, the early rumblings of rearmament began to be felt; in the next six years, the infusion of hundreds of billions of dollars into the economy produced full employment. Millions of women and men began to embrace their long-deferred vision of marriage and babies. And the marriage rate boomed in the early 1940s (Carter & Glick, 1976, pp. 40–43).

It is ironic that it was during wartime, not peacetime, that women and men formed families and began to envision and embrace the future. The marriage rate slumped somewhat beginning in 1943, but it remained at high levels for the rest of the war. And in 1946 it skyrocketed again, thus reflecting the consummation of a second large category of postponed marriages – those legal unions that war-separated couples had delayed for the duration of the conflict.

Clearly, the upturn in the business cycle had coincided with men and women's wartime-heightened needs for romance and intimacy – for someone to hold onto *and* to return home to. "World War II," observed two sociologists at war's end, "saw not only the largest number of families in the nation's history but also the largest percentage in history of men and women who were married" (Truxal & Merrill, 1947, p. 282). And could anyone doubt, under these conditions, that within a year of marriage many of these couples would also be parents, thus creating a boom in births as well?

Political and military events served as powerful stimuli for the wartime baby boom. An example is the Selective Training and Service Act, which Congress debated throughout the late summer and early fall of 1940. Paralleling the public debate were countless private discussions between men and women over whether marriage – and, in time, a child – would afford an exemption from military service. In fact, during the summer months of 1940, while Congress discussed the peacetime draft, the marriage rate soared.

But this marrying activity was "only the beginning. The attack on Pearl Harbor set off a frenzied rush to the altar" (Tenenbaum, 1945, p. 531). Marriage bureaus issued record numbers of licenses. In the months following the Pearl Harbor attack, newspapers and magazines discussed the issue of "war brides." And just as the press had pondered the question "shall they marry in wartime?" so too it asked, "shall they have babies?" Here also the preponderant issue was the uncertainty of the future. Dr. Katharine Taylor, a family life consultant for the Seattle public schools, was one expert who grappled with the problem:

There will be many war babies during this war epoch and many of them will be left fatherless. A major concern of our nation must be to provide really adequate nurture for these builders of a stronger democracy. (1942, pp. 218–219)

Was the nation up to the task? Did Americans even want to shoulder this burden? No one knew for sure. Meanwhile, Americans would ask, "Shall war brides have babies?" And as in the case of marriages, the answer often was "Yes" (Popenoe, 1942, p. 61).[2]

The Second World War ushered in a rapid increase in the number of newborn in America, after a decade of declining births. In fact, in the 1930s, the number of children relative to the rest of the population was the lowest ever for the United States. But then came the Second World War.

Although most writers and scholars refer to "the postwar baby boom," the baby boom actually began not in 1946 but in 1941, about a year after the

Table 2.1. *Wartime marriages and births*

Year	Marriage rate[a]	Total marriages	Birth rate[b]	Total births
1939	73.0	1,404,000	77.6	2,466,000
1940	82.8	1,596,000	79.9	2,559,000
1941	88.5	1,696,000	83.4	2,703,000
1942	93.0	1,772,000	91.5	2,989,000
1943	83.0	1,577,000	94.3	3,104,000
1944	76.5	1,452,000	88.8	2,939,000
1945	83.6	1,613,000	85.9	2,858,000

[a]Per 1,000 unmarried women over age 15.
[b]Women, aged 15 to 44.
Source: Bureau of the Census (1975), Part 1, 49, 64.

marriage boom. It then accelerated throughout 1942 and 1943. Indeed, with 3,104,000 births in 1943, the Census Bureau announced that the birth rate was the highest in the nation's history to that time. Earlier, during the Great Depression, the birth rate also responded to events, but negatively. According to demographer Wilson H. Grabill (1944, p. 108), "The trend in the birth rate between 1934 and 1940 bears a striking resemblance to trends in economic activities 9–10 months earlier."

"Among all its other booms," Vance Packard wrote in the spring of 1945, "America is enjoying its greatest baby boom in history. About 3,000,000 future citizens have made their debut in the past year" (p. 24). (See Table 2.1.) Writing 35 years later, Landon Y. Jones, author of a study of the baby-boom generation, agreed that "as World War II broke out, something changed. Spurred by military 'good-bye marriages,' births rose steadily from 1940 until 1943" (1980, pp. 18–19). What is more, the upsurge in births that began in the early 1940s continued for a full 20 years (Taeuber & Taeuber, 1971, p. 143). During the war, desire for family and family life was very strong in the United States. D'Ann Campbell (1984) presents an excellent discussion of American women's domestic ideology in *Women at War with America*.

England also experienced marriage and baby booms during the Second World War. The reasons were similar: improvements in economic and social conditions, changes in governmental social policy, and a revival of domestic ideology, particularly on the part of women (Winter, 1985).[3]

Children's health

Beyond the Second World War's demographic consequences, what else can be said about the war's impact on America's home front children? One of the most notable developments was that these children were healthier than they had ever been. Indeed, both maternal and infant mortality declined markedly not only during the Second World War but also during the preceding New Deal years. Between 1933 and 1945 American medical care registered its most dramatic improvements to that time – partly because of the government's financing of maternity and infant care, first under the Social Security Act of 1935 and then under the program of Emergency Maternity and Infant Care (EMIC) for military dependents of men in the lower enlisted grades.

Other factors included rural-to-urban migration, which gave more people access to doctors and in-hospital care; the benefits of wartime prosperity; and improvements in diet and nutrition. Also significant were developments in medical science, particularly the introduction of penicillin, antibiotics, and the sulfonamide "wonder drugs." For example, sulfadiazine, introduced in the late 1930s and early 1940s, reduced children's deaths from meningitis, pneumonia, and dysentery, and sulfanilamide helped to neutralize the threat posed by scarlet fever and measles (Crimmins, 1981).

According to Crimmins, the period from 1940 to 1977 was marked by three distinct phases in America's mortality decline. First, from 1940 to the mid-1950s "mortality declined at a pace unprecedented in American history" (p. 229). Second, "a marked slowing in the rate of decline occurs after 1954, presumably because the diffusion of antibiotics has been largely accomplished by that date" (p. 240). Third, beginning in 1968, "a new decline in mortality set in at rates close to those of the 1940's and early 1950's" (p. 229). In the third period, there occurred "a new trend – a sharp decline in mortality due to cardiovascular diseases" (p. 241), especially for people over 35.

Even before the government established its Emergency Maternity and Infant Care program in 1943, infant mortality had slumped to all-time lows, dropping by almost one-third between 1933 and 1943 (Gooch, 1945, p. 77). But it declined further in 1944 and 1945 when EMIC funded one of every six or seven births in the United States.

The family experience of children

The items discussed so far – migration, family formation, health – might not be the most fruitful topics for collaboration between developmentalists and historians. There is a question, however, the answers to which would enlighten family systems clinicians as well as historians: What was the war's impact on family members' roles, responsibilities, and relationships to each other? Therapists using the family systems theory draw genograms to highlight important structural questions about the roles of family members and how they change when the family is confronted with situational crises. Clinicians in this tradition have also begun to assess significant cultural variations in American society and to urge that therapists practice "ethnotherapy" (McGoldrick, Pearce, & Giordano, 1982). Similarly, historians could employ family systems theory and construct genograms to understand more fully the impact of social change in people's lives. Perhaps an example would help to illustrate the point.

Unlike the centripetal momentum of the Great Depression when many families pulled together to make ends meet, during the Second World War the momentum seemed to be centrifugal. And as before, when people's roles changed outside the family, so too they changed within it. Invariably, children's lives were affected. For example, full employment offered jobs outside the home for men, women, and youth alike. A psychiatrist identified the overwhelming allure of wartime job opportunities in one family; he described how the family's members rearranged roles, though not always happily, to make the most of the situation.

A very intelligent 11 year old boy is working in a store every night from 6 to 11. Both parents are working. They have been in considerable debt since the depression and hold onto the present opportunity to consolidating [sic] their financial situation with feverish tension and to such a degree that everything else, even the personal welfare of their children, seems of lesser importance to them.

The family had three other children. One, a 14-year-old girl, "has to take care of the youngest children after they come from the nursery. She complains that she has no recreation and no time for her school work" (Levy, 1945, p. 150).

Elder has studied the impact of economic loss on family life. However, he and others also have suggested the need to study the implications of "economic *gain* as well as loss . . . for family relationships and behavior" (Moen, Kain, & Elder, 1983, p. 216).

Historians have pondered the effects of family systems changes brought about by the "Rosie the Riveters" who left the home to work in the shipyards and aircraft factories. During the war the female labor force grew by 6.5 million women, or 57%. "For the first time," historian William H. Chafe has written, "more wives were employed than single women, more women over thirty-five than under thirty-five" (1972, p. 148). As large as this figure is, probably an even larger number of women worked at some time or other during the war, since women were more likely than men to move in and out of paid employment. In fact, paid work, according to historian Susan Hartmann, "constituted a part of the wartime experience of half or more of adult women" (1982, pp. 31–32, 77–78).

Still, it is difficult, for two reasons, to evaluate the experiences of the latchkey children of wartime. First, there is a great deal that historians do not know about the subject – beginning, for example, with how many latchkey children there actually were. Second, psychologists appear to be of several minds as to the effects of child care.

Unanswered historical questions include: What arrangements did working mothers prefer for the care of their children? Their choices included grand-mothers, older sisters, or other in-home baby-sitters, neighbors or nearby rela-tives, and in many cases, husbands and wives working different shifts. How widespread was the incidence of children left in locked cars or at all-day or all-night movies? Is it possible that journalists during the war distorted reality by generalizing – first, from the wartime instances of child neglect publicized by Agnes E. Meyer (1943, 1944) and others, and, second, from the federal govern-ment's admittedly slow and limited response to the need for child care – to reach the conclusion that there were many latchkey children victimized by war mobili-zation? Above all, considering the variety of child-care arrangements in practice, How available, or unavailable, was adequate care during the war? For an effort to answer these questions, see Tuttle (in press).

There is a need for a fresh perspective on the child-care story. To open its pages, one must begin by challenging the assumption that because the federal government never gave its highest priority to building child-care centers and training child-care specialists, children necessarily suffered neglect. Many did, but the vast majority did not. Moreover, hidden within this notion of federal neglect is yet another assumption, and an equally persistent one: that during wartime many working parents – perhaps even most of them – failed to fill the void caused by the federal government's failure. This notion, too, is question-able. Historians have not looked into the underside of the much-heralded latchkey children problem. They have not adopted the perspective of the parents – and especially of the working mothers – who made the decisions to take war-production jobs, who made the arrangements for the care of their children, and who clearly wanted their children to be healthy and happy.

Doubtless many wartime children did suffer neglect, but it is important to remember that during these years, most mothers did not work, most fathers were not away at war but were at home, and that unbroken nuclear family was the norm. Moreover, certain allegations of child neglect were clearly part of a general attack on the idea of mothers joining the work force at all. Even the president of the National Association of Manufacturers, whose members had benefited handsomely from the employment of women in war-production work, asserted that "from a humanitarian point of view, too many women should not stay in the labor force. The home is the basic American institution" (Chafe, 1972, p. 176).

The second difficulty in evaluating latchkey children's wartime experiences stems from disagreements among today's scholars in child development. This lack of consensus among developmentalists is a problem for the historian, who needs to know, for example, whether child care has been shown to result in poor parental bonding. Jay Belsky has employed the Stranger Situation Test in concluding that "a good deal of evidence now exists that extensive day care experience during the first 12 months of life . . . seems to be associated with . . . an insecure attachment relationship, as well as increased aggression and non-compliance" later on (in Bass, 1988, p. 30). Other experts disagree, arguing that more important factors include the mother's personality and sense of self-esteem, her relationship with her husband, and her own experiences as a daughter. Recent studies at the University of California at Los Angeles, for example, contend that infants placed in high-quality day care are just as developmentally happy, if not more so, than those reared at home (Bass, 1988). So where does this leave the historian who would hope to gain a deeper understanding of child care through reading studies done today? The most important realization is that the historian is not in a position to second-guess the experts. There is an area, however, in which the historian can turn to the developmentalists for insights and understanding. It too deals with a situational crisis for the family structure. That area is father absence.

Wartime separations accompanied by the rearrangement of family roles caused great changes in the lives of numerous American families. Clearly, children's home front experiences varied widely from family to family, depending on the challenges the families confronted and the manner in which they adapted to wartime changes and dealt with wartime stresses. Some children, for example, had to contend with father absence and older brother absence. And for some of these families, the most traumatic wartime event – though ostensibly the happiest one – was the return home of the soldier or sailor father. Readjustment was difficult, especially for families with "war-born children" who had been born while the fathers were overseas. In these cases, as Lois Meek Stolz (Stolz et al., 1954) explains in *Father Relations of War-Born Children*, the fathers and children had never before laid eyes on each other.

In the secondary literature to which historians turn for information – for example, periodicals of the Second World War era – there are case studies of families, and of children, in distress. One study (Cavan, 1953) involved a young wife, who spoke sadly of the "helpless, anxious, lonesome feeling" that marked the two years during which she was separated from her soldier husband. Married during the war after a four-year courtship, the couple had decided that Nancy "should go with him, working wherever he was sent. However, just after he left [in 1943], I discovered that I was pregnant and so had to make other plans." Nancy moved to another city to live with her folks. "George and I saw each other twice in the next eight months, when he was sent overseas. Our son was born after he left. We remained with my parents, where a sister and sister-in-law with her child were also living." There was "some tension," so

when little Tommy was three months old I returned to the city where we had lived and moved into an apartment, where I remained with the baby until he was a year old. I had felt sure the war would be over soon. I did not work as I could not conceive of leaving the baby with anyone else. We passed the time with friends who were in the same situation. Many of them also had babies whom the fathers had not seen. I moved into an apartment with a serviceman's wife who had one child a little older than Tommy and was expecting another. The children were not happy together and I was running short of money. I again returned to my parents where we stayed for about eight months until August, 1945. I felt sure George would soon be home and as I wanted him to return to his own home I again moved to our home city. (pp. 551–552)

George's return to his family was not only extremely difficult for him but also stressful for his son and wife. One can generalize tentatively from George's experience because it so resembled that of other veterans returning from long stretches overseas. "George came home after an absence of more than two years," Nancy recalled:

We were more or less strangers. Many of my friends were people I had met after he left and were strangers to him. His experiences had been so different from mine that at first there was little to discuss. He could hardly imagine he had a two-year-old son and didn't know how to respond in any way to him. He would say that I had pampered and spoiled him, that strict discipline was what he needed. At first Tommy was jealous of the attention I gave George and vice versa; but in time they became *fairly* [italics added] well adjusted to each other. (Cavan, 1953, p. 552)

In February 1944, 2.7 million married women were separated from their husbands by war – almost one-third of married women aged 20 to 24 (Cavan, 1953, p. 547). Being more aware of posttraumatic stress syndrome now because of veterans' suffering after the Vietnam War, we can be more understanding of some of George's readjustment problems and the damage they did to him and his family. But certainly at that time, too, wives, children, other relatives, and friends appreciated both the potential trauma as well as the joy in the return of the veterans. Hollywood also understood. The Academy Award-winning film for 1946 was *The Best Years of Our Lives*, the painful story of the postwar readjustments of three veterans.

Another example of father absence occurred in the Burns family. Burns, a merchant marine officer, periodically left his home for long cruises. During these absences, Mrs. Burns turned to her young son Edwin "for the companionship and affection she missed." She would move his cot into his parents' bedroom, and he would have his mother's "undivided and constant attention. His father's return always cast him into exile in his own little room. . . . His resentment toward his father flared up anew at every shore leave." Edwin also had adjustment problems in school and was referred to a family social worker. At the same time that Edwin deeply resented his father, he seemed to share his mother's concern for his father's safety. Twice during the war when Mr. Burns was rescued from torpedoed ships, "the child reacted so violently to his father's danger that . . . [medical] treatment had to be secured for him" (Clifton, 1943, p. 125; see also Igel, 1945).

It is difficult to generalize about the effects of father absence on families and children. "Reactions to their absence," one therapist wrote during the war, "are as varied and numerous as were the reactions to their presence" (Clifton, 1943, p. 125). Families adapted in different ways, depending on the family's prior history and the ages of family members during the period of rapid social change.

Long before the outbreak of the war, for example, many of America's fathers had relinquished their paternal responsibilities to other family members, such as older sons. Having suffered from joblessness during the Great Depression, many fathers had become demoralized and had turned to heavy drinking. These fathers became less important to a family's functioning than older brothers who had assumed the duty of directing younger siblings' lives. Two doctors from the Judge Baker Guidance Center in Boston told of a 10-year-old boy, "the youngest of 7 children, of poor family background in that both parents drink, the mother to excess." The boy "was referred for bunking out and picking up food and clothing wherever he could find them." His older brother, who had become the surrogate father, had been the only family member the boy had admired, and they got along well. But then his brother had enlisted, later to be killed overseas. The boy received a portion of his brother's life insurance, which he gave to his mother so that she would enter a hospital for the treatment of alcoholism. Even though he was the youngest member of the family, in this way the boy was assuming some of the role-responsibility that his oldest brother had formerly shouldered (Gardner & Spencer, 1944, pp. 40, 41–43).

Moreover, in dealing with the evidence, the historian needs to look not only at what is there but also at what is not there. It is clear from reviewing the periodical literature detailing children's psychological reactions to wartime disturbances that the published cases focused only on boys' experiences and not at all on girls' efforts to deal with father absence. For example, articles on father absence were entitled "A Boy Needs a Man" (Kelton, 1943), "What Shall I Tell Him?" (Robbins, 1944), and "Sons of Victory" (Nichols, 1944). No article on father absence asked "What Shall I Tell Her?"

War's legacy in lives

Obviously, the effects of wartime father absence did not cease with the end of the hostilities abroad. What have been some of the life-span consequences? Can the historian turn to the developmental literature for help? The answer clearly is in the affirmative. Two articles written almost 20 years after the war discuss the possible outcomes of father absence for home front boys. This research probed the effect of early father absence on Scholastic Aptitude Tests (SAT) taken by these young men 15 and 16 years later.

The first of these articles, by Lyn Carlsmith (1964), focuses on freshman men of the Harvard classes of 1963 and 1964. All of the young men in her samples had been home front boys, born between 1941 and 1945. Her father-absent group consisted of students whose fathers went away before their sons were 6 months old and were away for at least two years. A matched sample consisted of students whose fathers were not in the service at all.

Carlsmith cited the evidence accumulated "from a large number of studies on Math and Verbal aptitudes" as clearly demonstrating that, on standardized tests, "females are generally superior to males in Verbal areas, while males are superior to females in quantitative pursuits, particularly numerical reasoning" (p. 17). These studies suggested to Carlsmith that perhaps there were two styles of conceptualization:

an "analytical approach" which is characterized by clear discrimination between stimuli, a direct pursuit of solutions, and a disregard for extraneous material; a "global approach," characterized by less clear discrimination of stimuli and a greater influence from extraneous material. The first approach is more typically used by boys while the second is more typical of girls. (p. 17)

What Carlsmith found in examining the SAT scores of these young men, however, was that although the father-present boys achieved the predictably higher math than verbal scores, the father-absent boys achieved the opposite result. Their test performance was similar to the pattern typically achieved by girls. Moreover, Carlsmith found that "the relative superiority of Verbal to Math aptitude increases steadily the longer the father is absent and the younger the child is when the father left" (p. 10).

Carlsmith explained that the purpose of her research was to "provide evidence relevant to any general theory of identification by showing certain strong effects of father absence at various ages." As a premise, she argued that

theories of identification, whatever their form, usually agree on two points: for the boy to identify successfully with the father, the father must be present during at least some portion of the boy's childhood; development of an appropriate masculine identify or self-concept is predicated upon the success of this early identification with the father. (p. 3)

Carlsmith borrowed her explanatory framework from John W. M. Whiting's (1960) theory of cross-sex identification.

In recent years, critics have accused standardized national tests of being culture bound and having been written essentially for white, middle-class males. For them, an example of such bias would be the statement in the SAT booklet handed out in 1960 by the College Entrance Examination Board: "In general girls do less well than boys on the Mathematical parts of the test and should not be surprised if their Mathematical scores are noticeably lower than their Verbal." Some will argue that the attitude embedded in this statement was a social and cultural construction, which in turn had become a self-fulfilling prophecy. Moreover, in recent years gaps between men and women on mathematical problems and between women and men on verbal problems have been disappearing. In 1989 Marcia C. Linn and Janet S. Hyde argued that gender differences reported in 1974 in math "now are so small as to be negligible" (Turner, 1989, p. A10).

Still, there seems to be no gainsaying Carlsmith's statistical finding that among father-absent boys in her sample of home front children, "early and long separation from the father results in relatively greater ability in Verbal areas than in Mathematics" (1964, p. 16). The challenge is to find an explanation, and perhaps that explanation should be as much historical as developmental.

The second article was written by Edward A. Nelsen and Eleanor Maccoby (1966). Their samples included boys entering Stanford University in 1959 and 1960 – the classes of 1963 and 1964. Their findings tended to reinforce those of Carlsmith, including that, for boys, "a high-verbal, low-mathematics pattern was associated with reports of father absence, punishment exclusively by the mother, fear of father, and reports of having been a 'mamma's boy' or 'daddy's boy' " (p. 282).

Taking the perspective that cross-sex typing is a result of learning by imitation, one can test this view by looking at published research in other social-scientific fields. The sociologist, Gregory P. Stone (1971) provides a heart-rending example in an observational study of "a boy and girl playing house in a front yard."

The little girl was very busy sweeping up the play area, rearranging furniture, moving dishes about, and caring for baby dolls. The boy, on the other hand, would leave the play area on his tricycle, disappear to the back of the (real) house, remain for a brief while, reappear in the play area, and lie down in a feigned sleep. The little girl had a rather extensive knowledge of the mother role, but, for the boy, a father was one who disappeared, reappeared, and slept, *ad infinitum!* (p. 11)

Other psychological studies done of father absence – for example, by George R. Bach (1946), Robert R. Sears (Sears, Pintler, & Sears, 1946), and David B. Lynn (1959) – buttress the points Carlsmith and others make. Lynn provides validation when he says that "the process of identification" follows the "laws of learning." Whereas female and male infants learn to identify with their mothers, "boys, but not girls, must shift from this initial identification with the mother to masculine identification." Lynn thus offers a helpful explanation for children's adoption of sex roles when he states (p. 134): "Males tend to identify with the cultural stereotypes of the masculine role, whereas females tend to identify with aspects of their own mothers' role specifically."[4]

Historians and psychologists – reflections on cross-disciplinary research

The historian – if operating prudently and with full recognition of the limitations of her or his data – can make good use of psychological research. At the same time, using this literature to illuminate historical change can be highly frustrating. First, some developmentalists are hostile to such an approach. They contend (quite correctly) that historians, especially psychohistorians, leave the evidence far behind in positing unprovable, and sometimes ridiculous, theses.

Such theses are ahistorical as well. An example related to father absence during the Second World War was published in 1986. Its author, a psychiatrist (Rinsley, 1986), wrote:

I relate the social upheavals of the 1960s in substantial measure to the attainment of adolescence and young adulthood of the damaged offspring of wartime families, antecedent to which had been the more extended erosion of masculine authority and leadership during the Depression years. The various rights "movements" of the last quarter-century symbolized challenges to the attenuated authority of the white male, the symbolic plantation owner, by assorted minority subgroups who perceived opportunities to get for themselves what they believed the symbolic Simon Legrees had long denied them. The associated vacuum of national leadership found graphic expression in the nation's post–World War II military operations: the ill-starred . . . "police action" in Korea, the failed action of the Cuban Bay of Pigs, and, last and most horrendous, the debacle of Vietnam. (p. 24)

Now this is, indeed, quite a leap from the careful and reasoned research on father absence conducted by Stolz, Carlsmith, Maccoby, and others. Most historians realize that it would be presumptuous to attempt to formulate universal laws of human behavior on the basis of studying one nation's children only. The business of historians is not to make predications about future behaviors. It is, rather, to deepen our understanding of the relationship between social change and individual development.

For purposes of interdisciplinary collaboration, it is more important to focus on similarities than on differences. There are signs that the gap is not as large as it once was. This is the opinion of the developmental psychologist Dale B. Harris, who in a letter to a former doctoral student wrote that developmentalists "retain some measure of an appreciation for history!" (personal communication to Liz Pemberton, March 14, 1987). The developmentalist is, or should be,

aware of maturation and the time which those processes require. She is aware of the organismic character of her subjects, the intricate interrelatedness of the total organism, and the artificiality of the "parts" or "variables" into which her analytical procedure has segmented the functioning whole. So, fuzzy though it may seem, the developmentalist tends to think in terms of history, and in terms of influences which cannot readily be reduced to mathematical equations. I can recall a time when many in our field eschewed the term "developmentalist" in favor of "experimental child psychologist." But the radical position is not so popular today; I sense a return to a greater willingness to do descriptive work before launching into the more precise experiment.

Above all, social historians and developmentalists share a commitment to the study of human life. One wonders whether this should be not only a humanistic and social-scientific endeavor but an artistic endeavor as well – that is, a challenge to the imagination. We have come full circle at this point, returning to the artistry of Wilhelm Grimm and Maurice Sendak in *Dear Mili*.

Sir Isaiah Berlin (1978) has suggested that art should accrue from the study of human life.

History, and other accounts of human life, are at times spoken of as being akin to art. What is usually meant is that writing about human life depends to a large extent on descriptive skill, style, lucidity, choice of examples, distribution of emphasis, vividness of characterization, and the like, But, there is a profounder sense in which the historian's activity is an artistic one. Historical explanation is to a large degree arrangement of the discovered facts in patterns which satisfy us because they accord with life – the variety of human experience and activity – as we know it and can imagine it. (p. 132)

Mili was a child of war, and from her plight we can learn about separation and death in a child's life. Most would agree that it would be ironic if the studies of human history and human development met, at last, at the juncture with art. But perhaps we should have known all along that it is at this juncture that wisdom resides.

Acknowledgments

For their helpful suggestions, I wish to thank Aletha C. Huston, David M. Katzman, Michael Lamb, Paul H. Mussen, Lia Rudnick, David L. Thomas, Marilyn Yalom, and my co-participants in the Child Development/Social History Workshop, particularly its organizers, Glen H. Elder, Jr., John Modell, and Ross D. Parke. Thanks also to Dale B. Harris for allowing me to publish part of the contents of his letter to Liz Pemberton.

Notes

1. For an appreciation of historians' use of Erik Erikson's psychosocial stages for the study of children, see Demos (1971) and Hunt (1970).
2. Many people during this period were sexually inexperienced and prudish by today's standards. To them, sex before marriage was unthinkable. One can only speculate about what the history of their children's cohort would have been – specifically, its size – had the birth control pill been available during the war.
3. In another work, Teitelbaum and Winter (1985) have studied fertility trends over time in 27 industrialized countries.
4. Perhaps these differences are narrowing today because of changes in family structure. Marybeth Shinn (1978), who conducted a study in the late 1970s of single-parent families in which, usually, the father was absent, found that among the children, sex role identification did not play an important role in cognitive development.

3   Rising above life's disadvantage: From the Great Depression to war

Glen H. Elder, Jr., and Tamara K. Hareven

> In one life span, Americans had moved from scarcity to abundance, from sacrifice to the freedom made possible by prosperity.
>
> Glen H. Elder, Jr. (1974, p. 296)

Life-course continuities from childhood across the adult years seem all too expectable in American life, a predictable outcome without mystery. Until recently, social scientists have given little attention to the timing of historical events in lives and their biographical influences. As Everett Hughes once noted (1971, p. 124), "Some people come to the age of work when there is no work; others when there are wars." For others the timetable may offer a better match between life stage and historical stage, whether increasing or decreasing hardship or prosperity. At issue here is the synchronization between life history and social history and the subsequent ripple effects of that match or mismatch through adult life.

The synchrony between individual life stage and historical time for Americans born during the *early* 1920s minimized vulnerability to the Great Depression; those cohorts were too old to be wholly dependent on hard-pressed families in the 1930s and too young to face a stagnant labor market when they were coming of age. However, they were just the right age to be mobilized into World War II and to experience the economic recovery it prompted (Elder, 1974). This global war counteracted the impact of the Great Depression for members of this cohort, just as it ended the depression generally.

In our examination of several cohorts who came to adulthood during the depression, we asked, Why did the Great Depression not produce a "lost generation" as had been generally assumed? In an effort to answer this question, we examine the impact military service had on the subsequent lives of men (born during the late 1920s and early 1930s) who experienced deprivation as young children during the Great Depression. We compare, in particular, the experiences of two cohorts of young men who were members of two very different communities – the textile-mill community of Manchester, New Hampshire (Hareven, 1982), and the California city of Berkeley in the San Francisco Bay Area (Elder,

47

1979). In each case, the long-term impact of the war on the lives of young men encountering it depended on life chances that were structured by class, community setting, adversities inflicted by the Great Depression, and options provided by World War II. Of special interest are the children of working-class families and their life chances within a declining textile-mill community and the vibrant urban setting known as the Bay Area. How did community differences in their life chances affect the ability of young men to overcome the devastating effect of the Great Depression? How were those differences expressed in responses to military mobilization and its subsequent impact on careers?

Depression children in the Bay Area and in Manchester

The influence of historical times on life experience generally depends on the point in people's lives when they first encounter the new situations. According to this life-stage concept, adolescents in the 1930s were too old to be wholly dependent on their highly stressed families and too young to be looking for a job in a stagnant labor market. By comparison, younger children experienced the harshness of depression losses through their family – through heavy drinking and withdrawn behavior of father or frantic concern of mother.

Hitting the Great Depression

As noted in chapter 1, members of the Oakland and Berkeley cohorts encountered the Great Depression at different ages, which entailed an important difference in risks of lasting impairment. The Oakland cohort experienced the depression during early adolescence, well after the early years of development, whereas members of the Berkeley cohort were still highly dependent on parents at the time of family misfortune.

Consistent with this life-stage difference, the younger Berkeley cohort, and especially the boys, was most likely to be disadvantaged by family strains and conflicts associated with heavy income loss. The Oakland boys were least harmed by the experience. Hardship markedly increased a lack of self-confidence for the younger boys but not among the older ones. Similar differences in adolescence appear on assertiveness, social competence, and aspirations. Young women in the two cohorts ended up in the middle of psychological well-being in adolescence.

In much the same fashion, the younger Manchester men, who were born from about 1925 to 1934, were more adversely influenced by depression hardship than were the community's older men born before 1924. All of these men were the children of former workers of the Amoskeag Mills. Once the world's largest textile mill, the Amoskeag Company reached its peak of prosperity in the early 1900s and shut down in 1936, after a precipitous decline (Hareven, 1982). The children's generation, whose careers are being discussed here, consists of two cohorts: those who reached adulthood in the Great Depression (similar to the Oakland cohort), and those who reached adulthood in World War II or in the immediate postwar era (this younger cohort matches the historical time of the Berkeley cohort). Data on the Manchester children's cohort include extensive open-ended interviews gathered between 1980 and 1983 and demographic, career, and migration histories constructed from the interviews and other vital records. Data on the children's life histories were linked to those of the parents, thus making comparisons across generations possible.

Manchester was a one-industry town. The Amoskeag's shutdown left the entire labor force stranded. The shutdown deprived entire families of jobs and tore these families apart, as their members wandered around New England or returned to Quebec in search of work. The blow of unemployment on Manchester's laborers was particularly severe, because these immigrant workers had already been deprived through low wages and the ups and downs typical of the textile industry prior to the depression (Hareven, 1982). The first opportunity for relief in Manchester came with the arrival of war industries, following the United States's entry into World War II.

Considering all aspects of the depression experience, we have many reasons to expect an impaired future for the younger sons of hard-pressed parents in the California cohorts. Nevertheless, studies show (Elder, 1979) remarkably little evidence of such impairment on socioeconomic achievements. With adjustments for class origin and IQ, men from deprived homes were just as likely as the nondeprived to be in the upper middle class by their 40s and 50s.

The community context

Berkeley was a city of approximately 82,000 residents in 1930, and the local campus of the University of California loomed over the economic and cultural scene. Scattered evidence suggests that a university education for offspring attracted families to the city. As able children passed through the public schools, they were shaped by an ever-present standard of achievement and opportunity represented by the university. At the time, the state offered all residents a tuition-free higher education if they had a high school diploma. But only the most talented had access to the research universities, such as the Berkeley campus. The message for ambitious and able children of the working class was clear enough. An educational route to a better life was available and manageable.

Just as the University of California at Berkeley ranked as one of the finest public universities in the land, the Amoskeag Mills in Manchester was the world's largest textile mill at its peak of prosperity in the early 1900s with a labor force of more than 19,000. In 1907, *The Manchester Mirror* (cited in Hareven,

1982, p. [iii]) vividly described the enormous flow of humanity that left the great gateways of the mill at 6:00 p.m.

The first to leave the plant were men and boys, some with dinner pails and some with bicycles. Then came a steady stream of men and women, boys and girls. . . . The great majority of the younger of the toilers were chatting amiably, and appeared to be thoroughly happy and contented with their lot.

A workday from 6:30 a.m. to 6:00 p.m. for teenage Manchester boys and girls was clearly another world from the experience of working-class youth in Berkeley, and Amoskeag's demise in the Great Depression increased the difference. By the end of 1935, fewer than a thousand workers were still employed by Amoskeag – a hundred-year-old institution had come to an end for the Manchester working class. In 1936 the mills shut down completely, devastating the economy of this one-industry town, and leaving the entire community of 100,000 stranded. Only the economic recovery resulting from the unparalleled mass mobilization of a global war put an end to the crushing effect of this event.

Considering these contextual differences, the opportunity function of military service most certainly varied between the two communities and populations. Two questions, then, are central to our exploration.

1. Did military mobilization open up opportunities and the possibility of a better life for children of the Great Depression in the two communities?
2. How did military mobilization vary by community, especially among members of the working class?

Keeping in mind the life stage of each cohort at the beginning of World War II, the story of mass mobilization applies mainly to the older men – the Oakland and Manchester men who were born around 1920, the older cohorts. We begin with this account because it left a powerful impression on the minds and military aspirations of the younger men, who were teenagers during the war. Some of these teenagers managed to get into the war before it ended, though most entered in the postwar era and through the Korean War. Empirical evidence of the military pathway to greater opportunity comes from the younger cohorts in the two urban areas, the Bay region and Manchester. These young men were especially vulnerable to depression hardships and thus had much to gain through the social advantages of the military. The two studies, Bay region and Manchester, rely on different types of data and we attempt to integrate them as much as possible in the analysis.[1]

Recasting men's lives through military service

A major explanation for these unexpected developments centers on the positive effect of war mobilization in reversing the adversities of the Great Depression, from World War II through the Korean War. In view of maturing opportunities during World War II and the educational benefits of duty in the armed forces, military service represents a promising source of clues to the work-life accomplishments of the depression cohorts, despite the adversity they experienced during the 1930s.

In the nation as a whole, 4 of 5 American men born in the 1920s served in the armed forces of World War II (Hogan, 1981). Approximately 9 of 10 men from the older Oakland cohort (birth dates 1920–21) were inducted into the armed forces (Elder, 1974). The young Berkeley men (born 1928–29) were generally too young to be mobilized in this war, although 73% entered the service through the Korean War. In the Manchester cohorts, older and younger, 75% of the men served in World War II or shortly thereafter. Taking all of these figures into account, we have good reason to view military mobilization as a prime influence in changing the life-course direction and prospects of men reared during the Great Depression.

The military has long been seen as a pathway to opportunity for youth from disadvantaged backgrounds, but the full meaning of this statement requires examination of the impact of service experiences on the careers of young men from the working class who were caught in hard times during the Great Depression in communities such as Berkeley and Manchester.

The outbreak of war in Europe, September 1939, spurred America's initial mobilization for war – the draft in the fall of 1940. Between the surrender of France to Germany in 1940 and Japan's surrender in 1945, the number of men and women in the armed forces increased to over 16 million. By pulling tens of thousands of young men from diverse and highly insular communities and placing them on large training bases, service mobilization established conditions that favored dramatic life changes, breaking the hold of family hardship, frustration, and vanishing opportunity caused by the Great Depression.

This account applies only to men who survived their term of service and wartime events. Thankfully, war casualties were relatively light in these cohorts, and consequently we must weigh this fact and the legacy of combat with the recasting influence of mobilization. Only a fifth of the Berkeley veterans faced combat, compared with nearly half of the Oakland veterans, but the impairing legacy of heavy combat can still be observed in the later lives of some men in both cohorts.

Symptoms of posttraumatic stress disorder are still reported by a fifth of the heavy combat veterans (Elder & Clipp, 1988), including sleep disturbances, depression and anxiety, and flashbacks of combat scenes. Whether pathogenic or health promoting, the service experience and war events clearly have long-term implications across the life course. The effect of wars reverberate across lives and generations in human populations. War mobilization promoted social independence, a broadened range of knowledge and experience, a legitimated time out from age-graded careers and their ever-present expectations, and greater access to the means of educational and work-life achievement. The war experience also exposed young men to other areas of the United States and other countries in the world.

Entry into the service also meant separation from family influences and a measure of social independence coupled with establishment of new social relationships. Induction "knifed-off" (Brotz & Wilson, 1946) the recruit's past experience. In particular, basic training fostered peer equality and comradeship among recruits by separating them from their pasts. It provided, at least temporarily, new identities (except where race was concerned), required uniform dress and appearance, minimized privacy, and viewed performance on the basis of group achievement or failure. An Oakland veteran spoke about "the unforgiving environment" in which the consequences of personal failure were felt by the entire unit.

A second feature of the military experience is the extent to which service time represents a clear-cut break with the conventional expectations of an age-graded career – a time out or moratorium from "adult" responsibilities. Military duty provides a legitimate time out from educational, work, and family pressures in a structured environment. As a rule, presence in the service is not questioned, and neither is the lack of career progress or work plans resulting from being in the service. The very act of military service provides adequate justification for nonconformity with age-related expectations of career development. Indeed, Stouffer and his associates (1949, p. 572) note that for many soldiers in World War II, "perhaps for a majority, the break caused by military service [meant] a chance to evaluate where they had gotten and to reconsider where they were going." For individuals deprived of job opportunities and the normally expected transition into careers, the service provided a temporary respite from the desperate, often circular, search for employment.

Especially among men from deprived circumstances, the older Oakland and Manchester men, military service and its situational imperatives provided an escape from daily poverty by promoting independence and exposing recruits to new ideas and models. It offered a legitimate time out or moratorium for those unsure of the course to follow in life. For deprived youth lacking self-direction and a sense of adequacy, military service also offered developmental alternatives to the course charted by their families – separation from maternal control through involvement in a masculine culture and the opportunity to sort things out in activities that bolstered self-confidence, resolve, and goal setting. Some of these themes appear in the life reviews of veterans from deprived households. The break from a confused and painful family situation is a recurring theme (Elder, 1987b). One man recalled that he "finally realized what was happening and broke away." He entered the navy. Another described the time he joined the army at 18 as the end of his mother's domination and the start of independence.

Several men recalled the novel and rewarding experience of mastery of military tasks, or of skills learned in the military, of doing something well and on their own. Across this period, we see a contrast between descriptions of self before and after time in the military, from the implication of being "such a flop" in adolescence – "I couldn't do anything" – to the claim that from "the day I went into the service, I was almost on *my own* [an extraordinary statement from someone regimented into military discipline] . . . figured out my own situation and went on from there."

A third feature of mobilization entailed a broadened range of perspectives and social knowledge. Mobilization increased the scope of awareness of oneself and others through an expanded range of interactional experiences, including encounters with new people and places that promote greater tolerance of social diversity. Willard Waller once likened the process to "stirring soup; people are thrown together who have never seen one another before and will never see one another again" (1940, p. 14). Out of this experience comes greater awareness of self and others, an expanded range of interactional experiences with their behavior models and social support, and possibly a greater social tolerance of diversity. A veteran interviewed just after World War II in the study by Havighurst and colleagues (1951, p. 188) spoke about the incredible diversity of his acquaintances in the service and their influence on his views. As he put it, the experience "sort of opens up your horizons. . . . You start thinking in broader terms than you did before."

Similarly, for young men who had never left Manchester before, military service provided an opportunity to "see the world," to experience for the first time other parts of the United States as well as foreign countries. As one former serviceman from Manchester put it, "Part of the change is people getting to know and experience other people from different parts of the country and maybe different parts of the world." A veteran of the Pacific theater explained, "a man's life can't help but expand when you go through things like that. You see things from a different perspective than you ever had before" (Havighurst et al., 1951, p. 172). This access to greater opportunity stems from some of the personal changes we have noted and from service training and G.I. benefits that encouraged efforts to get ahead.

Finally, the educational opportunities presented by the G.I. Bill of Rights, enabled veterans to expand their education and acquire new skills after the war. Remembered now for its educational and housing benefits, the G.I. Bill was prompted by fear of the social and political danger of widespread unemployment among returning veterans. In many respects, the bill was a "child of 1944; it symbolized the mood of a country immersed in war, recalling the depression, and worrying about the future" (Olson, 1974, p. 24). At least in the area of education, the G.I. Bill became a primary factor in the life opportunity that veterans from the California studies experienced. For example, nearly half of the California veterans reported having completed an educational degree on the G.I. Bill. The education portion of the bill was designed for men in their early adult years – men most likely to want to complete an undergraduate education. Thus, the usual structure of the life course made the bill and its benefits more attractive to the younger men who lacked the competing alternatives to higher education, such as marriage and a family or a full-time job.

Typically, military mobilization seeks young men not involved in families and careers. However, the enormous work force needs of World War II prevented strict adherence to this standard. As the recruitment boundaries included larger numbers of older men, the personal disadvantages of service also expanded. Beyond the formative times of adulthood, older recruits experienced more of the costs, through career and family disruptions, and fewer benefits (e.g., the G.I. Bill) when compared with early entrants. By comparison, early entry into the armed forces minimized the costs and increased the benefits. For these men, military service was truly a timely event, especially if they came from hard-pressed families. By enhancing opportunity and achievement for men who grew up in the depression, military service functioned as a turning point, or change, in the life course.

There are thus two parts to our interpretation of military service as a turning point. One links Great Depression hardship to military service, and especially to an early entry into the military. In this scenario, deprived boys who lacked achievement options as well as feelings of personal worth are attracted to military pride and self-respect and the masculine appeal and status of military dress. They could, it seems, become someone of note merely by joining. The second part of the interpretation assumes that military service diminishes the persistence of prior disadvantage. From this perspective, the adult disadvantage of a deprived childhood in the 1930s would be least among men who entered the service at a relatively young age. Not surprisingly, the evidence shows that early mobilization was a major pathway toward life achievement and away from depression hardship among veterans in the California and Manchester cohorts.

The best single test of the turning point thesis is provided by the younger cohort of Berkeley veterans (born in 1928–29) and their counterparts in the Manchester working class. Members from the Berkeley cohort enjoyed higher status before the Great Depression than did members from the Manchester cohort, but they also had more to lose. We begin with the Berkeley cohort and then consider the life histories of the Manchester cohort.

Escaping hard times in the Bay Area

When war mobilization started, the younger Berkeley adolescents were in high school. A midwar survey found them surrounded by symbols of war mobilization (Elder, 1986). Signs of mobilization and consciousness raising were everywhere in Berkeley. A local radio series entitled "My War" dramatized "the wartime contributions of every man, woman, and child on the home front." Children at Saturday matinee movies saw war's reality through newsreels. Troop trains from nearby army bases chugged constantly through Oakland, and warships moved in and out of the bay. Families worked victory gardens on vacant plots – over 40,000 were reported in the East Bay Area during 1943. The energetic role of young people in the war effort and their resulting sense of significance are strikingly documented through the seemingly endless round of collection drives for fats, wastepaper, scrap metal, and even milkweed pods.

Among the Berkeley boys, "the war" became the most popular conversational topic with peers, outranking girls, school, parents, and "things I want." As military events began to shift in favor of the United States and the Allies, the boys were asked what they most often talked about with friends. The list included aspects of popular culture (such as movies), relations with girls, family and school affairs, and war items – the war in general, the armed service one would choose, the new defense workers and their families, and postwar planning. Over half the boys claimed that they often talked about the war with other boys, and the preferred branch of military service was only slightly less popular (53% vs. 41%) as a topic. For many boys, a major concern was getting into the armed forces although underage.

These preferences are revealing on the boys' future life course and reflect disadvantages extended back into the Great Depression. Slightly more than 70% of the Berkeley boys eventually served in the armed forces, and those who found the war an especially salient experience were likely to join up at the first opportunity, frequently during the last months of World War II. Early joiners entered the service before age 21; later entrants, at age 21 or older. Nearly 70% of the early joiners selected at least one military occupation on a "things to be inventory" in 1943–44, as did over half of the late joiners. Fewer than 40% of the men who never served also chose a military occupation during their high school career in World War II. Conversation (in the interviews) on this topic shows corresponding differences among these groups.

Disadvantage is a factor in the military preference of the Berkeley boys and in their mobilization. Frequent talking with peers about military roles during World War II is linked to disadvantages of one kind or another, such as low family status, deprivation, poor high school grades, and feelings of personal inadequacy. This background of disadvantage was more relevant to the timing of service than to entry itself. From all perspectives, the stronger the disadvantage, the *earlier* the military induction (Elder, 1986). Boys who entered the service early turned out to be the most disadvantaged group in the cohort. They were most likely to grow up in hard-pressed families during the 1930s, and their school performance was less than promising. They were less goal-oriented, less confident, and less assertive than other adolescents in this cohort.

But did the life disadvantage of entering recruits carry over to their postmilitary lives (Elder, 1986)? To answer this question, we must distinguish between veterans who entered the service relatively early and late. The early joiners stand out on family and personal disadvantage relative to late entrants. The early recruits have more in common on family disadvantage with the Berkeley men who did not enter the service at all. But they were actually more successful in terms of education – 70% completed at least some college, compared with 58% of nonveterans. For many early joiners, the G.I. Bill made college possible and a reality.

Consider the life experience of two men who came from deprived families in the 1930s. The first young man, from a working-class family, expressed a positive attitude toward the military during World War II. He listed a variety of military occupations; however, becoming a marine remained his primary goal. As his mother said at the time, "He'll be a marine regardless of what I want him to be." He followed through on this objective by quitting high school at age 17 and persuading his parents to let him join the marines. After a 4-year stint in the Middle East he returned to civilian life, launched an apprenticeship in printing on the G.I. Bill, and married his high school sweetheart. The other young man, with similar aspirations for military service, dropped out of high school and joined the navy. After the service, he became a member of the air reserve and earned a high school diploma. Eventually, his fascination with flying led to his enrollment in a university electrical engineering program on the G.I. Bill.

Not all of the Berkeley veterans went on to higher education and took advantage of the G.I. Bill in the 1940s and 1950s. Three observations are relevant here. First, military service did not reinforce or increase the educational aspirations of all men. Some with strong vocational skills (e.g., electricians) entered corresponding jobs after demobilization. Second, the experience of combat left some men psychologically impaired, and typically these were men who ranked lowest in ego resilience in adolescence. Third, some men who returned to demanding family responsibilities were discouraged from entering or completing their higher education. From another perspective, those men did not receive the support from wives, children, and parents that would enable them to take advantage of the G.I. Bill. The time for personal sacrifice had passed.

Occupational experience provides more conclusive evidence that military service became a turning point in the life course of men with backgrounds of disadvantage in the Great Depression. By the age of 40, men who entered the service early ranked slightly higher on occupational status than nonveterans. The two groups are evenly matched on family social class in 1929, although early entrants were far more likely to come from hard-pressed families, by a difference of three to one. More notably, we even find increasing similarity up to the middle years in the occupational rank of early and late entrants, despite their markedly different backgrounds and preservice educational achievement. For example, slightly more than half of the late entrants were college graduates, in comparison with a third of the early joiners. Status differences of this sort tend to diminish as we follow the men into their later years, but how does this occur?

Are there developmental gains over the life course, from an ineffectual pattern of behavior in adolescence to greater mastery and self-direction during the middle years? Consider a comparison of the early entrants and nonveterans (in California) on four measures of psychological functioning in adolescence and at mid-life (approximately age 40): self-inadequacy, goal orientation, social competence, and submissiveness. The content of each measure is identical for the two periods. In general, the data point to a convergence of psychological functioning by mid-life, with veterans who joined the service early showing a pronounced shift toward greater competence. However, these men still have not completely closed the gap with nonveterans; at mid-life they still rank slightly lower in all areas.

Our concept of military service as a potential turning point for children of the Great Depression is based in part on the assumption that service experiences markedly reduced the persistence of initial disadvantages. As noted, military service did weaken the usual cross-time correlation between adolescent and mid-life competence. In this case, adolescent disadvantage should be more predictive of military service than the latter is predictive of adult disadvantage. The data favor this interpretation, but other interpretations (such as regression to the mean) warrant consideration.

Developmental growth among men entering the service at an early age suggests another perspective on the service as a recasting mechanism. Military service may enhance life opportunities by enabling men to *use their personal resources* to good effect in education, work, and family. Motivation is part of the explanation, along with personal qualities that veterans frequently cite as benefits of their service experience (Elder, 1987b). Especially prominent among these qualities are self-discipline, ability to cope with adversity, and skill in managing people. Such qualities are most likely to be put to a test among children of the Great Depression, who had to use all they had to be successful in life. Neither a quality education nor a rewarding job is a given for this cohort.

Building on this account, we assume that military service is more predictive of occupational achievement among men from deprived families than among the nondeprived and, further, that the service effect occurs primarily through higher education. To put these ideas to a test, Elder and Caspi (1990) set up the same prediction equation for men from deprived and nondeprived backgrounds: childhood IQ and military service as antecedents of mid-life occupational status. The analysis shows that military service has a significant effect only among the economically deprived, whereas IQ is generally predictive in both groups. Second, the service effect occurs primarily through higher education. With education in the model for men from deprived families, military service no longer has any effect on adult occupational status.

These results suggest that some children of the Great Depression broke the cycle of disadvantage by entering the service and, if not mobilized, by virtue of their own intellectual ability. By contrast, the attainment of men from nondeprived homes most clearly hinges on their own abilities. Military service in young adulthood neither aided nor hindered their life success, in large part because these veterans generally entered the service later in life, often in response to induction processes.

Many years after the Great Depression and World War II, the director emeritus of the Berkeley Guidance Study, Jean Macfarlane (1963, p. 338), offered some reflections on the lives of the Berkeley men that summarize in many respects the turnaround we observe in the life course of veterans who grew up in deprived families. She notes that some of the Berkeley boys turned out to be more stable and effective adults than any of the research team, with its differing theoretical biases, had predicted. Most noteworthy, she observes, are the number of men whose poor adolescent scholastic records "completely belie the creative intelligence demands of their present position." A large proportion of the "most outstandingly mature adults in our entire group . . . are recruited from those who were confronted with very different situations and whose characteristic responses during childhood and adolescence seemed to us to compound their problems" (Macfarlane, 1971, p. 413).

These reflections are not scientific observations by any means, but they are remarkably attuned to the results we have presented. Macfarlane sought explanations for the disparity between early experience and the adult life course in the psyche and proximal world of the individual. First, she notes a common failure to recognize the potential maturation value of hardship experiences. As she puts it, "We have learned that no one becomes mature without living through the pains and confusions of maturing experiences" (1971, p. 341). Second, she decries our insufficient appreciation of experiences in late adolescence and early adulthood, including the potential of later events for altering life trajectories. According to Macfarlane, a large number of the Berkeley boys did not achieve a sense of ego identity and strength until later situations "forced them or presented an opportunity to them to fulfill a role that gave them a sense of worth" (p. 341). Thus, developmental gains may be associated with departure from home and community, changes that provide an opportunity to "work through early confusions and inhibitions" (p. 341).

Indeed, historical features of the transition to young adulthood offer promising explanations for the disparity between early deprivation and adult fulfillment among the Berkeley men as children of the Great Depression. After a decade of depression hardship, these men experienced the new prosperity of full-scale mobilization in World War II, followed at a short distance by the Korean War and postwar era affluence. Paradoxically, mobilization for World War II and the Korean War converged in ways that improved life choices or altered forever the depression's legacy of disadvantage, placing young boys of the Great Depression on a more promising route to personal growth.

Military service *and* higher education emerge in the lives of the Berkeley men as events that turned their lives around by enabling them to surmount childhood disadvantages in the 1930s. Another event of significance for changing the course of lives is marriage. Robins (1966) underscores the critical support a spouse provides in enabling the young to overcome problem behaviors in the transition to adulthood, and we find similar benefits of wife support in the lives of Berkeley and Oakland veterans from World War II and the Korean War (Elder & Clipp, 1988). Mobilization frequently brought the veterans in these cohorts together with their prospective wives on army bases or in hospitals; in some cases, the prospects of wartime separation lead to hasty or early marriages. For men who had lost confidence and hope in their future, an optimistic wife could turn around their dysphoric outlook toward greater vitality and ambition for a new day. Judging from available evidence, husbands and wives are likely to change in similar directions over time, far more so than unrelated men and women (Caspi, 1989).

From another angle, we find that the young women who managed to escape the hardships of the 1930s generally did so through marriage to a young man of potential. Indeed, the depression experience itself tended to orient women to life accomplishment through marriage by increasing the importance of interpersonal ties and reducing the value of higher education for daughters who, as one father put it, "are only going to marry." A middle-class mother from the Berkeley sample expressed aspirations for her daughter as "college, social popularity, and an early marriage." This young woman met her upwardly mobile spouse at college and promptly left school to marry (Elder, Downey, & Cross, 1986). Women of this generation frequently sacrificed both education and occupational careers for the work of husbands and presumed domestic claims of the home.

Wartime employment, the college campus, and population mixing through wartime demands played important roles in shaping the marriage experiences of the Berkeley women. By mid-life, these women of deprived childhoods had gained more through marriage than through personal accomplishments. Marriage turned out to be a more prominent route to high status for them than for women from more privileged backgrounds.

A respite from the Great Depression in Manchester

The coming of wartime imperatives to the depression-weary community of Manchester set in motion general change processes that drastically altered the lives of young people from working-class families. War production on the home front sharply increased job opportunities and earnings just as military recruitment siphoned off the young men for basic training and overseas duty. Both types of mobilization opened up a future of greater opportunity, if only within the working class. War pressures also increased the incentive to marry before the expected separation during overseas duty; the rate of marriage actually accelerated during the war. Finally, the loss of workers from the community and the opening of war industries expanded women's roles in particular, both within the household and in the community. Each of these developments is part of the mobilization experience for Manchester's children of the Great Depression.

Following the decision of the United States to join the war, the city's atmosphere was permeated with patriotic drives and appeals to Manchester's citizens to do their best in the war effort. Public buildings were plastered with recruitment posters from the military and the War Production Board, and churches acted as clearinghouses for information and as recruitment stations to the military and for various aspects of the war effort. The patriotic atmosphere was heightened by the Office of Civil Defense, which warned about the presence of submarines off the coast. Manchester residents' sense of connection with a distant war abroad was reinforced by the constant movement of troops through the city on their way to the adjacent Grenier Airfield, where they took off to Newfoundland and on to England.

The feverish excitement of the war and its patriotic effort was especially significant in Manchester where former mill workers still suffered from the double blow of the Great Depression and the shutdown of the Amoskeag Mills. The war effort united community members with a new sense of a common purpose and a commitment to the joint effort for survival. Sons and daughters who had left in search of jobs outside Manchester returned to find employment in the new industries mushrooming in the city. New feeling of hope overcame the sense of despair and loss of purpose in the wake of the shutdown of the mills.

The first stage of Manchester's recovery during the war entailed the opening of various war-production factories in the empty buildings of the Amoskeag Mills – a sweater factory for the military, a rubber plant for producing rafts and life jackets, a metal factory that made bullets, and a parachute factory. These industries restored the beat of life and activity into the desolate mill yard and recruited men and women of all ages. In addition, the Portsmouth Navy Yard, only an hour's drive from Manchester, and nearby Grenier Airfield attracted young working men in large numbers.

Jobs were available again after a hiatus of about 8 years. (Even though the Amoskeag Mills shut down officially in 1936, the company had actually employed only a rump labor force from about 1933 on.) Manchester's teenage boys and girls and even their older siblings were surprised at the sudden return of opportunity: "And they paid well. Boy did they pay," reminisced one of the Amoskeag's young workers who had remained unemployed after the mill's devastating shutdown.[2] Manchester youth who had been wandering around in other parts of New Hampshire and New England, working on occasional, temporary jobs, began to return home and start regular employment at unprecedented high wages.

For Manchester's young men, the war counteracted the deprivation imposed by the Great Depression in two stages. First, war industries provided employment, some of which involved learning professional skills. These opportunities benefited the entire community and provided new employment for women as well. Second, the war opened up new opportunities for young men through military service. When the war industries were first inaugurated, people were seized with excitement: "You could make yourself three to four hundred a week, no problem at all. Big money!" recalled a former shipyard worker. "My father was working for $54 a week for that job he had all his life. I told him 'Quit it Pa! Quit it. Come down to the shipyard and we will get you in there.' "

For some of Manchester's young men, the jobs that opened up in the initial war industries had a more lasting impact on their subsequent careers than military service by itself; but the military experience provided young men with excitement and a stage for heroic performance. Those who went to work in the war industries before military service felt for the first time a sense of self-respect as workers and enjoyed the kind of sociability with fellow workers that their parents had enjoyed in the Amoskeag Mills. These young men had missed that experience entirely because of the shutdown of the mills and the Great Depression. In many cases, the military also taught young men new skills they could use after the war.

Manchester's young men and women, born between 1920 and 1924, were the cohort that came to work when there was no work (E. C. Hughes, 1971, p. 124). They were the "lost generation" of the Great Depression, the children of the shutdown of the Amoskeag Mills. As they were growing up, their parents dreamed that they would escape mill work by graduating from high school and entering "middle-class" occupations. The decline and the shutdown of the mills in the midst of the Great Depression set this cohort's progression into the middle class back by one generation. Not only were they unable to escape blue-collar occupations, they felt fortunate to have a chance to return to or enter such occupations once the war industries opened in Manchester.

One long-time resident, Carl (born 1922), was able to embark on a steady job in a textile mill in Manchester in 1941 because of employment opportunities created by the war. The availability of textile work enticed him to quit high school. Carl got his job because his father was a foreman.

So he got me the job with the intention that by September I'd go back to high school. Well my intentions were all the time that I'd never go back to school, because I hated it. . . . [S]o come September I really fussed about going back to school and my mother forced me or tried to force me and ah, from one thing to another my father said, "Look, he's old enough to know what he wants, he's 18, almost 19 years old, it's up to him to make his decision. If he wants to work in the mill, he can work." Which is what I did.

Pete, also born in 1922, was first able to improve his chances by entering the war industries after a long period of floundering and unemployment during the depression. "In those days (I'm talking about 1939) there was no work . . . and I was happy to work even for nothing, to learn something." Pete first worked as a plumber's apprentice to learn a trade. He subsequently worked in a shoe company gluing soles and finally found a job assembling typewriters at the Royal Typewriter Company in Hartford, Connecticut. After 9 months Pete was laid off because the company was being converted to produce Colt firearms. He was finally saved from unemployment by the war industry at Pratt and Whitney Aircraft. "It was good work and it was a lot more money than I'd ever made in my young years."

The draft diverted Pete from the chance to make money in the war industries: "As a patriotic American I had to enlist. I was actually drafted into the army, but I didn't want to go into the army, so I volunteered to go into the navy." Because he was making aircraft engines, Pete did not have to enter the service if he preferred to continue working. But he said, "I would not hear any of this" and volunteered.

Pete was sent for training to the submarine school in Newport, Rhode Island. He became a torpedo man and served on a submarine in the Pacific until the end of the war.

I enjoyed serving my country. I enjoyed every minute of it. If I had to go back in the service that's what I'd want. Of course it wasn't a picnic, but you had to be doing something to save your country. And to me that was what I did and I enjoyed it!

After Pete's return from the service, he sold hardware in Manchester. Two years later he joined the family beauty supply company his brother headed. Family ties proved eventually to be more critical in finding Pete a steady career than his navy experience.

My brother was after me to go to work for him, so I decided to start working for him, on a basis that I would be looking for something else later. And obviously I didn't find anything else better because I've last[ed] for 35 years.

Pete's large family could stay together in Manchester because of the availability of jobs.

I think the big factor that the family stayed here so close is that we all found work here. That's what it amounts to, we all found a job and something to do and the something that we had in common, the beauty business.

The war industries were also extremely significant for those family members, especially wives and daughters, who did not join the military and who were able, therefore, to work and support the family members who remained at home, while the men were away.

One of the women in the Manchester study (born 1924) worked in several war industries and managed to support herself, her children, and her mother-in-law during her husband's 4-year absence. At Manchester Metal Products Company,

We were making 15-millimeter bullets. I was inspecting bullets – I was a little squeamish in there. I was afraid if you don't do it right it might backfire. It might kill your own man.

Helen soon quit to work in a sweater factory for military supply as a hand cutter. "I was the only one who could cut army sweaters; 50 dozens a day, by hand."

The war provided Manchester's young men with an escape from parental and societal pressures to attend college or obtain steady work. As noted for the Oakland and Berkeley men, it offered a moratorium from the usual expectations that young men move through orderly sequenced transitions, such as graduating from high school and embarking on a continuous, stable career or continuing with higher education or technical-professional training. The war provided an excuse for the men's delay in following such regular career patterns, especially where deprivation during the Great Depression had rendered regular careers impossible.

For some young men, the war also offered an escape from oppressive employment conditions. Consider an 18-year-old working in a shoe factory. He had a conflict with his boss.

I had damaged a shoe. And he came over about nine-thirty in the morning, started chewing me out. Well, I shut off my machine and told him where he could shove his job, and I took off, and I went downtown, and I enlisted in the army.

His wife remarked during the interview, "That's a patriotic way of going in the army."

For Manchester's young men, like for their California age counterparts, the war provided an opportunity to regain their self-respect, acquire skills, demonstrate their aptitude, and perform well even under trying circumstances. For Jerry (born 1920), the service provided such an opportunity. It also counteracted to some extent his educational deficiencies resulting from lack of a high school education. During technical training in the navy, Jerry felt under a severe disadvantage for not having graduated from high school. "I had to work three times as hard as anybody who had finished high school to get the same passing grade."

Before going into the service, Jerry could find only casual jobs (such as dishwashing in a grill or delivering for a meat market where his brother-in-law worked). He enrolled in a Civilian Conservation Corps camp for unemployed youth in the White Mountains where he worked in a forestation project for 6 months. After that, Jerry could find work only in Vermont, where he was buffing leather for the International Shoe Company. "Work was very hard to get in Manchester" before the war. The period just before the war was "the hardest time in my life."

Jerry joined the navy in 1941 and trained as a radio operator. He reminisced,

That training made my subsequent advancement in the area of electrical technician possible. When I went in the service, I joined the navy and became a navigation radioman. I knew absolutely nothing about radio and electronics.

After the service, he enrolled in a technical school under the G.I. Bill, where he learned to repair electrical motors. Following graduation from the technical school, Jerry worked steadily as a turbine tester for General Electric until 1955, when he became a supervisor, a position he still held at the time of the interview in 1983.

In assessing his own progress, Jerry speculated on how far he actually might have gotten had he started with a high school education.

I picked myself up by my bootstraps as you might say, because I came out of the navy as a chief petty officer and worked my way into General Electric to a supervising position. So I think if I had had an education, I might have been dangerous.

The war had such a profound impact on his life that when asked to describe the main periods in his life, Jerry designated the war years as a distinct period:

Well, I'd say the start of my life, when I was a child in the city of Manchester would be one period of life – very stable. And then the Second World War which is a period of turmoil, trials, tribulations, separation . . . and then I'd say the third period was bringing up the children . . . which is a period of responsibility. Now we are coming to the fourth period, which I'd say would be leisure.

Another cohort member (born 1923) viewed the military as an opportunity for education before the war broke out. Raymond grew up in Greenfield, Indiana, and married a Manchester woman. While in high school, he worked at various odd jobs.

I started passing newspapers . . . at 4 in the morning; and then I started working in the soda fountain at the local drugstore, naturally. All of us kids went through that I believe. I worked at the swimming pool, at the park; I also helped take care of the clay tennis courts in the summertime. And I hoed corn for a dollar a day from sunup to sunset and believe me that was rough, but I was tickled to death to make a buck.

After Raymond graduated from high school, his parents wanted him to train as a butcher. "And I says 'forget it.' So I went into the service hoping to get some education, so I could maintain a job. And I didn't realize that we were so close to war." After his release from the service four years later, Raymond went to Tri-State College in Indiana under the G.I. Bill. He then made his career as a civilian employee for the military. In the 1960s Raymond worked at a satellite tracking station in New Hampshire. The war provided him with a critical turning point for his education. It also enabled Raymond to meet his bride in Manchester and eventually to settle in New Hampshire.

Beyond teaching specific skills, military service also expanded the horizons of many young immigrant men in Manchester, by enabling them to learn the English language. One member of the Manchester cohort study, Henri (born 1927), who grew up in Manchester's "Little Quebec" on the West Side, attributed his acquisition of English and the ensuring benefits to his subsequent employment to his military service:

We spoke French outside, we spoke French inside, and when I went to the service this is where I learned [English]. Grammar school was all French even in the English class. I learned the hard way so I didn't want my kids to go through what I went through.

After 8 years of grammar school, Henri worked in a shoe shop. He entered the service at age 17 and left after 4 years. Next came work in a canteen for 2 years – a job made possible only by Henri's knowledge of English. After that he worked as a bread salesman. (His military pay, $20 a week for 52 weeks, enabled Henri to search for a job after he left the service, while contributing to his family.) He has continued to work as "a bread man ever since."

As it did for the California young men, the service opened new social and psychological horizons for the Manchester men and provided them with a new experience and an understanding of the world. "The war made me a better person," said Paul (born 1926), who had enlisted at age 17. "The war opened up my eyes. I learned a lot." As a gunner's mate on a ship, he went to France, England, and Africa, "all through the invasion," and then to the South Pacific and Japan. These travels were his first time outside Manchester. After observing conditions in Asia, Paul came to idealize the United States:

It made me appreciate the United States more than I ever did [before]. I feel that we're living in the greatest country in the world. Actually you can get away with everything here. Really it's so free. It's unbelievable. . . . And what I saw out in Japan and in that area there . . . I feel that we're very fortunate. Well, the way the people were living and they weren't as free as we were.

He was deeply moved by the poverty he encountered in Asia. By contrast he welcomed "coming back here and having a nice home."

Despite his having grown up in abject poverty in Manchester and his disrupted childhood family life, Paul gained a new perspective on poverty and suffering from his observations in Asia beyond those of his family background. His father had deserted his mother, who was left struggling with work in the mill and rearing her children without outside assistance.

We were a poor family, because mother was left alone with all the family. She was working in the mills. She was all alone to take care of the whole family. That's why she died young [at age 51]. She died right after we came out of the service. Six of us were in the service during World War II.

Paul gained no special skills from the military to apply directly to subsequent work. The war did provide him, however, with a sense of self-respect, maturity, and a perspective on the world that enabled him to assess his own poverty and unfortunate childhood experience in the context of a broader world scheme. In addition, the service also facilitated Paul's marriage. He met his spouse on the train from Boston to Manchester, the very day he was mustered out of the navy. He was returning home, and Arlene was returning from a day's excursion with "a bunch of the girls." "I got married young because I needed a home. I had no home. My mother had died and we were all alone. So I wanted to make a home for myself."

For most members of Manchester's war cohort, as for their California counterparts, the war reversed some of the disadvantages imposed by the Great Depression on community and individual levels. However, the pattern of reversal and the ensuing levels of achievement were different. Whereas most of the California men started from a middle-class base, the Manchester men were from the working class, and many of them had grown up in poverty or on its margins during the depression. They had few resources to fall back on.

Members of the Manchester cohort were textile-mill workers, shoe workers, metal workers, and semiskilled laborers. Their fathers had been textile workers or shoe workers and their mothers had been textile workers, maids, and waitresses. The war did not afford these men opportunities to advance to the next rung of the occupational ladder or to escape their family's working-class status. At best, the World War II experience saved them from falling below the economic level of their parents prior to or during the Great Depression. It gave them a chance for a "new start" within their own class.

Accelerating the timing of life transitions

As it did in other places in the United States, for most of the members of the Manchester cohort, the war had a direct impact on the timing of marital decisions (Modell & Steffey, 1988). The war hurried the process along among couples who already knew each other. It also exposed Manchester's young men and women to new potential marriage partners from other parts of the United

States and even to local ones whom they met through war activities. Marriages in this cohort typically occurred in the early stages of the war or at its end.

Those who married during or at the beginning of the war eloped with their sweethearts before they left for duty. Most of the interviewees, husbands and wives, admitted that the timing of their marriage (the husbands age 20–21, the wives usually 3 years younger) was early by comparison even with the immediate prewar years and that elopement had been common. Thinking back, they were conscious of this early timing; those who married during the war did so in the face of the emergency and threat of separation for an indefinite period. Marriage after a service member's return was encouraged by postwar affluence. By contrast with depression times, the men who were returning now had prospects for a job and felt they could afford to marry and establish a family.

A Manchester resident who married in 1947 explained that depression hardships and obligations to one's family of orientation had caused delays in marriage. Conditions changed after the war "because then everybody was in the money . . . not lots of money but everybody had a job. There was work all over the place." The war, as he pointed out, also exposed people to the opportunity of meeting spouses from other places in the United States and other parts of the world. But the shutdown of the mills had already started the process of sending Manchester's laborers afar.

Consider a Manchester couple married in 1941. The new husband was already in the service, and he planned to take his bride from Manchester to a Florida military base. However, he was sent overseas a day and a half after the wedding. "Got married on a Friday night," reminisced his wife, "and on a Sunday morning I was all alone again for two years. . . . Never, never saw him [during those two years]. I had quit my job, packed my bags and everything." She stayed with her mother in Manchester and worked in a textile factory folding parachutes.

Another woman eloped at age 17 just before the war and eventually suffered through 4 years of loneliness. Even though the war precipitated young marriages, elopement was not unusual for Manchester's working class. "[Eloping] was an accepted thing to do in those days, because nobody had any money for weddings. Everybody was very poor before World War II, that big depression, it was terrible."

Many of the youth in Manchester had little family backing or control anyway:

Well he didn't have any father; he was on his own, and I didn't have anybody either. I was on my own more or less. He was a mechanic, but he had lost his job. He was A-1 in the draft, so after this it was Pearl Harbor. So every eligible man was called. He was 22, so he was called right away. He forgot to inform them that he had gotten married.

Left alone when she was 7 months pregnant, this bride reluctantly decided to return home to Manchester. "I swallowed my pride and I asked my folks if I could come there until the baby was born. . . . So my father took me in, and I had the baby alone."

Another young Manchester woman, Ellen, was attracted by the presence of large numbers of servicemen in Manchester. "We had a whole bunch of men at first in Manchester. And then I met my husband there . . . my first husband." Both were age 20. "I remember when it happened too. It was December 7, 1941. I was listening to the radio when it happened [Pearl Harbor]. I didn't quite understand what they were talking about." Ellen's fiancé then called her from North Carolina and said "he wouldn't be able to see me for a while . . . and from then on we wrote letters, and finally we eloped." They were married despite her parents' objection. Karl was German, and Ellen's parents wanted her to wait. They said, "We don't know too much about him and we have to wait until the war is over in case something happened to him." Ellen took her fate into her own hands:

Well, when you're in love, everything seems great and you just take a chance because you don't think of tomorrow; you want to do it right now; because tomorrow is too far away, at that time.

Ellen then became a "migrant" army wife through the war.

The war thus precipitated two transitions to adulthood for Manchester's youth. For young men it facilitated and accelerated the transition to a regular adult work life, preceded by skill acquisition and completion of high school or a technical education under the G.I. Bill. Similarly, the war enabled young women to enter into regular, well-paying employment in the war industries after they had been deprived of that role by the Great Depression and the mill's shutdown. The war also accelerated the transition to marriage and in many instances, the transition to parenthood. Sequencing of the transitions to work and to marriage was erratic, however. Prior to the war, the young couple's economic self-sufficiency was a precondition for marriage; however, during the war, marriage often preceded regular employment (especially the husband's steady employment).

Customarily, marriage would lead to the couple's establishing a separate household (one of the main conditions for independent adulthood in American society). In Manchester's working class, despite the high incidence of immigration and poverty, the residential separation of the new couple from their families of orientation was consistently respected, except in cases like the Great Depression, when temporary "doubling up" became frequent. During World War II, marriage placed young couples in a status of semidependency; the bride usually continued to stay in her parental home or with other relatives. While the groom was in the service, even among those who married at the end of the war, the wife continued to reside, at least temporarily, with parents or relatives until her husband returned. In many cases, the young couple continued to reside with parents until they were able to establish a separate household. Thus, although the war accelerated the transition to adulthood, on one hand, it also slowed the establishment of independent nuclear families.

The nature of this adult transition undoubtedly reflects the age at which men were mobilized. Entrants out of high school were seldom married, and their service frequently entailed overseas duty. We find marital delays in this subgroup. Older men involved in serious dating relationships often turned intimate friends into marital partners over a weekend.

A persistent historical theme in the study of the life course has been the interdependence of individual life transitions and collective family ones (Hareven, 1978). The common pattern among the families of orientation of Manchester's young people had been that of a strict subordination of individual members' career choices to the family's collective needs and strategies. This traditional pattern governed the early lives of Manchester's war cohort and cramped their chances for achieving greater occupational mobility by leaving home and seeking new opportunities elsewhere. The war partly counteracted this pattern of individual members' subordination to the family of orientation by providing opportunities for young men's separation from their families of orientation and by thrusting them into new environments and circumstances. That many young men enlisted voluntarily at age 17, even when they were not drafted, suggests their view of the war as an opportunity to break away from home and familial control. Both the Manchester and California cohorts' experience suggests that this desire to break from home was rooted in family hardships during the 1930s.

The war thus imposed a new pattern of timing on the transition to adulthood: it accelerated departure from the family of orientation and, at least temporarily, offered young men a chance to become "independent" without having to support themselves or their brides and without having to carry the usual responsibilities for kin support at home. The situation was somewhat different, however, for young women. Their entry into the labor force as part of the war-industry effort enabled them to contribute to their families of orientation while continuing to live at home. In this way daughters' work made up for the absence of income from sons who were in the army and cushioned the family from deprivation during wartime.

Any discussion of the career advantages that war opportunities and the service offered to the California or New England young men would be incomplete without viewing these individual men as part of a family configuration. In terms of careers, the war promoted a certain degree of individualism, expressed in the servicemen's temporary independence from their family of orientation. That independence was mitigated, however, by a persistent commitment on the part of servicemen to their families of orientation, or to their new spouses and their families of orientation, as the case may be. All the men interviewed emphasized their efforts to send remittances back home, meager as they were. From a life-course perspective, it would be inaccurate to interpret the young men's career accomplishments as strictly individual achievements. Their educational and career development during the service was backed up by the efforts and sacrifices of family members who stayed on the home front (most commonly women).

Despite the relief brought about by war industries, the families left behind were still coping with the ripple effects of the Great Depression, while being deprived of the economic contribution as well as personal support from loved sons, brothers, husbands, or fiancés. "He could have stayed home," reminisced a Manchester son about his father, "but he didn't want to, so he joined the merchant marines. We missed him terribly, and my mother kept writing letters." The division of labor was very clearly defined, as one woman put it:

The war came shortly after my father died, and the boys were all in the service and we girls [mother and three daughters] stuck it out until they all came home. And you pulled together. I think that's where your basic pulling together of families is. It was the hardship that everybody went through. You don't have that today to keep your families together.

Women served as a matter of course as back-up for male relatives who were in the service. One Manchester woman stayed home and worked in a newly re-opened textile mill in the old Amoskeag building while her brothers were in the service. She left school after eighth grade: "So my high school years were mostly the war years. I had no choice when I came out of grade eight, I was only 13 or 14. There was no question of going to the mill then." Emma went to work because "I wanted to help my parents and the boys were gone, and I didn't want to leave home until the boys came back." She contributed her earnings to her family. "Well you paid board, you know; you helped with the food and you were given a certain allowance."

A full understanding of men's ability to avail themselves of the challenges and opportunities presented by the service and to realize their potential depended on the support of family members on the home front. The back-up services family members provided at home by caring for young children and older relatives were crucial not only for the family's survival but also for the servicemen's ability to concentrate on resettling when they returned.

The careers of these men by themselves do not provide the whole picture, unless one takes family configurations, needs, and supports into consideration. Even the servicemen's ability to find a job often depended on kin connections after their release from the army. Several returnees entered their relatives' businesses, and many who acquired a house did so because their relatives, taking advantage of low prices, had already purchased one for them. Mutual assistance among kin had been a strong tradition among Manchester's working class all along. Members of the cohort studied here were raised in that tradition and retained a commitment to kin despite their transition to a more individualized career during the war.

Discussion

We set out originally to ask: Why did the Great Depression not produce a "lost generation" as was generally assumed? By placing the careers of the young men in Berkeley and Manchester in the context of World War II and the Korean War, the significant role of military mobilization becomes apparent in reversing or mitigating the injuries of hard times. The service had a positive impact on both the Berkeley and Manchester cohorts, but it did not affect the two communities uniformly.

In both cohorts, the service turned around the lives of men from disadvantaged backgrounds by enabling them to reverse the impact of the Great Depression. The extent of this reversal and its impact on their subsequent careers differed considerably by community. Most of the Berkeley men who started from a lower middle- and working-class base were able to advance far into the middle class. Their advancement, facilitated by the service, enabled them to move beyond the status of their parents.

In contrast to the experience of the men from the San Francisco Bay Area, the war did not have the same "elevating" impact on the lives of the young Manchester men. Although it considerably redressed the adverse impact of the Great Depression, by enabling Manchester men to enter relatively stable careers, the war made it possible for them only to remain floating and to keep their heads above water. Few members of the Manchester cohort managed to rise above their class origins. The Manchester men were more likely to start from a working-class base and did not rise much beyond their level. Rather than propelling them into the next level, the service prevented them from slipping below their parents' working-class status.

Other contrasts by place revolve around the fate of dominant institutions in the 1930s. In Manchester, the Amoskeag Mills shut down in the depths of the Great Depression, literally paralyzing the community and leaving an entire labor force unemployed. In Berkeley, on the other hand, despite the severe impact of the Great Depression, a variety of employment opportunities were still available because of Berkeley's diversified economy and the presence of the university.

Berkeley's young men, even within the working class, were better equipped to cope with adversity than the Manchester men when they encountered the Great Depression. The mill workers' families in Manchester had survived marginally even before the Great Depression and depended, therefore, on the labor of their children. Thus, even when military service offered veterans new opportunities, such as the G.I. Bill, the Manchester ex-servicemen were less prone to take advantage of them than were the Berkeley young men. Manchester men could not afford to take the time out for an extended education, whereas the G.I. Bill became one of the main avenues of advancement for the Berkeley men.

The positive impact of military service on these young cohorts was closely related to the community contexts in which the men lived. The differences in the life trajectories of young men in Berkeley and Manchester were thus the products of the interaction of *time* and *place*. Life in the working class has different meanings in historical time and in different places.

It is a tragic commentary on American society that an entire generation caught in the Great Depression had to wait for a global war to escape the lasting effects of economic deprivation. Nevertheless, even the effects of war industries and war mobilization on the cohorts of young men encountering them in Berkeley and Manchester differed in the two communities.

Acknowledgments

The first part of this chapter is based on the senior author's program of research on social change in the life course within the Carolina Consortium on Human Development and the Carolina Population Center. Elder acknowledges with appreciation support from the National Institute of Mental Health through Grant MH41827 and a Research Scientist Award (MH00567). He is indebted to the Institute of Human Development, University of California at Berkeley, for permission to use archival data from the Oakland Growth Study and the Berkeley Guidance Study.

Hareven's research for the Manchester data has been supported by two research grants from the National Institute on Aging. Hareven is indebted to Kathleen Adams for managing the interviewing in Manchester, to Michael Weiss for qualitative data analysis, and to Nancy Wilson for valuable assistance and editing. An earlier version of this chapter was presented at the annual meeting of the Social Science History Association in Chicago, November 1988. The authors are grateful for the comments of Karl Ulrich Mayer presented at that session.

Notes

1. The Berkeley and Manchester studies used different regimes in collecting and analyzing data. The Berkeley data are longitudinal records based on recurring interviews and observations that extend to 1928–29 and follow an annual schedule across the 1930s up to 1945. Adult follow-ups were carried out in 1960, 1972, and 1982. Using these data, it was possible to construct life histories from early childhood to the later years of life. Much of the data analysis on which the Berkeley study is based is quantitative. By contrast, the Manchester study relies on retrospective data that Hareven and her associates gathered through extensive life history interviews. These interviews were then augmented by demographic data on family histories and immigration and employment histories for each interviewee. The Manchester project uses both quantitative and qualitative analysis of the interview data. In preparing this chapter, we have sought to blend these two styles of research as much as possible.

2. Throughout the remainder of this chapter, we have used unpublished quotations from Hareven's Manchester data. Respondents' names have been changed to protect their anonymity.

4 Child development and human diversity

John Modell and Robert S. Siegler

Are American children becoming more different from each other?
Question posed at Belmont Conference (1987)

Liberal capitalist theory in the nineteenth century raised individual achievement to a uniquely exalted position. An individual's achievement was understood as both the measure of his or her worth as a person and the measuring rod by which rewards might most efficiently be meted out (Halévy, 1928; Polanyi, 1957). The focus on the individual in this accounting contrasted sharply with the group or communal focus of precapitalist systems. Paralleling the spread of this ideology has been the development of increasingly clear-cut expectations for individual achievement *at particular ages* (Ariès, 1962; Gillis, 1974; Katz, 1975; Kett, 1977). Increasingly explicit lifetime schedules have been established for how much of what kind of work ought to be accomplished by particular ages.

Providing resources so that children can achieve appropriate goals has in many ways been defined as a public responsibility in the United States. Universal schooling has played a particularly important role in this mapping between age and achievement. Over time, public education has come to provide a formal schedule for which goals should be achieved by which ages and a means for measuring and marking the extent to which these goals were achieved. The public school system has been charged with simultaneously increasing mean performance (so that individuals will be more productive workers) and decreasing interindividual variance in performance (to maintain some degree of equality within the society) (Fishkin, 1983; Jencks, 1972; Levine & Bane, 1975; O'Neill, 1985; R. H. Turner, 1960). Providing more and better schooling has been reasonably successful in attaining the first goal – to raise mean levels of performance. However, it has been less apparently successful in attaining the second goal – to decrease the variance.

Schooling, indeed, often contributes to individuals' becoming less equal, as more-capable individuals continually learn more than less-capable ones. The cumulative effect of many years of schooling is often to compound initial in-

73

equalities rather than to reduce them.[1] A recent study of parental behavior toward twins of whom one was of low birth weight found that mothers so profoundly compensated for the lighter twin's initial disadvantage that by 1 year the initially lighter twin, although still weighing less, usually had better coordination, dexterity, and muscle tone. The researchers found that mothers talked to the underweight twins more often. The parents, apparently realizing that one twin was considerably smaller than the other, gave that baby enough compensatory attention to facilitate its development (Goleman, 1988).

Our collaboration seeks to shed light on this ingrained paradox in American democracy by exploring some ways in which individuals come to be different from one another. Alone, neither developmentalists nor historians quite tell us "how it happens" that individuals are as different as they are. Both developmentalists and historians are concerned (sometimes even theoretically concerned) with the balance between mechanisms that promote homogeneity and those that promote heterogeneity, but they characteristically look at different levels. Developmentalists focus on mechanisms that influence the pace of developmental change by operating either within the individual organism or between the organism and its environment. Typically, they treat the environment as essentially exogenous, however relevant. Social historians, for their part, ordinarily focus on changes in the construction of the environment, most typically on institutional arrangements that with or without intent amplify or mitigate inequality among individuals. Typically, they do not examine individual development.

The connection that we seek to establish between these distinct disciplinary approaches is, in effect, a demographic one. It seeks to examine the aggregate characteristics of a population at a given moment, seen as the sum of the prior developmental paths of the individuals in the population, in relation to an ecology of planned and unplanned environments (Bronfenbrenner & Crouter, 1983). We also focus on relations between changes in these environments and associated aggregates of developmental paths. Having thus established an aggregative link between individual development and social change, we then suggest the possibility of feedback between the two levels.

The demographic link we develop here is an integral one in that it does not merely supplement the questions or evidence of one discipline with those of the other, but it seeks a method (and appropriate evidence) that answers a question that lies right at the intersection of the concerns of the two disciplines, driven by the shared outlook on the logical possibility of attaining equality with which we have opened the introductory section. But it is not the only kind of integral link one might find. Social-historical approaches, for instance, seem a priori to be ideally suited to carrying out satisfying research that fulfills some of the analytic goals (albeit at a lower level of variability) proposed in Urie Bronfenbrenner's ecological approach to human development.

In this perspective, the contexts in which people develop are themselves made problematic rather than controlled, as they would be in a laboratory study. Disciplinary collaboration between developmentalists and social historians would answer Bronfenbrenner's call for approaches that turn attention from the "ecologies of family disorganization and developmental disarray" (1986, p. 738) to the kinds of families and children ordinarily treated as control groups, that is, essentially as background whose "normal" functioning is taken for granted. Such collaborative research would testify "to the existence and unrealized potential of ecologies that sustain and strengthen constructive processes in society, the family, and the self" (p. 738; see also Bronfenbrenner, 1979).

A simplified example will serve as an introduction. Consider first the distribution of heights in a stylized population consisting of girls at three ages: neonate, early adolescent, and late adolescent. The neonates differ relatively little in height, all being breast-fed by healthy and well-fed mothers. Nevertheless, because of differing genetic endowments, their developmental paths will diverge as the girls grow into childhood, and, as a population stratum, the children will differ more in height than did the neonates. Girls' growth in height usually stops by late adolescence (Tanner, 1970), and, on the whole, once-prominent differences in height are damped. Thus, the girls' population variance in height will have reached a maximum in early adolescence and will have declined somewhat by late adolescence.

Now, let us complicate the example slightly by assuming that there are two (and only two) genetically similar socioeconomic classes in the society, the poor and the rich, and that under existing levels of economic development and institutional redistribution the rich can afford considerably better health care and nutrition than can the poor. In this case, the growth in height of some of the poorer girls will have been less between birth and early adolescence than it would have been under richer or more egalitarian child-care circumstances. And, arguably, the impact on attained height will be a widening one, the more so the more literal the "class" designation is and the more continuing the malnourishment and poor health care suffered by girls in the poorer class. Under such circumstances, the neonate population stratum will be about as variable in height as had been that in the first example, but the early adolescent stratum will be more variable. The height of the late adolescents will be considerably more variable – perhaps so much so that this stratum is (as it was not in the first example) more variable in height than the early adolescent stratum.

Finally, let us add one further complication to our example – an institutional feedback loop relating the diet individuals receive to the heights that they have already attained. We will suggest two variants of this loop: one designed to exaggerate the growth in height of the tall – and thus amplify the differentiation of height within the girl population; and one designed to promote greater growth among the short – thus reducing the variability in height within the girl population.

The first institutional mechanism sounds a bit bizarre, but some reflection will suggest that this is probably because of the particular capacity being exaggerated rather than because the institutional exaggeration of some particular capacity seems inappropriate: consider a highly regarded activity in which height is at a premium, such as girls' basketball. Neonates probably do not differ enough in height for a differential feeding program to be established, but, as we have earlier noted, girl children do. A year-round, nutritionally spectacular, full-scholarship basketball camp for tall girls (practically speaking, girls of poor-class origin, few others having parents willing to see them enter this brief career) might profitably be established. If so, it would promote the production of tall basketball players, exaggerating thereby the growth in height of certain individual developmental paths and amplifying the amount of height variation in the population.

Conversely, one could quite easily imagine targeted compensatory nutrition programs offered to short girls (typically poor). These programs would aim to maximize the girls' growth and reduce height differentials in the late-adolescent girl population as a whole.

Historically, state-provided secondary education in Britain has followed a pattern that should serve to suggest the complexities of real-world experience that underlie the purposely stylized example we offer. When first developed, around the turn of the present century, state-supported secondary schooling was explicitly and intentionally differentiated by the social-class background of the children who might wish it. The schooling appropriate to each child was that which fit the child for his or her same-sex parent's position. The inefficiency of this system in recruiting technical and other skill-based elites, however, led to an evolution that, by 1944, retained the notion of "streamed" schooling appropriate to different kinds of children but divined the kind of child one was by a test at age 11. Individual characteristics rather than categorical ones were to define placement; but, of course, students who tested best on the IQ-like examinations employed tended to be those from advantaged class backgrounds.

Finally, in the last two decades, the comprehensive school movement has come to dominate large areas of state-provided secondary schooling. This system explicitly (although not without some internal contradictions) seeks to *damp* developmental differences based on social-class background by actively integrating schools by social-class background and measured IQ. Debate now centers over whether individual excellence is not also lost in the process (Fogelman, 1983; Halsey, Heath, & Ridge, 1980; Rubinstein & Simon, 1973). Lacking parameters of class size, class differences in nutrition, and biological propensities concerning variance in height at the three ages, we cannot actually say how much height variation, and how much class differences in height, even our simplified examples actually would imply. Indeed, the "wrong" combination of parameters would upset some of the putative consequences we have just proposed. Even a one-sex, two-class, three-age model of the development of and differentiation in a single characteristic is thus quite complex. But, it does lay out the way in which the population is the point of intersection between the individual-level concern of developmentalists and the macroscopic, often institutional, concerns of social historians.

We examine the relation between variability in resources available to children and variability in developmental outcome. The analysis treats the development of variability in two senses: (1) *development of variability* within the individual life span, and (2) *changes in variability* over the past hundred years or so of historical time. First we examine some likely trends in "inputs" to children. Next, we examine in suggestive, not definitive, fashion age-related changes in individual differences. Here we develop the notion that individual development involves the progressive differentiation of a population of young people along a large number of dimensions. We examine how this differentiation occurs, partly through the increased scope of individual activity made possible by development but also through experience with various cultural institutions such as schools.

Following this procedure, we examine some historical changes in age-related individual differences, touching on changes in the relation between group membership (e.g., race or gender) and individual differences. We use height and measured IQ as examples. We have chosen these two from a large list of individual characteristics worthy of study because the two are inherently important and have been widely measured over the past half century and more. This combination is vital to what we are trying to do and is not common. We anticipated that mean height and mean measured IQ would increase over the period we studied – as they did – but we were unsure, indeed in disagreement, about how and whether their variance would change. We developed no a priori hypotheses about what kinds of individual characteristics would undergo progressive historical homogenization. Such a typology would be a valid goal of our interdisciplinary collaboration, but we correctly anticipated that it would be challenge enough to describe and account for what trends we discovered. Our most significant preliminary finding is a negative one: *there seems to have been a contrast between the really quite considerable changes in the ways in which resources have been made available to children and the decidedly modest changes in the shape of the distribution of individual capacities.*

In this essay, we aim to provoke thought by raising an important issue that integrates child development and social history. And we seek to begin the task of finding and assessing data adequate to develop empirically the several aspects of the theoretical problems we have opened. We make no case for inclusiveness, or for exhaustiveness. Rather, we press the evidence hard in the expectation that readers who find our questions intriguing will locate sources and devise measures that will be able to answer more definitively questions that we are here concerned mainly to frame.

The development of individual variability

Interindividual variability in cognitive capabilities appears to increase considerably between birth and adulthood. Biology, the environment, and the adaptation of parents and others in the social environment to biologically given capabilities all contribute to the increase. The precise relations of these factors at different ages almost certainly have varied in separate historical eras (Lerner, 1986), but it seems likely to us that the natures of children conspire to make the general trend in intellectual variability over age hold in all historical periods. Note that this statement refers explicitly to intellectual development; given the large personality differences observed in infants and young children (Thomas, Chess, Birch, Hertzig, & Korn, 1963), it is not at all clear whether the statement would hold true for social and personality variables. In this section, we focus on intellectual development within the individual lifetime, in particular, on intellectual development in childhood and adolescence. In the next section, we examine changes in the variability of these aspects of development over historical time.

Early in development, biology seems to impose consistency across individuals in cognitive and perceptual domains. By age 6 months, all but biologically impaired infants have attained considerable skill in seeing, hearing, and other sensory capabilities. The development of many of these capabilities is strikingly regular. For example, stereopsis, the ability to infer depth from purely binocular cues, is consistently not present at age 3 months but is consistently present by age 5 months (Birch, Gwiazda, & Held, 1982).

These early consistencies across individuals are not limited to perception. Language is another early developing skill that shows impressive regularities. Few children say words that are recognizable to anyone except their parents before 9 months. By 18 months, however, almost all nonimpaired children can say at least a few recognizable words. Vocabulary growth is quite slow before 18 months and then explodes between 18 months and 5 years (McCarthy, 1954). Few children are exceptions to these general rules.

The acquisition of prototypic cognitive capabilities, such as those Piaget studied, also shows considerable regularity early in life. Perhaps the central acquisition within Piaget's account of infant cognition (the sensorimotor stage) is object permanence, the understanding that objects continue to exist even when they cannot be seen, as when a ball rolls behind a screen. Until the age of 8 months, the large majority of infants fail Piaget's task for measuring this capability, yet almost all master it before their first birthday (Piaget, 1954). The nature of the acquisition and the age of acquisition is similar among children throughout the world (Flavell, 1963).

This early consistency is not matched in later childhood and adolescence. Infants acquire sensorimotor capabilities in all societies and at about the same ages; young children also acquire concrete operational reasoning in all societies, though the ages vary with the particular society and individual; formal operational reasoning is not acquired at all by some adolescents and is present in many others only in their areas of greatest interest and expertise (Goodnow, 1962; Piaget, 1972). Virtually all children learn to talk, though not all children learn to read. Likewise all children typically learn to count, though not all learn to do algebra and geometry. In general, the cognitive capabilities of 1-year-olds differ considerably, but not as much as those of 15-year-olds (Jones & Conrad, 1933).[2]

Some of the reasons for this increase in variability with age are straightforward products of increasing environmental variability. One large difference is the presence or absence of schooling, and of schooling in particular subjects. All children learn to talk from being exposed to speech. However, children not exposed to books do not learn to read; only the rare genius will discover algebra or geometry on her or his own. And without science courses, formal operational concepts such as inertia and torque are unlikely to be discovered.

Beyond the sheer presence or absence of schooling, there is considerably greater variation in the schooling children receive at older than at younger ages. In the elementary grades, the curriculum is highly standardized. Almost everyone takes the same courses. In junior high school and high school, there is greater freedom to choose electives and greater variation in which courses students take. By college, there often are few if any required courses. Often, two students graduate from the same college in the same year without ever having taken a single course in common. When some students take mostly science courses, others mostly business courses, and others mostly music courses, individual differences cannot help but increase.

This structuring of the curriculum reflects certain assumptions about both equality of opportunity and diversity of talents. It would be possible to begin the specialization process earlier than is done. Exceptional talent in areas such as mathematics and music is often apparent from early in development (Feldman, 1986), yet it is not until high school that special schools for children gifted in these areas are often available. That the U.S. school system delays separating students according to specific abilities for as long as it does suggests a belief that children should be given every opportunity to display their talents in as diverse areas as possible. That the school system ultimately does direct students of different abilities to different tracks and sometimes to different schools suggests a belief, at least among American educators, that the diversity of ability levels is sufficiently great that children (and society) would benefit from children of different abilities being educated separately.

Exposure to specialized schools and classes is one factor in increasing cognitive variability among children, but it is certainly not the only one. Even during the period when children are taking the same school courses, interindividual variability in cognitive skills increases with age. This can be seen in achievement test performance of children from different school systems. The state of Pennsylvania each year administers the TELLS test for the purpose of providing remedial education funds to the districts with the greatest number of low-achieving students. Students in the third, fifth, and eighth grades take the test. The deviation of districts from statewide means clearly increases between these grades. Based on data from the *Pittsburgh Post-Gazette* (June 27, 1987), the standard deviation of the 43 school districts in Allegheny County in percentage of students below the cutoff on the test (and therefore considered in need of remedial education) was 13 for third graders, 18 for fifth graders, and 22 for eighth graders. Illustratively, the range separating the highest and lowest scoring districts (the districts with the fewest and the most children deemed in need of remedial education) was 2% to 32% in third grade, 3% to 41% in fifth grade, and 3% to 54% in eighth grade.

As might be expected, these differences among districts in test scores were correlated with unemployment rates, income levels, percentage of minority students, and other demographic variables. Districts with higher per family incomes, lower unemployment, and fewer minority students generally had lower percentages of children deemed in need of remedial education than districts with lower family incomes, higher unemployment, and greater numbers of minority students. The pattern is consistent with a commonplace rule of thumb that by third grade, lower-class children as a group are 1 year behind middle-class children in school achievement, by sixth grade 2 years behind, and by eighth grade 2.5 to 3 years behind. Thus, increased individual differences in cognitive attainments with age are accompanied by increasing differences among socioeconomic groups as well.

Increasingly diverse environments are not the only contributor to the increase in variability with age. The cumulative effects of differing levels of mastery of early-acquired cognitive skills also lead to diverging achievement levels. For example, Chall (1979) noted that prior to about fourth grade, children "learn to read"; after this point, they "read to learn." The effect of not acquiring good basic reading skills early in schooling is a weakened ability to learn later in schooling. Not only will poor readers have trouble learning about history and geography, but they also will have difficulty learning algebra and geometry, because of difficulty in understanding the textbook. The handicap increases with age, as more and more skills are not acquired, or are acquired to only a limited degree, because of difficulty in the basic skills. Thus, divergence in achievement with age reflects not only increasingly diverse environments, and the increasingly close matching of environments to individual capabilities, but also persisting effects of earlier learning on later learning.

Height is a characteristic of individuals that does *not* become more differentiated over the ages 6 to 11. As we have earlier noted, populations do not continuously differentiate on all characteristics. Variance in height, however, is considerably greater among children (of any given age) whose parents were relatively poor. Using the data on heights of children from Cycle II of the National Health Examination Survey (U.S. National Center for Health Statistics, 1972), we see that children of parents with less education (we use this measure rather than parental income because it is more completely filled out and easier to compare with population estimates for earlier and later dates) on the average are shorter than those whose parents were more educated, whether for genetic reasons or for reasons of nutrition and health. The proportion of variance in height that is statistically explained by differences in parental education is small – in the neighborhood of 2% for boys and 2.5% for girls. For boys and girls, the greater height variance differentials are generally present in children with a parent who had less than a full high school education (perhaps one in three of the entire child population). This pattern was slightly more pronounced among girls than boys and among older boys than among younger ones.

The greater variance in height for children of parents of lower socioeconomic status could also have a genetic basis, but one must suspect that the relatively greater presence of malnourished and medically impoverished children among poorer families explains at least some of this greater variance. It seems likely that the majority of children of each socioeconomic group, in our economically advanced society, received fine care and feeding throughout childhood, and reached their genetic potential, but that some number did not – a number that probably approached zero among middle- and upper-class children but was greater among children of poorer parents. Tanner (1962), reviewing numerous studies documenting socioeconomic height differentials *within* populations, attributes at least a portion of the differential to "nutrition . . . and with it all the habits of regular meals, sleep, exercise and general organization that distinguish, from this point of view, a good home from a bad one" (p. 140; see also Douglas & Simpson, 1964). Within American populations,

low per capita incomes are systematically associated with smaller size. . . . With increasing per capita income, increasing household income, and increasing incomes relative to need, boys and girls are systematically taller. . . . The generalization holds, within ethnic and racial groupings, though at somewhat different levels. (Garn & Clark, 1975, p. 307; see also U.S. National Center for Health Statistics, Vital and Health Statistics, 1973, 1981)

We have described a historical increase in "inputs" to child development, including nutrition and medical care. We cannot actually measure how much children's nutrition has differed, but we can easily do this for another input to children – education. Census data indicate that as children on average were educated for more years, they were less likely to differ sharply in how much education they received. The duration of education for children coming of age around 1940 was only about 90% as variable as it had been for children 20 years earlier. But this figure was still 20% more variable than it would be in 1960, which, in turn, was slightly more variable than it would be in two more decades (Taeuber, 1965, Table 6; U.S. Bureau of the Census, 1984, Table 262). More education meant more uniformity in educational attainment.

Resource change for children and changes in children's variability

Over the past century, commitment of resources to physical and cognitive aspects of child development appears to have increased in absolute terms and become more equal across social classes. To assert such secular trends is not to maintain either (1) that they hold in all areas of child development or (2) that there have not been reversals over significant periods of the century, nor (3) that the past decade has not seen interrelated shifts in demography, the institution of the family, the national economy, and social policy that place our own time within a long, and probably historically significant, period of increasing denial of fundamental, developmentally significant resources, such as adequate food, clothing, housing, and medical care, to major categories of children (F. Levy, 1987). We assert merely that in the time perspective we take in this chapter, a first pass through the evidence suggests that a higher proportion of children has received most resources that we consider essential to achieving developmental potential. Because most of these basic resources provide developmental returns that probably diminish after a certain threshold is reached, we will assume that the effect of an increasing *average* level of provision will be a *homogenizing* one.[3]

The most encompassing change here has been the increasing productivity of the national economy, coupled with the reduction in number of children per family. The joint result of these changes can be seen in the per capita sum available for personal-consumption expenditures, the amount that families have available to devote to all the things pertaining to any or all of their members, including children, on a more or less discretionary basis. This index grew substantially and fairly regularly from the 1870s to about 1905, was roughly stable until World War I, grew thereafter until the onset of the Great Depression, picked up again in the late 1930s, and continued to enlarge from then into the 1970s. In constant dollars, per capita personal consumption approximately doubled between the 1870s and the first decade of this century, and it had increased by half or more again when the Great Depression intervened. By the end of World War II, per capita personal consumption was four times that in the 1870s. The next generation very nearly saw a doubling once again (U.S. Bureau of Economic Analysis, 1973).

This amount is, of course, an average based on an aggregate figure. It might be argued that disproportionate amounts of this economic gain were arrogated by the wealthier segment of the population, so that material life for the children of poorer people actually improved less than one might expect. The economic evidence, however, is otherwise. The close examination of Williamson and Lindert (1980), thoroughly alerted to other possibilities by a controversial literature, sum up trends in income inequality thus:

Inequality in income and wealth rose sharply in America between 1820 and 1860. An inequality drift continued after the Civil War, although at a much diminished rate. The upward drift accelerates from the turn of the century up to America's entrance into World War I. Inequality fell between 1920 and the early years after World War II. It has changed little since. (p. 95)

On the evidence of Williamson and Lindert, there can be no question but that over the century poorer people became, in absolute terms, much better off than they had been previously. Inasmuch as there is no evidence of secular increases in differential fertility by socioeconomic level that might offset poor families' overall gains in disposable income, and in view of the important diminishing returns that limit just how much health one can buy with good nutrition and medical care, we have reason to suspect strongly that in these regards, children raised in poorer families came, over time, to be relatively better off.

We are not surprised to discover, accordingly, that estimates drawn from studies of working-class family budgets conducted from the end of the nineteenth century to 1961 reveal that the total amount of family food expenditures (in constant dollars) has increased (U.S. Bureau of the Census, 1975). The amount of food per child has grown, conservatively, by a half. We can safely infer that the nutrition of the poorest among American families has increased sharply during this period, converging upon that of the wealthier, whose nutrition was already quite substantial at the beginning of the period.

Historical change, of course, need not be unilinear. The Great Depression was a period of some duration in which there was a sharp drop in average income. A series of careful investigations in the rather prosperous town of Hagerstown, Maryland, compared the mean and variance of white children's weights (which we would take to be more variable with depression changes in the family economy than would be their heights) in the early and mid-1920s, in the depths of the depression, and in the period of modest economic upturn at the end of the 1930s (Palmer, 1933, 1934; Wolff, 1941). Socioeconomically related *variability* in body weight at given ages was present at all dates, but at particular phases in children's physical development *increased* in the midst of and toward the end of the depression. It is apparent from the data as presented that governmental welfare provisions kept this variance from becoming even larger than it was and that the gain in variance in the last period under study can at least in some part be attributed to a phasing out of welfare provision.

No one could dispute that almost all children in the population, however situated, have benefited from scientific advances in medicine, which changed diphtheria, for instance, from a disease that in the early years of the century may have struck as many as one in three as they passed through childhood to a threat to virtually none (U.S. Bureau of the Census, 1975). The specifically *differential* effects of these changes are harder to document, but on balance, the health conditions of relatively disadvantaged people – children included – seem to have improved somewhat more rapidly than those of the best-off, although the relative change is swamped by the overall improvements (Lerner, 1975). Institutional changes, especially the growth in third-party payers, including the government, for medical services, have presumably worked to the relative benefit of the economically less well-off. Between 1939 and 1970, the proportion of the whole population covered by at least some hospitalization insurance increased from 6% to 86%; between 1948 and 1970, the proportion of all personal health-care expenditures accounted for by consumers' direct payments declined from over two-thirds to less than one-third (U.S. Bureau of the Census, 1975).

Inputs to children's formal education are especially relevant to the kinds of children's capacities that interest us theoretically. Proportions of children enrolled in school expanded at both ends of the age spectrum. The proportion of 6-year-olds in school at some time during the year increased from about half in 1910 to seven in ten by 1940 to 98.7% in 1983. Only about a third of 17-year-olds were enrolled in 1910, but over the next three-quarters of a century, this figure, too, reached nine in ten (U.S. Bureau of the Census, 1943, 1975). Retrospective data indicate that as many as 8% of Americans living in 1940 and born between 1865 and 1870 had had no formal education whatsoever, a proportion declining to fewer than 1% of those born between 1915 and 1920. With the increase in special educational opportunities for even this fringe over the next decades, the proportion of those born in the early 1960s who had received no formal education by 1980 had declined to three-tenths of 1% (U.S. Bureau of the Census, 1943, 1984).

Between 1870 and 1890 the average length of the school year in public schools was steady at about 130 days, but then it started climbing steadily, reaching 170 days before 1930. Since then, it has grown slowly, reaching 179 days in 1968. The proportion of enrolled children who actually attended on any given day – reflecting, roughly, the day-to-day willingness of parents to forgo income or assistance with farm work or other chores from children to allow (or to force) them to attend school – also increased. The average number of days children actually attended school rose from about 60% of the already short term in 1870 to about 70% in 1900 and around 80% in 1930, reaching 92% in 1968 (U.S. Bureau of Economic Analysis, 1973). It is self-evident that at least some of these changes would have had more of their impact on the least-favored portion of the population than on the more-favored.

Educational resources have not been uniformly available to boys and girls, but the inequality has decreased. In 1909, Ayres noted that "the United States is the only nation having more girls than boys in her secondary schools" (p. 150). That year there were 10 high school freshman girls for each 8 boys and by senior year no fewer than 2 girls per boy. Ayers attributed the girls' edge to the boys' superior job opportunities, but his evidence points to a further reason: many more boys than girls failed to be promoted, at all grade levels; discouraged, the boys dropped out of school. The evidence on grade retardation points to decreasing gender differentials as schools became more and more reluctant over the decades to refuse students promotion because educators knew that being left back led students to drop out. Because more boys than girls were in a position to benefit from this administrative decision, more male than female dropouts were averted. Gradually, over the twentieth century, boys' and girls' educational attainment through high school has converged almost entirely (Karpinos & Sommers, 1942, pp. 684–685; U.S. Bureau of the Census, 1943, 1984; U.S. Department of the Interior, 1921; Williams, 1945).

Whether overall educational stratification has actually decreased in the United States is a complex question, one to which the work of Robert Mare (1981) has added subtlety. Some of Mare's argument is worth reproducing here. Mare notes two concurrent facts: the generality of the expansion of educational inputs, as indicated earlier, and the stability over the twentieth century in the extent to which the number of years of education received by individuals has been influenced by family socioeconomic status. (About one-third of the variance in individual educational attainment can be explained by a battery of parental socioeconomic variables; this has been true for cohorts born as early as 1907–11 and as late as 1947–51.)

Mare's work is on this paradox: Why have the enormously more available educational opportunities not reduced "inherited" educational inequality? His empirical answer involves distinguishing *levels* of educational attainment, rather than treating attainment as a single continuous variable. When he does this, he finds that whether or not a child attended high school, given his or her having completed elementary school, over time *became increasingly determined* by parental socioeconomic characteristics. So also did completion of high school for those who had entered; and so also did college attendance for high school graduates. At the same time, each of these transitions was always more dependent on parental characteristics than was elementary education. Multiplicatively, then, the overall level of attainment remained roughly as determined by parental characteristics as it had been, although several of its more important details became more socioeconomically stratified. Mare invites the reader to choose which notion of inequality fits one's model better, and he admits that

one can . . . conclude that if, say, 95% of a cohort completes a level of schooling, the chances of completing that level are highly equally distributed. . . . On the other hand, such a conception ignores the degree to which that small percentage of the cohort who fail to complete the schooling level is selected from the poorest families. (p. 86)

Even if we are justified in assuming declining developmental returns to marginal increments in basic resources like food or medical care, it is not at all self-evident that this is the case for formal education. A model that mechanistically translated equalization of educational inputs into child-development outputs would probably predict that children have become cognitively more alike over the course of the past century, but we are uncertain of this model, however one might measure the cognitive differentiation of a population.

How might these changes in resources influence changes in group-related variability over time? First consider arguments that favor the position that between-group variability has decreased over time.

- The *availability* to different groups of inputs that influence variation in admired or rewarded capacities may have converged. For example, at one time, formal schooling was available only to children from relatively wealthy families. The change to the present situation, where almost all children attend school at least to high school age, would be expected to reduce variation in academic skills between social classes.
- The *relative quality* of input variables may have converged. For example, since the 1954 *Brown v. Board of Education* decision outlawing segregated schools, the quality of schooling available to black and to white children should have become more similar, if the goal of the policy shift was achieved.
- *Changes in absolute levels* of an input variable may have increased sufficiently that children in all groups have risen above the level to where further increases of inputs would not greatly promote enlarged capabilities. For example, even if the nutrition received by lower- and middle-class children continues to differ, if all groups have risen

above some minimum requirement needed to attain genetic potential for height, differences in height between social classes will have declined.

- *Correlations between group membership and input variables* may have decreased. For example, in the late 1960s and early 1970s, the percentage of middle-class white children who attended college declined, while the percentage of children from lower-class black families increased (Siegel & Bruno, 1986, Tables A-1, A-2). This would be expected to have reduced variability across racial groups in skills acquired in college, though the overall amount of variability in the population may have remained unchanged.

The first three of these sources of variation would be expected to influence individual variation as well as variation between groups. The last would not, however. This source of variation is particularly interesting because of the social policy issues it raises. Suppose that after some policy were adopted, variation in individual income remained the same but differences between blacks and whites decreased. This could occur, for example, if jobs such as computer scientist and maid, now held disproportionately by members of one group, became more integrated, but the overall distribution of jobs and the salary paid by each job remained the same. Would such a change be a victory for equality? If the money incentives used to encourage blacks to become computer scientists were to become high enough, relative to those offered to white computer scientists and to maids of both races, the total amount of inequality and also the amount of inequality within the black group might actually increase (Fishkin, 1983).

Now consider why differences among groups and/or individuals may not have converged and may even may have grown greater in the past 50 or 100 years. The reasons parallel those just cited for expecting convergence; they differ only in their focus. As an example of changes in absolute availability of resources, some resources that previously were not available to anybody (and thus were not a source of variation between groups or individuals) may have become available to some but not (yet) to others. Microcomputers are one prominent contemporary example, widely available to middle-class children but not as often to lower-class children either in schools or at home (Greenfield, 1980). The microcomputer example can also be used to illustrate how changes in relative quality of resources can lead to divergence between groups. Even when such computers are available in middle- and lower-class areas, teaching and software may be superior in the middle-class areas.

Turning to the third factor, increases in overall levels may allow the higher group to attain the minimum level needed for some additional advance but not allow the lower group to reach that level. That is, some capacities are subject not to decreasing returns to inputs but to increasing returns over the relevant part of the input–output curve. For example, increases in disposable income may have widened the gap between the percentage of middle- and lower-class children who have had the opportunity to travel to other countries and thus to learn about them at first hand.

The fourth type of change, decreases in correlations between group membership and input variables, seems unlikely to increase variability between groups. However, increases in correlations between group membership and input variables may also have occurred over the past 50 or 100 years. For example, the difference between whites and blacks in the percentage of children growing up in homes where both parents are present probably has increased (Furstenberg, Hershberg, & Modell, 1975; Hofferth, 1985b) rather than decreased.

Historians' accounts ordinarily focus on the provision of inputs to various activities and categories of people in society; indeed, more often than not, they focus on the mechanisms underlying the provision of inputs rather than on the provision itself. From this, historians commonly infer the effect on recipient activities or individuals but do not observe such effects directly. Developmentalists, by contrast, will concern themselves directly with the developmental impact of more or less adequate provision of a given resource but will rarely look to the aggregative consequences of changes in provision. As a first step toward developing empirically the area of theoretical overlap between our two disciplines, we now turn to our somewhat schematic "history" of the provision of developmentally significant resources over the past century, followed by a highly empirical but narrowly focused examination of two aspects of developmental variability: height and measured IQ.

Trends in children's height differentials

Before we lay out some further empirical data regarding changes over time in height, we must address a measurement question with substantial theoretical importance for our analysis. In this chapter, we often use the *coefficient of variation*, the standard deviation normed by the mean, as our measure of population variance. In using the coefficient of variation, we implicitly argue that the pattern we are most interested in examining is that of difference relative to the mean and, again by implication, that in a society, individuals measure their own situation *in comparison with* that of others. Thus, the American "poverty line" has risen numerous times, as definitions of what constitutes the minimum standard of living have risen along with the average standard of living (McClymer, 1986). Correspondingly, "short" infants are fewer centimeters short of the average for children their age than "short" adults are short of the average for adults.

In the end, our argument's implications have to do with individual capacities.

By employing the coefficient of variation we are arguing, for instance, that as formal education came to include an increasing emphasis on scientific topics, a pupil considered "accomplished" at science probably had an advantage in scientific knowledge over an "average" student that was absolutely greater than the corresponding advantage of an "accomplished" pupil of the same age half a century before. We argue that *the social rewards for individual capacities depend on rough comparisons of diffuse capacities implicitly calibrated by a socially constructed average.* One would look to the absolute standard deviation rather than to the coefficient of variation if one were concerned with *the capacity to perform particular tasks,* rather than with the social reward for individual capacities.

In the course of the past century, American boys and girls have grown faster and taller, but the heights of individuals at a given age have remained roughly as dissimilar to one another as always – they have neither converged nor diverged (Hamill, Johnston, & Lemeshow, 1972; E. A. Martin, 1954; Meredith, 1978; Tanner, 1979). Such stability speaks to the complexity of how the flow of inputs is translated into the development of children's capacities.

Much of what we know about the distribution of heights among the populations of nations at differing levels of economic development, and of socioeconomic differentials in height within given nations, would lead us to anticipate a historical decline in height differentials within the American population. *At a given historical moment,* the height of children within poorer countries tends to be more variable than the height of children in richer countries. As an illustration, in the mid-1960s, height measurements were made on large nationwide samples of children aged 6 to 11 in the United States, Egypt, and India. For boys and girls, the coefficient of variation among the Americans was the least, among the Indians, the most (U.S. Health Services and Mental Health Administration, 1970). As economic development progresses, presumably fewer children suffer deficits of growth (as compared with their genetic potential) as a result of undernourishment or sickness. Accordingly, we are not surprised to find that the variance in the height of native-born Trinidad slave children in 1813 and that of (usually) native-born American slave children in the first half of the nineteenth century was considerably greater than that in any of the contemporary samples already discussed (Friedman, 1982, p. 494; Margo & Steckel, 1982, p. 518). They also varied considerably more in heights among themselves than did the nineteenth-century American schoolchild samples that will be discussed shortly.

We examine height partly, of course, out of convenience: height is easy to measure accurately, and it long has been measured for the mundane administrative purposes of the military and as an indirect indicator of correlated phenomena of broader social interest (Tanner, 1982). But we measure height also because it may itself produce subsequent social reward, because it complexly

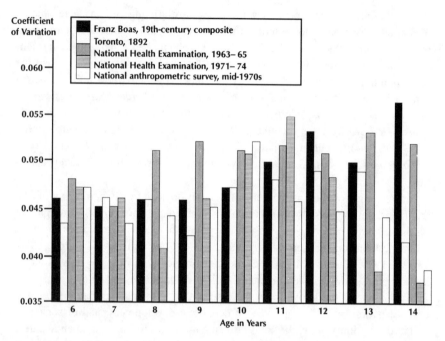

Figure 4.1. Coefficients of variation of American children's heights – girls.

registers the effects on the individual organism of a wide variety of environmental influences in development (Fogel, Engerman, & Trussell, 1982), and because it correlates positively, though weakly, with other valued capacities, including intelligence (Fogel et al., 1983; Humphreys, Davey, & Park, 1985; Tanner, 1966, 1982).

Tanner (1962) notes that the evidence on trend in the extent of the socioeconomic differential in size is weak, but it leans in the direction of supporting the idea of a reduction. At the same time, he infers this in part from declines in socioeconomic differentials in the age at menarche and notes that "the magnitude of the secular trend [toward younger maturity] is very considerable and dwarfs the differences between socio-economic classes" (p. 143). Overall differentials in height, however, do not seem to have declined in the United States over the past century or so. Beginning in the 1870s, a number of investigators explored American children's growth in height, depending on measurements of large and essentially representative samples of schoolchildren.[4] The six best of these nineteenth-century urban height studies were collated by Franz Boas, with the total sample size amounting to 88,449 (Boas, 1892, 1895; Boas & Wissler, 1905; Burk, 1898; Hastings, 1902; Hathaway, 1957). From these, we retabulated (cor-

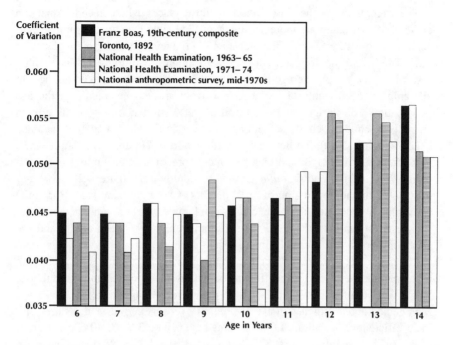

Figure 4.2. Coefficients of variation of American children's heights – boys.

rectly presuming a degree of computational error in those precomputer days) age-specific standard deviations and coefficients of variation. We drop tabulations at age 13, because of the increasing risk of underestimating population heterogeneity by selecting only the children who had remained at school.

American schoolchildren from the late nineteenth century were smaller but no more dissimilar from one another than are contemporary children of like ages. Figures 4.1 and 4.2 compare coefficients of variation at given ages for the composite nineteenth-century Boas sample with those for an 1892 Toronto sample (Meredith & Meredith, 1944),[5] for National Health Examination samples of the 1960s and 1970s, and for national anthropometric survey data of the mid-1970s (Snyder et al., 1977; U.S. National Center for Health Statistics, 1977). Initially, we should note the upward trend (in all samples) in variance with age, beginning to turn down by the teens for the girls, especially in the twentieth-century samples. Although there are numerous exceptions, it would be difficult not to conclude from these figures that *the height of children at given ages has not become more alike*. In fact, it would be rather difficult not to conclude from Figures 4.1 and 4.2 that heights have been becoming somewhat more *dissimilar*.[6]

The exceptions to the observation – those places where recent American children of given ages are more homogeneous in height than are their nineteenth-century counterparts – are at the oldest end of the age spectrum, particularly for girls. This is, presumably, a product of the timing of maturity, which is not only becoming younger on average but also becoming more concentrated in age.[7] In all samples, coefficients of variation rise from around the middle of the age period shown on the graphs, as a result of the dissimilar timing of the growth spurt from child to child, something only modestly correlated with attained height at some slightly earlier age. A birth cohort of children, that is, becomes more dissimilar in height and then becomes more similar, becoming – by comparison with childhood – *quite* similar in adulthood. Figure 4.1 shows unmistakably the homogenizing of girls' heights at the right-hand side. But, quite relevantly, it does so far more clearly, and rather earlier, among the recent samples. And, in fact, there are signs of homogenizing between age 12 and age 14 among boys, too, but only in the recent samples.

The general conclusion of increased heterogeneity in height is consistent with a comparison between the coefficient of variation in height among American World War I draftees and a representative sample of like ages a half-century later. Men gained about 2 inches in average height over this period, and, as they did, the coefficient of variation of their heights rose from 0.30 to 0.40 (Davenport & Love, 1921, based on the first 870,000 men measured; U.S. National Center for Health Statistics, 1981).

Any explanation for the positive trend, toward increased heterogeneity, which we find more nearly counterintuitive than otherwise, would be quite speculative. One simple possibility is that improved heroic medical treatment has outstripped improved nutrition and routine medical care, so that more defective (some exceptionally short) children now survive to be measured (or are "mainstreamed" into measured populations). A more intriguing possibility amounts to a variant of the sometimes curvilinear impact of improved resource provision on developmental differentiation, for which we earlier offered the example of the microcomputer. Perhaps subsequent height studies will continue the trend already observed toward decreasing heterogeneity as the growth spurt becomes younger and more uniformly so within the child population.

Trends in individual variation in IQ

Torsten Husén's international comparison (1967) of mathematics achievement for 13-year-olds, carried out in the first half of the 1960s, shows that among 10 countries to which a uniform test was administered, there was a correlation of $-.69$ between average score and variability of score, measured by coefficient of variation. Homogeneity was promoted by whatever school and study activities overall produced higher mean achievement. We assume (without data) that school skills (and, by extension, IQ) are more variable in economically (and thus educationally) less-developed nations, as we saw to have been the case with children's heights (Flynn, 1983; Stevenson & Azuma, 1983). Extended universal formal education provides an obvious explanation, one that would suggest historically convergent IQs within the United States and other nations that have moved historically to universal education.

No one can deny that there is much controversy about just what IQ is and about what any particular IQ test may measure. Both the history of IQ measurement and recent discoveries of cognitive psychology suggest that any notion that "intelligence" as measured by IQ tests is a fundamental capacity of individuals is misplaced; and one can hardly fail to recognize some rather crude political purposes underlying the gathering and publication of at least some of the old IQ materials that we employ in this chapter.

But to take IQ seriously as *an indirect indicator of a socially relevant capacity,* as we do here, does not require that we take on much of this baggage. We need only assert:

- that over time there is some stability in measured individual IQ, within the same test (Bloom, 1964) and across different tests (Anastasi, 1968).
- that IQ testing was created to fill bureaucratic needs – in the military, in schools, and in occasional industrial applications – and has been consistently used for such purposes, so that at least to this degree one's social rewards have depended upon one's measured IQ (Fass, 1980).
- that IQ is an indicator of a capacity connected with the *achievement* of subsequent rewards, such as high grades in school, rather than merely the *ascription* of them to the high-IQ individual (Cleary, Humphreys, Kendrick, & Wesman, 1975), at least to the extent that one can maintain that the measurement of IQ is not *simply* a bureaucratically convenient way of masking the rewarding of other socially relevant traits.

James R. Flynn (1984a, 1984b, 1985, 1987) presents a broad range of successive, identical intelligence test administrations in several national populations including that of the United States. His statistical scruples allow him cautious generalizations about historically increasing IQ, understood as a particular form of generalized intelligence. But the decreased variance that these runs of IQ tests superficially seem to imply depends significantly on the reduction of scores at the tails of the distribution; and because on almost all of these tests the central tendency for the population as a whole has approached the upper tail, the observed contraction of variance may well be spurious (J. R. Flynn, personal communication, 1987; Girod & Allaume, 1976). Professor Flynn also points out that the vagaries of standardization sampling become particularly acute at the extremes of the distribution.

Three clear and careful empirical examinations of IQ trends that we *have* been able to examine, however, based on relatively large and statistically representative samples, do suggest a reduction of the variance of IQ within samples of child populations. Cattell directed a study in Leicester, England, in 1936, that sought to test every 10-year-old in the city with the Cattell Scale I, form A, a *nonverbal* scale designed for ages 8 to 11. Hypothesizing on the basis of the dysgenic implications of his analysis of the first study that 10-year-olds in Leicester would not on the average be as bright by 1949 as their predecessors had been in 1936, he was startled to discover, and forthright to publish, that mean IQ had risen over 1 point, largely because the bottom half of the distribution had tightened up somewhat. There was also a modest decline in the coefficient of variation, from 0.022 to 0.020 (Cattell, 1950).

An extraordinary 1932 study by the Scottish Council for Research in Education of all Scottish children born in 1921 was replicated in 1947, using the same group IQ test. Like Cattell, the council found that (contrary to expectation) IQ was not declining (Maxwell, 1961). In Scotland, as in Leicester, the amount of variance in the population declined slightly, from a coefficient of variation of about 0.45 in 1932 to 0.41 in 1947.[8]

A comparison of New Zealand national samples in 1936 and 1968 – 26,000 and 6,000 respectively, almost randomly selected, and with nearly identical sampling procedures to permit comparison over time – offers the most powerful evidence of a decline in variance (Elley, 1969). In New Zealand, measured IQ rose considerably, at each age for which comparable data were available. Elley does not comment on changes in variance, but at age 10, the coefficient of variation of the Otis test declined from 0.52 to 0.45 between the two dates; at 11, the decline was from 0.45 to 0.36; at 12, from 0.39 to 0.30; and at 13, from 0.34 to 0.25.

Unfortunately, we have been unable to locate strictly comparable population-based IQ surveys of American children that have used entirely identical tests (U.S. National Center for Health Statistics, 1973).[9] We discover some evidence in a comparison of the extremely wide-based administration in World War I of the Army Alpha test to white enlisted men in the U.S. Army with a sample of almost 800 gathered from inductees entering the army in 1943 (Tuddenham, 1948).[10] The data presented show a sharp rise in measured intelligence and also an interquartile range that drops from a value equal to 0.84 of the mean to 0.67. The trend study, however, quite properly notes (in connection with the rise in the mean Alpha score) that World War I soldiers were wholly unfamiliar with objective tests, whereas most soldiers in World War II had had ample experience with them.

We have, in addition, three near-comparable vocabulary-recognition-based "IQ" measures taken on random samples of the *adult* American public at three widely removed dates. The first of these was a section on a Gallup Poll that Thorndike commissioned in 1942. The test consisted of 20 vocabulary words, understood to be an easy-to-administer way of estimating IQ. The words were handed on cards to the respondents, who were told that they were (you have to love their deviousness, at this remove) "some words which may be included on a quiz program, depending on how many people understand their meaning" (Thorndike & Gallup, 1944). The resultant coefficient of variation was 0.40.

Eleven years later, in 1953, Miner (1957) intentionally used a like procedure to estimate the intelligence of adult Americans in a representative sample of 1,896 cases. The standard deviation was considerably narrower than on the 1942 study, as was the coefficient of variation – only 0.32.

Finally, a shorter, 10-word version was placed on occasional versions of the annual General Social Survey, conducted annually by the National Opinion Research Center. For the years 1972–78, over four thousand people were administered this brief IQ test. The coefficient of variation was 0.37. After having seemingly declined from 1942 to 1953, the coefficient had again gone up. The population changes these trends *might* reflect involved (1) the dying out of the less-educated cohorts who had been born abroad in the latter part of the nineteenth century and (2) the addition of large, young cohorts who had received relatively differentiated education in the post-Sputnik era. But this is highly speculative.

What is clear is that the national data give little comfort to an interpretation that sees unilinear decline in population variance in measured IQ, even as educational inputs increased and IQ's average level responded (Stedman & Kaestle, 1987). Whether we consider these tests for what they literally were – brief vocabulary tests – or as actually tapping a far more general underlying capacity, it is apparent that rising educational levels did not directly "produce" populations more uniformly capable in measured IQ. Other mechanisms – perhaps even mechanisms of "forgetting" IQ when it is not called upon – may be involved in changing fashion as the nature of work and leisure evolve.

Gender differentials in measured IQ

The history of gender differentials in measured IQ is a story of apparent paradox. In the resolution of this paradox lies a small success story for the promotion of homogeneity of capacity in the population as a whole. The documentation is, as we have come to expect, a bit tenuous, but the paradox itself can be expressed in a nutshell. We have found that:

- over time, American boys have continued a modest superiority to girls in measured IQ *within school grades,* and
- at the same time, they have moved from a situation of modest inferiority to girls in measured IQ *within age groups* to one of modest superiority (Elley, 1969).[11]

The fundamental historical change, we will argue, is one of *institutional change:* schools used to be better suited to girls than to boys and have been changed so that they are no longer so. Boys have been induced (and compelled) to give more and longer attention to school, and have done so, with measurable improvement in their IQs, relative to that of girls.

Boys and girls historically have not passed through the schools in exactly the same way, both because of differing institutional structures established to handle the two sexes and because of differing gender-role expectations. A set of interrelated differences should be remarked here for their relevance to our arguments about measured intelligence. *Boys tended to receive lower marks* in their classes than did girls whose IQs were no greater. Teachers and other contemporary observers remarked that the boys seemed to have had a harder time applying themselves in the highly structured classroom situation and in persuading teachers that their demeanor did not call for demerits (Lentz, 1929; Rock et al. [1985?]; Rundquist, 1941; Stroud & Lindquist, 1942).[12] As a consequence of their inferior marks, *boys were considerably more likely to be left back* in school than were girls, when such administrative practices were common. Partly on account of the discomforts that derived from such a visible sign of failure as having been left back – and no less on account of the more vivid lure of the young-adult labor market to boys than to girls – *boys were more likely voluntarily to drop out of school.* This pattern persisted until dropping out was strongly discouraged, that is, until the age homogenization of school classes was encouraged by making promotion more dependent on chronological age and less on marks, and the amount of grade skipping was reduced.

The IQs of children in a given grade at school would be more varied, even as their chronological ages would be less varied (Maller, 1932; U.S. National Center for Health Statistics, 1973).[13] The earliest near-representative data we have that allow us to estimate gender differences *by age* in measured IQ is a study based on a total sample of schoolchildren ages 8 to 16 in three cities in Indiana in 1918 (Pressey, 1918). The Pressey test was used; medians and quartile scores were tabulated. From these, we make estimates (on the assumption of a normal distribution), finding that the average raw scores of girls regularly exceeded those of boys by approximately 0.2 standard deviation. *At each year of age, girls in Indiana proved to be better at what the Pressey test examined.* A few years later, Whipple (1927) administered the National Intelligence Test to 2,198 pupils at age 11 in the public school systems in four midwestern cities – nearly the whole number attending at that age – to compare scores properly for the two genders. Whipple, like Pressey before him, *found girls to be superior students, by about 0.14 of a standard deviation* (Jones & Conrad, 1933; Rigg, 1940; Whipple, 1927).

We contrast these findings to a pair dating from the 1960s. Project Talent in 1960 examined girls and boys at a single year of age – 15 – including those who were in and those who were not in high school (Shaycoft, Dailey, Orr, Neyman, & Sherman, 1963). For the whole age group, *boys' vocabulary-based IQ had a mean score that exceeded that of girls by about 0.25 standard deviations.* Boys, to judge from this study, had now passed girls in vocabulary-based IQ. And in the mid-1960s, another nationally representative IQ test (Wechsler, vocabulary portion) confirmed this finding. *From ages 12 to 16, boys' IQ superiority averaged slightly above 0.2 standard deviation* (U.S. National Center for Health Statistics, 1973).

Assessing historical trends in gender differentials in IQ *within grades at school* will give us clues about the ways in which institutional change may have influenced the process by which change in these differentials may have taken place. As far back as we can measure, boys in given school grades have had higher IQs than girls, even in the earlier period in the century in which *within a given year of age* boys were seemingly, on average, not as smart as girls. Thus, Colvin's 1922–23 study of Massachusetts high school seniors found that *boys' IQs* (measured with the Brown University Psychological Examination) *exceeded girls' by 0.45 of a standard deviation.* But there were only 60% as many boys among the Massachusetts seniors as girls, and the girls were younger (Colvin & MacPhail, 1924).

Book's broad application (1922) of a Pressey test carried out upon all high school seniors in cooperating high schools in Indiana in about 1921 found that *boys had a higher median IQ than girls, the spread being about 0.1 of a standard deviation.* Having gathered Otis test scores on a sample of 11,321 high school seniors in Illinois in 1923 (almost the whole senior class in 368 schools), Odell (1925) found that boys (who constituted only 44% of the seniors) had a very slight superiority in IQ of about 0.02 of a standard deviation. Among a sample of almost 25,000 Pennsylvania high school seniors in 1928, boys' mean Otis score exceeded that of girls by 0.29 standard deviation (Rhinehart, 1947). The large (20,000 pupils) mid-1930s national study, done for the American Council of Education and applying a specially devised test, discerned "national norms" for the two sexes, derived directly from the collected data, that indicate that *at each grade boys had higher IQs by differences that ranged from 0.16 to 0.26 standard deviations* (Eells, 1937).

Half a century ago boys had a harder time than girls did staying in school. Dropping out earlier, boys received on average less formal education than did girls. In the child population as a whole, boys had slightly lower average IQs than girls. More recently, however, boys have been coerced and cozened to remain in school, and, doing so, they perform slightly better on vocabulary-based IQ tests than do their female classmates. Let us grant the schools – and the less-comfortable boys – this: as educators have learned how to keep boy and school together, they have also learned how to teach and learned the cognitive capacities that IQ tests measure.

But have *individual* differences in cognitive capacities been reduced by the evidently successful series of institutional interventions that have reduced the variance in the formal education input between boys and girls? Evidently not. On IQ tests, boys simply score about as much *better* than girls score, as their grandfathers scored *worse* than their grandmothers. Inputs of formal education have been successfully redirected, with discernible categorical results. But equalization of individual capacities is not among these. Nor, in view of the tiny proportion of individual variance in IQ attributable (now or ever) to gender differences, should this be surprising.

Racial and socioeconomic differentials in IQ

Evidence drawn from a large number of local studies (28 had adequately drawn samples and included all the statistical apparatus needed to make the calculations) comparing the IQ scores of whites and blacks from the 1920s into the 1960s suggests a persistently greater difference between measured IQ of blacks and whites in southern rural contexts than in southern urban contexts, which, in turn, had persistently greater differences in measured IQ as compared to northern urban contexts. Over time, the only trend that indicates an inclination toward decreasing racial differentials in measured IQ was that in the urban North. The persistent differences in the size of differentials, however, point to the probability that historical trends in black population mobility have reduced national differentials in measured IQ between the two races, as blacks have moved to cities and toward the North, in part because of superior educational opportunities. (A plausible explanation for the lack of convergence in measured IQ within the South is differential migration: blacks with higher IQs may have moved to northern cities) (Shuey, 1966).[14]

When we turn to changes in socioeconomic differentials in IQ, we also find little evidence for homogenization of capacities within the population. Because the difficulty of measuring socioeconomic status consistently over time compounds that of measuring intelligence over time, it is difficult to inquire into socioeconomic differentials in IQ over time. Although we know that at least modest levels of formal education have become considerably more widely distributed over the past century, our most solid historical comparisons in socioeconomic differentials in cognitive capacities, however, leave us with a fairly persuasive negative finding.[15]

Our data on socioeconomic differentials in children's IQs rest on three studies:

1. Haggerty and Nash's New York State studies (1924) of grade school and high school students early in the 1920s, using the Haggerty test, which was said to measure the capacity of children to profit from school instruction.[16]
2. Byrns and Henmon's publication (1936) based on state-mandated tests administered to *all* graduating seniors in Wisconsin, 1929–33.
3. The vocabulary portion of the Wechsler IQ test administered to a representative national sample of 12- to 17-year-olds in 1966–70 (U.S. National Center for Health Statistics, 1973).

Socioeconomic differences were quite substantial in the 1960s, accounting for 18% of the total amount of variance within a given age group.[17] And they were visible in the older studies as well, but they were nowhere near so substantial. The Haggerty-Nash high school study suggests that perhaps one-third as much of the individual variance as in the 1960s might be explained by parental status; the Wisconsin senior data suggest an effect slightly less substantial than this.[18] By high school, of course, many students, especially of lower socioeconomic status, had dropped out, which tended to reduce the measured socioeconomic differentials in IQ within school populations (Maller, 1933).[19] But if we substitute the far less exclusive *grade school populations* tested by Haggerty and Nash, the impact of socioeconomic status on individual variance in IQ was still only about half as great as it was to be in the 1960s.

A portion of the explanation for what we have found, may be that it is a figment of comparing *student* samples to recent *population*-based samples, although it seems intuitively likely that recent student samples would far more nearly resemble recent population-based samples than in the more distant past, and in this sense our finding is real. But, from this set of large, carefully administered IQ tests, we seem to have found that, if anything, *socioeconomic variation has become more prominent among differentiators of children's IQs*. Not impossibly, increases in school provision interact powerfully with aspects of home learning climate to produce this finding, the perversity of which, however, ought to invite closer examination with more and sounder data and more varied and powerful analytic methods. If sustained, the finding would fit unhappily well with the experience of "Sesame Street," to be treated in the next sections. If, as we have tentatively concluded, American IQs have not much converged, we can probably say that the broadening of public schooling has not produced a much more "democratic" distribution of school skills by reducing socioeconomic differentials in schooling inputs, even to relatively young children.

Interventions explicitly intended to reduce categorical variance

In the past 25 years, the United States has instituted a number of programs aimed at decreasing differences between groups. Two of the most prominent of these have been the Public Broadcasting System television program "Sesame Street" and Project Headstart. In addition to being important, large-scale efforts in themselves, "Sesame Street" and Headstart are representative of two main alternative approaches to reducing intergroup differences. The approach embodied by Headstart is to provide the disadvantaged group with a resource not available except at a price to the advantaged group: preschool education. The approach embodied by "Sesame Street" is to provide to all takers a resource that is expected to be especially valuable for members of the disadvantaged group, in this case to provide televised instruction in simple academic skills. The history of the two programs illustrates the difficulty of reducing variance between groups, even through plans explicitly designed to achieve this goal.

"Sesame Street"

The original proposal for the funding of "Sesame Street" expressed its goal as "to promote the intellectual and cultural growth of preschoolers, particularly disadvantaged preschoolers" (Cooney, 1968, p. 2). This statement makes clear that increasing the general intellectual level of preschoolers and providing special aid to disadvantaged preschoolers were major purposes of the program. Because the world was becoming increasingly complicated and was demanding increasing knowledge and understanding from everyone, it was important to raise the overall mean level of preschoolers' knowledge. Because inequality between lower-class blacks and middle-class whites was a serious problem, and because lower-class blacks started out in school seriously behind their middle-class white peers, it was important to reduce differences between the groups.

The actual impact of "Sesame Street" on mean level of achievement and on intergroup variability has been analyzed thoroughly by Cook et al. (1975). The program was quite successful in achieving its instructional goal: children who were exposed to the program learned more about letters, numbers, and relations than did those who were not. It was, however, less successful in its "democratic" goal. It not only did not increase the equality of economically advantaged and disadvantaged children, it appears to have increased their inequality. That is, the gap between advantaged and disadvantaged children appears to have grown as a function of exposure to the show.

One prominent reason for this unsought outcome was that advantaged children watched the show more. A 1971 Harris Poll indicated that among families who viewed public television, "Sesame Street" had been watched at least once by 65% of children with parents who were not high school graduates, by 83% of children from homes with parents who were high school graduates, and by 88% of children whose parents were college graduates (Cook et al., 1975, p. 295). Similarly, a Nielsen Survey indicated that among families with 2- to 6-year-olds, the average viewing audience for "Sesame Street" was 12% of preschoolers in families with incomes below $8,000 and 17% in families with incomes above $8,000. Encouragement from experimenters to watch the show led to increases in viewing among both disadvantaged and advantaged children, but it did not reduce the difference between them. Indeed, the encouragement seems to have increased the differences. Encouraging disadvantaged children to watch the program led to an increase in the percentage of heavy viewers from 50% to 62%. Encouraging advantaged children to do so led to an increase of from 60% to 81%.

Greater viewing of "Sesame Street," probably in combination with greater frequency of parents watching together with their children and the head start in learning that middle-class children already had, led the advantaged children to learn more from the program. The most dramatic data attesting to this greater learning involved asking children to identify six main characters from the program. Of the advantaged children, 58% correctly identified all six. Of the disadvantaged children, only 6% did so (Minton, 1972).

Thus, making available similar educational resources to advantaged and disadvantaged groups cannot be assumed to reduce automatically intergroup differences. The advantaged children's superior, existing ability to learn and the greater involvement of their parents in helping them to learn may often lead to such interventions' increasing group differences. This recognition led Cook et al. (1975) to conclude that the only way to reduce the social-class gap in preschoolers' achievement was differentially to provide educational experiences to disadvantaged children.

Project Headstart

Project Headstart is an example of the differential type of approach. Only children from families with low incomes could participate. Numerous outcome studies have demonstrated that participation in the program has increased intellectual achievement of children who take part and thus has reduced the difference between them and middle-class children (Lazar & Darlington, 1982).

Intraindividual differences are tenacious, however. The most extensive follow-up study of Headstart programs (Lazar & Darlington, 1982) reveals a mixed picture of reductions and nonreductions in intergroup intellectual variability. First, consider the reductions of differences between middle- and lower-class children. Participants in Headstart were significantly less likely to be assigned to special education classes than were children in control groups. They also were somewhat less likely to be retained in a grade. Mothers of program graduates had higher aspirations for their children than did control mothers. In all of these ways, program participants and their parents become more similar to middle-class children and adults.

The picture was quite different with regard to direct measures of intellectual outcomes. Immediately after the program and for 2 years thereafter, children who participated in the program scored significantly higher on IQ tests than those who did not. This was no longer the case by ages 10 to 17 years, however. By these ages, no significant IQ benefits were present. Similarly, by sixth grade (about age 11), none of the four programs for which achievement test data were available found significant differences between participants and nonparticipants in reading achievement, and none of the three programs for which data were available found significant differences in mathematics achievement. Analysis of the combined data also yielded nonsignificant results for reading and math. As Ramey (1982) notes in his commentary on the Lazar and Darlington monograph:

The mean IQ performance at follow-up for the children from the four projects having more nearly randomized designs is approximately one standard deviation below the national average, for both program and control children. Clearly, then, this represents a group of children who are likely to experience major hardships in an increasingly technological and sophisticated culture. That these results obtain in spite of the efforts of some of our leading social scientists and educators testifies to the difficult and complex set of conditions associated with lower socio-economic status in this country. (p. 149)

Thus, the effect on intergroup variability produced by Headstart participation depended on the type of outcome examined. On some measures, notably assignment to special education classes and retention in grade, significant progress was made toward reducing differences between middle-class white and lower-class black children. On other measures, notably IQ and achievement test scores beyond age 10, the intergroup variability was substantially unchanged. Thus, even planned interventions made available only to members of disadvantaged groups, and implemented by dedicated and knowledgeable social scientists and educators, are often inadequate to reduce intergroup variability in many of the ways we would like.

Conclusion

The long-term waxing tide of material well-being that raises all boats seemingly has raised all boats *proportionately*. Developmental inequalities of children seem to have remained fairly stable over the past century or at least seem not to show any pronounced downward secular trend, despite marked improvements in such resources devoted to child development as nutrition, health care, and formal education. From one perspective, this is to be expected: children's capacities have never varied as much as did the resources devoted to developing them. The underlying balance of human biology has seen to this. And the assumption of diminishing returns to developmental inputs is just that: an assumption, albeit one worthy of systematic review. Such work would be a fine contribution on which historians and developmentalists could collaborate.

Indeed, we might go further in this hortatory direction, hoping that we have persuaded our readers of the theoretical significance of work at the intersection of our disciplines. How can we account historically for what we have (so tentatively) found? In this case, we would ask for a more thorough effort to:

1. catalog developmentally significant resources, the availability of which varies and has changed;
2. search the developmental literature for empirically based parameter estimates of effects, with due respect to nonlinearities;
3. search the historical literature for accounts of trends in provision of these resources, both central tendency and dispersion;
4. from these searches, make real hypotheses, and test them.

At such point, failed hypotheses ought to suggest more satisfying ad hoc explanations than we have been able to supply here. From another standpoint, however, the tenacious ability of developing individuals to distinguish themselves from one another does not give enormous comfort to those who hope to bring about reductions in the inequality of individual attributes, to reduce the inequality in reward accruing to them.

Despite the rather coarse grain of our study, however, the historical materials we have examined provide a basis for insisting on the variety of human capacities and of the environments that encourage their differential development. And the very complexity that our investigation has indicated about the phenomenon of inequality and its transmission suggests why liberal theory must necessary translate crudely into an applied theory of social justice.

Notes

1. In this regard, public policy may differ from intrafamilial tendencies, at least in a prosperous society with a strongly egalitarian belief system, like ours.

2. A conclusion of Jones and Conrad's exceptionally careful study (1933) of homogeneous New England village populations in the late 1920s is a propos: "More rapid growth of bright than of dull children would cause an increase in the standard deviations [of measured aspects of intelligence] from age to age; this increase in standard deviations during adolescence is observable, not only for the total [Army] Alpha test, but for each individual subtest" (p. 267).

3. Evidence for the approach to growth potential is found in "the marked diminution and near cessation of the trend to constantly increasing size of successive generations of American children," as revealed by comparing the first, second, and third rounds of the U.S. National Health Examination studies (U.S. National Center for Health Statistics, 1977).

4. These samples, of course, were themselves increasingly less representative of all children the further they went beyond the age that children started leaving school, perhaps 11 or 12.

5. Comparison of a 1939 replication of the 1892 Toronto height study indicated a marked growth in average height and *increased* variance, whether measured by standard deviation or coefficient of variation. The samples differed only in that parochial-school children, excluded in 1892, were now included and in that, of course, a higher proportion of the total population at a given age – especially at the older ages tabulated – were now pupils.

6. We must remember that the nineteenth-century data are exclusively urban, whereas the twentieth-century data, being national, have thereby included what urban/rural variance the urban data had eliminated and that the twentieth-century data, being *population-based,* have eliminated whatever variance the *schoolchild-based* data may have excluded.

7. This phenomenon is well-established with regard to menarche.

8. Reviewing these two British studies of trends in child IQ and seven others that seem to have been based on less than representative samples, and employing a cruder measure of variance than we employ, Lynn and Hampson (1986) conclude that there is no consistent pattern of decrease or increase of variance.

9. Scanlon, U.S. National Center for Health Statistics (1973), compares his empirical results with the vocabulary subtest from the short form of the Wechsler on a national sample with those found for the standardization sample, selected to be representative of the entire U.S. population, not random, but representative by region, urban/rural, and occupational group among men. He found a significant reduction in variance at 10.5 and an insignificant reduction in variance at 13.5 but a *widening* of variance among children at 7.5.

10. The test administered in 1943 was a revised version of the Alpha but was said to yield distributions very similar to the original version.

11. In New Zealand, girls' Otis scores exceeded boys' slightly in 1936 and by considerably more in 1968, at given years of age.

12. In 1972 and in 1980, girls' high school grades still exceeded boys', on the average, by about 0.4 of a standard deviation. The girls' reported time on homework assignments also exceeded boys' by just about this same amount. However, the intervening 8 years were a period in which – behaviorally and attitudinally – girls were converging on boys' comparative disdain for formal schooling, even as each gender declined in measured academic attainment (Educational Testing Service, 1986, Tables 5-4, 6-37).

13. A comparison of a four-city survey of high school seniors who took the Terman and/or Otis tests about 1930 with the national Wechsler Intelligence Scale for Children (WISC) vocabulary subtest data on ninth graders in 1966–70 reveals that the average difference in measured intellectual capacity between younger (and, on average, smarter) students with those of average age for the grade and with those who were rather old for the grade *essentially remained the same*. But, because of changes in institutional policies on grade promotions, there were very many more students of modal age in the later year, and very many fewer who were either relatively old or relatively young. So, overall, the entire grade's *population of students* had homogenized on IQ.

14. We included only studies that offered means and standard deviations, where the sampling was relatively wide or inclusive of some relatively representative sampling unit. The measure used

was the difference in mean measured IQ between whites and blacks, divided by the mean of the standard deviation of IQ for each of the two racial groups.

15. The three adult U.S. vocabulary surveys allow us, in a rudimentary way, to develop a sense of trend in the amount of variance in outcome associated with socioeconomic status. Unfortunately, the 1942 study published only a three-way breakdown by family income. Income is much contaminated as a measure of socioeconomic status by age's relationship to earnings. Accepting the published threefold distribution as heuristically defining the relative size of the class categories we will compare, we discover that in 1942, 1953, and the 1970s (using occupation as our socioeconomic indicator in the two later surveys) approximately the same z-score of IQ separates the lowest from the middle and the middle from the highest socioeconomic levels. Arguably, there is some convergence between 1953 and the 1970s, but, in light of the enormous expansion of schooling and the special attention paid in public schooling to the disabilities suffered by the rural poor, ghettoized urban blacks, and other economically disadvantaged persons, the degree of categorical convergence along this dimension is somewhat disappointing. The 1942 sample offers no tabulations by race, which is unfortunate because in this realm we would expect rapid changes in the extent of categorical difference within the population. And in fact we do find this situation between 1953 and the 1970s. In the earlier year, race differences were quite large, amounting to more than the difference between two adjacent socioeconomic groups – nearly 0.9 standard deviations. In the 1970s, this difference was still very substantial, still more than the difference between two socioeconomic groups, but the race differential had declined to about 0.7 standard deviations. Equally encouraging, the racial differentials in the 1970s data are far stronger among older than among younger respondents.

16. Sample sizes are 6,688 children in grades 3 through 8 and 1,433 children in high school, constituting, according to the authors, a satisfactory sampling of the rural population (those living in places with fewer than 4,500 residents) of New York State.

17. Results are the same whether we take parental education or parental income as our indicator of socioeconomic status. Occupation, necessarily our indicator for the earlier studies, was not tabulated in the 1960s study.

18. Because the WISC offered raw scores whereas Haggerty and Nash offered instead age-normed "intelligence quotients," the proper comparison is of *a single* late-1960s single-year age group, with either of Haggerty and Nash's samples. Furthermore, paternal occupation (as in Haggerty & Nash) probably is not as well-related to IQ as is paternal education, at any date, and the Haggerty occupational categories, despite massaging, could not be grouped as evenly as were the 1960s educational categories – weakening the proportion of variance explicable by between-categories. Further, the Haggerty and Nash data were grouped; we scored each at the midpoint, and assumed the small extreme categories to be at midpoint had they not been open categories. These techniques somewhat reduced total variance.

19. Maller's study of IQ and school progress in New York City in 1930–32, an ecological study of neighborhoods, found a correlation of .70 between average IQ and school progress in fifth grade. Maller reports a coefficient of variation of 0.08 in district average IQ, but one of 0.024 for district proportion of grade retardation. Environments (schools, families, labor markets), that is, differed more sharply in the way they acted on students than could be explained by IQ variation alone.

Life transitions across historical time

In Part III, we explore various life transitions that individuals undergo across development. By viewing these transitions through the dual lenses of the historian and the developmentalist, we can gain new insights into how life transitions are modified by the historical context or era in which they are embedded. In this part the first two chapters focus on adolescent transitions, and the third addresses a role transition – in this case, the transition to fatherhood.

In chapter 5, Steven Schlossman and Robert B. Cairns illustrate how our society has shifted in its treatment of girls who exhibit deviant behavior during their transition to adolescence. The authors compare contemporary and earlier eras, focusing on how our treatment of the same broad domain of social behavior either has changed or has remained constant across time. Socialization is always a product of the social norms of a culture at a particular time and of the particular institutions that have been given responsibility for enforcing these norms. This notion is nicely illustrated by Schlossman and Cairns. They show us, first, how social norms that help us to decide which behaviors are to be regulated at different points in development are products of a particular historical period. In the 1940s and 1950s, girls were brought into court mainly for "status offenses" such as disobeying parents or truancy, or for being sexually active. In the mid-twentieth century, then, the courts were vehicles for regulating sexual morality – at least among girls. By the 1980s, however, girls were rarely being arrested for these classes of behavior. In short, the same behaviors treated by the justice system as offenses in the 1940s were ignored by the system in the 1980s. Clearly, even across the last 40 years in the United States, our definitions of illegal behavior have changed markedly.

Second, the cross-time comparisons in chapter 5 suggest that different institutions play the major socialization role in different eras. Whereas the court system served an important regulatory function in the socialization of female behavior in the 1940s, the school and family played a more prominent role in this process 40 years later.

Moreover, little is known about the consequences for society of institutions

107

such as the courts publicly labeling different behaviors as deviant. Further historical analyses could provide important insights into the consequences of such labeling on the rates and qualities of deviant behaviors.

Finally, these cross-time comparisons provide an opportunity to track shifts in the frequency with which different forms of deviant behavior occurred over time. With this data on rates at different historical periods, we can make better decisions concerning the most useful periods for historical comparisons.

Joan Jacobs Brumberg and Ruth Striegel-Moore provide in chapter 6 a fascinating review of how historical circumstances can shape the expression of physical symptoms and our explanations of disease. They use as their example the issue of anorexia nervosa. The investigators trace the history of this disease and show how the same set of symptoms – such as food refusal or starvation – may flow from very different underlying causes unique to particular historical eras. The meaning of food and eating in female identity formation in the nineteenth century and in the present are radically divergent. In turn, these cultural meanings shaped the explanations and interpretations of the same symptoms in each historical period. Distinct forms of the same disease emerge as a consequence of changes in historical circumstances; for example, bulimia, or overeating and purging, is a modern variant on anorexia nervosa and could have emerged only in an era characterized by a high degree of privacy, solitary eating, and easy access to food. This analysis shows how historical period can determine the expression of underlying psychopathology. Understanding even the biological and medical aspects of development is closely tied to understanding the historical period in which they are observed. The benefits of a historically sensitive approach to development are clear as well in cases such as those biological processes where environmental inputs often are assumed to be limited.

In chapter 7, Ross D. Parke and Peter N. Stearns provide a historical analysis of how the role of father has changed in concept and reality over the last century. Of central importance is the corrective function of their essay in reminding us that many of the modern trends toward a new definition of the nature of fatherhood – one purportedly qualitatively and quantitatively different from those of the past – are, in part, mythical. Many of these trends were anticipated by earlier patterns, and continuity between earlier eras and the current era is evident. The dual themes of increased nurturant fathers and absent/abandoning fathers are both modern and historical. Current ambivalence about paternal involvement and the surprising difficulty of achieving true equality for mothers and fathers as care givers have clear historical roots.

In introducing the concept of a cultural ideal, Parke and Stearns suggest how era-specific versions of this ideal serve to shape or even to distort our thinking about fatherhood. In earlier periods, the uninvolved father was assumed to be at least normative, which led us to underemphasize cases of highly involved fathers. At the same time, our current culture champions the concept of the in-volved father, which, in turn, has obscured the extent to which many fathers are today uninvolved or absent. Perhaps of greatest importance is the authors' artic-ulation of the need for more detailed descriptive historical analysis of actual father behavior and the ways in which variations in this behavior alter the trajec-tory of children's lives.

Finally, the essays in this part should be read on two levels. First, they represent progress reports on the advances that can be made through inter-disciplinary dialogue and collaboration. Second, these chapters can be taken as invitations to join the search for a better understanding of how children and adults develop and how they change in different historical circumstances.

5   Problem girls: Observations on past and present

Steven Schlossman and Robert B. Cairns

Sexual precocity in itself is no longer considered to be a crime for girls.
Steven Schlossman and Robert B. Cairns (1992)

In areas of social inquiry where there are few precedents and fewer data, one has an unusually free hand to be methodologically inventive. This chapter plays that hand with some abandon: we link data from two different time periods, locales, and institutions to sketch broad patterns of change and continuity in family characteristics, behavior, and social treatment of problem youth – with a focus upon girls – during the past half century.

If our methods seem unorthodox, that derives largely from necessity. Today as in the past, no research tradition has emerged to advance knowledge of girls who seriously misbehave and/or are adjudged formally delinquent. Few data have been regularly collected that are related to the subject. The absence of scholarly interest in problem girls – whether by historians, social workers, psychologists, psychiatrists, sociologists, criminologists, or educators – highlights the wider neglect and marginality of girls per se in social science research. Only when girls act out and/or become formally delinquent has the scholarly community, and society at large, shown sustained interest in them and recognized a need to develop appropriate and remedial responses. There are some exceptions, of course, including the important work of P. C. Giordano (1978) and her colleagues (Giordano, Cernkovich, & Pugh, 1986).

Changing times and some issues of comparison

Profound shifts have occurred during this century in the social expectations and legal machinery society uses to encourage conforming behaviors by girls and to punish nonconforming ones. Through most of this century, juvenile court was the arena of first resort for dealing with acting-out youth. The philosophy and machinery of the juvenile justice system were geared toward nipping behavioral nonconformity in the bud – in large part by facilitating access to the court by parents, neighbors, private agencies, school officials, and other, less formal, monitors of youth.

This philosophy applied with special stringency to girls: under the legal doctrine of *parens patriae,* whereby the state legitimately steps in as guardian or superparent for children at risk, the behavior of girls was subjected to especially rigorous scrutiny and disapprobation (particularly with regard to sexual behavior; see Odem & Schlossman, 1991; Schlossman & Wallach, 1978). The juvenile justice system was not unique in these respects; a similar dual standard where sons are provided greater freedom of movement and activity than daughters has been broadly observed in developmental studies of families (see, e.g., R. B. Cairns, 1979; Maccoby & Jacklin, 1974; B. B. Whiting & Edwards, 1973).[1]

Society's aggressive stance toward the monitoring of juvenile (especially female) nonconforming behavior changed rather dramatically in the 1960s and 1970s as a result of the sexual revolution, the "children's rights" movement, and the growing distrust of law enforcement per se as an agent of benevolent paternalism. Since then, juvenile court has gradually withdrawn from its historic role as general overseer of problem youth and has focused its authority more narrowly on persistently criminal youth. Social responsibility for problem youth who are not persistently criminal has moved formally from the courts and, *by default,* to various types of public and private agencies. As the role of the court has changed, and as social expectations for juvenile behavior have become increasingly latitudinarian, many of the problems that identified acting-out youth in earlier eras have been defined out of legal existence. Some behaviors once sufficient for legal action may no longer be considered adequate grounds for juvenile arrest.

Generational changes in what behaviors classify adolescent females as "delinquent" present a problem for efforts to understand problem behaviors in girls. Any inquiry into the types, frequency, and antecedents of legally defined "problem girls" must take into account the possibility that, over time, both the court attitudes towards deviance as well as the actual types, frequency, and antecedents of problems may all shift across generations. This possibility implies that the frequency as well as the psychological meaning of deviant actions are influenced by the social context.

Such changes in legal definition and in psychological interpretation has dampened enthusiasm for cross-disciplinary investigation among criminologists and psychologists in the past. The two groups have been at loggerheads for nearly the entire century. The difficulties are not merely in method or theory. They speak to the problems inherent when the core concepts of each discipline are not readily transplanted. Delinquency and crime speak to legal concepts; the causes of aggressive and sexual behaviors speak to psychological/behavioral constructs. Within each discipline, precise definition is achieved by embedding the construct within a network of relations specific to its application and use in that domain of inquiry. Furthermore, the networks of relations within the law or psychology typically are themselves not static. Even if a tolerable cross-disciplinary translation is achieved at one point in time or in one domain, there can be no guarantee that the translation will hold at other times or in other domains.

The shift across time in the legal meaning of female delinquency is a case in point. It not clear whether determinants of the actions now identified as "delinquent" have also shifted over time. Deviant behaviors and problem youth are very much with us – but the court seems to have changed which forms of adolescent deviance may be brought to it for sanction. We believe that many acting-out youth in school today who receive no firmer discipline than counseling or class reassignment in school would have been referred in earlier eras to juvenile court. The juvenile court's functions and clientele have thus been transformed, and there is today no good analogue to the role previously played by the court in overseeing the behavior of problem youth.

Where, then, does society turn first nowadays in order to deal with acting-out, noncriminal youth? Although not often acknowledged, an accepted agency of first resort for children and early adolescents has fallen by default to the public school. Schools today, unlike in the early twentieth century, find it difficult to exclude problem children prior to age 16. The legal constraints against early exclusion are many; we implicitly force upon schools a policy of containment, if not education, of problem youth. This represents a major policy shift: teachers and counselors are expected to tolerate, adapt to, remediate, or ignore nonconforming student behaviors that in earlier eras would have led to immediate expulsion or referral to juvenile court. Hence, one reasonable way to proceed is to compare problem girls identified in the school today with problem girls who appeared in juvenile court several decades ago.

In line with the preceding discussion, we will examine evidence from the courts and the schools and give special attention to court records in the first half of the century and information from schools in the last decade. In particular, we will examine the types, frequencies, antecedents, and attendant punishments for seemingly similar behaviors across time. Through a convergence of methods, we hope to examine the major transformations in social function that have occurred in both institutions – the courts and the schools – in defining and dealing with deviancy in adolescent females.

To obtain data on problem girls in schools and juvenile courts over the course of the twentieth century is not a simple matter. Neither schools nor juvenile courts have been very receptive to researchers who wish to acquire detailed, systematic, intimate data about their juvenile clientele. In our analyses, we will link information obtained from two unique, ongoing studies. The common concern is with problem girls. But there are large differences in terms of the measures employed; the years, locales, and populations on which the information was gathered; the data available for analysis and comparison; and the disciplines represented by the investigators.

Some might conclude that comparisons are impossible because of such differences in concepts, methods, and measures. In our view, this objection reflects a misunderstanding of how advances in the social sciences can be achieved. The independence of the procedures and methods can be more an advantage than a liability. Indeed, multiplicity of methods and perspectives is necessary to extend our understanding of complex processes and to invigorate research. Rather than gloss over differences in procedures or homogenize methods, social sciences must understand key phenomena from multiple perspectives. Only when the richness and diversity of behavioral processes are explored will it be possible to achieve an adequate understanding of their multiple determinants. As observed by the statistician R. A. Fisher (1937), heterogeneity in sampling is required to identify generality. And at this early stage in our understanding of the historical contexts of child development, such heterogeneity provides occasion for imaginative work rather than despair about inconclusiveness.

Collaborative since its inception, this project has required an intermingling of concepts and ideas from two disciplines – history and psychology – that in the past have been virtual strangers. Schlossman, the historian, heads a project that is analyzing several thousand original case files of problem youth in Los Angeles Juvenile Court during the first half of the twentieth century. The data reported in this chapter deal primarily with youth on whom delinquency petitions were filed in 1950 and exclude children brought into court solely as dependents or as victims of abuse or neglect. Cairns, the psychologist, helps direct a longitudinal research project that has been ongoing since 1981. Two groups of youth – 695 in all – have been individually followed each year from late childhood to early maturity. The data reported in this chapter deal with girls and boys identified as serious problems in the transition from childhood to adulthood. Although the original samples began in two counties – one suburban and one rural – of a Southeastern state, the subjects had dispersed throughout the United States by late adolescence. To help place these findings into context, we also refer to other investigations of these issues.

Five questions

The data enable us to address, albeit in different ways, five questions regarding the backgrounds, behaviors, and treatment of problem youth in the past and the present. Briefly stated, these questions are

1. What is the distribution of problem girls relative to problem boys, and are gender differences increasing or diminishing over time?

2. Are there significant differences in the types of offenses problem boys and girls are accused of, and have the differences been narrowing over time?
3. Are girls becoming more violent?
4. Do the problems of problem girls generally appear as single entities or as configurations?
5. Are there changing expectations of appropriate youth behavior and shifting thresholds for social intervention into the lives of problem youth?

We offer tentative answers to these questions, drawing primarily on our own research, and then assay some synthesis of these answers to generate further directions for future empirical inquiry.

The distribution of female and male problem youth

Boys accounted for the great majority of problem youth in Los Angeles Juvenile Court at midcentury: 79.5%. This share was virtually identical for every decade year between 1920 and 1950. Of course, this pattern does not necessarily mean that boys were four times more likely than girls to manifest serious behavior problems. Our data involve only youth with filed delinquency petitions.[2] Juvenile courts were not passive, impartial reflectors of general social patterns but, rather, active participants in determining whom to identify as "problem youth." All that might be said with confidence is that boys were far more likely than girls to engage in problem behaviors that would trigger intervention by the juvenile court, society's chief overseer of youth misconduct in the first half of the twentieth century.

National crime statistics in the United States in the 1980s continued to show a large gender difference among adolescents in the likelihood of arrest (Federal Bureau of Investigation, 1990). Boys were over six times more likely to be arrested for violent crimes than girls. For example, in 1987 the age-specific arrest rate for violent crime for boys was 765.3 per 100,000 population. For girls, the violent crime arrest rate was 118.7. The differential was smaller for property crimes: 15-year-old boys were twice as likely as girls to be arrested for non-violent crimes, such as shoplifting and theft.[3] The gender difference in arrests persisted from childhood to late adolescence, with the greatest difference being observed in 18-year-olds (see Stattin, Magnusson, & Reichel, 1989).

The issue remains how legal definitions of delinquency relate to psychological definitions of problem behavior. One bridge has been established by a statewide program in North Carolina, initiated to identify extremely aggressive youth. This identification is of special interest because it was made independently of the child's court history.[4] "Problem" children and adolescents 18 years and younger could be referred for treatment by community agencies, schools, and parents; and a full psychological assessment was given to those nominees who passed the first filter of problem severity. For our purposes, it should be emphasized that the judgment of "aggressive and assaultive" was made on the basis of psychological criteria rather than legal ones. Despite these differences in criteria, the gender differences in the juvenile arrest statistics paralleled the gender differences in the psychological assessments. In the first 1,300 cases (1981–85), males constituted four out of five youth certified as "assaultive and violent" (79.5% males and 20.5% females).

The longitudinal methodology of the Carolina Longitudinal Study (CLS) investigation permitted us to study the development of gender differences in problem behaviors. According to these findings, gender differences in aggression are not static across development. They are accentuated with the onset of adolescence. In the fourth grade, marginally fewer girls than boys were identified in a normal school population as being problems in school (e.g., arguing, getting into fights). By the seventh grade, the difference between genders increased, and approximately twice as many boys (30.6%) as girls (13.7%) were cited· by their teachers as being extreme with regard to problem behaviors (see R. B. Cairns, Cairns, Neckerman, Ferguson, & Gariépy, 1989b, for an extended discussion). Entry into adolescence is thus associated with the emergence of serious acting-out, aggressive behavior, and more boys become at risk than girls. Though fewer girls were judged to be aggressive in elementary school than boys, the dimension proved to be relevant for predicting problem behaviors in high school.

Offense patterns of problem girls

Gender was a major determinant in the identification of problem youth in mid-twentieth-century America. Boys were brought to court primarily for major and minor crimes, whereas girls were brought to court mainly for so-called status offenses (e.g., disobeying parental authority, violating curfew, truancy, running away), or for being sexually active.

To be sure, no rigid dividing line separated each gender's offense patterns. A minority of girls were accused solely of crimes, and a minority of boys were accused solely of status offenses. Moreover, anecdotal information contained in each youth's case file makes the dividing line fuzzier still. Boys were sometimes accused rather casually of specific crimes, when, in fact, a long history of insolence to parents or school officials explained their referral to court. Girls were sometimes accused of "incorrigibility," when, in fact, quite specific crimes preceded their referral to court. Boys were sometimes sexually active, but, unlike the situation for girls, the court tended not to count this as a mark against them.

Nonetheless, despite these vagaries of social labeling, major gender differences still existed in the behaviors of problem youth. Furthermore, the court viewed status offenses no less seriously than crimes as symptoms of major personality maladjustments that required active public intervention and correction.

Only 12.2% of the boys were referred to Los Angeles County Juvenile Court for status or sexual offenses by parents, schools, or social agencies. A majority of the boys, 58.8%, were referred by law enforcement officers for serious crimes – felony-level offenses, especially burglary and auto theft. In addition, a significant minority (29.1%) were referred by law enforcement officers for misdemeanors, principally petty theft or simple assault (e.g., a school fight). Thus, the overwhelming majority of male problem youth were involved in criminal behavior.

Many of the criminally active male youth in Los Angeles in 1950 were also status offenders. That is, many had long histories of disobedience to parents or school misconduct or curfew violations that, technically, could have led to court referral independently of their criminal conduct. By and large, however, this had not been the case: the petition filed on these boys in 1950 was generally their first, and the precipitating behavior for their court referral was a specific criminal act rather than diffuse problem behaviors at home or in the neighborhood.

Problem girls, unlike problem boys, were referred to the Los Angeles Juvenile Court in 1950 mainly for status and especially sexual offenses. Only 22% of the problem girls were accused of criminal offenses; of these, most committed misdemeanors, mainly petty thefts. Of the 78% of the girls charged with noncriminal offenses, nearly half (47.6%) were accused of sexual offenses (sexual activity of various kinds, mainly intercourse, but not prostitution); most of the others were accused of running away (17.5%), truancy (16.5%), or incorrigibility (10.7%).

Sexual activity was actually more central in the problem behaviors identified by the Los Angeles County Juvenile Court in 1950 than these statistics indicate. Many of the girls formally charged by their parents with incorrigibility were, in reality, brought to court for sexual activity. Moreover, over half (54.5%) of all the problem girls (including felons and misdemeanants) were identified as being sexually active. Whether or not a girl was formally charged with sexual misconduct, her sexual activity was always central to the court's deliberations about how to punish her.[5] Thus it seems fair to conclude that whereas the characteristic problem male youth in midcentury Los Angeles was a felon, the characteristic problem female youth was a sex offender.

By the 1980s, girls in the longitudinal study were rarely arrested for status offenses, whether sexual activity or incorrigibility. It is of interest that there was only a single arrest for vagrancy in the 364 girls and 8 years of longitudinal study – a girl who had run away and become associated with a motorcycle gang.[6]

There were no arrests for status offenses. This arrest pattern does not mean that there were fewer status offenses among the females than in the previous era. To the contrary, running away and sexual activity were common among girls in the longitudinal study. Over one-fifth of the girls (23.2%) and boys (20.9%) ran away from home (left home without permission and stayed away at least overnight). Boys rarely stayed away for more than a week, but girls often remained for an extended period or permanently. Over half of the girls (53%) and boys (62%) reported they had run away – or seriously contemplated it – before they were 18 years old.[7] Even in those cases where incorrigibility and/or sexual offenses could have been claimed, parents sought arrests of their daughters on other grounds (e.g., theft and larceny when running away with a boyfriend with the family car and a parent's credit cards).

A significant proportion of the girls in the longitudinal study in the 1980s were active sexually. Almost 7% of the girls gave birth at least once (24 of 364) before they completed the 11th grade. Most of the girls were unmarried when they became mothers (72%, or 18 of 24). No females themselves were brought into court for sexual offenses, save for the one vagrancy charge and the small number of instances (1%) where the fathers/stepfathers were adjudicated for sexual abuse of their daughters/stepdaughters.

In summary, there are large differences between the two studies in the behaviors that define "problem girls." The principal actions that led to juvenile arrests in Los Angeles in 1950 (running away, incorrigibility, sexual activity) were no longer predominant "crimes" in the 1980s. The arrests for girls in the 1980s were primarily for actions that would be crimes for males and females regardless of their age. The differences are large, despite a possible "regional lag" that could have reduced the generational effect.[8]

Are girls becoming more violent?

Violence is at the center of public perceptions about problem youth today. The belief is widespread that youthful misbehavior is often violent and that this was not the case in the past. Our historical and contemporary data shed new empirical light on the validity of these perceptions.

As noted previously, burglary and car theft were the most frequent felon offenses charged against males in Los Angeles Juvenile Court in 1950. Felonies involving personal violence – such as robbery, rape, assault with a deadly weapon, manslaughter/homicide – were much rarer. Weapons were on the scene in 15.2% of the males' offenses. Even when present, however, weapons were rarely used in the commission of a crime, whether to injure or to threaten. Thus, while the characteristic male referred to juvenile court in 1950 was a felon, he was unlikely to have committed a violent crime.

Not surprisingly, violent crimes were even rarer among the girls referred to court. Only 1.5% (2 girls) were accused of violent crimes, one for murder and the other for assault with a deadly weapon. Although these crimes accounted for a large share (22.2%) of the girls' felony offenses, only a small portion of the girls' total offenses (6.7%) were at the felony level. Thus, violent crimes were an extreme aberration among problem females in 1950 in Los Angeles County.

The longitudinal study suggests that aggression and violence are not rare events in the lives of girls in the 1980s. On the basis of juvenile court and probation department records, self-reports, and published information, it was ascertained that 6% of the girls (22 of 364) were arrested for at least one serious charge before age 18. (Motor vehicle offenses were not included in this tabulation.) The arrests were diverse, with the most frequent involving drug abuse or sales (55%), physical assault (22%), and theft and larceny (22%). The infrequent charges included embezzlement, vandalism, and injury to property. Fewer adolescent girls than boys became involved in direct physical assaults, but it was not unusual for fights to be observed among girls in middle and junior high school. Interview reports of physical attacks indicate that 25% of the girls reported physical fights with other girls in the 7th grade, and 12% in the 11th grade (R. B. Cairns et al., 1989b).

Direct aggressive acts that do occur become more dangerous and potentially harmful as the individual grows older. This increase in the stakes of direct confrontation – as individuals gain access to lethal weapons and become capable of inflicting serious injury – could simultaneously appear as an increase in arrests and a decrease in overall frequency. It should also make attractive the use of alternatives to direct confrontation for girls, such as social aggression. The gender difference in the proportion of girls and boys who are violent seems to be part of a larger age-gender difference in the normative standards for the expression of aggression. As girls enter adolescence, indirect hostility – through ostracism, rumors, and social alienation – became the most frequent form of aggressive expression in female–female conflicts. Boys, however, continued to adopt a "brutality norm" in male–male conflicts, and they continued to rely upon direct confrontations in their disputes with other males. The outcome observed was that fewer adolescent girls than boys became involved in direct physical assaults.

But some girls who are highly aggressive as children become assaultive as adolescents. Twenty girls (from a sample of 364 females) had been identified as at high risk for aggressive behavior while they were in elementary school (4th grade) or middle school (7th grade). These girls were compared over the next 6 years in behavior and arrest records to an individually matched control group (matched for classroom attended, sex, socioeconomic status [SES], and physical size), as well as to the remaining 344 girls in the normal population sample.

When the longitudinal records of the at-risk females are examined, a high proportion (80%) became subsequently involved in serious problem behaviors. The incidents range from multiple cases of stabbing (of sisters, brothers, or fathers) to arrests for simple assault and violent fights with other females. None of the girls in the control group reported similar instances of violence.

There are large gender differences in normative activities related to violence and injury. For example, firearm ownership was virtually nonoverlapping for adolescent boys and girls in this investigation. Approximately half of the boys reported gun ownership (49%) and only 4% of the girls (Sadowski, Cairns, & Earp, 1989). The rate of serious injury in conflicts among males would increase when impulsive weapon use was coupled with the strategy of direct confrontation. This relationship should hold even if weapon use in conflicts were rare and if the proportion of highly aggressive males actually diminished in adolescence.

In summary, the combined data are consistent with the hypothesis that there has been a generational increase in the occurrence of assaultive behaviors by adolescent girls outside the home. Two aspects of the data relevant to this matter require comment as well as caution. First, it appears that arrests for physical assault have increased for girls from the 1950s to the 1980s. Along with the arrest information, our direct observations and the annual self-reports indicated that brutal fights with other girls were not uncommon events for many adolescent girls in the 1980s. The reported physical assaults extended beyond the at-risk girls to include many girls within the general population. In addition, some of the more serious acts of violence – stabbing a sibling or a stepfather, suicide, suspected infant abuse – occurred in the home, and arrests were not made.

Second, it seems likely that physical attacks within the home were also underreported in Los Angeles in the 1950s. Embedded in the available court records are reports of family violence where the adolescent girls seem to have played active instigating roles. Hence it would be inaccurate to assume that physical assaults did not occur in the 1950s, although arrests were made for other violations. All this is to say that some adolescent girls were physically assaultive in the 1950s, although the behavior tended to be concealed in the home and/or by the courts.

But in the 1980s, physically aggressive behaviors involving adolescent girls seemed to be becoming more frequent, more public, and more often adjudicated. We may speculate that there have been generational changes in female behavior and in criminal justice policy. First, public confrontation and "male-typical" assertive responses appear to have become more acceptable for female conflicts in the 1980s than in the 1950s. Second, this shift in behavioral standards for girls seems to have been correlated with, and perhaps helped to provoke, counter-responses by the institutions of society (including schools and the courts). The process may not be unlike the earlier response of the Los Angeles Juvenile Court to female sexual misconduct, whereby actions tolerated in males were deemed unacceptable for females. The phenomena and alternative explanations merit vigorous exploration.

Are the problems of problem girls entities or configurations?

Do the problems of problem girls appear as isolated, single entities in their life histories, or are they embedded in a configuration of problem behaviors and circumstances (both of the juvenile and her family)? If the latter, were the configurations of difficulties that occasioned the petitioning of girls to juvenile court at midcentury mainly similar to or different from those presented by problem girls in the 1980s?

These questions speak directly to theoretical issues of behavioral organization and indirectly to practical issues of treatment and change. In looking for determinants of problems in girls after they have been identified as being "delinquent" or "difficult," one must look in retrospect for causes. Such backward tracing invites errors of selective sampling and biased interpretation. There is a tendency to identify differences as determinants, and cross-sectional surveys provide no controls for girls who show comparable differences but who do not show problem behaviors. On this count, longitudinal studies have the advantage of permitting researchers to study all girls, not just those who get into trouble. Hence, our linking of two such different data bases permits comparisons as well as internal checks of the social contexts in which problem behaviors emerge among girls and of how those contexts and behaviors may have changed over time.

The problem girls in our Los Angeles County sample were socially and personally disadvantaged in a number of ways. For one, they came from poor and economically marginal families. Of the girls' resident male guardians, 85% had working-class occupations, the majority as unskilled laborers with records of intermittent employment. Only 7% were executives or professionals. At a time when public relief was much harder to qualify for than it is today, 22% of the girls were subsisting entirely on welfare.

A variety of additional uncertainties and dislocations also characterized the backgrounds of problem girls in 1950. Their families were highly unstable. Although few of the girls' parents had never married, disruption of the parental household through divorce, desertion, or death was common. Only 34% of the girls' natural parents were still married. At a time when divorce was less common and less accepted socially, 45% of the parents' marriages had been disrupted by divorce or separation. Although many parents had remarried, the share of girls who lived in single-parent households was still strikingly high. Of the girls, 43% had no resident male guardian; an additional 14% had no resident female guardian. Maintaining a stable family arrangement was thus highly precarious for parents of problem girls. It was probably also a contributor to their being adjudicated as problem girls.

Family disruption per se, of course, does not necessarily translate into family dysfunction. But other indicators shed light on the darker side of everyday life for a substantial segment of these problem girls. Among them, 29% of the girls had lengthy histories of running away from home, and 30% had previously been placed out of their own homes to live (on one or several occasions) by their parents or by social agencies. Of the girls' families, 36% (surely an underestimate) also had histories of physical or sexual abuse, chronic substance abuse (generally alcohol), or jail and/or prison experience by siblings and/or parents. Reflecting the tenuous hold that many of these girls had on a secure family life, 24% were petitioned to court by their own parents or guardians.[9]

Although the evidence presented so far indicates that the problems of problem girls often appeared in clusters, rather than as single entities, other evidence suggests that the extent of clustering should not be exaggerated. For example, the school drop-out rate was minimal: though 18% of the girls were age 17 or above, only 12% of the entire sample had dropped out and only 10% were currently employed. Moreover, even though few of the girls were stellar scholars, only 1.5% were behind in grade.[10] In addition, for a group of girls who had been brought to court primarily for sexual activity, the 10% who were currently pregnant does not seem excessively high. Furthermore, for the great majority of these girls, their court appearance represented their first contact with law enforcement agencies of any kind. Of the girls, 77% had no prior police, probation, or court contacts; the petitions filed against them did not represent the culmination of an escalating confrontation with the criminal justice system. Finally, some of the data presented earlier need to be placed in perspective. For example, although 34% of the girls had resided with an abusive, alcoholic, or criminal parent, 64% had not. Similarly, although 30% of the girls had run away, 70% had not.[11]

All of this is to say, then, that for a substantial portion of the girls who were brought to juvenile court at midcentury, perhaps even for a majority, a lengthy trail of horrendous home experiences or of overt, long-term maladaptive behaviors was not in evidence.[12] To be sure, many of these girls were very unhappy with the course of their lives at home, at school, or in the neighborhood. However, despite the low threshold at which the juvenile court and other social agencies at the time were obviously willing to intervene, the girls' unhappiness had generally not manifested itself in clusters of problem behaviors likely to elicit social intervention: for example, falling behind in or dropping out of school, getting pregnant, drinking alcohol in public, hanging out on street corners, committing petty thievery, vandalizing property, or assaulting peers or adults. The misconduct for which many of the problem girls were brought to court was often their first serious breach of law, social convention, or both. And this, after all, is not that surprising once we recognize how often sexual activity alone provided the explicit or implicit justification for court intervention into the lives of girls.

We tentatively conclude, then, that problem girls in midcentury Los Angeles were of two major types: on one hand, those whose difficulties were embedded in a configuration of problem behaviors and, on the other hand, those whose difficulties came to public attention mainly through the highly interventionist goals of the midcentury juvenile justice system, especially with regard to sexual activity among unmarried adolescent girls.

We now shift our attention to the configuration of difficulties presented by problem girls in the 1980s. The longitudinal method – tracking individual girls from age 9 through their early 20s – provided us with detailed information prior to the girls' encountering problems that required social intervention. One strategy we adopted was to compare problem and nonproblem girls in terms of their school and social adaptation at the beginning of the study – when they were in the fourth or seventh grade. Consider, for example, the factors associated with three types of adolescent problem behavior: (1) running away from home, (2) dropping out of school, and (3) becoming a teenage mother.

Running away from home. Recall that a large proportion of the girls (one-fifth) in the "normal" sample of the 1980s ran away from home at least once, and some permanently. How did the girls who ran away compare to girls who did not run away? A unique feature of longitudinal data is that comparisons can be made in childhood, years before the incident. In general, runaway girls differed from nonrunaways as children in terms of personal characteristics (aggressive behavior in elementary and middle school) and social conditions (lower socioeconomic class) (see B. D. Cairns, 1989). Running away was itself associated with further difficulties. Over half of the girls who left home subsequently dropped out of school before completing the 11th grade. If they managed to become employed, they held menial, entry-level jobs. By late adolescence, virtually all of them were experiencing major financial problems. For the runaways who married, approximately a third split up with their husbands within two years.

Dropping out of school. The overall likelihood of school dropout was higher in this Southeastern sample in the 1980s than in Los Angeles in the 1950s.[13] The overall dropout rate prior to the end of the 11th grade was 17% for the girls and 20% for the boys. To plot the relations between school dropout and earlier problem behaviors, we employed a multivariate statistical technique to identify clusters of girls who had similar demographic and behavioral profiles at the beginning of the study. To establish such clusters, we employed only data available from 7th-grade assessments, prior to dropout. This included information about socioeconomic status, peer popularity, school performance, maturation level, appearance, peer reputation, and peer conflicts/aggression. In one cohort, each girl was placed in one of seven clusters.[14]

Once these homogeneous clusters were defined, the rate of early school dropout was determined for each cluster. The highest dropout rate was observed in the cluster of girls characterized by low academic success and high aggressiveness in the 7th grade. Almost half (47%) of the girls in that cluster subsequently dropped out of school prior to completing the 11th grade. These at-risk clusters were also comprised mostly of girls in the lower socioeconomic class status. In contrast, the dropout rate was virtually nil among clusters of girls not defined by serious problem behaviors in the 7th grade (0–2%), even if they were lower SES. Parallel findings were obtained for boys. Over 80% of the boys in the cluster defined by high aggression and academic failure dropped out of school prior to the end of the 11th grade. These findings indicate that in the 1980s, for girls as well as boys, school dropout is associated with a confederation of problems.

Becoming a teenage mother. In the longitudinal sample, 7% of the girls became mothers before they completed the 11th grade. When these eventual teenage mothers were in the 4th grade, they differed from the girls who would not become teenage mothers in both behavior and social circumstances. The teenage mothers were, as children, reliably more aggressive in school than were non-teenage mothers when they were children. The mothers-to-be were also from the lower end of the socioeconomic distribution. But they were not less able students, a finding quite in line with the Los Angeles findings from an earlier era. The school problems of the teenage mothers were primarily behavioral, not cognitive. Nonetheless, there was a correlation between school dropout in the 1980s longitudinal sample. Two-thirds of the girls who became mothers also dropped out of school, a dropout rate over twice as high as that among girls who did not become mothers. Which came first, dropout or motherhood? The longitudinal analysis indicates that about half of the girls had already dropped out before becoming pregnant.

One further observation concerns the social dynamics and social support for problem girls. Girls who later become teenage mothers tended, in elementary school, to hang around with other girls who themselves would become teenage mothers. There was selective affiliation among teenage mothers-to-be as early as the 4th grade. Because affiliation patterns show large changes over time, it cannot be assumed that the same girls stayed together and influenced each other from childhood through adolescence. What happened was that girls shifted social groups from year to year, but they tended to associate selectively with other girls who shared their values, behaviors, and aspirations.[15]

Risk–control group comparisons. One other research strategy permitted by the longitudinal design is germane to the entity–cluster issue. At the outset of the investigation, contrasting groups of girls were identified on the assumption that they would show different developmental trajectories with respect to psychological adjustment. One group was considered to be at high risk, based on their aggressive behavior in school. For each nominated subject, we identified an individually matched control subject who was the same sex, race, and physical size, enrolled in the same classroom, and with roughly the same SES, but who was not nominated. After 8 years, we compared the two groups on a composite index of adjustment, with the positive points on the scale indicating school graduation, lack of serious difficulties with police or at school, and success in the community, sports, or work. The negative points on the scale indicate arrests for nonstatutory crimes, school dropout, serious morbidity or mortality, unwed parenthood, substance abuse, or serious injuries from fighting.

The longitudinal findings of high-risk girls can be summarized by two points. First, the longitudinal contrasts indicate that an overwhelming majority (80%, or 16 of 20) of the girls identified as being at risk in the fourth and seventh grades showed extremely poor social adjustment in late adolescence. In contrast, only 3 of 20 (15%) of the individually matched control females were classified as having serious difficulties in subsequent adjustment. Second, there are only modest sex differences in the prediction of difficulties. Indeed, the outcomes for the at-risk females in late adolescence were more dismal than those for the at-risk males.

These outcomes help answer the question of why chronic behavioral problems resisted change. For the most serious problem girls in the longitudinal sample, the constraints on their behavior were convergent and redundant. These were the girls in the multiproblem cluster. Problems at one level of experience – the values promoted in the home – were correlated with those that operate at other levels – the values supported by intimate associates and the girls themselves. The social systems in which the problem girls were embedded tended to collaborate rather than compete; together, they served to funnel and direct the girls' deviant behaviors. Problems of being aggressive, low academic performance, being poor, and having a disrupted family tended to go together. These redundant forces can operate to keep problem girls on a trajectory of problem behaviors throughout adolescence. Benign changes did not endure for most problem girls in the longitudinal observations because of constraints from within and without. On this score, recidivism in female delinquency may not be an exception so much as it illustrates a general developmental principle.

In both data sets, the problems of many of the problem girls appeared in configurations and clusters, not as single entities. But the problem girls of Los Angeles in the 1950s appear to have been identified as "problems" for at least two reasons. One group only demonstrated sexual activity that was unacceptable, and the other group showed a co-occurrence of sexual misconduct, low socioeconomic class, family pathologies, and family disruption. In the longitudinal study of the 1980s, however, it was possible to plot the configurations of problem girls with surprisingly high accuracy. This may have been because of the availability of detailed life-course information about each girl's behavior (social and cognitive) as well as her circumstances (economic, race, family). In any case, extreme aggressiveness and deviant peer affiliations in late childhood and early adolescence were associated in the 1980s with multiple problems of living in late adolescence, including arrests, unmarried pregnancy, and early dropout.[16]

Are there changing expectations and punishments for youth behavior?

Treatment and punishment provide one indication of societal attitudes toward the problems of problem girls at midcentury. How did the Los Angeles County Juvenile Court in the 1950s respond to the acting-out behaviors of delinquent girls? Perhaps the least understood component of juvenile court procedure concerns the use of short-term detention facilities (jails), both prior to and following a youth's initial hearing. As an outcome of the charges lodged against them, 55% of the girls first spent time in Juvenile Hall, usually for two or three weeks. Thus, *before* the court actually heard their cases, most girls were punished by confinement in jail for a significant period of time. A short-term "jolt" thus formed an unstated but integral component of the legal processing of problem girls.

In Los Angeles 11% of the girls had their cases dismissed, and 15% were committed to reform school. The court disposed of most cases (73%) by placing the girls on probation in their own homes or the homes of relatives. Girls who were returned home on probation remained under the court's jurisdiction. If they continued in delinquent behavior, their probation could be revoked and they could be placed in long-term custodial facilities. All together, 26% of the girls in the Los Angeles sample in the 1950s were sent to reform schools by the court while their cases remained active.

Information from the longitudinal investigation of the 1980s indicates that there has been a shift in the kinds of behaviors considered to be serious enough to bring adolescent females to the courts. There was no direct legal intervention in the lives of the 364 girls because of sexual conduct (with the exception of one arrest for vagrancy), although sexual activity was common in this population of girls.

If girls in the 1980s were no longer being arrested or brought to court for sexual behavior, for what kinds of infractions were they being punished, and how harsh was that punishment? Generally speaking, girls in the longitudinal sample were rarely incarcerated, even when they encountered the police and/or the courts for felony offenses that would have been regarded with the utmost seriousness in the 1950s. When placed in jail, girls were typically left for only a short period (hours or overnight). Dismissal and suspension of sentences were very common dispositions among girls who did appear in court. If the girls' removal from the community was deemed necessary by the court, alternative "treatment" placements were made for virtually all the offenses, even for those involving serious assaults, thefts, or major drug violations. These placements included state mental health facilities, county drug rehabilitation units, half-way houses, private residential drug treatment homes, or foster-home placement. Such placements reflect in part the policy adopted by the courts to employ the "least restrictiveness" alternative for juvenile offenders. They also reflect the general unavailability of detention facilities for girls.[17]

On the broader issue of whether it has fallen to the school to enforce behavioral norms no longer enforced by the courts, we must be modest in our claims. Two points can be made. First, it was our impression that nonsexual acting out (e.g., fighting, vandalism, theft) was tolerated less among girls in the 1980s than among boys. Girls who violated the behavioral standards in elementary school and middle school were punished by the school at least as severely as were boys. Although there were proportionally fewer problem girls than problem boys in school, the girls identified as being at risk were as likely to encounter subsequent problems in living as did at-risk boys.

Second, some criminal laws were enforced in the schools in the 1980s that were not vigorously enforced by the legal system in the community. The use of illegal drugs is a case in point. A minimum of half of the longitudinal subjects reported illegal drug use while in high school. Accordingly, we found that only flagrant violations tended to be punished in high school or when our college-bound subjects reached the university. In elementary schools, however, the laws against use and possession were often vigorously pursued for preadolescent and early adolescent children, both boys and girls.[18]

General discussion

From its origins at the turn of the twentieth century, the juvenile court served as a prime vehicle for society to punish precocious female sexuality. Our review of Los Angeles Juvenile Court records in the 1950s leaves little doubt that the court was then, as earlier, seeking to act as a guardian of female virtue. But times do finally change: in the 1980s longitudinal data, there was virtually no indication that sexuality played a role in court contacts for problem girls. Arrests for status offenses were rare, and girls were arrested for behaviors that were crimes for anyone, regardless of sex or age. Examination of the longitudinal evidence indicates that it is unlikely the incidence of precocious sexual activity had diminished in frequency. If anything, sexual acting out, running away, and unwed motherhood seem to be more prevalent in the 1980s than in the 1950s.

Why then fewer arrests for sexual behaviors in the contemporary period? One hypothesis is that the standards of the community, including those of the courts and police, have shifted such that sexual precocity in itself is no longer considered to be a crime for girls. The increase among girls of more serious offenses, including crimes of violence, may have propelled the shift. A related hypothesis is that following World War II the prevalence of one or all of the "status offense" behaviors expanded so rapidly among adolescent females that law enforcement had little practical choice but to "decriminalize" them in order to concentrate resources on the increasingly criminal and gang-related activities of male delinquents.

This chapter should be viewed as a progress report rather than a finished product. It is incomplete on at least two counts. First, more adequate information is called for on contemporary judicial policy and the treatment of girls. This information should be obtained not only from the courts where the longitudinal work was conducted but, in addition, from the Los Angeles Juvenile Court of the 1980s. Second, a more detailed review is called for on the factors associated with sexual acting out among girls in the first half of the twentieth century. Given the embeddedness of problem behaviors, it seems unlikely that there would not be significant correlates of precocious sexuality in the 1950s as well as in the 1980s. Such correlates could include early maturation.[19]

In the course of this essay, we have raised questions that seem deserving of further investigation. Consider, for instance, the role of the school in enforcing behavioral standards that the courts have abandoned. We found merit in the picture of schools as regulators-by-default. But we also found the high schools we have studied to be reluctant to take on the roles abandoned by other agencies in the society.[20] To be sure, schools continue to enforce some social standards at some times. However, it appears that the age at which they exercise such authority has shifted downward, from late adolescence in high school to late childhood in elementary and middle school. This age-graded shift in school responsibility – as well as changes in the expectations for and behaviors of adolescents and children – merits further study.

Our focus in this chapter has been on problem girls. The problems of boys have been relegated mostly to footnotes. In light of the neglect of problem girls in the delinquency and developmental literatures, there is ample justification for our priority. But we have told only half of the story. In future work, it would not be inappropriate to reintroduce the problems of juvenile males. Such a comparative analysis could further clarify the issues covered in this chapter (e.g., the generality of changes in standards and punishments, the role of the school in the enforcement of standards for children, or the extent to which problems occur in configurations as opposed to entities). It could also provide additional information about the changing relations between the courts and the kinds of behaviors that are seen as crimes in juveniles.

Looking backward, we found that the collaboration has been enriching and enlightening. Enriching, because the insights that emerged from sister disciplines deepened our understanding of issues within each of our areas. Enlightening, because collaboration demanded reexamination and reformulation of assumptions that were dear to each orientation. To be sure, collaboration between history and psychology cannot achieve advances that are won only by within-discipline rigor. But it can help each discipline understand the meaning, limits, and importance of those advances.

Acknowledgments

Schlossman's research was supported by funds from the Rand Corporation, the Rockefeller Foundation, and the California State Department of Justice. He thanks Barbara Williams, James Rasmussen, and Phoebe Cottingham for their assistance and support, and Paula Wenzl for her several contributions in project design and data analysis.

The CLS Project (Robert B. Cairns and Beverley D. Cairns, co-directors) has been supported by the Spencer Foundation, W. T. Grant Foundation, and NIMH grant 45532. Beverley Cairns, Holly Neckerman, and Tamara Flinchum made several contributions to this chapter as well as collaborating in the conduct of the research.

Notes

1. There are some exceptions. Sons are typically not permitted to participate in stereotypic "feminine" behaviors, although daughters are often allowed to take part in male-type patterns of play and dress.
2. A "petition" in juvenile court functions much like a "complaint" in adult criminal court to initiate formal legal proceedings. In Los Angeles in 1950, parents, schools, and social agencies regularly filed petitions alleging delinquent conduct against juveniles, although the majority of petitions were filed by law enforcement officers (especially the police).
3. Information on "assaultive and violent" adolescents is from a study of 1,320 at-risk subjects in the *Willie M.* program (R. B. Cairns, Peterson, & Neckerman, 1988).
4. Behar (1985) describes the *Willie M.* program.
5. Most girls readily admitted their sexual activities. The court often went beyond a girl's admission and conducted a vaginal examination to determine whether the hymen was intact.
6. There was only one known instance of a status offense, namely, failure to attend school by a 14-year-old girl.
7. These results on runaways are generally in line with previous analyses, including studies by the Colorado group (Brennan, Huizinga, & Elliott, 1978). The exception is that our incidence rate is higher. Whether this difference reflects variation because of decade – 1970s versus 1980s – or because of region – Rocky Mountains versus Southeast – remains to be determined.
8. One possible explanation for the generational difference is that the comparisons are confounded with differences on the urban–rural dimension as well as in region (Southeast vs. West Coast). However, in light of the directionality of the difference, this interpretation is not compelling. The regional and/or urban differences should have operated to diminish, not accentuate, the generational effect if Los Angeles in the 1950s might be considered a priori to be similar to the Southeast in the 1980s.

9. These various problems of economic marginality, family instability, and family dysfunction tended to be more severe among minority females. For example, among minorities 9 of 10 resident male guardians were unskilled laborers; 1 of 8 girls lived with her natural married parents; 1 of 3 households subsisted on welfare; 2 of 5 girls lived with chronic substance abusers; and 2 of 5 girls had parents or siblings with criminal records. In short, the foundations for a secure family life were even shakier for minority than they were for white problem girls.

We are less certain how to interpret the extraordinary geographic mobility among problem girls and their parents. California is known as a state of newcomers, both immigrants and internal migrants. This pattern was evident between the two world wars, with the first mass movement of Mexicans across the border, the explosive growth of Los Angeles, and the Dust Bowl exodus from the nation's interior. Nonetheless, the degree to which the girls in court, and especially their parents, were newcomers to the state is startling. Half of the girls were native to the state, and although we have no comparable data for nondelinquent girls, we suspect that this was an unusually high rate of geographic mobility for midadolescent California females during this period. More notable was how few of the girls' parents were born in California: only 9% of the fathers and 10% of the mothers. It remains to be determined whether, and how, the migration experience per se – whether from overseas, as was common in the East (and explored in the classic study by W. I. Thomas & Znaniecki, 1918–20), or internally from other states, as was common in the West – set apart the experiences of problem girls from those of the general female youth population. (See note 15 for a discussion of the relations between moving and behavior problems in the longitudinal sample.)

10. This failure and dropout rate must be interpreted in the context of policy within the Los Angeles schools at midcentury. Grade failure was extremely uncommon because of school policy from the mid-1930s through the 1940s, the period in which the girls would have been enrolled in elementary and high school. A more sensitive measure of school adaptation would be the extent to which the problem girls (relative to nonproblem girls) had been disciplined within school for behavior or academic problems.

11. A note of caution on interpretation is in order. It would be helpful to have more detailed pre-arrest behavioral information on the "delinquent" girls and a comparison group of "nondelinquent" girls. Comparison on pre-intervention measures, such as disruptive activities in the school and involvement with deviant peers, are necessary to track the life-course trajectories to sexual activity and court involvement.

12. This was surely not for lack of trying on the part of the probation officers, who often went to great lengths to latch onto any piece of "dirt" that would shed light on the origins of the girl's delinquency.

13. School policy in this region in the 1970s and 1980s was such that grade failure and subsequent dropout were not uncommon. By the 7th grade, 58% of the minority boys and 28% of the white boys had been held back at least one grade. Among the girls, 23% of the minority females had been held back by the 7th grade and 13% of the white females. A strong association was observed between grade failure and subsequent school dropout.

14. The statistical techniques and outcomes are fully described in R. B. Cairns, Cairns, and Neckerman (1989a). An unpublished analysis of the younger cohort of girls confirms the importance of the combined effects of school failure and lack of achievement, along with difficulties in social adjustment, upon subsequent school dropout. See Elliott, Huizinga, and Menard (1989) for a discussion of multiple problem youth.

15. Recall that problem girls in Los Angeles in the 1950s came from families who had moved into the state. By contrast, mobility in the Southeast in the 1980s was considerably less than in California in the 1950s. More than 9 out of 10 of the girls in the total longitudinal sample remained within the state of their birth through late adolescence. Some movement did occur, however. In light of the association between migration patterns in the families of problem girls in Los Angeles in 1950, it was of interest to find that more problem girls had a history of moving in

the 1980s than nonproblem girls. In this regard, girls who moved during their school years were twice as likely subsequently to drop out of school as girls who did not move. Moreover, the act of moving was as much diagnostic as it was causative. Even prior to moving, girls who moved in elementary and middle school were poorer students and more aggressive than girls who did not move.

16. About 6% of the girls could be identified as "problem girls" in the 1980s. This proportion of girls accounted for virtually all of the arrests. It would be of interest to determine whether a similar small proportion of girls were identified as "problems" in the earlier era. It may be that the community and the courts are likely to define a small proportion of girls as "seriously deviant" regardless of the period. The proportion of "problem girls" in the society may remain constant, even though societal definitions of deviancy change.

17. There were few dedicated short-term facilities for juvenile males in the areas where the longitudinal data were collected, and even fewer for juvenile females. Incarceration was an important option for juvenile boys and young adult males. A significant proportion of the most serious male offenders in the longitudinal sample were incarcerated in county jails prior to court hearings and placed in state training schools prior to age 18 or in state prison after 18. Given the limited facilities for detaining girls, the actions of the court for probation or "treatment" may reflect a combination of social norms and lack of physical accommodations.

18. But conflicts may arise among the courts, communities, and schools even in the younger age groups. In one instance, despite compelling evidence of student possession, all charges against the students were dismissed by the court, and the principal was fired by the school administration.

19. In this regard, Magnusson (1988) found that very early maturing girls in his large-scale longitudinal study in Sweden were more likely to show precocious sexual behavior and to become involved in a variety of problem behaviors, including difficulties in school and drinking. Interestingly, these girls when followed up in adulthood, did not differ in significant measures of adult adjustment (e.g., marriage, psychopathology, criminal behavior) from girls who did not mature early and who did not become involved in early sexual behavior. Beyond the Swedish studies, studies of very early maturing females indicate that they are generally at a social disadvantage relative to late-maturing girls (e.g., Simmons & Blyth, 1987).

20. We may speculate that today, as in the past, the family is held primarily responsible for the upbringing of children and adolescents, with the courts, school, church, and community-at-large still considered to be backup. As families have backed off from responsibility for the problems of adolescents, so have the courts and the schools.

6 Continuity and change in symptom choice: Anorexia

Joan Jacobs Brumberg and Ruth Striegel-Moore

The post-1960 epidemic of anorexia nervosa can be related to recent social change in the realm of food and sexuality.

Joan Jacobs Brumberg (1988, p. 268)

In the past two decades, anorexia nervosa has become an increasingly prevalent disease in the United States, and eating disorders are regarded as commonplace among women students on our nation's campuses. Patients with anorexia nervosa are drawn largely from the middle and upper classes; they are Caucasian, female, and largely adolescent and young adult. Despite many confusions (and lapses) in the historical epidemiology of the disorder, most medical and mental health observers agree there has been a real rise in incidence in the number of patients with anorexia nervosa since the 1960s. Since the 1970s, the number of women patients seeking help with eating disorders has increased steadily in clinical settings across the country (Brumberg, 1988).

These changes in incidence and presentation of symptoms are of concern to social historians and mental health professionals. For historians and psychologists, the current situation prompts an important theoretical question: Why does a psychopathology become more prominent in one time period than another? What one thinks about the causes or etiology of this particular disease will obviously determine an answer. For the purposes of this essay, however, we will set aside the discussion of etiology and proceed from the following shared assumptions.

First, in mental illness, basic forms of cognitive and emotional disorientation are expressed in behavioral aberrations that mirror the deep preoccupations of a particular culture. Second, anorexia nervosa is a multidetermined disorder involving biology, psychology, and culture. We regard these three etiological components as interactive and reciprocal; no one model can be used in isolation (Brumberg, 1988; Garner, Garfinkel, & Bemis, 1982). For purposes of studying the disorder, however, we follow a two-staged conceptualization of the disease

131

(Brumberg, 1988) that is useful for clarifying the relationship of sociocultural influences to individual biological and psychological variables.

In Stage 1 – *recruitment* – sociocultural factors play a critical role. In this period, dieting and the pressure to be thin are extremely salient. Not eating, or eating very little, is culturally sanctioned among elite women in the West (Brumberg, 1988; Chernin, 1981). Individual psychological and biological variables, however, ultimately explain why some women but not others move from chronic dieting to the full-blown clinical psychopathology. (Does the symptom have some larger meaning in the patient's emotional and family life? Does starvation actually make her feel good and energetic?) Then, in Stage 2 – *career or acclimation* – we see biological and psychological responses to starvation: these physical and psychological responses are relatively uniform from patient to patient and from time to time and serve to perpetuate the illness (Garfinkel & Kaplan, 1985). The study of Stage 2 is within the realm of medical science (broadly defined), but Stage 1, recruitment, represents an important arena for historical inquiry in collaboration with clinical, developmental, and social psychology.

In this essay we explore change and continuity in the meaning of the primary behavioral symptom in anorexia nervosa – refusal of food – and comment on how the symptom constellation in this disorder has changed over time. Our analysis is based on a comparative investigation of patients with anorexia nervosa in the late nineteenth century and clinical and research experience with contemporary anorectics. Admittedly, our methodology is highly qualitative, and, because of the limitations of the historical material, it has been based on only about a dozen cases. Yet, we have been able to compare our "patients" on a number of important dimensions, particularly the issue of presentation and symptomatology.

For the psychologist, the historical material did, of course, have a striking limitation: in nineteenth-century case records, doctors concentrated on somatic issues and said little about the psychology of their anorectic patients. Moreover, there is virtually no primary source material – diaries or letters – written by Victorian anorectics explaining their behavior. Thus, it is very difficult, if not impossible, for the historian to explain why a particular individual developed anorexia nervosa. As a result, we are unable to say a great deal about the psychodynamics of individual cases in past time. This is a frustration, but also an important reality, in collaborative research between historians and clinical psychologists.

If the individual psyche was hard to approach from a historical perspective, the family was somewhat easier. Again, historians of medicine generally do not have primary materials that describe the daily functioning and emotional environment of the families of individual patients. Yet, because of the importance of intrafamilial dynamics in explaining contemporary anorexia nervosa, we felt that we must try to penetrate the family world of the nineteenth-century anorectic. By coupling what we knew about patterns of Victorian middle-class nurturance (culled from primary and secondary historical literature) and the psychodynamics of modern anorectic families (described by Sargent, Liebman, & Silver, 1985; Strober & Humphrey, 1987; and Yager, 1982), we did come to some understanding of the emotional milieu that surrounded anorexia nervosa in the nineteenth century.

A brief history

Anorexia nervosa was named and identified in the 1870s by William Gull and Charles Lasègue in England and France. This is not to say that it had not existed before. Published reports from at least one American asylum, as early as the 1850s, reveal that there were adolescent girls, aged 16 to 23, from "good families," who refused to eat their food and suffered no other physical or mental disorder. At that time, American anorectics were classed as "sitomaniacs," those who feared or loathed their food (Brumberg, 1988). These patients clearly did not have commonplace "wasting diseases" such as tuberculosis or consumption; nor were they explicitly delusional or insane.

Because wasting diseases were so prevalent and so critical in the nineteenth century, the doctor's first task was to determine the source of emaciation. In general, nineteenth-century physicians concentrated on the problem of differential diagnosis (how to tell one disease from another) and on the cure of physical symptoms. Because of the somatic emphasis in nineteenth-century medicine, not much attention was paid to the psychology of anorexia nervosa or to the question of the patient's motivation. Before Sigmund Freud, the meaning of noneating was not explored; few questions were asked about "feelings." A cure was accomplished when the patient gained weight, or "added flesh," and appeared to be out of physical danger. In essence, anorexia nervosa was a relatively rare disorder, and therapeutics in that day centered on relieving the primary physical symptom: emaciation.

The rarity of anorexia nervosa as well as the pattern of treatment in the nineteenth century makes the task of historical documentation and analysis particularly difficult. In the nineteenth century, young women of respectable social backgrounds were generally not treated in public institutions of any kind. Anorectic patients were most often treated in their own homes or on an ad hoc basis. Some went to private "hysterical homes" for a brief respite; others took extended recuperative trips and sea voyages. The bias against institutionalization of respectable girls means that few records were kept. Consequently, documentary materials on this disorder are scanty and hard to come by.

Having acknowledged these problems of documentation, a great deal can still be garnered from a comparative study of anorexia nervosa in past and present. Using published and unpublished case reports, the social historian of medicine can assess the nature of the Victorian anorectic's presentation, the involvement of her family, and the nature and pattern of her symptoms. The historian can also move beyond case materials on individuals to the larger cultural milieu that surrounded bourgeois Victorian girls, specifically to the language of food and the body in that era.

We argue that to understand and treat anorexia nervosa, some attention must be paid to the meaning of food and eating in female identity in both the Victorian and the contemporary world. Ultimately, our joint investigation illustrates two basic but important points for the behavioral sciences: first, that the same psychopathology may change over time despite numerous continuities; and second, that symptoms and symptom constellations are quite responsive to culture.

The language of presentation

The nineteenth-century patient understood implicitly that the doctor was primarily interested in the physical signs and sounds of disease. As a result, the Victorian anorectic presented somatically rather than psychologically. "I have no appetite" or "It hurts when I eat" were the most common explanations of noneating in the Victorian era.

Today, in a medical world that is becoming increasingly more sensitive to psychological issues – particularly among adolescents whom we expect to see struggling with issues of sexual maturation and autonomy – anorectics present their refusal of food in a quite different way. Today, the formulaic statement is "I do not need to eat" or "I am too fat." Often, the modern anorectic denies that her eating behavior is unusual. She maintains that she is not ill or sick and that her jogging, swimming, and aerobics are proof of her good health. Typically, she denies her problem and her need for professional help or therapeutic intervention.

Today, her therapist is likely to see her problem as a developmental one: the eating disorder typically emerges during adolescence, a life stage that ushers in several developmental tasks. These tasks include coming to terms with the physical changes of puberty, establishing stable peer relationships while becoming increasingly independent from one's family, and developing a cohesive personality structure (Attie & Brooks-Gunn, 1989). Although girls *and* boys experience these challenges, achieving mastery is more difficult for girls because they are faced with ambiguous messages or ideals. Acceptance of the mature female body, for example, has to be accomplished in a cultural context that values the prepubertal shape more than the mature female shape. Furthermore, appearance plays a more central role in peer relationships for girls than boys; popularity figures more prominently into girls' self-esteem than it does for boys. Finally, girls receive conflicting messages about the ideal female personality: although they are encouraged to be autonomous, they also are urged to be empathic, caring, and helpful to others. Developing an autonomous self is difficult for girls who have been raised to be obedient and conformist, personality characteristics often ascribed to anorectic girls (Friedlander & Siegel, 1990). Dieting represents a seemingly "ideal" solution for the adolescent girl who is struggling to live up to our culture's developmental tasks. By reducing her weight, the adolescent girl can approximate the beauty ideal and hope for popularity among her peers; by restraining her food intake, she signals to others and to herself that she is in control of herself and her life, that she is "mature."

By contrast, in the Victorian era, the ideal of female fragility and debility was incorporated into personal identity, family interactions, and medical assessment. Ill health in women had a certain currency and social value. Women who suffered were admired; robust women were considered uncouth or déclassé. Consequently, Victorian ideas about the superior moral and aesthetic sensibilities of frail women underlay presentations that stressed physical pain and suffering. An adolescent daughter who did not eat was a source of enormous concern to the middle-class family. In an age of medical somaticism that concern was legitimated by complaints of organic discomfort and gastrointestinal or digestive pain. Although some nineteenth-century doctors (such as Lasègue) saw anorectics who denied their illness, the general cultural milieu promoted discussion rather than denial of ill health in women and dependence rather than autonomy in relation to medical personnel. In essence, anorexia nervosa was a medical rather than a psychological problem of adolescent development.

Family dynamics

Although we recognize that the psychogenesis of anorexia nervosa is not strictly familial, historical materials confirm the continuing influence of family and class factors. In the earliest nineteenth-century case reports, there is a connection between socioeconomic class and anorexia nervosa. Anorectic girls did not work outside the home; many had formal schooling well into late adolescence; they came from families able and willing to expend financial resources on them. Today, as in the late nineteenth century, anorexia nervosa is confined largely to middle- and upper-class young women in the West, a phenomenon that explains its classification as a "culture-bound syndrome" (Prince, 1985).

The emergence of anorexia nervosa as a modern disease entity was intimately linked to the emergence of modern adolescence. By the late nineteenth century, family life had intensified as a result of social and economic changes that accompanied industrialization, urbanization, and class stratification (Brumberg, 1988). Families became smaller; corporal discipline declined and "spoiling" increased; and children lived at home with their parents well into their late teens and early 20s. In this environment of material and emotional privileging, adolescence and anorexia nervosa were "born." Thus, anorexia nervosa has been and remains largely an adolescent disorder for reasons that are social and historical as well as developmental.

In fact, the middle-class families described in nineteenth-century clinical case records appear to have been "enmeshed" much in the manner Salvador Minuchin and other family systems theorists describe. *Enmeshment* refers to a style of family interaction characterized by an overinvolvement of family members in each other's affairs. Needs and moods of others are often inferred; family members are highly sensitive to one another. The good of the whole is often put above the needs of the individual. Criticism is discouraged because it threatens an ideal of harmony and unity. Although parent–child enmeshment is functional when the child is young, failure to disengage gradually undermines the child's development of an autonomous self. For example, in enmeshed families exploration and independent problem solving are discouraged, depriving the child of the opportunity to experience a sense of self-efficacy (Minuchin, 1974; Sargent et al., 1985).

The nineteenth-century middle-class family appears to have another characteristic hypothesized to play a role in the development of anorexia nervosa among women today. According to Minuchin and colleagues (Minuchin et al., 1975; Minuchin, Rosman, & Baker, 1978), families with an anorectic daughter exhibit relationships characterized by overprotectiveness. Family members feel a strong sense of vulnerability and respond by being overly protective and unable to take risks or allow for risk taking. Highly nurturant interactions dominate, at the expense of constructive criticism and the chance for the development of a sense of mastery and autonomy.

In terms of intrafamilial psychodynamics, the historical evidence for enmeshment and overprotection is highly suggestive but not altogether conclusive: nineteenth-century doctors had a sense that the family was implicated in the disorder, but they were imprecise about the nature of the emotional involvement. Although the Victorian physician recognized that the family played a role in the maintenance of the anorectic symptomatology, this assessment led to blaming the parents for failed moral leadership rather than to understanding the family from a systems perspective.

For example, doctors almost always considered both parents overly solicitous and indulgent in relation to anorectic daughters. It is important to understand that middle-class parents in the Anglo-American world prided themselves on their ability to protect their daughters and that their protectiveness set them apart from "heathens" and the working class (Brumberg, 1982). Middle-class physicians observing middle-class families regarded parental overprotectiveness in a positive way but often described the daughters as "spoiled" and in need of a firm moral authority.

At the same time, in a number of cases, the doctor observed "hostility" between the indulgent mother and her emaciated daughter. Unfortunately, the specific issues between mother and daughter are not usually elaborated. In at least one case, however, the patient told her girlfriends that her mother complained that she was too fat, suggesting that there were parental expectations and pressures surrounding the girl's body and her social persona. The unwillingness of the parents to follow medical orders – that is, to separate from their daughters – was a theme in early reports. At least one death from anorexia nervosa was attributed by the doctor to his inability to keep the patient isolated from a "nervous" mother. According to this 1895 case report, the concerned mother continued to visit her daughter in the hospital on a daily basis despite orders to the contrary. As a result, the effects of medical intervention were negated (according to the doctor) and the patient died.

The middle-class families of Victorian anorectics were, by virtue of their single-minded focus on their daughters' health, child-centered to a fault. The pursuit of health for the daughter was a centerpiece of the family's social activity. Lasègue noted that every visitor to an anorectic's family was expected to talk earnestly and continually about the girl's food and eating. Although William Gull never said anything explicit about the psychology of the disorder, he (and many others) advocated removal of the anorectic girl from her family, what is now called a "parentectomy." Once the patient was away from home, in a "new moral environment," the girl was expected to improve and return to normal eating. In fact, Gull's clinical reports suggest success after separation from the nuclear family.

In sum, bourgeois family life in the Victorian era was child-centered, overprotective (especially with girls), and sometimes indulgent. Not surprisingly, in this materially and emotionally privileged environment, some young women chose to express their unhappiness in a "ladylike" symptom – not eating – that clearly disturbed the family without being as flamboyantly disruptive as a tantrum or quarrel. The evidence suggests that Victorian anorectics were then, as they are today, extremely "nice" adolescent girls whose behavior combined overcompliance with hostile symbolic behavior.

Despite these striking behavioral continuities, we propose that enmeshment and overprotectiveness were motivated differently in the Victorian era than today precisely because contemporary parents have different expectations for themselves as well as for their daughters. For the Victorian mother, the central task was to ensure that a daughter was "marriageable." A daughter with social graces (the ability to make polite conversation, a restrained appetite, and a moral reputation) was visible proof that mother had performed her maternal role. Costanzo and Woody (1979) argue that when parents are highly invested in a domain of a child's life, they tend to use a restrictive parental style (including overinvolvement) to influence the child in that domain. Thus, by being overly involved with her daughter's social life, a Victorian mother was able to exert control with the expectation of achieving what her role as mother prescribed: launching her daughter into a proper marriage.

Mothers in the 1990s have different developmental needs and social expectations from their Victorian counterparts. A mother's expectations for herself as well as for her daughter are more diverse, possibly giving rise to anxiety about her performance as a mother. In fact, launching a daughter into marriage and/or career no longer signals that mother has reached a developmental milestone and can now retire. Modern mothers are expected to continue to have active lives, to be attractive, and, most of all, to remain young; at the same time that they aim for these personal goals, they may be ambivalent about what the "emptying nest" implies for their own lives and future achievement.

In contemporary society, a mother's overinvolvement in her daughter's life may be motivated in part by a desire to participate in her daughter's experiences and thus be a part of the younger generation. Mother–daughter relations around clothing provide a telling example. As much as being able to wear her mother's clothes signals that the adolescent girl is growing up, wearing her daughter's clothes proves that mother is not aging. It seems quite unlikely that a Victorian girl would have worn her mother's clothes and even more inconceivable that the mother would have chosen to wear her daughter's clothes. In all probability, the Victorian mother and daughter differed in size (as a function of repeated child-bearing as well as cultural acceptance of a matronly form). In this milieu, sharing clothes would not have been possible, even if mother or daughter desired to do so. Today's mother and daughter commonly have a number of clothes items that are interchangeable; mother is as busy trying to look young as the adolescent is trying to look sophisticated.

Thus, although it is useful to underscore the continuity of enmeshment as a contributing factor in the genesis of anorexia nervosa, we must also consider how new social arrangements and personal expectations have changed the motivational dynamics that underlie enmeshment. From a clinical perspective, we have little idea of what new parental values, styles of parental behavior, or family interactions may be contributing to the current "epidemic" (post-1960).

The literature on recent family change provides few clues and concentrates on structural issues such as divorce and remarriage or number of children. But there is no positive correlation between divorce and anorexia nervosa, suggesting that we push for more intense investigation of parental inputs within stable, nuclear families. This question suggests that students of the family and the life course take a closer look at the parents of the anorectic generations in terms of their personal achievement values and parental styles.

Efforts are needed to assess more carefully the role of fathers in the etiology of anorexia nervosa because an expanded research focus reduces the likelihood of blaming just mothers. Certainly the role of fathers in relation to daughters has changed considerably.

In the seventies, our culture seemed to have "found" fatherhood, as exemplified by the numerous popular and scientific books on fathers and fathering. Our culture now upholds an ideal of fatherhood that encourages men to be more involved in parental activities and to expand the father role to include caring for the emotional needs of one's children. How this ideal relates to modern anorexia nervosa remains to be explored. It appears that being male no longer is a guarantee of freedom from body-image concerns. In fact, even though women continue to be more likely than men to feel fat (Silberstein, Striegel-Moore, Timko, & Rodin, 1988), survey data suggest that men are catching up with women (Cash, Winstead, & Janda, 1986; Striegel-Moore & Kearney-Cooke, 1991). At this point, we can only speculate about the significance of fathers' increased preoccupation with appearance and shape for their daughter's body esteem. Research has already established a relationship between mothers' dieting and food behaviors and the severity of the daughters' disordered eating (Drewnowski, Yee, & Krahn, 1988). It is quite plausible that fathers' attitudes as well as dieting and exercise efforts may also contribute to the development of eating disorders in adolescent daughters. Thus, although the overt behavioral symptom (food refusal) has remained the same, the social and personal dynamics that underlie enmeshment may be quite different because *both* parents have changed.

The language of food and the body

In societies where food scarcity is not a problem, the appetite appears to become more of a social and emotional instrument (Brumberg, 1988). Moreover, food is an important analog of the self. Food choice is a form of self-expression made according to aesthetic, literary, and social ideas as well as economic and physiological requirements (Barthes, 1975; Lévi-Strauss, 1966). In anorexia nervosa, today and in the past, young women use the appetite as a voice, as a way of saying something about personal identity.

Ideas about food and eating circulating in popular culture are central to the anorectic experience today and in the Victorian era. The Victorian anorectic was likely to say, "I cannot eat because I have no appetite" or "When I eat, I feel bad." The modern anorectic generally says "I am too fat and I need to be very careful with my food." Although we recognize these statements as rationalizations for the symptom's deeper emotional meaning, it is useful to understand the changing language of food and the body because the language provides an important context for understanding a disorder such as anorexia nervosa.

In Victorian society, food and femininity were linked in such a way as to promote restrictive eating among privileged adolescent girls. According to the bourgeois perspective, only peasant or working-class women ate with gusto; their bodies were robust. By contrast, privileged women and girls cultivated "birdlike" appetites and slim bodies that marked them as ethereal and spiritual. Meat eating was considered an inflammatory or socially aggressive act among privileged young women; many women thought it was necessary to hide their eating from public view. Doctors reported that many adolescent girls became phobic about certain foods and about eating itself. Displays of appetite became problematic for young women who understood appetite to be both a sign of sexuality and an indication of lack of self-restraint.

We live in a social and cultural environment where food is also loaded with complex meanings. In our society, some young women fear normal food and eating because eating constitutes the first step on the way to being fat. In this obesophobic culture, rigid dieting constitutes a popular form of perfectionism and competitiveness. For example, anorectic clients report that when they enter a room at a party they immediately rank all the women in the room in terms of body weight. The anorectic experiences her greatest satisfaction if she ranks lowest; if she has not achieved the prized place in the order, she feels despair. Many anorectic clients talk about how they compete with a sister over who is thinner.

Moreover, today the act of eating may no longer induce feelings of shame because of a sexualized meaning of food. However, eating may evoke shame because of the anticipated consequence of gaining weight (Silberstein, Striegel-Moore, & Rodin, 1987). Not uncommonly, women talk about their embarrassment about eating in public, particularly in front of others whose opinions they value. "Eating lightly" is a culturally prescribed strategy to attain the thin body ideal and is clearly linked to femininity. Data from social-psychological experiments suggest that women who "eat lightly" are perceived to be more feminine than women who eat normal meals (Mori, Chaiken, & Pliner, 1987). Furthermore, women appear to adjust their eating behavior to the social context in which it occurs, presumably in the service of "impression management." For example, women ate significantly less when asked to interact with a desirable man than when they interacted with an undesirable man or another women. In contrast, the eating behavior of men was not influenced by the attractiveness of their women partners (Mori et al., 1987). Hence, modern women seem to be aware that their eating and weight serve as a primary form of communication about their femininity.

In addition, our society is characterized by an extraordinary amount of attention, particularly in the educated middle and upper classes, to the notion of "right" foods. Food cultists and food fads are coupled with a constant stream of new diet regimens aimed at promoting beauty, health, and happiness. Clinically, today we see a fair number of anorectic and bulimic women who are vegetarians (Kadambari, Gowers, & Crisp, 1986). In effect, it is easy to see how a young woman can become preoccupied with food and, in the name of purity and health, begin to restrict her food repertoire to a small number of foods or maybe even to a single item eaten only at one specific time of day.

In fact, the ritualistic intensity with which the anorectic diets suggests that the disorder has obsessive–compulsive features (Rothenberg, 1986; Solyom, Freeman, Thomas, & Miles, 1983; Strober, 1980, 1985). A central characteristic of individuals who display obsessive–compulsive symptoms is a preoccupation with control. Impulses, wishes, fears, or fantasies unacceptable to the individual are controlled by means of obsessional thoughts and compulsive behaviors. In this case, weight regulation serves as a metaphor for self-regulation and self-control as the patient confronts various sources of adolescent anxiety: a changing and maturing body, the mandate to develop interpersonal relationships, and the expectation to become autonomous.

It appears that the typical obsessive–compulsive individual, today and in the Victorian era, exhibits excessive perfectionism, stubbornness, and rigidity, along with a preoccupation with order and cleanliness (Rothenberg, 1986). In the late nineteenth century, women showed they were in control of themselves by being asexual, meticulous about cleanliness, restrained, and slim. This package implied a superior spirituality.

Today, the same characteristics also imply a superior morality and a high degree of control. (Cleanliness is less central because it is taken for granted.) Being in control implies being able to get what one wants to get. Modern concepts of control include being able to restrain one's needs in the service of long-term goals (e.g., career achievement) as well as satisfying one's needs instantly (e.g., buy now, pay later). Thus, our contemporary culture holds up an ideal for women that may be more complicated to actualize, in part because it entails contradictory components. This ambiguity may give rise to considerable anxiety, which in turn may feed the development of compulsive rituals – such as obsessive dieting – as a way of managing anxiety.

The changing symptom constellation

In the history of anorexia nervosa, food refusal represents a basic continuity: anorectics in both the Victorian and modern eras do not eat, although they articulate different reasons for their behavior. There are, however, two "new" symptoms: hyperactivity and bulimia (bingeing and purging). Our final collaborative effort assesses the sources (and consequences) of these new symptoms in light of historical evidence and clinical practice. We argue here that the new symptom constellation is a function of changed social opportunities and greater options for young women as well as of the cultural environment in which they find themselves.

Hyperactivity was not a central feature of anorexia nervosa in the Victorian era, although some published clinical case reports do describe anorectic girls who insisted upon taking long solitary walks, playing at badminton all day, or doing somersaults in bed until late at night. The Victorian physician generally regarded frenetic physical activity on the part of the anorectic patient as a form of "moral perversity" (Brumberg, 1988). Clearly, jogging, swimming, and aerobics were not culturally sanctioned for women a century ago. Doctors in that era also observed anorectic patients who were frenetic about doing charity and philanthropy work (Albutt & Rolleston, 1905).

For contemporary women, exercising is a socially sanctioned and prescribed way to control weight. Not surprisingly, more women than men report that their primary reason for exercising is to control their weight (Klesges, Mizes, & Klesges, 1987; Silberstein et al., 1988). Over the past two decades, exercise studios have sprung up throughout the United States, and women who represent the ideal of American beauty (e.g., film stars, media celebrities, and models) promote different exercise regimens that have kept them healthy, young, and trim. The current fitness movement has also brought about a redefinition of female beauty so that some muscularity is now seen as desirable. Freedman (1986) argues that this creates a double burden for women that generates even more anxiety. For most women, aspiring to be fit is a thinly veiled effort to achieve thinness. That women who exercise religiously are admired for their efforts explains our tolerance for behavioral extremes in this area and also serves as a source of satisfaction to the hyperactive anorectic.

Yet, the symptom of hyperactivity has received relatively little empirical attention despite its being a central feature of anorexia nervosa in our time. In clinical treatment, we see a pattern of excessive and compulsive running, swimming, and exercise that persistently accompanies not eating and diminishes with successful treatment (Kaye, Gwirtsman, George, Ebert, & Petersen, 1986). The more one runs and the less one eats is the prevailing moral calculus in contemporary anorexia nervosa.

Clinical experience suggests that hyperactivity serves a number of functions for the anorectic. For example, excessive exercise provides a way to regulate body weight, to manage the fear of weight gain, and to make up for real or feared transgressions in one's diet. Aside from these weight-related functions, excessive exercising may constitute a compulsive symptom that serves to contain feelings of anxiety by providing a distraction. Furthermore, hyperactivity serves as an achievement ritual to the anorectic, who seeks to compensate for her profound sense of ineffectiveness by aspiring to perfection (Druss & Silverman, 1979). Compulsive exercising also provides a way of punishing oneself and punishing the body that has become the focus of the anorectic's discontent with herself. These examples show a variety of ways (that are not mutually exclusive) in which the role of hyperactivity can be understood in an individual case. Regardless of the particular reason, the contemporary anorectic's frantic physical activity occurs in a climate of acceptance, admiration, and even envy.

The issue of bulimia in anorexia nervosa is more difficult to explain. Since the 1980s, an increasing number of patients appear to "mix" bulimia with anorexia nervosa. This condition may be referred to as *bulimia nervosa* or *bulimarexia* (American Psychiatric Association, 1987; Boskind-White & White, 1983; Russell, 1979). In the historical material that Brumberg examined, there was no evidence of bulimia in anorexia nervosa. Victorian doctors did identify and write about "hysterical vomiting," but that was a different phenomenon altogether and did not involve the same patient group. It could be that bulimia was a hidden or covert activity, kept secret from parents and physicians. Yet, we hypothesize that covert bulimia was unlikely on the basis of what we know about Victorian girls, their families, and their homes.

First, the degree of privacy needed to support covert bingeing and purging was not generally available to young women in the Victorian era. If there were an indoor toilet with plumbing facilities, it would be shared with parents, siblings, and guests so that chronic regurgitation and its telltale signs and smells would be hard to hide on a regular basis. To eliminate all traces of regurgitation, a flush toilet of some kind is required, but in the late nineteenth century many homes still used chamber pots where the "evidence" collected.

Second, eating in the nineteenth-century middle class was a highly visible and interactive activity, arranged for certain times of the day, and organized around a fixed center of sociability: the family dinner table. The kitchen (in contrast to the dining room) was the territory of domestic servants, and leftovers from the family were for servants to eat. It is difficult to conceive how the Victorian girl could have acted autonomously enough to secure large amounts of food on her own and, then, have had the time to eat it undetected. Where did she binge? (At the family table? At teatime while visiting an aunt or neighbor?) Where did she secure large amounts of easily digestible foods? (Did she raid the larder when everyone was in bed? Was she able to purchase food items for herself whenever she wanted?) On historical grounds, we argue that these opportunities were simply not available to Victorian young women and that bulimia nervosa was probably not part of the symptom repertoire of the earlier age.

Bulimia in anorexia nervosa seems to be a recent development suited to the pace and psychology of our contemporary society. To a large extent, the characteristic bingeing and purging of the modern bulimic depends on personal freedom, a desocialized eating environment, lack of supervision, and the availability – at almost any time – of food for purchase. Personal reports from bulimic women include regular mention of picking up "fast" or prepared foods in supermarkets or convenience stores and eating alone in cars or other solitary settings. Brumberg (1988) suggests the ways in which the contemporary epidemic of eating disorders may be related to (1) the availability of food in our society; (2) desocialized eating, particularly on college campuses where rates of anorexia and bulimia are quite high; and (3) "learning" the behavior from others who know how to do it (Striegel-Moore, Silberstein, & Rodin, 1986).

The emergence of bulimia as a symptom may also be related to two other important but essentially contradictory aspects of our culture: the extraordinary emphasis on dieting (a form of denial) and the equally powerful push for instant gratification. Many current psychological theories of bulimia nervosa propose that the increasingly thin beauty ideal plays a major role in promoting bingeing and purging. The data on the effects of starvation on mood and behavior make a compelling argument for a link between dieting and binge eating (Polivy & Herman, 1985). In other words, the emphasis on the former makes the latter possible. Astute clinicians increasingly discern that chronic denial around food sets the stage for bulimic behaviors.

Despite this pervasive American preoccupation with dieting, our society also promotes instant gratification and the notion that "you can have it all." Traditionally, Americans admired persons who attained success through hard work. Today we admire and envy those who are happy and successful without observable effort. We are told to "work smarter, not harder" (Machlowitz, 1980). At the same time, the ability to indulge oneself – in exotic foods, an elegant perfume, a massage, or a sensual vacation – is now regarded as a sign of mental health, whereas once these same self-indulgences generated moral indignation if not vilification.

The bulimic symptomatology mirrors these contemporary cultural characteristics. Bingeing behavior – almost always involving easily digestible foods high in carbohydrates, sugar, and fat – is based on instantaneous gratification. There are no appetizers to tease the palate and no delays between courses. A lot of food (as much as 10,000 calories at one sitting) is consumed as quickly as possible (Abraham & Beaumont, 1982; Fairburn, Cooper, & Cooper, 1986). In the act of regurgitating this food, the bulimic finds a temporarily efficacious compromise: a way to offset the caloric implications of indulgence without the hard work of chronic dieting. In effect, she has found a way, albeit a dangerous one, to beat the metabolic system.

The two "new" symptoms we describe seem to have real physical conse-quences for anorectic patients and for treatment. Anorexia nervosa is a more dangerous disease than ever before because of the extraordinarily low weights of its victims. An index of body mass in anorexia nervosa hospital admissions since the 1930s shows a marked decline over time, suggesting that more patients with severe weight loss are being admitted today than were admitted 50 years ago. In short, today's anorectic is thinner than ever before (Agras & Kraemer, 1983). The severity of anorexia nervosa today could be the result of delays in treatment or more extended outpatient therapy before hospitalization, but this scenario is unconvincing given our current sensitivity to the disease. We suggest that the severity of current cases probably reflects the patients' zealous commitment to both exercise and diet as well as peer, parental, and/or medical tolerance for thinner bodies. And, quite importantly, bulimia in anorexia nervosa complicates the therapeutic picture: clinical data suggest a worsening of symptomatology once a young woman begins to engage in regular vomiting as a way of undoing the caloric effects of her binges (Garfinkel & Garner, 1982).

Conclusion

The modern symptom constellation in anorexia nervosa – chronic re-fusal of food, hyperactivity, and bulimia – did not (and could not) exist a century ago. Although individual and family variables contribute to the psychogenesis of anorexia nervosa, our present cultural infatuation with extremely thin women, our preoccupation with exercise, and our desocialized style of eating have all contributed to an acceleration in the number of women who are at risk for anorexia nervosa (and bulimia nervosa). Our joint investigation suggests, how-ever, that more than incidence is at stake here. In fact, the past two decades have witnessed the expansion of the symptom repertoire in a manner altogether in keeping with the spirit and direction of contemporary culture.

For the purposes of our collaboration, we had to put aside the individual psyche and focus instead on patterns of symptoms and family life. We have not done "psychohistory" as it is usually practiced because we offer no analysis of the psychogenic origins of anorexia nervosa in any particular person. Yet, it is our contention that the collaboration of psychology and history can be quite fruitful, particularly in understanding psychopathologies that are clearly linked to particular stages of development and/or socially constructed sex and gender roles.

Ultimately, history serves psychology as an important vehicle for understand-ing the pattern and variability of psychiatric symptoms, and psychology serves history as a suggestive model for interpreting human behavior. Both disciplines gain from a fuller understanding of this fact: today, as in the past, psycho-pathologies exist in reciprocal relationship to the culture in which they occur. It is our hope that clinicians can incorporate this insight as they work to understand how individual patients construct their reality and that social psychologists will begin to take seriously the issue of social contagion, particularly as it affects adolescent women.

7   Fathers and child rearing

Ross D. Parke and Peter N. Stearns

> There is still the widespread belief that a man does not belong at home
> taking care of children.
>
> James A. Levine (1976, p. 153)

Fatherhood, long a neglected subject in scholarly and popular discussions of child rearing, has been treated to a substantial reevaluation during the past 15 years. The contributions of fathers to child development now seem more important and more varied than was assumed in the long heyday of maternalism. This reassessment has coincided with unquestionable new needs for changes in parental balance, given women's characteristic work commitments, and with some measurable shifts in parental procedures such as paternal presence at childbirth.

These varied developments have won an approving chorus from many family experts that may at points verge on the uncritical. They also carry interesting historical implications, as the undeniable reevaluations by experts may be extended to a larger scenario in which a century or more of paternal eclipse yields to revolutionary new patterns of fathering by the 1960s or 1970s. Assumptions about widespread change have not yet been subjected to extensive historical scrutiny, yet each scrutiny is essential to place the recent findings about fatherhood's potential into clearer perspective. The need for establishing historical trend and for situating current beliefs is to discover not only what fathers can or should do (or could or should have done) but what actually goes on and how current practice flows from past precedent.

Most current judgments about the state of fathering – and they continue to be diverse – involve at least implicit assumptions about the past. Some reformers, blasting heavy-handed authoritarians, condemn what they see as a hoary paternal tradition. Optimists, heralding the new-style father, assume his contrast with the peripheral figure of a generation or two earlier. These and other uses of the past are interesting, but many are simplistic and some wrong outright. Whatever their degree of accuracy, however, they rightly suggest the inescapability of history at least as a baseline by which current fathers can be measured.

147

This essay, examining the state of relevant research and then turning to the central, and surprisingly complex, themes of the modern history of American fatherhood, delineates the historical baseline but goes a step beyond. It suggests that historical trends be seen as an ongoing framework, subject to change but seldom abrupt reversal, within which fathers and children alike continue to operate.

The state of historical inquiry

The need for an integrated approach to fatherhood and its role in child development that includes a focused historical perspective has not thus far been matched by scholarly output. Some important findings are available, however, and it is also possible to sketch some of the more obvious opportunities for research in terms of available knowledge of recent family history.

On the strictly historical side, although family and childhood research has blossomed in recent years, researchers have paid insufficient attention to fathers and their activities and particularly to what actual fathers did with young children. A promising literature exists for the premodern period, including some rich debates on distinctions between Western Europe and colonial America (where father–son relations may for a time have been softened by abundant available property) (Greven, 1970) and on the nature and severity of patriarchy (Hunt, 1970; Ozment, 1983; Pollock, 1983). Erik Erikson's classic psychological study of Luther (1958) includes data and assumptions about prevailing father–son relations, though some historians would now insist that traditional patriarchal styles were milder, more infused with affection, than Erikson allowed.

For the period since 1800, however, serious historical work has been missing, partly because so much of the commentary or advice on parental behavior shifted to focus exclusively on mothers (Gordon, 1983). Some nineteenth-century auto-biographical evidence has been mined to reveal substantial father–son tensions, but wider patterns – including the possibility that childrens' input could condition fathers' choices about the extent of domestic involvement – have not been pursued; nor has there been a twentieth-century follow-up.

On another front, there has been some debate over what husbands (as fathers or potential fathers) might have contributed to decisions to limit the birthrate, from the nineteenth century onward, with one line of argument holding that men, as primary breadwinners, might first have realized children's shift from asset to cost and so taken the lead in arguing for smaller family size (Banks & Banks, 1964). Recently, however, most historians interested in this subject have assumed that women, whose bodies were involved in childbearing and who were in fact the daily budget keepers, probably took the initiative, as witness the fact that the most effective birth control devices were female controlled, though there is considerable evidence that decisions in this area were often mutual (Branca, 1975; Gordon, 1983). A related though implicit argument has developed over paternal and maternal roles in motivating middle-class baby boom family size. The Easterlin hypothesis on family size in the baby boom argues implicitly that fathers' economic outlook set the framework for decisions to have more children. But Modell and others, dealing with data, lean toward arguing that mothers' expectations and child-centeredness played the greater role (Easterlin, 1980; Modell & Campbell, 1984). These discussions are relevant in determining fathers' interest in children in past time, but they may or may not be germane to an inquiry into what fathers did with children once born.

Demographic changes that did occur have obvious bearing on fatherhood, but no effort has yet been undertaken to find out what this bearing was. Here is a clear research challenge, given recent cycles of baby boom and bust and the attention lavished on their relationship to women's roles and maternal expectations. For example, lower birthrates may increase father–daughter interaction, as more men have only girls to guide; this could correlate, at least in the middle class, with changes in women's career choices toward more male-model directions (e.g., turn of the century and post-1960). Some recent biographical work suggestively points to the importance of paternal guidance or at least the paternal model in spurring high-achieving professional women precisely in these time periods. More generally, declining maternal mortality from the 1880s reduced the likelihood of widowers raising children, which might well have further limited attention to paternal roles and the principles of fatherly guidance.

A more recent shift occurred during the baby boom decades, as men became fathers at an earlier age than they had before (particularly in the middle classes). Young fathers, often without much experience with young children because of the previous low birthrate and resultant limitations on sibling interactions, additionally faced increasingly late ages of career entry. They often had their first children before they were fully entered on a career and thus encountered key parental responsibilities while also trying to master basic job demands. It is easy to imagine severe distractions from active parenting in this context. On the other hand, children might have served as a relatively manageable and pleasant compensation during late-student and early job years, thus enhancing father–child interaction and the father's sense of reward.

From the early 1960s onward, again particularly in the middle class, fatherhood occurred later in life, with fewer children born, and with greater equality in age and economic role between father and mother. Age of career entry continued to go up a bit but not nearly so radically as did age of first fatherhood. Some men may thus have gained a certain sense of rhythm, even of initial mastery, in their job sphere before children entered the picture. This might have facilitated paternal attention and care (a possible result also of the fewer children being born per family), though it might also have made the presence of children less relevant and more disruptive (and we will offer some evidence in this direction later). Again, we know a good bit about key shifts in the structure of fatherhood, as in the demographic area, but we have yet fully to penetrate their significance either for fathers themselves or for father–child interactions (Demos, 1982; Modell, 1989; Vinovskis, 1986).

Inquiry into fatherhood as a changing phenomenon is also hampered by commentary bias toward white, middle-class norms and behaviors; this is true in both historical and contemporary materials. Some modern constraints on fatherhood undoubtedly cut across class and ethnic lines, but subcultural diversity and its impact remain vital topics for focused research.

Granting the inadequacy of available data and treatments of fatherhood that offer serious, empirical analysis over time, certain patterns can be discerned, though they apply particularly if not always exclusively to middle-class families. These patterns, and the changes they suggest, lead to two related conclusions that will organize the remaining discussion as we turn from gaps in historical knowledge to the thrust of recent historical change. First, it is vital to separate conventional image and reality at most points in the evolution of modern fatherhood – fathering over the past century was not as "bad," nor has contemporary fathering become as "good," as much public and expert imagery suggests.

Second, it is essential to recognize a durable tension in fathers' role and expectations. This tension seems to be built into modern fatherhood, informing both the "bad old days" and the enlightened present. To be sure, the most obvious line of historical inquiry, at least until the 1960s, emphasized negative features – the various new deterrents to active paternal involvement. But another, less familiar strand worked actively in the opposite direction. This ambiguity showed not only in differences among fathers but also in conflicting impulses within individual fathers, and, though modified, it has persisted into contemporary paternal styles. Here is a key link between present and past. Actual paternal roles, and divisions among types of fathers, have played out in a complex interaction between new barriers to paternal activity in child development and promptings toward a redefined but engaged fatherhood (Parke & Tinsley, 1981).

Modern constraints on fatherhood

We certainly know that a number of developments over the past century or more have had negative implications for an active paternal role in child rearing. It is worthwhile to consider this fairly long time frame not, as we will argue, because it set irreversible trends that run neatly into the contemporary era, but because it does establish part of the context within which contemporary fatherhood still operates.

Most obvious in setting new constraints on fatherhood was the separation of work from home brought by the industrial revolution. By the late nineteenth century most urban fathers of whatever social class worked at some distance from the household. The trend had begun earlier, particularly for factory workers, but it became a general urban pattern by the 1890s. The ramifications did not uniformly separate fathers from older children, particularly sons. Working-class fathers often carefully arranged to have their sons join them in the factories, an arrangement normally congenial to employers as well in insuring a more stable labor force. Interestingly, the practice of sending teenagers away from the family to work, a staple of preindustrial life, dropped off. But the contacts of fathers with their older daughters and with their younger children of both sexes undoubtedly diminished. The rise of schooling and later ages of entry to work extended this separation, first for the middle class.

Even the time fathers had at home could be affected by new work arrangements. Many reports, some from fathers themselves, cite the difficulty of dealing with children after a tense day at work, along with a tendency to be harsher with little children than the men desired because of work-induced strain and fatigue (Stearns, 1975). Although this theme has been most often cited in dealing with the working class, it surfaces in middle-class accounts as well, as in homes in which young children were carefully enjoined (by their mothers) to be quiet and respectful when their fathers came home, because the latter were simply not up to the noise and pranks the mothers cheerfully indulged when they had the house to themselves (Spencer, 1983).

From the late nineteenth century onward, men themselves reported discomfort and ineptitude in dealing with young children. One sign of this feeling, of course, was the novel establishment of maternal custody when families split up and particularly the "tender years" doctrine, which assumed, with apparently widespread paternal agreement, that as a matter of natural course mothers knew best for children under age 12. Another sign was the virtual monopoly that women established outside of the home in young-child care (a monopoly that also had the merit of being cheaper than employment of men would have been). The one exception, based on the primacy of science over "normal" gender lines, rested in the growing use of male pediatricians.

The impact of less active fatherhood

Several corollaries have been developed within the general framework of declining paternal involvement with young children. First, it is obvious that paternal abandonment of children became easier from the nineteenth century onward. It was by no means an entirely new phenomenon. The decline of community controls, the decline of the family (and of children's work) as normal prerequisites for economic life, and, quite possibly, the growing distance – even discomfort – that some men felt in dealing with children, plus the need for geographic mobility in seeking jobs, all made paternal delinquency a growing problem, one that, though dressed up in new guises, has continued into our own day (Furstenberg, 1988). Some historians have tried to draw consequences from the rise of absent fathers, as in noting a correlation between this phenomenon and daughters who grew up to be feminists in the late nineteenth and early twentieth centuries (McGovern, 1969–70).

More widely still, it seems probable that relatively inactive fathers ironically encouraged strong male–female differentiations in children. The basic contention here, again focusing on the late nineteenth century onward into our own time, is that relatively distant fathering promoted assertively masculine standards for boys (Filene, 1986; Parke, 1981; Pleck & Pleck, 1980).

This argument has three interrelated prongs. First, adult men themselves encouraged aggressive masculinity because of a widely publicized fear that boys were otherwise being smothered by women, by female schoolteachers as well as by mothers. Certainly this concern was voiced by the early twentieth century. Thus, fathers (as studied in the 1920s and 1930s) were much more tolerant of aggressive behavior by boys, and were much more concerned about passivity, than were mothers or teachers (Stearns & Stearns, 1986). Second, women themselves, though not in full accord with fathers, also reflected their growing responsibility for the care of young boys by emphasizing gender differences, lest they be guilty of coddling.

Third, boys themselves, aware of their masculinity but often deprived of daily male role models with whom they could interact in detail, defined their necessary separation from their mothers by stressing what they saw as masculine traits, as in enthusiasms for sports, intolerance of boys who were "different," and so on. Girls, in contrast, cleaved more readily to their mothers, all the more in that paternal traits seemed so remote. Encouraged by part-time fathers who touted masculinity, a tough, unemotional standard developed for many boys, a standard that in recent years has been lamented, along with deep condemnations of the fathers' style, by many male liberationists (Pleck & Sawyer, 1974).

A third corollary of the basic "industrial" framework for fathering involved the guidance available for fathers themselves. From the 1840s onward the preponderance of expert literature written for parents was directed almost exclusively toward mothers; in the nineteenth century much of this literature was explicitly titled "for mothers." It was assumed that mothers had almost exclusive daily responsibility and, in accord with gender imagery that arose in the nineteenth century and endured well into the twentieth, that mothers also had necessary virtues that men largely lacked in dealing with and moralizing children. Women could provide nurturance and comfort along with exacting physical care;

they could restrain their tempers and other noxious impulses; they were the true standard-bearers of civilized behavior.

Although some paternal advice was not explicitly gender specific, there was a dearth of comment on anything that fathers as fathers could usefully do aside from bringing home the bacon (Wishy, 1967). Some manuals did note, though often vaguely, an important role for fathers in providing a character model for boys and the kind of support for girls that would permit them to deal successfully with men in adult life. Beyond this, jobs for fathers, if sketched at all, were clearly secondary and often intermittent. Standard twentieth-century treatments of sibling rivalry, for example, urged that fathers jump in when a new baby was born, to help provide compensatory attention to the older child. This was a temporary assignment, however, and most child-rearing manuals left primary responsibility for the compensation to mothers.

A vast outpouring of expert advice thus largely shunned the father, building on but also perhaps exacerbating the barriers to daily father–child interaction. Dr. Spock's first edition (1946) devoted a mere nine pages to the father's role, specifically noting that fathers should play but an occasional role in child care and mainly to give mothers a periodic rest. Most specific advice sections explicitly addressed mothers alone.

The pessimistic historical perspective on the trajectory of modern fathering bears obviously on our judgments about current patterns. First, it reminds us that many of the now-touted trends of involved fathering are not only probably new but also for this reason potentially fragile, as they work against some powerful inhibitors from the past century or more. The division of work and home, which continues to allow many men to assume that primary responsibility for young children lies elsewhere, is an obvious case in point (and we will discuss recent studies that confirm its persistent impact); but so is the modern tradition of expert advice that looks almost exclusively to mothers for child rearing. Although increased divorce rates create a superficially new setting for some paternal neglect, they in fact build on earlier patterns of transience and abandonment.

In another connection between tensions generated by industrialization and contemporary concerns, one historian has argued, plausibly though not definitively, that child abuse itself (not exclusively of course a paternal practice) is a modern phenomenon in the United States, building from the nineteenth century onward, as urban, industrial conditions pushed parents, and particularly fathers, to take out on their families a violence they did not manage to express fully elsewhere (Demos, 1986). Certainly not only neglectful and uninvolved fathers but also pushily masculine fathers remain part of the contemporary child-rearing scene, and they are the products of some important and persistent features of modern society as established over the past century or more.

It is also obvious and understandable that many modern trends make it difficult for many women – even some who profess to want assistance in parenting – seriously to envisage a male role, or at least a male role that goes beyond supporting bit player. Even with all the changes and new diversities in women's lives during the past several decades, the temptation to argue for a special maternal province remains an ongoing inhibition to more active fathering.

The negative appraisal of the modern history of fatherhood may come as a scant surprise, particularly in the child development field where by the early twentieth century authorities were calling attention to the need to compensate for absent fathers. Insistence on the durability of some of the modern constraints on fatherhood may jar a bit in an area where some have rather facilely assumed a parenting revolution in recent decades, but the idea of a difficult modern past is in itself compatible with many current perspectives. For this very reason, however, it is important to insist that the negative appraisal must be balanced by an understanding of some real complexities in the trajectory of modern fathering, even if we assume further change since the 1960s.

Some important modern trends worked against the grain of the home–job separation and other deterrents in encouraging new paternal engagement and new styles of father–child interaction. The familiar impacts of the Great Depression and World War II on families and children, economically but also emotionally, as a result of absent or thwarted fathers remind us that industrial-style fatherhood still counted (Elder, 1974; Elder, Caspi, & Van Nguyen, 1986; Stolz et al., 1954).

The standards of good fathering

One key to understanding the complexity of modern fatherhood lies in the meaningful adaptability of paternal standards. The trends working against active fathering, in terms of daily, nurturing involvement, did not prevent many fathers from asserting *and fulfilling* extensive paternal commitment.

There was an increase in "bad" fathering in the nineteenth century, in contemporary terms as well as in today's, as in the case of outright abandonment and possibly abuse, but most fathers had no reason for harsh self-judgment. The concept of "bad" fathering indeed helped many fathers feel rather confident about their own adequacy. Publicly articulated goals of good fathering changed to fit and guide the situation, as a colonial belief in fathers as moral mentors gave way to a primary nineteenth-century emphasis on the provider function. This belief in turn was modified by a new concern for serving as role models for boys, characteristic of the turn-of-the-century decades, which has more recently yielded to the nurturance model by which we tend to judge good fathering today.

Despite the absence of detailed advice on how to behave in intimate interactions with children, then, between the colonial moral guidance and the contemporary nurturing norms, middle-class culture did generate a real sense of the functions at which good fathers could succeed and that would allow men to maintain that their roles as fathers formed a cornerstone of their lives (Lamb, 1986). And the progressive adaptation of standards, in turn, helped generate a second underlying framework for modern fathering, one that worked against the distancing tendencies of work and maternal monopoly by urging that fathers develop new styles and purposes in dealing with children to establish more positive relationships than traditional patriarchy had presumably allowed.

Historical impulses toward more active fatherhood

The most important point to emphasize here is the development, by the eighteenth century in Western society, of a redefinition of the family in more emotional and democratic terms, as against older style patriarchalism and male reliance on community rather than primarily familial contacts. One of the key findings of family historians has been a widespread tendency to emphasize the importance of family, and close emotional bonds among family members, from the seventeenth century onward, at least in propertied classes (Shorter, 1975; L. Stone, 1977; Trumbach, 1978). Men, particularly, were urged to develop a new closeness with their wives and children and to abandon harsh, hierarchical discipline. They even, in some cases in the eighteenth century, attended at childbirth.

A number of causes account for new paternal relations with children. An increasingly commercial economy reduced community closeness, prompting men to look to family for emotional support. New religious and political ideologies urged some familial as well as political democracy. Emotional control received new emphasis, as fathers were urged to curb anger in dealing with children, and corporal punishment began – though slowly –to recede under the impact of new standards of discipline.

The trend of growing family closeness, including the novel degree of emphasis on its emotional importance for men, has played itself out in modern American history as a significant counterpoint to the distancing impact of industrialization. This trend generated a tendency in methods of discipline to shift away from physical chastisement and, by the nineteenth century, to emphasize the importance of initiative and individuality, and not just docility, in the goals fathers sought for their children. The same trend contributed to the sometimes sentimental valuations that men in the late nineteenth and early twentieth centuries claimed to place on family members and in the rewards of dealing with children and providing for them. It promoted men's willingness to increase their economic outlays for individual children, as part of an inflatable "provider" function, toward spurring new opportunities for education or mobility (Zelizer, 1985). In some cases, to be sure, once the industrial context was installed, the values that men placed on family might become somewhat abstract – believed in theory even as, in practice, the effective care of children was turned over to wives and mothers. But often the reassessment of family encouraged a more substantial commitment in terms of resources and emotional engagement, even when the time spent with children perforce declined.

The modern history of fathering must be seen, then, in terms of a dialogue between very real deterrents to active involvement and important new emotional and cultural promptings toward a more positive redefinition of paternal role, promptings that urged an attack on purely patriarchal control efforts and some kind of new, emotional engagement with one's offspring. This dialogue shows in a number of features of fathering history visible in the later nineteenth and twentieth centuries.

First, though this is unsurprising on reflection, paternal roles and outlooks have varied greatly in modern history. Despite the barriers to regular attention and the undeniable examples of abusive, withdrawn, or absent fathers, many modern fathers have been actively involved with their children, including young children, playing a central role in their lives (T. Thompson 1981).

Examples of involved fathers – including cases of primary care for young children – come from all social groups. Nor, as against some editorial exaggeration from contemporary liberation movements, did fathers earlier in the twentieth century hold up a uniform standard of masculinity. An important turn-of-the-century history stresses the complexity of the standards fathers hold up to their sons, for example, in sexuality or the management of aggression, as against any macho mindlessness or simple reliance on mothers for gentler influences (Filene, 1986). Although systematic inquiry remains to be done, it is clear that fathers were more diverse and, on balance, probably more active, beyond a mere provider or role model function, than expert child-rearing literature allowed for. A growing body of work on child guidance issues in the first half of the twentieth century, while it reveals many abusive fathers and many fathers who left initiatives on behalf of problem children strictly up to mothers, also sketches many cases in which fathers took strong roles in dealing with troubled children (Horn, 1984).

Another aspect of the proinvolvement side of modern fathering trends (this one, too, worth more attention than it has received prior to the most recent decades) was the inclination of many men, by the late nineteenth and early twentieth centuries, to devote a considerable portion of their growing leisure time to explicitly family activities, despite the fabled attractions of bars and other nonpaternal diversions. Men defended the idea of greater leisure time in family terms quite often, and they meant at least a good bit of what they said.

Thus, shared leisure with children, used among other things to instill certain skills and values, became an important part of modern paternal life, from weekend romps to the birth of the more formal practice of a family vacation, an explicitly modern invention. Playing with children was not, of course, new for fathers, but playing as a means of serious contact and even explicit training unquestionably increased over the past century, thereby allowing fathers some balance between their active family goals and work commitments.

The playful style

There have been important signs since the 1940s of efforts by fathers to adjust their styles of interaction with children still more and, as part of this, to develop new kinds of contacts with their young children. Obviously, not all fathers have been involved in this effort, and there have been all sorts of complications, including family disruption at a rising rate. Attempts by fathers to develop a friendlier style with their children, deliberately to depart (at least in their own view) from the styles of their own fathers, and sometimes to reallocate disciplinary roles with mothers, deserve serious attention. In some cases, the modifications after 1940 seem to relate to shifts in the kind of personality that fathers hope to develop in their children, away from heavy emphasis on competitive achievement and toward more cooperative social modes. Various observers have noted (and some have lamented) a tendency of fathers to reduce certain traditional tensions with older children (Lasch, 1977), but a new interest in young children is often involved as well. This recent historical change blends into the new roles for fathers urged, since the 1970s, by experts, feminists, male liberationists, and others, but it seems to antedate it and, therefore, to require a somewhat separate causal explanation, in terms of fathers' own desire to redefine their family role, more home-based leisure time, and some changes in child-rearing goals.

The variety of actual fathering roles in precontemporary American history, the powerful movement to emphasize men's family involvement and to define it in emotional terms, and the more recent but not brand-new shift in some fathers' styles feed into some of the expert reassessments of fathers' actual and potential impact on child development today, just as the more negative aspects of the modern historical framework help explain some of the ongoing limitations that have been discovered. The point is, as against some of the simpler uses of history in this area, that the modern history of fathering is complex, not unidirectional, and that this complexity helps explain some of the cross-currents revealed in current research on paternal impacts.

We must not, as a result, expect to deal with contemporary fathering patterns and possibilities in terms of some stark contrast with a dreadful past – both because the past was not so uniformly dreadful and because some of the negative modern factors surely persist. Indeed, the possibility exists, given the reality of modern fathering history, that some previous modern strengths could be lost amid more strictly contemporary factors.

The contemporary scene

We turn now to quite recent developments, mainly over the past two decades. This allows some application of recent empirical evidence to the historical trends, though because the empirical base is largely of relatively recent origins the extrapolations backward to earlier historical eras are rather speculative. More directly, recent developments allow a statement of some significant changes in paternal patterns and their impact. The most obvious change involves a major reversal of expert theory about paternal roles, but there is also solid evidence of new activity by actual American fathers as well.

Theoretical shifts in our views of early development

One of the major historical tenets that has justified and sanctioned limited father involvement is the concept of natural maternal superiority in the child-care and child-rearing realms. This argument has assumed various forms ranging from invocation of a maternal instinct to a concept of biological preparedness on the part of women. This biological determinism argument gained further support from the dominance of Freudian theory from the early 1900s to the 1960s. According to this doctrine, the feeding situation was the critical context for adequate social and emotional development. Because mothers were the primary feeding agents, their primacy in shaping the development of the infant was further reinforced. However, support for the concept of the biological superiority of women as care givers and the theoretical legacy of Freud have both waned in recent years, in favor of more complex ideas about child–parent attachment.

Two recent shifts have contributed to the decrease in feasibility of the older views. At the theoretical level, there has been a serious questioning of the value of the Freudian position for understanding the development of early paternal behavior. Specifically, there has been little empirical support for the view that infants' social relationships with their parents develop as a result of being associated with the feeding context. The classic studies of Harlow (1958) with monkeys, in which he demonstrated that the degree of attachment to the surrogate mother was independent of whether or not the mother was associated with feeding, were an early contributor to the downfall of this doctrine. The early work of Schaffer and Emerson (1964) revealed that human infants' attachment to their care givers was independent of the degree of care giving.

Instead, research over the past two decades has clearly indicated that the quality of parent–infant interaction, especially the degree of parental responsiveness, is a more central ingredient for promoting attachment between children and their care givers. This shift then provided new meaning to the potential role that the father might play in early development. Although the father's role as feeding agent is less than the mother's, the kinds of stimulatory interactions that characterize father–infant as well as mother–infant interchanges are sufficient to promote infant–father attachment. In fact, over the past decade a number of studies have demonstrated that fathers as well as mothers are the objects of infant social attachments (Lamb, 1977, 1981). The studies provide strong support for alternative, non-Freudian-based views and permit the recognition of the father as a vital social contributor even in his child's infancy.

The other strand of evidence derives from studies of father–infant interaction. Observations of father–infant interaction with newborn infants suggest that fathers are just as competent as mothers to care for newborn infants. Indexes of competence include the ability to feed infants – as measured by the amount of milk consumed – as well as paternal sensitivity to changes in infant behavior or to cues in the feeding context. Success in care giving, to a large extent, depends on the caretaker's ability to correctly "read" or interpret the infant's behavior so that his or her own behavior can be modified to respond appropriately. Research suggests that fathers and mothers are equally competent as measured in these ways (Parke & Sawin, 1975, 1976, 1980) and so are equally capable of performing early care-giving roles. Other evidence suggests a similar pattern with older infants. For example, Lamb and his colleagues (Lamb, Frodi, Hwang, & Frodi, 1982a) have found that mothers and fathers are equally responsive to the smiles and cries of infants. This evidence provides little support for the doctrine of biological superiority of women.

Other evidence presents a more direct challenge to this biological doctrine. Although there is evidence in support of the role of maternal hormones in the maintenance of maternal behavior in rats (Fleming & Orpen, 1986; Rosenblatt & Siegel, 1981), there is no evidence of a clear link between maternal behavior and hormones in human mothers. Fleming and Orpen found no relationship between levels of estradiol and progesterone and measures of maternal behavior during pregnancy or in the first 10 days postpartum. Moreover, even in rats, Rosenblatt (1969) has shown that males as well as females that have been surgically altered so that hormones were inactive were capable of exhibiting parenting behavior as a result of exposure to rat pups. Clearly in rats as well as for humans, the tyranny of hormonal control has been overestimated. Together these findings seriously question the historical limitations on the fathering role on the basis of biological superiority of mothers for parenting.

Evidence of change in level of father involvement

In spite of a great deal of variability in the extent to which different segments of the population of fathers has changed, there are clear indications of overall shifts in the amount of father involvement over the last half century. In a unique follow-up of the Middletown study conducted originally in the 1920s, Caplow and Chadwick (1979) reported that in 1976 only 2% of fathers spend no time with their children in contrast to 10% of fathers in 1924 – at least according to mothers' reports. Similar results were obtained by Daniels and Weingarten (1983), who interviewed parents who began their parenting careers in the 1950s, 1960s, or 1970s. These investigators noted that fathers were twice as likely to be involved on a daily basis if their children were born in the 1970s than in the preceding two decades. Similarly, Vanek (1981) found an increase from 1967 to 1977 in the amount of time fathers spend with infants and toddlers but no increase for fathers of older children. Perhaps there are cohort and/or period effects in operation that account for younger fathers with younger offspring being more responsive to recent trends (Parke & Tinsley, 1984).

Further evidence of modest shifts in father involvement comes from a recent study in Great Britain. Lewis (1986) interviewed first- and second-time fathers in 1980 when their infants were 1 year of age and compared their level of involvement with a matched sample of fathers in 1960. Several changes were found. First, there was a sharp increase in the percentage of fathers who attended and were present during labor and delivery. In 1960, when nearly 60% were home births, fathers attended only 13% of all deliveries. In 1980, only 2% of all births still took place at home, yet 84% of fathers attended their wives' labor, and 67% stayed through delivery. "Father attendance, like delivery itself has become institutionalized" (p. 61).

Half of the fathers in families with one or two children in 1960 never got up at night to attend to the baby, whereas by 1980, 87% of a comparable sample participated in this way. Moreover, in 1960 only 30% became involved at home in the period following delivery, whereas 77% did so in 1980. Other indicators suggest, however, that the real shifts may be less marked. There was little alteration between 1960 and 1980 in the extent to which fathers participated in routine care giving (e.g., bathing or diaper changes), but there was a significant increase in the proportion of men who put their child to bed regularly (35% in 1960 vs. 48% in 1980). Even in the cases of the increases in father participation over time, mothers still played a more active role than fathers. There is clearly a gradual shift toward greater father involvement, but the sexes are far from equal in their contribution to child care. Whether the trend will move toward fuller equality may depend on whether the paternal role ceases to be so differentiated from its maternal counterpart and on whether men come to be seen as equally "natural" in child nurturance, as the research cited earlier suggests could be the case.

scientism naturalism

The distinctive roles of mothers and fathers

In spite of the modest changes there remain clear differences in styles of interaction of mothers and fathers. Recent evidence has confirmed that mothers and fathers still play distinctive roles in the family. Moreover, this evidence places on a firmer foundation our assumptions about shifts in the paternal role from disciplinarian and teacher to a more relaxed and potentially more nurturant and friendlier style of interaction. A number of studies over the past decade have provided a clear portrait of the father as playmate.

Both mothers and fathers are active playmates for their infants and children. However, fathers devote a higher proportion of their time with children to play than do mothers, and this provides an important paternal role though a rather specialized one. For example, in one study of middle-socioeconomic-status (SES) families, Kotelchuck (1976) found that fathers devote nearly 40% of their time with their infants to play, whereas mothers spend about 25% of their time in play. Further evidence comes from Lamb (1977), who observed interactions among mother, father, and infant in their home when the child was 7 to 8 months and again at 12 to 13 months. Lamb found marked differences in the reasons that fathers and mothers pick up their infants: fathers were more likely to hold the babies to play with them, whereas mothers were more likely to hold them for caretaking purposes.

Fathers and mothers differ not only in quantity of play but in the style of play as well. Fathers' play is more likely to be physical and arousing, whereas mothers' play is more verbal, didactic, and toy mediated (see Parke, 1979; Parke & Tinsley, 1981, 1987; Power & Parke, 1982). Mothers and fathers provide distinctly different types of stimulation and learning opportunities (Power & Parke, 1982).

More recent evidence suggests that father play may be an important opportunity for children to learn how to regulate their emotions in social interaction with others, such as their peers. Specifically, children may learn to recognize other people's emotional signals and learn to use their own emotional cues in social situations, in part, in the course of father–child play (Parke, MacDonald, Beitel, & Bhavnagri, 1987). In short, the fathers' role as a play partner may be an important source of children's learning about the social environment. Unfortunately, little is known about the extent to which the father operated as a play partner in earlier eras. If evidence can be found to substantiate this role in earlier eras, it would support the need to rethink our current assumption that the father as an emotional and social partner with his children is a contemporary innovation.

Equally interesting is the picture that emerges of the maternal role in play. In contrast to the earlier historical portrait of father as a teacher, it is mother who emerges as playing a didactic role in the context of play. Other evidence supports this role difference between parents. Neville and Parke (1987) surveyed approximately 300 families of children from infancy to adolescence and found that fathers were less likely to be operating in a teaching mode than mothers. Fathers were less likely to be involved than mothers in helping their children with schoolwork or with arts-and-crafts projects.

This finding suggests that these stylistic differences between parents are not limited to infants and young children. Moreover, observational studies (Power & Parke, 1982) suggest that the mother – at least in the first 2 years of a child's life – functions as the disciplinarian who sets boundaries for the infant's activities and limits the infant's access to household objects or spaces. This is consistent with the finding that mothers act more frequently than fathers as managers of their children's activities (e.g., making appointments or supervising activities with friends) (Parke & Bhavnagri, 1989).

Continued evidence of variability

The data on ongoing differences in parental roles lead naturally to more general inquiry about the limitations of paternal impact on child rearing, limitations that in part suggest the continuity between contemporary fathering and the historical constraints developed earlier in the modern era. In the first place, just as previously in the nineteenth and twentieth centuries, though with some important new twists resulting from new family forms, the contemporary period continues to be characterized by a considerable diversity in the types of roles modern fathers play. Just as historically there was no single portrait of the father role that accurately captured the range of ways in which fathering was executed, this remains the case.

At the same time, it can be argued that the cultural ideal of fatherhood maintains important limitations across historical time. The ideal has changed, even in a predominantly middle-class context, as we have seen. Yet from the nineteenth century to the present the fact of a cultural ideal continues to represent a stereotype that is positively valued at any point in time and that serves as a useful heuristic device for comparing and contrasting the ways in which actual practices conform or deviate from its standard. This concept also helps explain the frequent failure to recognize the variability that characterizes fathering. The concept of the uninvolved father was characteristic of the precontemporary era, before the late 1960s, and examples of involved fathers were given little weight or even credibility because they were inconsistent with the dominant concept. In contrast, the uninvolved or disinterested father in the contemporary era receives less recognition because this example violates the current ideal concerning father involvement.

In each era a different set of fathers may go unrecognized depending on the currently dominant ideal. Others (Lewis, 1986) have argued that the concept of the involved father has been slowly evolving over the last 40 years and that contemporary beliefs about father involvement may have been prefigured in social science writings since the 1940s and 1950s (e.g., R. A. Elder, 1949; Mogey, 1957). This evidence of historical precedent, however, does not take into account the altered social and economic climate of the 1970s and 1980s, which may have led to an acceptance of this new ideal by a wider section of the parent population than in previous periods.

Diversity in the contemporary era takes a variety of forms. First, as already indicated, many traditional families retain role definitions that limit father involvement with children and child care. Moreover, these families – mothers as well as fathers – are content to retain these more traditional orientations. Contrasted to this family type is the other extreme, represented by a small minority of families who have explicitly explored alternative family arrangements such as role sharing and role reversals (Russell, 1982).

Another form of diversity in contemporary culture occurs in the form of variations in fathering as a function of ethnicity, race, and social class.[1] A further major source of diverse fathering roles flows from the proliferation of forms of family organization that has accompanied recent demographic shifts in divorce and remarriage as well as in the timing of the onset of parenthood (Daniels & Weingarten, 1983; Furstenberg, 1988).

Evidence of the difficulty of shifting levels of father participation

More important to father involvement even than ongoing variability is the considerable evidence that overall mother–father roles are more difficult to change than current rhetoric would suggest. Three sets of studies will illustrate this situation: (1) studies of maternal and paternal employment provide one kind of evidence; (2) cross-cultural studies of social experiments in which shifts in government policy have provided increased opportunities for involvement offer another source of evidence; and (3) follow-up studies of the stability of role-sharing families – that is, families in which fathers and mothers more equally share care-giving activities – yield further signs of continuity.

We have argued that shifts in the patterns of men's and women's work modified the fathers' role historically. Recent shifts in employment patterns of mothers represent one source of data relevant to this issue. A large number of studies have demonstrated that fathers show an increase in the proportion of time they spend in child care when their wives are employed. However, this relative increase is often due not to an absolute increase but to a reduction in the amount of time that mothers devote to child care. There is some evidence that fathers increase their level of participation when their children are younger (e.g., Russell, 1982), but the overall bulk of the evidence supports the proportionate argument (Lamb, 1986; Pleck, 1981, 1983). To be sure, even these shifts in the relative proportions of time that mothers and fathers devote to child care may be psychologically meaningful for children in that they provide a more equal or balanced exposure to maternal and paternal interactive styles.

On balance, however, the recent shifts toward greater equality of participation of males and females in the work force have not in any dramatic way altered the balance of care giving by mothers and fathers. One explanation for this substantial persistence lies in the continuing value that our society places on the male role of breadwinner and the links between work involvement and family life. Does work still interfere with basic family commitments and activities? One approach to this issue involves examination of the relationship between commitment to work and participation in parenting activities. In a short-term longitudinal study, Feldman, Nash, and Aschenbrenner (1983) found one predictor of paternal involvement in infant care giving was low job salience. Fathers who rated their job more salient were less involved in parenting activities. Until social norms concerning the importance of outside employment for men shifts, there is likely to be a continuing tension, especially for fathers, between home and work commitments. In fact, as women's sense of identity becomes more closely tied to their outside work activities, similar tensions may become apparent for mothers as well.

Another source of information that testifies to the difficulties of shifting men's work and family roles comes from cross-cultural studies. Lamb and his colleagues (1982b) took excellent advantage of a unique national family policy adopted by the Swedish government. The Swedish government has offered the equivalent of paid sick leave (up to 90% of the individual's regular salary) for 9 months to any parent who wishes to stay home to care for a new infant. Although between 1974 and 1979 fewer than 15% of new fathers in Sweden took advantage of this opportunity, Lamb and his co-workers studied the growing minority of men who took parental leave for more than a month, during which time they had primary responsibility for their infant's care. The nontraditional families were compared with traditional families in which mothers served as primary care giver. Based on home observations at 3, 8, and 16 months, some surprising findings emerged. Mothers and fathers – regardless of how equally they were involved in care giving – differed in characteristic ways: in general, mothers exhibited more of the classic "nurturing" behaviors (e.g., smiling, touching, and vocalizing) than did fathers, with only a few exceptions. This pattern is, of course, similar to prior observations of parents in traditional families, and it contrasts with the theoretical quality of mothers and fathers in competence in young-child care, as established in the experiments noted earlier. The fact is that, regardless of their family type, mothers and fathers behaved in characteristically different ways:

Differences between maternal and paternal behavior are remarkably robust, remaining stable inter- and intra-culturally despite variations in the relative involvement of mothers and fathers in childcare. This suggests that these behavioral differences are biologically-based . . . or that they are deeply internalized during years of socialization. We will not be able to evaluate these alternative explanations until we are able to study parents who were themselves reared in a nonsextyped fashion and assign primary parental responsibilities to the fathers. (Lamb et al., 1982b, p. 139)

The other source of evidence comes from the small minority of families that have explicitly explored family arrangements such as role sharing and reversing family roles. In one study, Russell (1982) examined 50 Australian families in which fathers took major or equal responsibility for child care. In these families, fathers and mothers shared about equally (12 hours a week for mothers, 9 hours for fathers) the full range of child-care tasks such as feeding, diapering, bathing, and dressing. In traditional families, by comparison, fathers performed these tasks only 2 hours a week or 12% of the time. A similar pattern emerges for play and for other significant interactions, such as the parent helping the child with homework, the child helping the parent prepare a meal, and so forth. Fathers and mothers again were approximately equal in their division of playful interactions (18 hours for fathers and 16 hours for mothers), whereas in traditional families fathers spent an average of 10 hours and mothers 23 hours a week in such interactions. However, the two types of families were comparable for the absolute amount of time spent by both parents combined (53 hours a week in shared-care-giving families and 56 hours a week in traditional families).

However, as Russell (1982) found in a sobering follow-up of his role-sharing families, only about one-fourth of his families were continuing with the arrangement 2 years after his first study. A number of factors may account for the small number of families that chose these alternatives and persist in them. For example, in general, men are still paid more than women, so that most families may find that it makes better economic sense for the father to be the breadwinner. Men may be reluctant even to request leaves of absence that may jeopardize their job security – particularly in times of scarce jobs and inflation. In some cases, such as when the mother is breast-feeding a child, role reversals may be difficult to implement. The basic problem, however, may still be one of attitude; as Levine (1976) points out: "There is still the widespread belief that a man does not belong at home taking care of children" (p. 153). Until there is some change in this traditional view about the roles that men and women can or should play in rearing their children, few families will either try or persist in alternative patterns for extended periods of time. Together, the evidence suggests that there is still considerable fragility to the concept of the newly involved modern father.

The yin–yang of contemporary fatherhood

As previously in the nineteenth and twentieth centuries, the contemporary period in the United States and other advanced industrial societies presents mixed evidence about the prospects for extensive paternal involvement in child rearing, even setting aside the variety of styles that continue to proliferate. Expert opinion has decisively shifted in favor of more credit to the paternal potential, but many child-rearing manuals, including Spock, despite having made rhetorical strides against sexism, continue to credit an implicitly inherent maternal instinct for love that fathers cannot really rival (J. S. Modell, 1988). New signs of activity by fathers are unquestionably important, but they are balanced by continued work distractions and, overall, by an approach that suggests that fathers have moved into a more prominent supporting-actor stance, rather than earning equal billing with mothers.

Fathers themselves, furthermore, continue to reflect deep ambivalence in outlook as well as in behavior. The emphasis on playful interactions between fathers and children, though it does constitute an important change in fathering over the past half century, embodies its own ambiguities. It leaves fathers as the less "responsible" parent. It acknowledges the primary teaching role that mothers, schools, youth groups, and peers have acquired in modern society. To be sure, paternal play teaches children, and many fathers intend a transmission of skills and values through play that deserves further examination. And the play style does self-consciously cut into earlier disciplinary or control emphases. "Wait until your father comes home" is a threat no more. But although oriented toward new emotional expressiveness, the play style also has its selfish qualities: "Give me fun with my children or I'm going out."

Indeed, the changes that have occurred over the most recent decades in the time that fathers spend in caretaking may actually have reduced men's pleasure in children, because of the tenacity of prior values and because of more recent tendencies to stress freedom and self-indulgence and to downplay intrinsic pleasures in parenting. A specific comparison, between a point just prior to the contemporary era (defined in terms of new women's roles and expectations and the general cultural challenges of the 1960s) and the mid-1970s, certainly suggests the complicated relationship between recent paternal outlook and prior modern ideas.

Questionnaire responses[2] from married men in 1957 and in 1976 definitely reveal change, suggesting that the contemporary pattern has to some extent moved away from previous modern patterns of fatherhood. But they also reveal the complexity that the larger historical overview leads us to expect, as the earlier responses show real commitment to active fatherhood, at least in principle, and a vigorous sense of the rewards of children, just as the more recent statements reveal a number of new hesitations as well as new points of father–child contact. The comparison of the modern and the contemporary, in terms of a single but rewardingly coherent data set, defies any beguiling hypothesis that would see married men moving from harsh or uninterested parenting (the modern nadir of fatherhood) to the happy engagement with child care so many authorities have now shown as possible (Veroff, Douvan, & Kulka, 1981).

According to the Veroff et al. study, married men in 1957 already noted an increase in responsibility, once a child was born, as their most common response to a set of questions on "how parenthood changes things." Interestingly, more married men than women responded along these lines in 1957. Expectations of responsibility and obligation went up substantially by 1976, from 24% of all responses to 39% (still, puzzlingly, a higher rate than that of married women whose increase was roughly comparable). The sense of children as an undesirable limitation on freedom rose as well (though here, much less rapidly than with women), from 8% to 12%.

In the Veroff et al. study, a stake in children as character builders or purpose givers declined (again, among women as well). Married men became less likely to see in children the advantage of making them less selfish or more stable, and less than half as many of the men, in 1976, hailed children for providing them with a major goal in life. Probably reflecting the decline in breadwinner ideology, there was also a massive proportionate decline, from 6.5% to 2.8%, in the married men who saw children as a spur to their working harder.

An interesting increase in the married men who viewed children as an opportunity to teach was balanced by a decline in the idea of setting an example – but here the change may well have reflected a shift in the way fathers behaved, toward greater interaction and away from remote role modeling (Veroff et al., 1981). Though the category involved infrequent response, there was an increase (by about 50%) in the men who saw children as providing love or companionship. But emphasis on nurturing children declined, from 5% to 3% (though single men maintained higher ideals here). Pleasure in seeing children grow increased, but the idea of children as fun remained roughly stable. Whereas 13% of married men thought that children increased happiness in 1957, only 9.5% stressed this benefit in 1976 – a slightly greater decline than among married women. Finally, there was a notable expansion in the number of men who saw children as an interference in relationships with their spouse.

These data clearly warn against seeing recent decades as a triumph of a new, active fatherhood. Male expectations of responsibility to children did increase, and a few small shifts – notably, the increase in pleasure in watching growth, the decline of the breadwinner spur, and the move from exemplar to teacher – may have followed from new paternal styles. But specifically emotional rewards, not a big category at either date, did not go up much – and, in fact, married women showed greater gains in some areas than men did. The nuisance aspects of parenthood received greater emphasis from fathers, which might, of course, have followed from greater day-to-day paternal involvement and the shallowness of some playful interactions, and the link between children and happiness receded.

These polling responses may suggest a decline in certain paternal myths, as fathers became more actively responsible for children and less likely to talk glibly of children as life goals or happiness creators. The responses are certainly compatible with the possibility of increasing divisions among fathers, between some fathers who stressed active engagement and others who viewed family in terms of relations with spouse and self-expression with children as a drag. The data do not paint a revolution in happy fatherhood – because fathers did not see themselves as uninvolved in 1957, as against some historical imagery, and because new-style fathers were not uniformly committed to parenthood in 1976. Fatherhood, and the expectations that attached to it, did change, but at both dates it was pulled by a number of conflicting impulses. The overriding trend saw a declining commitment to parenting, and in this trend men and women both shared.

One data set does not a recent history make, but in combination with a larger historical overview the interpretive implications are suggestive. Because modern fathering trends have long involved impulses toward creative redefinition, and not simply barriers to effective contact, there is room for deterioration in aspects of current fathering whatever the level of theoretical rehabilitation of the paternal role. More important still is the probability, even amid some change, of an ongoing tension in fathers' expectations and behavior, that is, of tension between fathers' impulses toward greater utilization of family on the one hand and commitment to a child-free work and leisure on the other. This now-hoary modern tension, juxtaposed with the real increase in daily involvement, most likely accounts for the souring of tone between the 1950s and the 1970s.

Hopeful signs: Availability of support for fathering activities

In spite of the pessimistic or at least qualified tone of this essay, some final signs of change may support the new fathering ideal. There have been significant shifts in the level of institutional support available to fathers, and fathers are increasingly viewed as appropriate targets of institutional assistance. This type of institutional backing is necessary in light of the fact that fathers may need disproportionate support to maximize their potential for involvement.

Support has assumed a variety of forms. There has been an increase in advice directed specifically to fathers (in magazine columns, books, and educational films). Hospital-based prenatal and to a lesser degree postnatal classes are more common than even a decade ago. Related to this hospital-based instruction is the liberalization of postpartum visitation rules as well as the increased opportunity for fathers to attend labor and delivery when their offspring are born. Moreover, there is accumulating evidence that men can profit from these shifts in terms of subsequent child-care involvement. (See Parke & Beital, 1986, for a review of hospital-based interventions for fathers.)

The research agenda

The complexities of contemporary fathering – the identification of significant change but also of ongoing concerns about limitations – suggest a context in which current approaches can be enriched by further exploration of historical perspective. Data from the past about fathers' outlook, behavior, and impact will doubtless continue to frustrate historical analysis through its limitations, but the absence of extensive efforts thus far to trace fathering through the later nineteenth and twentieth centuries suggests the possibility of some real advances that can interact with social and behavioral science approaches. Interestingly, the few available surveys of fatherhood that embrace a historical perspective at all, although often quite good, turn the perspective primarily to policy uses; they discuss how the tender reed that is modern fatherhood might be better nurtured by policies that take fathers' problems, as part of male adulthood and in light of pervasive maternal bias, into better account. There has been relatively little attention given to the developmental implications of changing paternal styles of the sort that would really link historical and contemporary research and deal with change and continuity in fathers' impact on their children (Furstenberg, 1988; Rotundo, 1985; Vinovskis, 1986).

Certainly it is important to try to distinguish between "universal" limitations on fathering, as suggested, for example, in the anthropological literature, and the special constraints and ambivalence that developed in the modern West. Even the limitations on standards may be culturally determined and reversible, of course, but the special features of modern structures and values invite particular redress. Knowing how modern work affected men's family values, as well as their behavior, may help us to grasp the obvious continued tensions between work commitment and fathering more fully.

The ongoing monitoring that many women apply to paternal activities also merits investigation from the standpoint of historical continuum. When, under the familiar blanket of modern maternalism, did many mothers develop specific "gatekeeper" strategies that could condition the functions and approaches taken by fathers toward their children? How do these strategies continue to constrain fatherhood and the satisfaction men take in this role?

Still more alluring is the need to connect historical inquiry with contemporary *new* !

findings about contrasts between fathers' playfulness and mothers' didacticism. When did fathers develop this emphasis, and for what reasons, and with what effects on children in the recent past as well as the present? How, indeed, have modern fathers developed expectations and standards for their parental functions, as the salience first of moral guide and then of breadwinner declined? Here is an opportunity empirically to connect historical considerations about men's activities in the absence of published standards, in most family manuals over the past century, with inquiry into the impact of the more recent literature directed at fathers. American fathers may be somewhat distinctive in their attempts to use play to interact with young children, which means that the causes and impact of the style deserve serious inquiry in connection with its current manifestations.

There is even some possibility, at least for the twentieth century, to link earlier data about distinctive paternal approaches to children and their apparent results, with more contemporary findings. School and child guidance materials back to the 1920s certainly suggest that, in regard to children's behaviors and emotional norms, fathers stood out in certain areas against mothers and experts alike; the results of this distinctiveness, for children themselves, might be explored through application of contemporary theory and in juxtaposition with our current understanding of the ways that their fathers' standards affect children.

The obvious point is that an approach to contemporary fathering, and its role in child rearing, is almost inherently historical in part. The identification of change means that we should know as precisely as possible when and why the change occurred: when the emphasis on playfulness or when the shifts in involvement away from adolescents and toward younger children took place. The further identification of the continuing impact of values and behavioral standards from the relatively recent past also calls for assessment over time. The need to understand recent innovations and the desire to encourage further rethinking both demand not simply the invocation of the perspective of the past but a new commitment to relate energetic historical inquiry – the quest for the lost fathers of the past 150 years – to the methods and findings of contemporary research.

Notes

1. There is also an increasing recognition of the diversity of fathers in other cultures. See Lamb (1986) for a volume devoted to cross-cultural studies of fatherhood. These variations may have long existed, representing durable cultural traditions that have shaped maternal and paternal roles. Studies of the impact of westernization on cultural variations would be worthwhile, particularly to evaluate the hypothesis that differences may be lessening as a result of modernization. Alternatively, the combination of unique heritage with exposure to Western traditions may produce a wide diversity of hybrid definitions of fathering roles (McAdoo, 1988).
2. Codings of both questionnaires allowed multiple answers and were open-ended.

Part IV

The cross-disciplinary collaboration

> Interdisciplinarity is a means of solving problems and answering questions
> that cannot be satisfactorily addressed using single methods or approaches.
>
> Julie T. Klein (1990, p. 196)

Up to this point, we have presented the end products of a cross-disciplinary
collaboration that began in the mid-1980s. This collaboration, we believe, offers
valuable insights into the nature of cross-disciplinary work. If joint efforts of this
kind are the answer to investigative needs when expertise is required from
different fields, it is important to give thought to ways of building cross-disciplinary teams.

Our first step in this direction is to follow the path of our workshop enterprise
(see chapter 8), beginning with the New York City meeting of historians and
developmentalists and concluding with the Belmont Center Conference and its
written papers. The New York meeting provided members of each discipline an
opportunity to know each other. The historians presented models of social
change in the twentieth century, and the developmentalists discussed various
behavioral outcomes. Out of this meeting emerged a plan to team members from
each discipline to work on specific research problems. The Belmont Conference
critically examined manuscripts based on these collaborations, resulting
eventually in the present volume. Wherever possible, we bring the exact words
and reflections of the participants into the text in an effort to convey the different
perspectives and interpretations.

The Belmont Conference had much to say about issues of method and approach, prompted, in part, by a thoughtful presentation, "The Elusive Historical
Child: Ways of Knowing the Child of History and Psychology" (chapter 9). In
this essay, Emily Cahan and her colleagues explore ways of drawing accurate
inferences about "children's actions and consciousness" from the available evidence in history. Some of this evidence pertains to children in field settings, in
experimental laboratories, in case studies, and in social experiments.

At the conclusion of the conference, William Kessen and Michael Zuckerman

171

(see chapter 10) reflected on the proceedings from their vantage points as developmentalist and social historian, respectively. Their commentary is properly skeptical about the practicality and authenticity of the cross-disciplinary collaboration. Zuckerman, in particular, challenges the developmentalists to move beyond contextual language to the formulation of research questions that actually incorporate contextual issues. Collaboration with a historian is an empty gesture if a joint study merely entails reference to historical settings and does not include a historical dimension at its analytic heart.

In a very real sense, Zuckerman's challenge speaks to the heart of our mission to discover ways to bring social and historical contexts to the questions we pose concerning children and their development. The empirical chapters in this volume vary greatly in their achievement of this standard, from giving more attention to historical influences than to developmental processes and outcomes to doing just the reverse and relatively neglecting historical context in favor of developmental outcomes. We bring this report from the field to a close by discussing these matters and by proposing what seems to us to be a promising and compelling agenda for collaborative research by social historians and developmentalists on children in time and place.

8   The workshop enterprise

Glen H. Elder, Jr., John Modell, and Ross D. Parke

> The necessary groundwork laid the first day was the realization that the
> psychologists had no grand theories to offer and the historians had few solid,
> interesting trends to offer.
>
> Steven Schlossman (personal communication, 1984)

The studies in this volume up to this point represent the end point of a collaborative process that began in the 1980s. In this chapter we will take you back on
our journey through this process, from the initial planning session to a series of
workshops and a good many research meetings. The authors of the preceding
chapters are not a perfect match for the authors of papers at the workshops.
Consistent with the nature of workshops, some new working arrangements developed out of the discussion sessions.

   The nature of cross-disciplinary study is best experienced by taking on the
roles of the historians and the developmentalists in their struggle to work out a
common ground. We hope that the lessons of this collaborative process will
inform and strengthen cross-disciplinary ventures in the years to come.

The proposal

   Responding to the rapidly expanding interest in aging across the life
span, a group of social scientists led by Matilda Riley of the National Institute on
Aging formed a committee (circa 1977) at the Social Science Research Council
to pursue a deeper, multidisciplinary understanding of human development over
the life course, with particular emphasis on the middle and later years (Elder,
1985; Sorensen, Weinert, & Sherrod, 1986). Developmentalists were well represented on the committee, and social historians frequently participated in topical
meetings.[1]

   In one of our meetings, at the end of 1983, we discussed a proposal that might
foster greater use of contextual influences by developmentalists – a plan to bring
child developmentalists and historians together around the theme of childhood

and children's development. To this end, we held a multidisciplinary planning meeting in January 1984 to explore the value of holding workshops on the general theme "Children and Their Development: Historical and Developmental Perspectives."

Following a lengthy exchange of views, we chose an agenda for the first workshop (fall 1984) that would draw upon the distinct strengths of each field using disciplinary working groups. As a first step, professionals from each field needed to learn about the other's perspective and state of the art. Three members of the planning session formed a social history group (John Modell, William M. Tuttle, Jr., and Peter N. Stearns) to prepare for the workshop, and developmentalists formed a working group (Orville G. Brim, Jr., Glen H. Elder, Jr., and Ross D. Parke) around the theme of behavioral outcomes.

Social historians are especially skilled in assessing the course of social change and the implications of specific trends and events for children and childhood. As one member of the history group put it, "Social change is, after all, the basic building block in historical studies" (J. J. Brumberg, personal communication, 1984). Accordingly, we asked the historians to recruit additional colleagues for the task of identifying at least five major historical changes since 1920 that have had important implications for the developmental experience and well-being of American children. We chose the years since 1920 in order to avoid a primary focus on the effects of industrialization as well as to overlap with the chronological emergence of the field of child development (R. B. Cairns, 1983). Each member of the group was asked to submit a succinct description of each proposed historical change along with a rationale for its selection and an account of its principal implications for children.

Linking historical change and children's lives

The decision to build on the strengths of each discipline through working groups of historians and developmentalists seemed reasonable at the time, especially as a first step toward genuine collaboration. But it entailed major unknowns for an enterprise that aimed to relate historical change and the development of children. The planning session concluded that our ultimate objective was to arrive at "connections between historical change and the development of children."

Different perspectives

The two disciplinary groups started from *different* vantage points. For the most part, historians are likely to begin their story of historical influences on children with an explanation of the macrochange itself and its times, such as the social institutions of the Progressive Era (Schlossman, 1977) or business cycles and the Great Depression (Elder, 1974). Having traced macrochanges to the microlevel, historical analysis may also proceed in the opposite direction by asking, What are the implications of widespread microchanges for society as a whole? Individual actions may be aggregated to address this question, with all of the methodological problems that this process entails (but see Spenner, 1988).

By comparison, developmentalists tend to view linkages between an individual and the environment from the perspective of the organism. Their research questions do not focus on social transformation and its behavioral effects, but rather on children's behavior and relevant social influences. Some of these influences may be historical and some may be environmental.

Both the historical and developmental perspectives may refer to the centrality of the environment in child development and yet have different concepts in mind. A sociologist observes that statements regarding the centrality of the social environment in life-span developmental psychology do not mean that research will be designed in a way that "apprehends social structure as a constitutive force in development, and that views the social environment as more than a setting that facilitates maturational unfolding" (Dannefer, 1984, p. 847). Psychological models fall short of offering this mode of analysis and interpretation.

No theory in psychology assumes this perspective on social structure in human development as a constitutive force in development because the field generally views the social environment from the perspective of the individual organism. This perspective poses questions that lack an informed knowledge of the workings of society, social structure, and social change relative to their psychological implications. Thus, it does not contribute to a theoretical account of how social factors and systematic influences shape the life course and human development.

These varied perspectives reflect different research questions and the probability that different models that link historical change and children's lives will be offered. What this means for communication between the two disciplinary groups is captured by Modell's reflection (personal communication, October 22, 1984) that the disciplines have different stories to tell and that "a certain amount of puzzlement resulted when we were both rowing hard but in different directions, given that we were both interested in a common subject." In Figure 8.1, Models A and B show a simple representation of the differences.

Developmentalists tend to follow Model A, in which a particular outcome of child behavior is analyzed in relation to relevant antecedent influences, both proximal to the child (such as the family environment) and more distal (as is social class or ethnicity). Note that the point of departure is the behavior of the child, such as being aggressive or adopting certain values, and not the changing environment. A question that might be asked about the most salient influences on children's self-control would not concern the developmental effects of an environmental change.

The full weight of social change in children's lives is understated by Model A

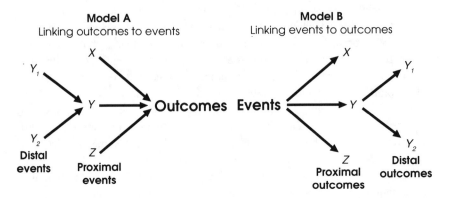

Figure 8.1. Studying social change in the life course.

in two ways. First, any historical factors among the selected antecedent influences represent only partially the historical changes underway or in question. Moreover, the linking process tends to be neglected because the analyst does not address how certain historical factors make a difference in children's development. Second, the model focuses on only one of the potential outcomes of a social change process, but a single social change may have multiple and diverse effects.

By contrast, Model B addresses questions that begin with a historical event or change process that leads, perhaps through the family or the school, to effects for children. Thus, the massive collapse of the economy in the Great Depression had wide-ranging effects for children, some of which were mediated by the family and others by welfare agencies and the schools. The full consequences of an event branch out, generating a number of outcomes in the lives of children. Proximal implications tend to emerge from an account of the change itself and then produce implications of their own for life experiences. This life change is most clearly observed within children's primary environments, such as the family or among age mates.

In search of the connections

Despite their different perspectives, the two designs in Figure 8.1 can be used together in a research program. A project might begin by assessing influences on children's sense of competence (a Model A approach) and then shift to a more intensive exploration of particular historical changes and their consequences for this outcome. In some respects, this sequence was followed in *Children of the Great Depression* (Elder, 1974). In this work, the developmental literature on children's sense of competence informs efforts to assess the impact of drastic family-income losses on children in the 1930s. The research sequence could also be reversed in ways that make sense. For example, an intensive study of the impact of family deprivation on children's relationships and self-image might require the analysis of a broader range of antecedent and contextual factors, biological, social, and historical.

Both disciplinary groups expressed an initial desire to learn about the other through relevant presentations of their state of the art, a common first step toward cross-disciplinary collaboration (Klein, 1990). Steven Schlossman, a member of the history group, observed that we need "to experience how each scholarly group thinks on common specific interests before we can seriously hope to crystallize and abstract common explanatory ground." For example, how might a developmentalist think about a particular historical change and its effects on children's lives? One way for the developmentalist to begin this process would be to learn what social historians think about the major social changes of this century and their implications for children. Their guidance might extend from the change process itself to a sequence of linking events and adaptations.

Historians with developmental interests likewise could benefit from state-of-the-art presentations by developmentalists. Misunderstandings and misrepresentations proved to be among the earliest casualties of our cross-disciplinary learning. Even in the planning session, historians were surprised by the developmentalists' view of organismic plasticity across the life span and by their lack of consensus on theories of human personality (Pervin, 1990). For their part, the developmentalists discovered that historians were more attached to the notion of individual variation across historical time than across the life span. These preliminary explorations underscored the work to be done before we could form meaningful collaborations.

We turn now to this collaborative venture as preparation for our multidisciplinary workshop. The logical meeting ground is the proximal environment of the child – the child's situations in family, peer group, school, and community (see Figure 8.2). Large-scale changes alter these environments, and developmentalists are most likely to point to such environments as influential factors. But the two disciplinary perspectives have very different views of these proximal settings. The historians were instructed to identify major social changes in the twentieth century that had consequences for children, and the developmentalists were asked to propose key behavioral outcomes.

All nominations from the history group involved large-scale changes in American society since the 1920s that have broad implications for the social development of children. We review these changes briefly and then turn to the behavioral outcomes proposed by the developmental group and to the task of bringing the two contributions together in a meaningful way.

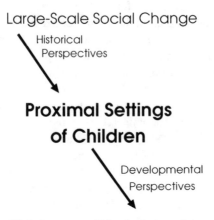

Large-Scale Social Change

Historical
Perspectives

Proximal Settings
of Children

Developmental
Perspectives

Children and Their Behavior

Figure 8.2. A meeting ground for disciplinary perspectives.

Historical influences

By the 1930s a number of major changes in the experience of children
were part of our rapidly urbanizing society. They include a small family system
and correlated changes in sibling relations, dramatic improvements in infant and
child health, the spread of formal education, and a diminished need for children's
contributions to the family economy.

Though there were many changes since the 1920s that deserved attention for
their consequences in children's experience, the history group narrowed the list
to five: (1) the growth of television and the telecommunications revolution;
(2) rising prosperity in the postwar years and the problem of economic inequality; (3) the Great Depression and World War II as an example of economic cycles;
(4) social change in women's lives; and (5) ideological change in child rearing.
As these sets of events suggest, we favored a view of history that slights the big
picture of neoevolutionary change across human societies and over a broad
expanse of time (Barkow, 1989; cf. Simonton, 1990). The larger view required
more resources than we could muster for this initial cross-disciplinary venture.

The historical nominations are also varied in their level and scope. Technological change is clearly of a different order than the changing lives of women
and ideological change in child rearing. Indeed, one might argue that there are
changes in women's lives that mediate the effects of some technological changes
on the developmental experiences of children. We should keep this diversity in
mind in our discussion of each mode of historical influence.

The historians sought to avoid the generalities of a modernization process and
to make as much headway as possible toward connecting specific macrochanges
to specific outcomes in children's lives. Nevertheless, the changes they selected

clearly represent exceedingly complex processes that may have diverse effects on children. Consider the following accounts.

Television and the communications revolution

Television and new program materials have diffused so rapidly over the past half century that they constitute a line of demarcation in the experience of successive cohorts. The proportion of families having TV sets grew tenfold to near universality in the 1950s, achieving for television a dominance that seemingly threatened the influence and survival of other entertainment media.

Television watching dominates the awake, out-of-school time budgets of children – especially youth – as neither movies nor radio has ever been able to (Murray, 1980). Its diverse effects on children's lives, culture, and mentalities are much debated. The impact on young children of exposure to scenes of explicit violence or sex is one of the more visible issues in this debate. Within a longer-term perspective, television can be seen as one phase in a larger telecommunications revolution, each phase of which further minimizes contact between children and adults.

Prosperity and economic inequality

The past half century has been one of a marked increase in real personal purchasing power, a trend that up to the mid-1970s extended across class strata. We see this general trend as a factor in the following developments that have consequences for American children.

- Children do not have to work gainfully as much as they had formerly, but they do have to go to school for many more years than in the past (Modell, 1989).
- There is a trend toward the right of children to have money they can allocate independently, whether they earned it or received it from their parents. Dependent children are no longer seen as contributors to the family economy (Zelizer, 1985), but rather they are expected to be economically selfish. Moreover, the "good parent" has become one who lavishes goods upon the child, and this characterization applies to even the poorest segments of the population.

The Great Depression and World War II

The historians proposed the Great Depression and World War II, two dramatic eras of change, as a package because these events together had an intriguing set of complementary effects on family life and on the world of children. Indeed, it is plausible that the historical discontinuity of 1929–45 constitutes a true watershed in American life. Consider the following family changes:

- *The Great Depression* (1) altered marital roles by threatening men's capacity to support their families reliably; (2) modified age roles by making age distinctions less important to household operations (children assumed adult responsibilities in hard-pressed families); (3) postponed family formation by influencing the timing of marriage and births; and (4) markedly reduced the amount of goods and services that families could either afford or hope to afford (Elder, 1979).
- *World War II* (1) altered marital roles by removing millions of married men from their homes to the front and placing wives in formerly male work; (2) changed age roles by drawing young boys into the labor force and by exposing them to heroic male role models in the service (see Tuttle, this volume); (3) accelerated family formation initially, then postponed the process; and (4) markedly increased the disposable incomes of families, in part through shortages of goods and services.

Such discontinuities made problematic the task of raising a child, but how were these breaks expressed in cohorts of children at the time? Other discontinuities occurred because of the culture of World War II, expressed in the family lives of returning veterans. As a result, children were socialized with images of war and of national service that would later clash with the realities of the Vietnam War.

Social change in women's lives

No change has produced more consequences for the social experience and development of children than the dramatic change in women's lives since the 1920s, from the sharply rising levels of gainful employment even among mothers with young children to the increasing likelihood of separation and divorce, marital postponement, and later childbearing, particularly among well-educated women (McLaughlin et al., 1988). In disadvantaged populations, by contrast, teenage pregnancy, childbearing, and single parenthood are commonplace. Children born to teenage mothers are at risk for school failure and for the repetition of their mothers' early life course (Furstenberg, Brooks-Gunn, & Morgan, 1987), though social intervention and resilient mothers can alter this prognosis.

Ideological change in child rearing

Child-rearing goals in contemporary America continue a pattern, established in the latter decades of the nineteenth century, of oscillating recommendations every 20 to 30 years. Thus, in the 1940s permissiveness replaced strictness, and this was followed by greater interest in discipline from the 1950s to the present. Underlying these oscillations, we detect changes away from the basic child-rearing paradigm of the nineteenth century – that is, away from hierarchical parental authority and control. Shortly after the Great Depression era, interest in harmonious relations between parents and children and among children tended to replace the emphasis on authority in parent–child relations. The advice literature also shifted toward the valuing of emotional release and expression.

A number of studies in the postwar era link broad cultural and institutional changes to standards for children and parental values and behavior (Alwin, 1986; Kohn, 1977; Kohn & Schooler, 1983; Miller & Swanson, 1958). More historical and comparative research is needed to assess the implications of such change for the socialization of children in their families and schools.

Historical influences considered

These proposed domains of historical change provide examples of different patterns of transformation. They range from secular trends in the status and role of women to sequences expressed in economic cycles of boom and bust and the interactive processes of change that link family and school to an evolving social order. Each domain can be thought of as a broad category of interdependent change events and processes.

Though much is known about each type of social change over the past 70 years, the processes that link them to the life experience of children are largely unknown. In part, the unknown territory has much to do with its scope. Consider, for example, the challenge of assessing the effects of the Second World War on children's lives (see Tuttle, this volume). Change in the lives of women brings us closer to the world of children than other suggested areas of social change bring us, and the literature provides even more detail on the potential implications of such change for child development. Three topics are especially prominent in empirical studies: (1) the gainful employment of mothers, part-time and full-time; (2) divorce and the single-parent household; and (3) the implications of day-care (Hayes, Palmer, & Zaslow, 1990).

Studies that examine any type of change in the lives of mothers generally find multiple consequences for children. That is, the effect of a social change branches out through different family processes. Thus, single-parent households headed by mothers tend not only to accelerate the growing-up experience for children (Weiss, 1979), but they also increase the risk of problem behavior and school failure. Each behavioral outcome is linked to different causal mechanisms. By comparison, studies by psychologists that focus on a specific problem behavior might not include the single-parent household as a relevant social or environmental factor. This contrast in research design is highlighted as we turn to the proposal of the developmentalists and its behavioral outcomes.

Children's behavior and social processes

The developmental group sought to identify several major behavioral outcomes for children and the processes linking them to the social environment. The following nominations emerged from this working group: aggressive behavior, achievement and aspirations, and intimacy and attachment, plus concepts of children's intelligence and cognitive development. Each nomination could be approached in three ways:

1. By focusing on the particular class of behavior, such as aggression or achievement, and outlining the key influences. Some of these influences might stem directly from a major current of social change since the 1920s.
2. By asking how the meaning of a behavior has changed over time and place. For example, have certain behaviors gained significance or meaning with respect to aggression, or have the behaviors classified as social aggression changed over the past century?
3. By concentrating on paradigm shifts in models of a behavioral outcome or process.

These three approaches vary in their relevance to the task of linking historical change to children's behavior and in putting propositions to empirical test, but all are represented to some extent in the developmental group nominations. Two nominations – aggressive behavior and achievement – draw on the "key influences" and "change in meaning" approaches, whereas the notion of changing paradigms applies to concepts of intimacy and attachment and of children's intelligence and cognitive development. Moreover, as a brief discussion of each of these developmental issues will reveal, they vary considerably in terms of their links with the social changes proposed by the history group.

Children's intelligence and cognitive development

From the beginning of twentieth-century research on child development, there has been steady interest in establishing exact descriptions of the changes in ability, knowledge, judgment, and learning that appear as children mature or grow up. From the Binet and Simon studies of children's cognitive development before the turn of the century and through the 1930s and 1940s with the work of Piaget (1983), Vygotsky (1962), and Werner (1948), scholars have been concerned not only with the description but also with the exploration of the impact of childhood experiences on cognitive development. The practical questions concern whether or how children at risk can be given enriched early experiences. The ideological questions center on the changeability of human nature and the wisdom of social programs for the disadvantaged.

These issues were energized following the 1957 Sputnik launch by an educational revolution that emphasized the need to start educating children at earlier ages. This emphasis reinforced a social reform movement that saw early intervention programs as an effective means to buffer socially disadvantaged children from the adverse effects of their environment. The social consequences of this movement included a national program of early childhood education and one designed for the education of handicapped children. Early intervention programs have traditionally been evaluated for their intellectual outcomes, but, increasingly, social and emotional outcomes have also become a concern.

This shift toward early education and intervention programs is linked to another historical change, the liberation of women from traditional child-care roles. The enrollment of children in day-care programs has raised many questions, including some regarding the impact of separation from the mother on the emotional development and the subsequent social adjustment of the child (Hayes, Palmer, & Zaslow, 1990). Although not defined as an intervention program, day-care shares many features with such programs, and its growth will have profound consequences for the family experience and development of America's children.

Children's aggressive behavior

In contrast to the study of cognitive development, the linkages with historical themes were less obvious in the case of aggression. Whereas we know a great deal about the antecedents of aggressive behavior (Parke & Slaby, 1983), we know less about the way in which the determinants change in their relative impact in different historical eras or in response to large historical changes. Some influences on children's aggression, such as the impact of television and movies (Pearl, Bouthilet, & Lazar, 1982), seem especially promising for cross-level linkages to the telecommunication revolution (one of the history group's nominations as a major social change). However, no such linkages were spelled out in research projects.

The challenge for developmentalists, in the considered judgment of the working group, is to generate theoretical models that permit a coherent integration of the multiple factors that affect aggressive behavior, from proximal influences to those most distal and macroscopic. This task is complicated by two issues. First, generational changes are likely in the ways that antecedent–consequent relations are organized over time and in the relative weight of particular factors in given historical periods. Second, the scientific community and larger population are subject to biases in behavior interpretations that vary over time. Interpretations regarding the major determinants of aggressive behavior have shifted from blaming forces within the person (such as genetics, gender, and race) to blaming those outside the person, particularly family structure and the mass media.

Intimacy and attachment in life experience

The developmentalists focused on shifts in scientific concepts regarding the development, antecedents, and value of intimacy across the life course. These shifts have broadened the range of influential figures in the development of attachment relationships and emphasized the malleability of social ties from early childhood to the later years of life. Attachment, intimacy, and other prosocial outcomes can be linked to a changing world of groups, communities, and social institutions through the interdependence of lives and its social dynamic. The logical starting point for such analysis is the family, a potential bridge between macroscopic changes in society and the developmental experience of children.

A variety of the historical themes, especially shifts in women's lives and changes in child-rearing ideologies, could be conceptualized as influencing the attachment relationship within families. The argument that the reduced availability of mothers through their work force participation may modify their attachment relationships is, in fact, being debated currently by social scientists. Similarly, less authoritarian child-rearing attitudes could result in more intimacy between parents and children. Finally, as Elder has repeatedly demonstrated, familial relationships are profoundly altered by major upheavals such as depression and war. In spite of these possibilities, few links were forged in our workshop discussions.

Children's achievement and aspirations

With much known about the antecedents of achievement and aspirations (Spenner & Featherman, 1978), the developmentalists brought up a number of issues concerning historical trends in child behavior in this area. Among the questions they posed were Have the self-respect and self-worth of children changed in any way? What can be said about temporal differences between the aspirations of boys and girls of different races and ethnicity in matters of education, athletics, work, and social acceptance? Has the fit between aspiration and achievement changed over the years under specified circumstances? Do children today have a greater or lesser capacity to change their plans, their interests, and the direction of their development? Have children's theories about themselves and their abilities changed in any way?

Forging the links between history and developmental psychology

The topics for developmental study were presented in a more elaborate form to the working conference, but their diversity clearly limited the possibilities for their connection to the proposed historical changes. The historians were looking for explicit behavioral outcomes, such as aggressiveness or achievement, along with explicit linkages to the larger environment. Paradigm shifts in views of child attributes and development define a challenging field of collaborative work between historians and developmentalists, but their relation to the heavily material view of social change among the historians is dubious at best.

In addition to the problem of the diversity of the developmental nominations, the historians had much reason to be startled by how little of the cross-level bridge had been constructed by the developmentalists and was ready for their additions. Of course, they too had made little progress in tracing macroscopic changes in society to the primary world of children. The conceptual distance between the two sets of disciplinary statements was very wide indeed. As one of the historians put it:

On reading the initial statements from each of the two disciplines I was particularly struck by the lack of mesh. What a developmentalist might most expect from historians – a clear statement of changes in children and in the developmental process – was lacking. Rather, the historians have focused on legitimate general changes without being especially clear about their impact on children. For their part, the developmentalists did not offer what historians most like from psychology: clear, causal links such that a historian might know, for example, what effects on children result from a measurable change such as father absence or a shift from authoritarian to permissive childrearing (P. N. Stearns, personal communication, 1984).

Another interpretation of the conceptual distance might fault the history group for not making more headway in specifying linkages from the changes in question to the proximal world of children. A clear statement of changes in children and in the developmental process would be more within the expertise of the developmentalists, assuming that they have a research interest in temporal changes at the level of individuals and situations.

The history group could not produce a clear statement about the impact of the selected social changes on children because the group had not spelled out the intervening processes. Thus, the general economic collapse of the Great Depression would elude understanding in terms of its effects on children until the links, such as the behavior of fathers, the state of the household economy, and the relationship between authority and affection, are identified (Elder, 1974). Contrary to Stearns's observation, linkages offered by the developmental group were strongest in relating the child to a primary environment, such as the family; they were weakest in locating the primary environment in a larger system of social structures and institutions, a potential strength of historical analysis.

Research on drastic economic decline suggests links to children's aggressive behavior that might be emulated in other cross-level domains. Why does a general economic decline tend to increase the rate of child abuse and children's problem behavior? A plausible explanation is suggested by studies of Berkeley children of the Great Depression (Elder, Liker, & Cross, 1984) and by contemporary research on family hardship in the farm belt. Drastic income loss in the depression among the families of children born at the end of the 1920s in Berkeley sharply increased the prospect of the children's acting out by increasing the aversive interactions within the family. Heavy income losses increased fathers' irritability, negativity in their marriages, and punitive and arbitrary behavior toward their children. Boys and girls became more ill-tempered and explosive as a result, and this kind of behavior reinforced the explosiveness of parents in an accelerating cycle of abuse. More than 50 years later, we find a similar process among hard-pressed families in the Midwest and their children (Conger & Elder, forthcoming; Elder, Conger, Foster, & Ardelt, 1992). Strong economic pressure increases the acting-out behavior of young adolescents by amplifying the explosiveness of fathers.

Economic decline is only one of a long list of factors that influence the expression of aggressive behavior by children. Among the other social changes that the history group listed, television watching has engendered much concern because of the medium's extensive coverage and even celebration of violence. We know that aggressive children tend to be heavy viewers of TV violence, and, research indicates, aggressive children elicit reinforcing aggressive responses from others. The more these children watch television and view violence, the less time they have for peer interaction and the more likely they are to enhance their coercive repertoire. Eron and Huesmann (1986, pp. 310–311) note that this cyclical pattern of amplification is associated with social and academic failure:

Children who behave aggressively are less popular and, perhaps, because their relations with their peers tend to be unsatisfying, watch more TV and view more violence. The violence they see on TV may reassure them that their own behavior is appropriate or teach them new coercive techniques that they then attempt to use in their interactions with others. Thus, they behave more aggressively, which in turn makes them even less popular and drives them back to TV. The evidence supports a similar role for academic failure.

The painstaking construction of conceptual linkages between macroscopic social changes and behavioral outcomes among children was not a primary objective of our disciplinary working groups. The respective lists of social changes and child outcomes identified points of disciplinary interest, but they could not become shared points in any fundamental sense. The common ground, as the discussion evolved, included a recognized need for the contributions of both disciplines to understand "children in time and place."

The historians sensed a need for developmental input in relating their environmental changes to the reality of children, and the developmentalists found historical insights essential in helping them think about the boundedness and variability of their causal models. Both fields were dealing with "moving targets," linked in uncertain ways – society for the historians and the child for the developmentalists. Given the complexity of studying the society–child connection, each working group no doubt wished that the other's territory would "hold still," as Stearns put it.

Based on presentations and discussion, the workshop analysis of social changes and behavioral outcomes generally convinced members of both working groups that the *initial disciplinary* approach was essential to the formation of collaborative groups on problems of common interest. Misunderstandings of each other's discipline were early casualties of the exploration. Historians quickly discovered anew the disarray of theories of personality in the developmental camp. For the developmentalists, historical analysis offered surprisingly little guidance on the key environmental variables relative to the selected behavioral outcomes.

The exchange moved at this stage to exploring common areas of research interest and to finding a way to draw on diverse disciplinary insights in the *multidisciplinary* phase of the project. One group of historians and developmentalists formed around the challenge of studying children in the past through the use of different kinds of data. The availability and quality of data on children across periods of the twentieth century were commonly noted issues in efforts to build collaborative research. Archives of longitudinal data that extend back to the 1920s (Verdonik & Sherrod, 1984) represent the best-known resource for such ventures; other sources include surveys, institutional records, and ethnographic materials.

A second working group formed around the question of whether American children have become more like each other across the twentieth century, owing to the standardization of pathways to adulthood, such as schooling. This presumed convergence has also been applied to gender differences. The logic here is that gender differentials can be explained by the distinctive aspects of the biosocial environments of males and females and thereby offer us an approach to finding the reasons behind the trends uncovered.

A third working group assembled around the domain of problem children and their life experience, with its attendant social and cultural definitions and private and public aspects (inside and outside of the family). Group discussion focused on aggressive behavior in adolescence, with initial commentary on the neglect of environmental variables by psychological research. For this group's historians, the rise in violent crime among contemporary adolescents posed a basic question about temporal changes in behavior. Had there been a real increase in aggressive behaviors among adolescents, especially girls? Had the repertoire of these behaviors expanded since the nineteenth century? The group explored some of the ways in which these questions might be addressed drawing upon developmental and historical insights.

A fourth working group identified changes in the role of children as a common interest. The actual functions of children and adult concepts of these functions changed dramatically from the later nineteenth century to the 1930s (Zelizer, 1985) and then to the 1990s. Children lost their role in the family economy by 1930 as they were excluded by law from working in a formal, productive sense (with some exceptions, as in farm families). But in adult eyes, children's economic inutility was balanced by a growing belief in their emotional value. And, in practice, growing numbers of children were given new functions – as students. This transition raised two questions: (1) From a developmental standpoint, what did this transition mean for children's own sense of worth and responsibility? and (2) To what extent did the paradigm of children's functions and value, observed around 1900, persist after 1950? It is possible that, despite the prolonged transition from earlier definitions of utility, children in recent decades have experienced the change more as a redefinition of utility than as cause for an ongoing sense of "uselessness."

As a whole, these common interests provided a much-needed forum in which to bring developmental and historical insights to bear on the development of children. By encouraging a working through of concepts, assumptions, and research strategies, we hoped the working groups would lead to collaboration on research and writing across disciplinary lines. The two-phase approach, from disciplinary presentations to multidisciplinary groups around common problem foci (cf. Klein, 1990), seemed to be effective when we considered the task at hand. To establish a meaningful ground for fruitful collaboration, each disciplinary group had to understand and respect the other's territory.

The conference drew to a close with plans for continued collaboration and for another workshop to be organized around papers, each of which would be written by a historian and a developmentalist. We had not achieved the cross-level expectations of our original goals, but the working groups were definitely headed in this direction. Moreover, the new working arrangements were producing the rewards that made the entire venture worthwhile. Topics and forms of collaboration changed in the months after the conference, but a good many of the original concerns of the four working groups led to jointly written presentations and papers for our final meeting in the Belmont workshop. We turn now to central themes from the workshop experience (October 1987) at the Belmont Conference Center outside of Baltimore and to our concluding efforts to bring historical and developmental insights to bear on children's lives and development.

Central themes from cross-disciplinary collaboration

Merely nominal collaboration was a constant temptation, because we could always follow tradition and divide the work into "background" (history) and "argument" (developmental psychology) or, alternatively, into "story" (history) and "theoretical significance" (development). The presenters, however, had already evolved their particular topics and more or less settled the most unavoidable questions of evidence, method of analysis, and theoretical framework. They had also evolved at least some sense of the contribution the work might make to the larger effort at mutual sensitization of the two disciplines. At Belmont, we sought to go beyond one-way borrowings by defining together a question that directly intrigued historians and developmentalists and by providing the beginning of an answer.

Historians for generations have, of course, called for scientific psychology to supplement or strengthen the psychology implicit in their conventional actor-centered accounts of events. At least since Freud, historians have recognized that intent stems from more than just conscious reasons, and they see psychology as a discipline that says that it can help them to discern connections. And psychologists, like others in the social and behavioral sciences, have long, if ritualistically, invoked historical-style accounts in describing "the setting" of those of their studies that they did not present as though they had been carried out in laboratories located, somehow, outside time and place.

But we were *developmental* psychologists and *social* historians, and although we could have fallen back on the easy, minimal mode of cooperation just described, we tried not to. "Social" historians have moved away from the parent discipline's focus on individual-level intentional behavior. Similarly, developmentalists, among psychologists, are especially concerned with holistic, processual accounts of modal individuals over their lives. They thus already have one element of change through time in their accounts and this makes incorporating a second macroscopic dimension of change, as other than "background," a genuine challenge. Five themes from the workshop reflect our mutual education as social historians and developmentalists as we worked toward the chapters that appear in this volume.

Evidentiary questions

Evidentiary questions occupied a fair amount of workshop time. Their discussion, generally, resembled discussions in historical circles on such issues as the biases in evidence at hand, potential alternative sources of evidence, and ways of extracting meaning from data. Discussions of this kind are almost always easy, comfortable ones for historians, for they largely represent adding on, which is relatively painless. At Belmont the developmentalists threw themselves into the historical spirit of things, becoming very inventive – especially, of course, in connection with the Cahan, Mechling, Sutton-Smith, and White paper (now chapter 9). Earlier disciplinary scruples, focused on the experimental and the observational traditions of psychology, were put aside for the moment.

Level of analysis

Far smoother, too, at Belmont than at the group's earlier meetings were the discussions that centered on the question of level of analysis – the individual versus the macroscopic (institutional, cultural, or society) level. Here, again (perhaps because more often than not the historians had taken the lead in drafting papers), the developmentalists tended to adapt themselves to the disciplinary predispositions of historians more than vice versa, although it is apparent from the essays in this volume that they were able to do so because of the policy and normative perspectives within their own tradition.

Situational variations

A developmentalist's theme that resurfaced at Belmont was the extreme situational lability of children and its putative age pattern and domain specificity. Developmentalists also reminded us that children might vary greatly according to their immediate setting. Children have great capacity to rebound, to achieve something like their old equilibrium, after adverse conditions are modified. Children are subject, too, to a very wide variety of influences as they grow up, and they experience these influences in manifold combinations.

This fact, together with children's own resilience, makes simple extrapolation from environment to development very risky. Indeed, this perspective obviously has major implications for the historians' initial, and occasionally persistent, hope of inferring what historical children may have been like (at any given age) from what can be learned about families, schools, cultural concepts of childhood, or whatever. In a sense, this was an often frustrating theme for historians, who, as viewed by the developmentalists, want to overgeneralize – in a way that may falsify the variety no less than the lability of the experience of childhood.

Different stories to tell

An important disciplinary difference centers on each field's preference for a different story line. Historians hope to tell of coherent change in historical time, whereas the preferred story for developmentalists concerns an interacting, multifaceted equilibrium system, moving through individual time. Social historians look for choices that have produced discernible change in society, including its children; developmentalists are only slightly concerned with choices and do not anticipate much cohort change outside the general path of development. Certainly, the three presentations (Stearns and Parke; Modell and Siegler; and Tuttle and Elder) that discussed environmental changes and hypothesized about the changes that might follow (although these hypotheses had been muted in the collaborative process) were richly greeted with enlightening instances of "yes, but then . . ." objections from the workshop.

Contexts of human development

Our last theme concerns the persistent evocation of context. History matters, somehow: this much we all agreed. But the content of our discussions revealed less than a fully shared understanding of just how it matters. As the reader will see, this theme provides the centerpiece of Michael Zuckerman's defiant challenge to the workshop, and it is hardly absent from William Kessen's more dulcet needle (chapter 10).

Note

1. Childhood and child development began to chart the committee's agenda through support from the Foundation for Child Development in 1981, and much of its work to 1987 focused on problems of the early life course (Hetherington, Lerner, & Perlmutter, 1988). A central issue involved the context or ecology of human development, a perspective made prominent through the writings of Urie Bronfenbrenner (1979, 1986, 1989).

The elusive historical child: Ways of knowing the child of history and psychology

Emily Cahan, Jay Mechling, Brian Sutton-Smith, and Sheldon H. White

> I proposed to myself a number of years ago, the task of studying the child.
> William Preyer (1888–89, p. ix)

The child eludes our understanding. The ubiquitous presence of children in our everyday worlds and the power of the memories of our own childhoods conspire to make the child deceptively familiar to us. Both the scientific understanding of the "natural child" inherited from the eighteenth and nineteenth centuries and our twentieth-century commonsensical, folk psychology of the child hold that childhood is a human constant. Knowing the child in history poses no special problem, according to this view, just as understanding the child from another culture offers no particular challenge. Children are children.

This everyday view of the child is losing its scholarly legitimation. The academic disciplines that study the child are increasingly inclined to view the child not as a natural object but as a social object, not as the product of developmental, biological forces alone but as a fiction constructed just as much by social and historical forces located in time and space. Social historians, of course, already are predisposed to view the child as a social object, but of significance is that developmental psychologists are coming to the same conclusion. Both disciplines are converging upon the notion of "the invented child," and both are undergoing what appears to be some fundamental reassessment of the epistemological foundations and goals of their research agenda.

History and psychology have always had such close affiliations with philosophy that it should surprise no one that recent developments in that discipline are at the root of the present trends in ways of knowing the historical child (Baynes, Bohman, & McCarthy, 1987). Historians seem more aware that they must make problematic their ways of knowing the historical past, even if they are still uncertain what new methods will emerge in this exercise. And social historians show increasing dissatisfaction with the discipline's conventional reliance upon the narrow case study. Social and historical forces in America in the 1960s and 1970s favored the retreat from grand synthesis to the safe turf of making "true" generalizations because one generalized only about inconsequentially narrow matters (McNeill, 1982). A number of historians now are calling for a return to the earlier agenda of grand theory and synthesis (Bender, 1986; Zuckerman, 1984), and many others are ready to join the movement.

Science's grip on the discipline of psychology has prevented quite the rout of positivism occurring in philosophy and history, but we see weakening around the edges. One should not overdramatize the case, but Gergen's assessment of social psychology (1982) and Bruner's move toward a narrative approach to psychology (1986) are important signals that positivism no longer is the single (or even preferred) epistemology for answering some of the discipline's most pressing questions. Within developmental psychology, in particular, is the making of a postpositivist revolution not only by some "young Turks" in the field (e.g., the sociopolitical critique offered in Broughton, 1987) but by some of its most prestigious members. This is "a time of deconstruction in developmental psychology," reflected William Kessen in a symposium devoted to thinking about the social, cultural, and historical contexts determining the history of the discipline (Bronfenbrenner, Kessel, Kessen, & White, 1986, p. 1218). Developmental psychologists seem to have lost a clear sense of where their discipline is going, and part of the reassessment has been the discovery of "the invented child" (Kessel & Siegel, 1983).

It is the coincidence of two disciplines in flux that makes the present moment seem so promising for drawing a new, shared research agendum on the historical child. We aim in this essay to lay some of the groundwork for the convergence of social history and developmental psychology on the task of knowing the historical child. We share with the other authors in this volume an excitement about the prospects for this new project. Neither discipline has done very well alone characterizing the ways in which social and cultural forces interact with developmental processes to create the socially constructed child. We wager the joint venture will succeed.

We first review briefly the new epistemological and methodological trends that seem to us to signal a readiness for this interdisciplinary project. The two disciplines have some new agreement on ways of "knowing" the historical child, that is, ways of making inferences about children's actions and consciousness from available evidence. Next, we survey the sorts of contextual variables we believe affect "the practice of childhood" and are also likely to show up in historical evidence. Finally, we look at four research settings – the field, the laboratory, the case study, and the social experiment – where the historian and psychologist can observe the child and learn something about the interactions of contexts and children's lives, about the possible "linkages" (Elder, 1973) between historical change and developmental issues.

Like the other essayists in this volume, we shall limit ourselves pretty much to the lives of American children from the late nineteenth century into our own. We emphasize, however, that our primary interest is in developing ways of understanding the historical child, regardless of the child's time and place. Much of what we say here speaks to more than the American materials.

The conditions of the practice of childhood

As intellectual historians and some social historians take the famous "linguistic turn" in modern philosophy, they turn away from psychology and sociology and toward the most clearly discourse-based disciplines – rhetoric, linguistics, philosophy, and literary criticism (Toews, 1987, p. 898). Perhaps that turn works well when the historian reconstructs the symbolic universes of adults and their relatively rich discourse, both verbal and nonverbal. But the historian of children's lives cannot afford to depend only on this linguistic turn. Children simply are not located in society in a way that leaves much evidence of their discourse. There is plenty of adult discourse *about* the child, but the child often is too silent for the historian's usual arsenal of methods. The historian of childhood must be far more resourceful than others, teasing evidence and meaning from unlikely sources.

Put differently, neither the historian nor the psychologist can treat the category of children like a social class whose interests emerge in an explicit ideological discourse of some kind. If our goals are to understand how children, as a category of humans, come to construct and sustain a consciousness or world view, to understand how historical "events" (broadly defined) affect the world views of children, and to understand how developmental processes interact with social forces and historical events, then we must look to the recent scholarship that puts *practice* at the center of our study.

Two intellectual traditions converge in recent attempts to put practice (or, sometimes, *praxis*) at the center of social and historical inquiry. The one tradition is Marxist, but it offers a more subtle approach than the "vulgar" Marxism so easily parodied. For English and American social historians especially, European models of Marxist cultural criticism fail to account very well for the dynamics of British and American societies. Thus, E. P. Thompson's historical analysis (1963) of the English working class and Raymond Williams's incisive scholarship on the entire scope of cultural products (e.g., R. Williams, 1980), from fine literature to television, share the project of attempting to understand how symbolic culture establishes the "totality" that short-circuits open class conflict in some societies.

Williams boosted the enterprise considerably by redefining and elaborating the too-simple Marxist dictum that base determines superstructure. "We have to revalue 'determination,' " writes Williams, towards the setting of limits and the exertion of pressure, and away from a predicted, prefigured and controlled content. We have to revalue "superstructure" towards a related range of cultural practices, and away from a reflected, reproduced or specifically dependent content. And, crucially, we have to revalue "the base" away from the notion of a fixed economic or technological abstraction, and towards the specific activities of men in real social and economic relationships, containing fundamental contradictions and variations and therefore always in a state of dynamic process. (1973, p. 6)

Williams seeks for any society in any historical period, therefore, "the central, effective and dominant system of meanings and values, which are not merely abstract but which are organized and lived" (p. 9). This system never accomplishes complete hegemony, or totality, over all citizens. Williams distinguishes between mere alternatives and genuine "oppositional cultures" not incorporated by the dominant culture, and he allows the possibility of traditional, "residual" cultures and of innovative "emergent" cultures as sources of alternatives to the dominant culture. Still, all cultures, dominant and alternative alike, are grounded in practice. The historian's task, accordingly, is to inquire into "the conditions of a practice," to recognize that individuals may have "related practices" with strong "resemblances," and to use those resemblances to speak confidently about the collective mode of cultural practice (p. 16; see also Lears, 1985).

The second scholarly tradition converging on the notion of "practice" as the key trope for undertaking historical and sociological analysis is a reinvigorated American pragmatism, one that builds upon the founders (Charles Sanders Peirce, William James, John Dewey, Margaret Mead) but seeks a synthesis between their old approaches and recent approaches to cultural criticism. Rorty (1979, 1982, 1989) provides the philosophical charter for the new pragmatism, Bernstein (1971, 1976, 1983) provides an ambitious synthesis of American pragmatism and European social theory, and Rochberg-Halton (1986), among others, provides concrete demonstrations of the sort of sociological and historical analysis possible "in the pragmatic attitude." Pragmatism's value to historians lies in its contribution to the historians' attempt to "address themselves to the promises and problems of sustaining the dialectical unity of and difference between meaning and experience (as all historians must) in the wake of the linguistic turn" (Toews, 1987, p. 882).

A tentative typology of the conditions shaping, limiting, and empowering the social practice of children's lives might include (1) the physical environment, (2) the social environment, (3) the "imperial" practices of adults, and (4) the "native" practices of the child's social group. This typology suggests too static and too neat a map of the complex dialectic among these factors. Moreover, each of these conditions is responsive to developmental forces, social forces, and historical events. In what follows, we intend our discussions of each condition of practice to be suggestive, not exhaustive. Our aim is to stimulate historians and psychologists to expand their notions of what counts as evidence of the practice of childhood.

We must offer one caution before launching our discussion of the typology we propose. In our drive for grand theory and for generalizing about historical children, we should not recapitulate the errors of the consensus historians of the 1950s, who ignored gender, race, class, and ethnicity in describing the patterns and meanings of American experience. Nor should we forget that birth cohorts can be smaller than cohorts typically used by historians and social scientists. Developmental and historical forces may converge in different ways upon the 2-year-old and on the 10-year-old, for example, and the institutional connectedness of children at different ages may leave different quantities and qualities of evidence of their everyday lives. In short, the term *children* may lump more than is good for our inquiry. These warnings issued, let us examine each of the four large categories of the conditions for the practice of childhood.

The physical environment

The physical environment of children conditions their social practices in several ways. Potter (1954), for example, shows how American abundance established in this century an environment of goods affecting child-rearing systems. Changes in children's clothing help set the limits for independence training; the change from buttons to zippers to Velcro fasteners and the invention of laced (now Velcroed) shoes, for example, increased the ability of children to dress themselves. Technology and medical ideology pressed for the change from breast-feeding to bottle feeding, washing machines helped make toilet training less urgent, and disposable diapers made the demand for control even less urgent.

American abundance also affects the larger scale of physical environment. The child's room, the number of siblings sharing it, and the panoply of things in that room changed dramatically in this century. The child's room, of course, is filled with objects: furniture, toys, game and sports equipment, wall decorations, even pets. Rheingold and Cook (1975) studied the rooms of nearly 100 children under age 6 and discovered myriad ways in which the parents reinforced sex role stereotypes through their choice of decor and playthings. Parke and Sawin (1979) have explored in detail the ecology of the child's room and its relationships to child-rearing antecedents and outcomes. And physical environments in the home may have something to do with the "privatization" of play with toys that Sutton-Smith observes (1986). Historians and social scientists clearly have a great deal of work to do both inventorying and understanding the ecology of the child's domestic objects (Csikszentmihalyi & Rochberg-Halton, 1981).

The architecture of the home creates a powerful set of conditions for the practice of childhood. Deetz (1977) combines archaeology and history to show ways in which evidence of room use and the arrangements of public and private spaces in early America might be used to infer substantial changes in familial social practices and world view affecting the child. Historians and folklorists working in the broad field called material culture likewise are building a view of the nineteenth- and twentieth-century American home and its furnishings, though few have addressed explicitly the child's material culture (Clark, 1986). The development of the multiple-family dwelling in urban America created a new space for the child, and the more recent trend toward "high-rise" apartment and condominium buildings limits parental supervision and increases the danger for children (Kornblum, 1974; T. M. Williams & Kornblum, 1985).

In ever-widening concentric circles from the child's home, the physical conditions of the neighborhood, street, and playground further condition the practice of childhood. Sutton-Smith (1981) uses an ecological approach in his history of children's play in New Zealand from 1840 to 1950, devoting separate chapters to the school, the child on the way to school, the playground, and the child away from school altogether. Zelizer (1985) describes the social and historical forces that made streets increasingly dangerous for the child, and Borchert (1980) describes the world of the alley communities in Washington, DC. Histories of the playgrounds often describe and analyze the physical features of those organized play spaces, including playground equipment, and a current journal, *Children's Environments Quarterly,* has devoted whole issues to schoolyards, playgrounds, and neighborhoods.

One helpful feature of the child's physical environment as a condition of the practice of childhood is that these conditions leave physical evidence that is likely to survive. Just as historians of antebellum African-American culture have been able to "read" such material artifacts as slave cabins, pottery, and quilts for clues to the symbolic world of an oral (as opposed to a written) culture, so the historian of childhood must learn to "read" the far more voluminous physical record of American children. Mergen's (1982) excellent survey of play and playthings includes a chapter "Space to Play" (on playgrounds and equipment) and one on toys and other artifacts of play. Mergen also provides in his four-page appendix, "Research Collections," a model for a research guide we do not yet have – namely, a comprehensive catalog of museum, historical society, and private collections of the artifacts of childhood. Mergen alerts the historian to collections of photographs that include children and their things. The study of material culture is a sophisticated specialty within social history, and historians can continue collaborating with social scientists to infer practice and meaning from known physical evidence.

The social environment

The social environment, consisting of social relations and values, conditions the child's practices of everyday life. Family size, structure, and interpersonal dynamics are most salient in this regard, but so are such elements as the racial, ethnic, and social class composition of neighborhoods and schools. One would expect that we know a great deal about the social environments of children. In fact, we know relatively little. Historians and demographers can reconstruct some of the larger trends in family size and composition over time, and social theories of the small group may help us understand the connections between these variables and various outcomes. For example, the social and historical forces that reduce family size for many American groups result in a setting rife with implications for practice and values. Smaller groups tend to be more egalitarian and less hierarchical than larger ones, which should affect family attitudes toward authority and affection. Gender roles may be more specialized within a small nuclear family, as Parsons and Bales (1955) suggest all too clearly.

The composition of the family affects the practice of childhood as much as does its size. The number, gender, age, and relationship of the child's primary caretaker(s) during specific developmental periods matter greatly in the socialization of the child and in the creation of the child's attitudes toward authority, aggression, and so on. Anthropologists see this in their work in other cultures, and the Six Cultures Project made much of these differences (B. B. Whiting & Whiting, 1975). Certainly in the American case the shift toward the small nuclear family, isolated from grandparents and other potential caretakers, considerably narrows the social experiences of children. The increasing likelihood that the mother is the exclusive caretaker of children has at least two profound effects. First, the stress upon the mother colors her performance of parental tasks. Second, the nearly exclusive pattern of early child care by mothers may create psychodynamics that reinforce certain gender roles and patriarchy (Chodorow, 1978).

Social relations within the family often reproduce the social relations of the larger society, or at least of the class to which the family belongs. This, after all, is Raymond Williams's point about cultural practice (1973), about the relationships between base and superstructure, but not only Marxian scholars are interested in the dialectic between the culture of the family and the political economy of the society. Miller and Swanson's now classic study (1958) of nearly 600 Detroit families described as either "entrepreneurial" or "bureaucratic" in style aimed at understanding the linkages between the father's work setting and patterns of child rearing within the family. Similarly, Sennett's goal (1970) in his study of middle-class families in Chicago at the end of the nineteenth century was to understand the connections between the political economy of the city and the changing textures of middle-class family life. Hareven (1982) also provides an excellent model for the historian's work on the connections between work and family life. The 1970s and 1980s, in fact, have seen possibly hundreds of books and dissertations do for one community or another what these early studies accomplished – a microethnography of the relationships between a community's political economy and family culture. Zelizer's study of the increasingly economically irrelevant child (1985) brings the sociologist's perspective to this historical pattern.

Consider, in addition to social relations within the family, the child's peer relations, including friendships, as a crucial element in the practice of childhood. Sutton-Smith (1982) criticizes the orthodox, adult-centered, structural–functional approach to children's peer relations and proposes instead a performance-centered approach to peer interaction as "life's interpretation in action" (p. 75). The performance-centered approach requires that the study of children's friendship and other social relations begin with the actual social practices of children in natural groups, as do some of the authors in the collection edited by Foot, Chapman, and Smith (1980).

As the social groups of the child become larger than the dyad or small, informal clique of "best friends," the historian discovers middle-level social groups that "mediate" between the public world and the home world (Mechling, 1989). Gangs, school classes, Boy Scout and Girl Scout troops, stamp clubs, athletic teams, and countless other sorts of midrange institutions constitute significant social environments for children in the nineteenth and twentieth centuries. Sometimes these social groups are able to create and sustain a rich symbolic "folk culture," and sometimes the groups remain simply a gathering. But in any case, these peer groups provide a socialization setting for the child to learn values and attitudes that may be continuous or discontinuous with the values and attitudes learned in the home world.

Schooling is a "forced" social setting that, nonetheless, can be very important in the child's social world. Access to schooling, length of the school day, duration of compulsory schooling, size of the school, the mix of gender and race in the school, the urban or suburban setting for the school, and similar factors affect the texture of a social world in which children can spend up to 8 hours a day. The suburbanization and growth of secondary schools after World War II, for example, has implications for the developmental dynamics of American adolescents. Barker and Gump (1964) demonstrate the developmental advantage of a small school, and Simmons and Blyth (1987) add to this point evidence of the adverse effects of large schools, where young people feel more anonymous and are more likely to be victimized by schoolmates.

Unfortunately, many social environments leave maddeningly little historical evidence. The researcher who tackles the problem of determining whether, for example, patterns of children's friendships have changed over time faces a formidable question – What can we take as evidence of friendships? Again, we must be resourceful, piecing together fragments of disparate evidence. Some sorts of material artifacts – autograph books and photographs, for example – attest to the dynamics of friendship, as might more traditional sorts of evidence, such as correspondence and autobiographies.

The "imperial" practices of adults

A third category of the conditions of the social practices of childhood consists of what we call, for lack of a better phrase, "imperial" practices. The imperialism here is of the adult world on the child's. Historians have written the history of the child largely from evidence of these imperial practices, such as child-rearing manuals, travelers' accounts, diaries, and the like. So our knowledge of the historical child to this point depends on the adult's considerably distorted viewpoint (Pollock, 1983). We have good reasons to be very skeptical toward that historical knowledge (Mechling, 1975).

This does not mean, however, that evidence of the imperial practices of adults has no value in writing the new history of the practice of childhood, only that we must use such evidence carefully and in relation to evidence of the three other classes of conditioning forces. We should not ignore the flood of discourse and objects that adults aim at children in an attempt to socialize them into the world of adults. One way to look at these materials is as cultural *narratives* that adults provide children, hoping the children will learn the lessons and internalize the values inherent in the practices. These narratives bear the cultural tropes and images of the adults' *ideology* of childhood.

A good many of the adult narratives meant for children are oral, ranging from bedtime stories to family proverbs to personal experience narratives meant to teach lessons. Some of the narratives enter print, however, becoming "children's literature" and wedding words with illustrations (Lystad, 1979). The messages in children's literature range from the obvious to the subtle. Thus, the practice of reading the Golden Book *Tootle,* to take Riesman's example from *The Lonely Crowd* (1950), was meant to teach the child of the late 1940s that conformity with the expectations of others is the best way to get along in life. Although it may be an error to assume that children always internalize and act on the oral and printed narratives originating with adults, the discourse may exert pressure upon the child's practices in certain directions. In fact, it is worth remembering that adults are the source of some forbidden literature that children read, from "dime novels" of the nineteenth century to the science fiction magazines and *Mad* magazine of the 1950s to the countercultural comic books ("comix") of the late 1960s and 1970s.

The rise of mass-media narratives aimed at children surely is one of the most significant conditions for the practice of childhood in this century. Some of the ephemeral children's literature bridges the mass print and electronic media, as was seen in the comic book versions of radio superheroes. Radio narratives and early television did not tend to segment their programming by age as much as later television has. Children's programming on television began in the 1950s and continues to explore new formats, including the much-praised "Sesame Street" of the 1970s, 1980s, and (now) 1990s and the widely condemned blurring of the boundaries between programs and commercials at the end of the 1980s. There is no doubt that television dominates a large portion of the average child's experience; by one estimate, the young child (aged 2 to 5) watches television 30 hours a week (Mintz & Kellogg, 1988, p. 221). American adults now commonly attribute a number of social ills to television's pernicious influence on children (Postman, 1982, 1985).

Sometimes the "narratives" are less like oral and written stories. Board games imply narratives, as do toys (Sutton-Smith, 1986) and organized action games (Sutton-Smith, 1959a). Anthropologists' increasing interest in process, ritual, and performance (V. W. Turner, 1977) leads some to formulate an "anthropology of experience" (V. W. Turner & Bruner, 1986) quite compatible with our developing a history of the practice of childhood. Psychologists and historians should experiment with ways to use processual anthropology in their own approaches to the games, rituals, and other processual genres adults create for children.

Of course, an important aspect of the imperial practices of adults is that they create institutions to back up their narratives, which in turn implicates the physical and social environments for the practice of childhood. C. Z. Stearns and Stearns (1986) demonstrate in their exemplary book on the intellectual and social history of anger in America how profitably a historian and a psychiatrist can collaborate in untangling the relationships between a human emotion and a cultural phenomenon. "Emotionology" is their neologism for "the conventions and standards by which Americans evaluated anger, and the institutions they developed to reflect and encourage these standards" (p. 14). They analyze in great detail what we would call the imperial practices of adults toward children's anger from the 1830s to the present. What we still lack is an account parallel to that of Stearns and Stearns of how children over this period dealt with anger, both in the individual and in the peer group. And that lack leads us to discuss our fourth and last condition for the practice of childhood, the "native" practices of the children themselves.

The "native" practices of children

Children have their own "native" practices, as well as those imposed by the adults, for while adults are striving to socialize the child into their world, other children are striving just as hard to socialize the child into the peer group's alternative culture. Children in relatively small, face-to-face groups create distinctive folk cultures that are an important condition of the practice of children's lives (Mechling, 1986a). Thus the child learns from peers the slang, jokes, insults, riddles, pranks, games, songs, superstitions, legends, and so on that establish a shared sense of identity in the child's folk group. Historians and child psychologists can learn from folklorists, sociologists, and anthropologists how to read the native symbolic cultures of children for clues to the themes and concerns of the group. Moreover, we can aspire to generalize beyond the small group, demonstrating Williams's point that there can be in a historical period a collective mode of practice. Thus, Fine (1987) not only describes in thick, ethnographic detail the folk speech and customs of preadolescent boys, but he shows as well the family resemblances of boys' practice across a sample of communities from Boston to Minneapolis, leading him to argue for the existence of a distinctive preadolescent subculture (what Fine calls their "idioculture").

Models of inference

Armed with a list of the conditions of the practice of childhood, such as we have outlined in the preceding sections, the historian and psychologist still are not ready to collaborate on writing the history of children's experience and consciousness. They need models of inference for generalizing from the particular to the general and for moving from the known in the historical record to the unknown in the child's everyday life. The unhappy fact is that even under the best of circumstances these scholars will have only fragmentary evidence of the practice of childhood and will need to find some way to use the fragments to create a plausible picture of the whole of childhood and its consciousness.

Let us acknowledge that the matter of models of inference provides simultaneously the most exciting and most difficult moments in the interdisciplinary cooperation among psychologists, historians, anthropologists, sociologists, cultural geographers, literary critics, mass-media critics, and whoever else might join the project of writing the history of the practice of childhood in America. The project requires that the scholars be as explicit as they can be about how they "know" things in their field, and then they can move toward agreement in their scholarly practice.

Glen Elder's (1973) notion of "linkages" provides one way to conceptualize the task of connecting social structure with individual and collective action. Elder has explored this concept over a number of years, making resourceful use of longitudinal and demographic data to connect social structure (which he defines as "persistent form of social interaction or relationship" [p. 786]), life-course dynamics, and various personality variables (see, for example, Elder, 1974, 1987a; Elder & Caspi, 1988; Elder & Liker, 1982; Elder, Van Nguyen, & Caspi, 1985). Several essays in this volume draw upon the notion of "linkages" as their model for connecting history and developmental processes in a specific case study.

As we have mentioned already, the concept of *practices* suggests an equally attractive approach to the basic problem of inferring individual and collective action from scant, indirect evidence. The growing use of practices, or *praxis,* deserves a much more extended treatment than we can offer here, but we can characterize the approach in the broadest strokes. We must recover a much more complex and subtle understanding of the dialectical relationships between the structures of everyday life and the actions of individuals living within those structures.

Both the linkages approach and the practices approach benefit greatly from observing settings in which living children practice their lives. The historian and the developmental psychologist can look to four research settings where scholars have observed the child in context. We turn next to these four contexts – the field, the laboratory, the case study, and the social experiment – and to some of the studies that provide evidence of the linkages we seek between sociohistorical contexts and children's practices.

Settings for studying linkages between contexts and the practice of childhood

The study of living children provides the occasion for gaining direct knowledge of the linkages between certain conditions of the practice of childhood and certain patterns of behavior and meaning. We review here research in four such settings – the field, the laboratory, the case study, and the social experiment. We want to raise some of the most important prospects and problems we see in these research settings.

The child in natural settings

Among the earliest field studies of children's lives are those of children's games. Newell (1883) and Culin (1891) did most of their collecting in the streets of New York and Philadelphia, but even then the formal playground was replacing urban streets and vacant lots as "the field," the setting where adult researchers would observe children at play. The playground is the historical legatee of both village green and urban street. By bringing children into universal schooling, the governments of the nineteenth century gradually displaced all other places as the central venues for children's play. Playgrounds provided space where children could play together with more regularity and ultimately with greater safety (though less adventure) than at any time in the history of childhood in Western society (Cavallo, 1981; Goodman, 1979; Mergen, 1982).

Adults collected playground songs and games largely out of the antiquarian and evolutionary drives to record these dying customs that were believed to have historical value because they contained remnants of earlier stages of societal development (Gomme, 1894–98). These "survivalist" theories themselves did not survive, and the early practice of explaining games in terms of their origins gave way to the practice of describing them in terms of their historical continuity. The outstanding example of this is the work of Iona and Peter Opie (1959, 1969, 1985) and their sustained belief in children's games as the living evidence of traditional continuity. Even though Sutton-Smith (1959b, 1972, 1981) takes the contrary position that such continuity is limited, he still provides an account of games largely in terms of historical issues. His account suggests that it is easier to find evidence of continuity in England, where traditions were continuous over a long period of time, and harder in colonial countries, where such traditions were broken (though there are exceptions in the colonies, such as the games among Welsh miners on the inaccessible West Coast of New Zealand or the Elizabethan folk songs in the Appalachian Mountains of the United States).

Parallel to psychology's history as a discipline, most of the nineteenth- and early twentieth-century data, with some exceptions, were derived from the use of questionnaires and written sources. At first the researchers were studying the child playing on the village green or in the street (Douglas, 1916; Strutt, 1801), but after World War I the public schools became the major focus of interest in children's games. Slowly the techniques shifted away from inventories (Lehman & Witty, 1927) to playground observations (Johnson, 1935).

The most impressive field study of children's lives on the school playground is that of Rivka Eifermann of Israel, in which she used over 100 observers to catalog the playground activities of thousands of children in many schools between 1964 and 1966 and has developed as a result an encyclopedia describing some 15,000 games and their variants. This mammoth, largely social psychologically oriented study has never been reported fully, though there are various articles indicating its coverage (Eifermann, 1970, 1971a, 1971b, 1972, 1973, 1974, 1978). Eifermann deals with such topics as age differences, group size, sex differences, mixed and single-sex play, variety of play, kinds of games, life span of games, Israeli versus Arab schools, town versus village schools, structured versus unstructured games, and so on.

In complete contrast is Polgar's (1976) miniature ethnographic study of a second-grade recess, using only the commentary of several children to show not how they appear as observed from the outside but how they themselves construe their playground world by categorizing it into games, goofing off, and tricks. Similarly, Sluckin's (1981) several-year study of two playgrounds in Oxford, England, is an insider's view (the "ethnogenic method," he calls it) of the children's playground world in terms of how the children choose each other for games, use framing devices, invoke access to rituals, and maintain sex differences.

Folklorists have provided the richest field studies of children's games and play on the playground, using intensive observations of particular games such as Red Light (von Glascoe, 1980), Four Square (L. A. Hughes, 1983, 1989), and jump rope (Goodwin, 1985) to explain school playground activity within the children's own social frames. All three of these studies are informed by feminist scholarship and show us that girls' games are not quite as simple as they seem from the male-centered, rule-structured viewpoint.

These recent studies may be too particular and too contemporary to contribute directly to historical ethnography, though they will help illuminate variables to be sought in larger historical contexts. We now know, for example, that playground surfaces, boundaries, walls, and apparatuses all make some differences to play; that age and sex groupings provide almost separate cultures within the same playground, and yet they interact in a highly systematic territorial and patterned manner; that within groups there are the usual group roles of bosses, bullies, and loners and hierarchies of dominance; that there are patterns of rivalry between groups with teasing and bullying; that teacher supervision varies from relative indifference to high concern and brings about a radical change in the children's play; that there are also differences of play at various daily times as the populations in the playground change dramatically; that there are playground legends and oral lore; that there are playground smells, splinters, tastes, and moods.

But in general what is most historically relevant is the way in which these playgrounds have been steadily *domesticated* over the past hundred years. The playground provides us with a psychologically revealing example of the changing character of American children. The histories of the playground and of childhood presumably have much in common, and our failure to analyze this history and its complex psychology adequately may be a striking omission in efforts to trace the confluence of history and psychology on our understanding of children's lives.

Also contributing to our understanding of the interaction of historical and psychological forces are field studies conducted in other natural settings of children's lives. These field studies tend to be of settings more or less under the control of adults. This means that the children's group cultures under study really amount to a dialectical culture at the border between adult and child culture, and it is this fact that legitimates the presence of an adult researcher and makes possible the intensive scrutiny these studies provide.

A few folklorists have done their fieldwork in the summer camps of children and adolescents. Mechling (1980a, 1980b, 1981, 1984a, 1984b, 1986b, 1987a) has documented and analyzed the large folk repertoire of a California Boy Scout troop over several years of its annual summer encampment. Ellis (1981a, 1981b,

1982) has done the same for a more limited range of genres in a summer camp population of disadvantaged urban children, and there are a few smaller scale studies of children at camp (Chandler, 1981; Savin-Williams, 1980a, 1980b). Krell's (1980) survey of children's folklore in a hospital wing remains the only study of its kind.

Fine's (1987) ethnographic study of Little League baseball provides the richest "thick description" to date of a preadolescent boys' culture in a natural setting. The special value of Fine's work lies in its simultaneous concern for minute ethnographic detail and larger theoretical questions. He combines the folklorist's appreciation for the importance of the expressive, symbolic culture of the small group with the sociologist's concern for the connections between group discourse and social structure.

Fine tackles an especially difficult question, one very important to the historian's goal of establishing linkages between sociohistorical forces and developmental outcomes. Recall that we quoted Williams (1973) to the effect that the historian's task is to look for "related practices" with strong "resemblances" in order to speak confidently about the collective mode of cultural practice. Fine poses the question whether he can speak at all confidently about an American "preadolescent subculture," based on his case studies of teams in five communities (two in New England, three around Minneapolis). Fine uses the folk speech and other folklore of the boys to show that there is a distinctive cultural tradition shared by preadolescents separated by space and time. Thus, Fine's approach and conclusions should comfort the historian worried about generalizing from fragmentary, local evidence.

Fine's work also interests us because he is one of the few ethnographers who has written about the special problems that arise while doing fieldwork on children's lives in natural settings (Fine, 1987; Fine & Glassner, 1979; Fine & Sandsrom, 1988). Adults attempting participant observation with children face problems concerning what social role – leader, supervisor, observer, friend – they may play while interacting with the children. Choice of research role leads to further problems, including ethical issues. How, for example, should the adult fieldworker handle situations that pose potential harm to the children? What should the fieldworker say or do in the presence of racist or other cruel insults? Can or should the fieldworker abandon the normal "policing role" adults play in protecting children? These ethical questions lead naturally to methodological ones regarding the ways in which an adult can establish rapport with the children, gain their trust, and thereby obtain access to children's practices normally hidden from adult caretakers. Fine cautions fieldworkers about the seemingly easy comprehension of the meanings of children's practices. Children once ourselves, we adults tend to project onto children our adult meanings or our memories of the meanings of our own childhood practices. This tendency may lead us to miss significant changes in the children's understandings of the meanings of their practices.

Short of intensive ethnographic accounts of children's games and play, folklorists have also collected fragments of children's expressive culture in homes, in schools, and on the sidewalk. Surveys of children's folklore (Bronner, 1988; Knapp & Knapp, 1976) collect these fragments, especially those deposited in folklore archives in universities around the country (Mechling, 1987b). Archive items vary greatly in quality and source (fieldwork v. memory culture), but with proper caution they can be a valuable source of evidence of the practice of childhood.

Some *longitudinal studies* of the life course count as another sort of natural-setting approach to the practice of children's lives. Elder's superb study (1974) of the lives of children during the Great Depression relies on longitudinal studies, and he continues to mine those materials for historical insights. *Middletown Families* (Caplow, Bahr, Chadwick, Hill, & Williamson, 1982), the first volume published by the team of sociologists that returned to Middletown (Muncie, IN) from 1976–78 to replicate the Lynds' earlier studies (1929, 1937), makes extensive use of questionnaires, structured interviews, and participant observation to trace the strains of continuity and change in Midwestern family life over three generations (the grandparents of the teenagers surveyed in 1976–78 were the teens surveyed by the Lynds in 1924–25). This "Middletown III" project is an extremely rich source of material on children's lives in the 1970s, and it is interesting for the historical project to note that Caplow and his colleagues found much more continuity than change in the Muncie families.

There is a special use of ethnographic records that has been of significant help to historians and ought to be revived. We are referring to the *cross-cultural study*, the use of large numbers of ethnographic accounts to test hypotheses about the relations between certain independent variables of social structure and dependent variables of children's lives. John W. M. Whiting and Child (1953) used the Human Relations Area Files to test a number of hypotheses about the child-training antecedents of patterns of adult personality. Later, John and Beatrice Whiting and their colleagues launched the Six Cultures Project, which included an elaborate fieldwork handbook (J. W. M. Whiting et al., 1966) and research protocol with an eye to improving the validity, reliability, and commensurability of ethnographic data to be used in testing cross-culturally the sorts of hypotheses Whiting and Child tested. The Six Cultures Project resulted in six high-quality ethnographic monographs and a number of thoughtful volumes analyzing the data (Minturn & Lambert, 1964; B. B. Whiting & Whiting, 1975). These volumes provide a rich source of cross-cultural correlations pertaining to the conditions of the practice of childhood.

Meanwhile, dissatisfied with the quality of much of the material in the Human

Relations Area Files, anthropologists at Yale University and elsewhere began to create better files, such as the Cross-Cultural Survey Files and Murdock's Ethnographic Atlas. Using these improved files, social scientists began testing a broader range of hypotheses, including some involving children. Roberts and Sutton-Smith (1962, 1966) collaborated on a series of provocative studies based on their "conflict-enculturation" hypothesis, which posited that

conflicts induced by child-training processes and subsequent learning lead to involvement in games and other expressive models, with the results that the conflict-developed motivations are assuaged and that buffered learning or enculturation occurs which is important to the players, to the groups to which they belong, and to their societies. (1966, p. 131)

Natural-setting studies of the practices of childhood are extremely promising for understanding, as Toews (1987, p. 888) puts it, "the complexity of mediated connections between experience and meaning." Not only does the ethnographic detail of natural-setting studies alert us to evidence we might otherwise miss, but ethnographic approaches also provide the material for comparing related practices and discovering their "resemblances" and for generalizing about collective cultural practices, as we see in Fine's work and in the cross-cultural survey work.

The child in the laboratory

There is some question about how well children's lives can be documented in laboratory experiments. One source of doubt concerns the "ecological validity" of the laboratory for understanding children outside of the experimental context. There are contemporary questions about whether laboratories are in *any* sense bona fide environments in which children can be themselves. Do we get authentic records of children's lives in laboratories? A second source of doubt concerns the possibility that much of our laboratory-based understanding of childhood mentality reflects a childhood that is not stable, but rather changes with secular, historical shifts. How can knowledge obtained with the presumption of stability shed light on a childhood that is known to vary widely by time and place? Third, the putative changes in children's practices in laboratory settings might simply be a product of changes in the experimenters' assumptions and attendant methods. If Heisenberg's Uncertainty Principle plagues modern laboratory physics, similar uncertainty makes us approach the childhood laboratory with great circumspection.

Our purpose in this section is to explore some of the common practices and rhetoric surrounding our laboratory-based understanding of children. We wish to suggest some ways in which these practices may gain some sensitivity for documenting the historicity of children's lives.

Most often, developmental psychologists encounter children in laboratory environments. A *laboratory,* according to Webster's dictionary, is "a room or building for scientific experimentation or research." Psychologists have taken the word from the natural sciences at a little cost. Not carefully considered for the use the *psychologist* makes of it, the laboratory environment has been taken for more and less than it really is. At times, the psychological laboratory is discussed as a privileged environment in which psychological observations can be made with great precision and replicability. Experimenters control the variables governing behavior, and universal, context-free psychological processes are rendered visible for analysis. Laboratories are specialized and designed to allow one to see facets of motor behavior, learning, and sociability and a limited range of emotional, familial, and voluntary aspects of the child's behavior.

Laboratories are not so powerful or universal, as anyone who works in them can attest. On the other hand, they are not completely "ecologically invalid" in a world in which people engage in formal relationships with one another and operate according to conventional rules and norms. These *arranged environments* are not totally unnatural to a child; they are one of a number of settings created by adults in which children are constrained to follow adult-stipulated rules.

Psychologists have limited entry into children's lives. Part of the challenge of psychological research is the art of using selected moments of restricted and circumscribed access to build up coherent and consistent pictures of children. The process is inherently clumsy. John Dewey (1900) once defined psychology as the ability to transform a living personality into an objective mechanism for the time being. Psychological knowledge is built on brief encounters, unobtrusive observations, and a little access to institutional records. Occasionally, with permission, we visit a family or a school and make systematic observations. Reduction is inevitable, the "whole child" one of those much-talked-about, elusive ideals. Structured laboratory environments nevertheless provide a powerful and flexible setting for studying various aspects of children's behavioral organization.

The generalizability of observations of children based upon laboratory encounters to a population larger than that observed in the laboratory is an experimental ideal. Such generalizability is limited by, among other things, the extent to which the laboratory observation reflects or represents aspects of the child's encounters with the world outside of the laboratory. Sources of compromise to generalizability can vary from the trivial to the profound. A particular task may be so foreign to the child that any generalization concerning his or her behavior based upon that task becomes suspect. Observations of children in one socioeconomic class or culture may not be representative of children of another class or culture.

Attempts to study children in everyday environments are said to be "ecologically valid." But difficulties surround anyone's attempt to define one superauthentic milieu for a child. The trouble, of course, is that the environment of a child is a system of hundreds of milieus and child development is, in part, a process of the child's progressive entry into more and more of that system through physical and symbolic excursions into larger and larger subsets of it (White & Siegel, 1984). Large-scale attempts to map the multidimensional environment of the child include those of Barker and Wright [(1954?)] and Bronfenbrenner (1979). These mappings all attempt to detail the kinds of milieus in which children live.

The problem of representativeness or ecological validity of the laboratory assumes a peculiar form of urgency when one considers the laboratory as a source for documenting historical changes in the lives of children. Developmental psychologists have for the most part designed laboratories at a time when it was assumed they were pursuing a natural science that might reveal the processes and sequences of an *unchanging* childhood. Child development was understood as a natural process, an extension of biology, and the general goal of research on childhood was to provide benchmarks for parents, teachers, mental health workers, and others who dealt with children. Psychological research would establish statistical norms of child development or, ideally, the specifications of universal stages of perceptual, cognitive, or moral development. In this view, children are considered to be "natural kinds"; they can be understood in terms of timeless, universal laws of development.

But if childhood is not everywhere and everyplace the same – and the anthropologists and social historians have been amply demonstrating to us that it is not – then the meaning and object of all forms of psychological research have to be reconsidered. Childhood is a cultural invention (Kessen, 1979, 1983). The child is a social and historical kind rather than a natural kind (Wartofsky, 1983). How do we use laboratories to explore a childhood that changes across time and place? How can we use knowledge generated with the assumption of stability over time to capture historicity? In particular, we wish to understand changes in children's lives as they may be brought about by historical and cultural circumstances – a depression, a war, a change in cultural institutions dealing with children, and so forth.

Laboratories allow us to examine brief, episodic snapshots of a child's directed activity. Presumably, we would like to be able to compare the laboratory encounters of one historical cadre of children with the laboratory encounters of another. One can do this, but it takes a little readjustment of one's approach to laboratory research with children. Psychologists consider it an empirical question how much laboratory-derived information will generalize, and we could use a technique for reassessing decades of experimentation as to the durability and generality of the findings. One might expect more generality from biologically based variables than from cognitive variables than from social variables because, in fact, these have been shown to have more stability in longitudinal studies in that order of priority.

For the purpose of our present discussion, it will be convenient to distinguish two broad uses of laboratory environments by psychologists: (1) the laboratory as a designed natural environment and (2) the laboratory as a convenient environment for the study of children's use of symbols. In addition, some laboratory settings are designed social environments, but we shall defer discussion of that use of the laboratory until our later examination of the designed social experiment as a setting for the study of the practice of childhood.

The laboratory as a designed natural environment. The oldest psychological laboratories were designed natural environments for the study of unchanging features of perception and learning. For many years, the canonical psychological laboratories were (1) scientific-instrument – and, later, electronic – laboratories for the psychophysical study of sensation, perception, and simple reaction time and (2) laboratories for the controlled study of animal and adult human male learning.

Both types of laboratories seek to relate stable features of the natural world to stable subjective reports of experience or predictions of behavior. Neither the perception nor the learning kind of laboratory has ever been widely used for the study of children and of child development. Although we have used such laboratories to establish some changes in children's sensory processes with age, their use to investigate higher order forms of childish reasoning about the physical and social worlds has been limited.

Jean Piaget (e.g., 1954) was interested in the child's reasoning about the physical world. When he turned to his "revised clinical method," he showed children physical phenomena with one or more exactly calculable features, asked children to make calculations about the physical and logical relations between these objects, and made inferences about the children's reasoning and judgment based on both the child's calculations and verbal justifications about them. Because most Piagetian research relates features of a stable physical world to aspects of psychological reasoning, one might say that such research is a kind of psychophysics.

The physically oriented laboratory environment is not, at first blush, a good place to examine responses to historical change. Could one use this kind of laboratory-based knowledge to document children's lives in a historically sensitive way? The question depends on assumptions about whether and in what way history changes the natural world of the child and the child's capacity to deal with and represent the world. Obviously, historical change modifies the physical environment of childhood. Over the past century, more and more American children have left the world of trees, rocks, streams, and fields and have grown up in a built environment full of houses, automobiles, newspapers, and airplanes. More and more of the physical world around the child is of human construction. More and more it is salted with communicativeness and intelligence. Can we bring into Piaget's little tabletop world (White, 1980) pieces of the historically changing physical world?

The laboratory as a convenient environment for the study of children's use of symbols. A second approach to the use of the laboratory is to focus on children's use of symbols. We know, from our research literature, that as children get older, their learning is increasingly mediated by symbol usage. Because some of these symbol systems reflect the culture's representation of the world at any given moment in history (symbolic representations in language and science, for example), many of the historical changes of interest to us might be captured by changes in children's representations of that world.

First, the psychological laboratory can provide a relatively open, quiet, useful context in which to explore the use of symbolization, by the child and by others, for the regulation and control of the child's activities. Second, such studies may help us to understand how the child acquires the cultural inventions of adult mentality.

Children become knowledgeable about the environment at two levels as they grow up. On one hand, the child physically moves into larger and larger excursions into her or his community and has an increasing number of concrete experiences with the places and scenes maintained by the adult society around the child. On the other hand, that child – talking, watching television and movies, reading, and given informal training in how to get things done and formal training in literature, history, and geography – enters ever more completely into the world of symbolic imaginaries used by that society (White & Siegel, 1984). The world of imaginaries may be a system of myth and magic; it may be scientifically given knowledge about things that are very small, very large, very old, or very far away. In any case, the child begins to range outside of the here-and-now and engages in forms of thinking that mix together calculations about the real and the imaginary. Technological inventions such as microscopes and telescopes, as well as literary products such as textbooks and works of fiction, serve to introduce the child to this world of myth, magic, and science.

Psychological laboratories are convenient environments for the study of children's use of symbols and symbol systems. Developmental psychologists now use a range of research paradigms to explore the child's use of symbols to represent the stable world of some aspects of the physical environment and the not-so-stable world of the culture's imaginary world of meaning. Habituation and conditioning studies provide indicators of the child's attribution of sign value to events of the physical environment. "Intelligence" tests and achievement tests and all their relatives assess the child's capacity for symbolic representation.

Piaget's research program is centrally oriented to the study of symbol formation in childhood, the "grasp of consciousness" that symbols make possible, and the powerful forms of judgment, logic, and mathematical thinking that the possession of symbols open up to the child. Piaget's studies of the symbolizations and genetic logics of childhood follow, in many respects, the program of James Mark Baldwin, an early American theorist of child development. Although Piaget was more interested in developmental logics of the physical world, Baldwin (1911) argues that still higher order forms of thought emerge in human development when people turn their thinking towards aesthetic objects. Perhaps the current body of research on aesthetic development (Gardner, 1980; Winner, 1982) will direct us towards those higher order logics.

Laboratories have proven to be extremely productive settings for the study of children's imaginaries and their ideals. Children want to grow up in all times and places, but their conceptions of what it means to grow up must change from one era to another. Over the past 200 years, as America has become an industrial and then a postindustrial society, its occupational structure has changed. The tasks of childhood as well as the jobs adults hold are different. Distributions of high- and low-status occupations to women, ethnics, and minority members have changed. Children have moved away from adult work. They lost their jobs and went to school near the turn of the century, a good thing on the whole but not a *completely* good thing (see Carnoy & Levin, 1985; Nasaw, 1985). They began to lose sight of what many adult workplaces and occupations looked like (Bronfenbrenner, 1974). The mass media – radio, movies, and television – gave children glimpses of imaginary adult worlds of work and play, as well as of imaginary lives of other children and families. At times, some of these glimpses are realistic, and at other times they are tremendously unrealistic. Caughey (1984) has given us a provocative portrait of the range of imaginary social worlds inhabited by adults, and much of what he says applies equally to the child.

We have a small opportunity to compare past and present children's images of adulthood. One of the more popular questionnaire studies of the 1900s involved asking children who they wanted to be like. Hill (1911) asked 1,431 children in two Nashville schools to write down who each child "would like to resemble." The children's nominations were categorized – Hill made an effort to practice coders and to obtain intercoder reliability – and the findings appear to have some solidity. They were quite similar to findings reported in an earlier, similar study by Barnes (1896–97).

Hill's youngest children, 6-year-olds, nominated people they knew – *acquaintance ideals* – including their parents, as people they would like to resemble. Public and historical figures gained popularity as children got older. Fictional characters had little appeal for the children; unhappily, Hill noted, the fictional characters children did emulate came from "the cheap novel." Unhappily, also, religious characters were nominated only a few times by the smallest children and almost never by the older. Finally, Hill reported a growing preference for male nominations with age. The youngest boys of the study nominated women, but the older boys chose female-ideals less and less. Girls, too, as they got older nominated a larger number of male-ideals.

There is a reasonable chance that findings like Hill's would not be repeated today because of historical changes in children's opportunities to examine adults, as well as in the definition of acceptable roles for men and women. For example, Hill's children moved from nominating direct acquaintances toward nominating public and historical figures as they got older because it took time for them to be able to read and, therefore, to be exposed to descriptions of such figures in newspapers and magazines. Today's preliterate children see public and historical figures regularly on television. Given children's enormous interest in toys and clothing linked to celebrities nowadays, one would guess that children today respond more strongly to the heroes and heroines of movies and MTV rock videos. Girls of today might make more same-sex nominations than girls did in 1900. Certainly, as opportunities have expanded for women, media people have made serious efforts to depict women in diverse roles, thereby creating more positive images of womanhood in the media. We might reasonably expect that the dramatic expansion in role opportunities for women during the last 20 or so years, may be reflected in a changing pattern of children's role models.

The images and icons and stereotypes in the public eye change over time with changes in the social fabric. Most of the popular stereotypes and slogans, heroes, sports figures, and so on of the 1920s would not be recognizable to people today. One reasonable use of laboratory settings would be to explore the gradually changing contents of children's minds and to connect such changes with changes in social roles and responsibilities and with the communication patterns of the society.

Another category of symbol use that can be studied in the childhood laboratory is the child's social motives and values. Hill's study explored children's knowledge of other people near and far, asking children what kinds of people they tended to choose as reference standards for themselves. One could ask similar questions of children about their sense of normative and ideal social relationships from among people in different historical circumstances. Beatrice and John Whiting (1975) report that as one moves from rural to urban societies one finds that children shift from viewing activities with their peers in a cooperative mode toward a more competitive outlook. McClelland (1961) reports that the stories children told in certain societies modeled and apparently taught children to have high motives for achievement.

Did American children move from a cooperative toward a competitive *ethos* as the United States industrialized? Did competition become a more central American value with the coming of industrialization? A historical understanding of children's social motives may reveal much about cultural values and the ways in which children learn about such values. If subgroups of American society achieve upward mobility from one generation to the next, are there conflicts between the motives parents would like to see children adopt and the motives children in school and with peers come to see as normal and positive? And who leads this shift, the parents or the children? If Margaret Mead (1942) and others are correct in arguing that American children are the cultural pioneers, unencumbered by tradition and more knowledgeable about the rapidly changing modern world than are their elders, then children's practices and the social motives connected with them might be the engine of change in the relationship between cooperation and competition in the twentieth century.

Finally, there may be historical changes not only in the contents of children's minds but in the structure of their thought processes as well. The laboratory, therefore, is a valuable setting for understanding historical change in children's "mentalities," a possibility that would link laboratory studies with the trend among some social historians to write the history of human *mentalité*. There is a long-standing tradition of developmental philosophies lying behind the establishment of contemporary developmental psychology. One of the ideas that recurs again and again in that tradition is the assertion of a relationship between the "intelligence" of individuals in a society and the "intelligence" embodied in, or demanded by, their social institutions. Baldwin expressed the idea in his *Thought and Things* (1911) in these terms:

If the development of the apprehension of self and things, in the individual's case, is correctly made out, we may be able to trace out the correlative stages in the historical evolution of the race. The social products could not rise higher, at any period, than the individuals' knowledge and practice would justify – so much negatively. And the notable and typical gains of individuals, in mental and moral progress, would show themselves, in time and in serial order, in the texture of the social fabric; in its institutions and in its theoretical speculations – so much, at least, more positively. (p. 6)

An individual's understanding of the social and physical world becomes embodied for Baldwin in social institutions. The thought patterns used by an individual and by social institutions have to harmonize with one another. Change one side, and the other will change to come into balance again. G. Stanley Hall (1904) made essentially a sociobiological theory of child development out of this idea. Biological maturation brings about successive "nascent stages" of children's thoughts, feelings, and will. With each stage, the form of governance that the child can accept and participate in changes. Very young children fit comfortably into familial associations; somewhat older children, preadolescents, tend to associate with their peers in leader–follower, Lord-of-the-Flies societies; still older children think and feel in such a way that they can participate in social aggregations marked by altruism, reason, and democratic social institutions.

Hall's framework is an interesting and plausible basis for thinking about children's social development. The recapitulationism to which Hall subscribed is incidental – consistent with his framework but not necessarily part of it. The thinking of older children ought to reflect the institutions and practices and conceptions of the society to which the child belongs, but the *history* of the child's own thinking does not necessarily have to match the *history* of the social institutions.

On a less grand scale, there are sporadic arguments that historic changes in technologies and social institutions are associated with cognitive changes. Among developmental psychologists, David Olson (1977, 1980) has argued that the use of written text elicits special forms of thought in the reader and may well stimulate significant intellectual changes in children. We know that historically the introduction of written script (Clanchy, 1979) and the printing press (Eisenstein, 1979) brought about large changes in the ways in which people normally dealt with quantities of information. Did those changes in handling information bring about changes in intellectual skills? Calhoun (1973) has offered the speculative argument that eighteenth- and nineteenth-century Americans, engaging in different activities, developed corresponding "intelligences." Radding (1985) has argued that early medieval changes in the use of ordeals in jurisprudence reflect historical changes in peoples' mentalities, changes that he aligns with Piaget's (1948) and Kohlberg's (1981, 1984) analyses of stages of moral development.

Can we detect intellectual changes as products of historical change? Luriia's (1976) study of traditional Soviet peoples who were introduced to education and collectivization has become well known as presumptive evidence that social change initiates cognitive change. Luriia thought he had found evidence that collectivization and education formed the basis for a dramatic shift in people's thinking from being predominantly concrete and functional to being abstract and representational. But the conduct of Luriia's study and the context in which it was undertaken have generated some doubts about its validity. The work was undertaken in an extremely problematic political situation, and Luriia was inexperienced in ethnographic work.

Laboratory environments might allow the use of sensitive indicators of movements and changes in children's mental processes linked with changes in the surrounding society. How would one so use the laboratory? A reasonable line of attack might be to try to confront directly one of the traditional sore points of mental testing, the issue of "culture fairness," by studies in which one deliberately tried to maximize and minimize differences in the performances of different subgroups of children. There have in the past been informal "Black IQ" and "Appalachian IQ" tests published, in which vocabulary and concepts have been so selected that minority children would have a much higher probability of passing than majority children. If one could, somehow, manage to set aside the enormous political and ideological overtones that such testing has aroused in recent years, it would be of considerable interest to explore the question of whether children in different social subgroups of American society show differences in information processing, or "intelligences."

Despite its limitations, then, the child development laboratory is a powerful setting for understanding some of the linkages between practice and meaning that will assist the historian in recovering the historical child. The laboratory is especially helpful in studying children's use of symbols. Psychologists in the laboratories need to begin collaborating with historians toward designing experiments that will get at the linkages historians posit or need in their construction of the child.

The child in the case study

There is an underground movement now in psychology that would like to see if we can move toward a fully developed method of the individual case study. Some of psychology's most important insights, it must be remembered, have been the result of the case study. Freud's intensive case histories and Piaget's observations of a single child are only the most famous examples. More recently, Kelly-Byrne (1989) conducted an intensive, ethnographic case study of a 7-year-old girl's "play and story relationship" with the researcher, a relationship that began as baby-sitter–client and evolved into a full dyadic play relationship. Over the course of the year, their "play" relationship shifted from enacting plays to discussing the staging of plays without enacting them to playful conversation about intimate life events.

The case study method is especially useful for the historical project when the psychiatrist or caseworker draws on experience across a number of cases to draw a larger portrait of the child's personality in a particular cultural milieu. Well known in this regard is the work of Horney (1937) and Erikson (1950, 1968, 1975), but there are others working in this tradition. Coles's five-volume *Children of Crisis* (e.g., 1977) project, for example, is full of sensitive readings of the lives of individual children. At the same time, Coles takes seriously the need to look for resemblances between the life practices of children who seem, at first glance, to have nothing in common. Coles has also used his conversations and psychiatric sessions with children to comment upon the moral and political lives of children (Coles, 1986a, 1986b).

Nonclinical genres of the case study also can contribute to the study of the practice of childhood. Biographies, especially psychobiographies, unveil the ways in which vectors of developmental forces, social context, and historical change collide in the individual. As in any case study, the psychobiography offers a challenging instance of the epistemological problem mentioned earlier – namely, how to move with confidence from statements about the particular child to statements about children in general. Historian Peter Gay (1985) discusses intelligently such problems and prospects of psychohistory.

The child in the designed social experiment

When child study became established in a few American universities at the turn of the century, people generally expected it to yield natural laws of child development. A natural sequence of psychological "growth" was proposed and assumed to correspond to or even be driven by sequences of physical growth. Child development was thought to be a universal process, governing the development of all children, and varying from one child to the next about as much as physical growth varies from one child to the next. Child development changes, but it changes so slowly, evolving over geological time, that in any one, brief historical period such development can be taken as a given. Scientific study should map such development for the benefit of teachers, parents, and other adults who design programs and institutions for children.

Schwebel and Raph (1973), introducing a book about Piaget, quote the author of an 1867 book for teachers, who is asking for such "scientific study":

> For many years there has been a growing conviction in the minds of the thinking men of this country that our methods of primary instruction are very defective because they are not properly adapted either to the mental, moral or physical conditions of childhood. But little reference has hitherto been had to any natural order [of] development of the faculties or to the many peculiar characteristics of children. (p. 3)

Presumably, Piagetian stage theory gives an answer to this 1867 question. Had that answer been fully satisfactory, then social reforms could have been put in place following an Enlightenment vision and a common set of nineteenth-century assumptions of the possibilities of social reform following scientific understanding. Natural laws, precisely ascertained, would dictate the necessary and the desirable in the design of social institutions.

Developmental psychologists have searched for natural sequences of ages and stages in the child's understanding of the physical, social, and moral worlds. Problems have accumulated because this approach has rested, more often than not, upon an exclusively biological orientation. The biological metaphor ignores the social and historical aspects of the child's development or takes them as secondary. The traditional biological approach has been characteristically finalistic, centering attention on what children are to *become,* and concerned with the child's march toward adulthood. Such approaches have ignored the scientific need to understand children as constantly viable, naturally adapted creatures in their own right, passing through a series of what might be called "ecologies of development."

Suppose we put the cart before the horse and consider "applied" programs of change in the child's ecology before we consider "basic" problems of the nature of children's development? Developmental theory has a long history, and we cannot find a time in that history when theory and practical experiments have not gone together hand-in-hand. Before G. Stanley Hall, there was Jean-Jacques Rousseau, with remarkably similar ideas about the basic character of child development and the right and proper governance of a child's education.

In the late eighteenth and early nineteenth centuries, Rousseau had the force of a theorist of child development. Widely read, his writings provoked thought and exerted a practical influence on educational practice – much like the influence of Freud's writings on psychotherapeutic practice in our own time. What marches from Rousseau's time toward our own is not simply intellectual history, an ideological lineage, but a reciprocating system of ideas and practical experiments. Sometimes, ideas lead into practical programs, and at other times innovations shaped by the exigencies and pressures of society give rise to ideas.

The reciprocating system is clearly in view immediately after the French Revolution, when the young physician Jean-Marc-Gaspard Itard, sponsored by the Society of the Observers of Man and influenced by the writings of Rousseau, John Locke, and Etienne Bonnot de Mably de Condillac, created his program for the civilization of Victor, the "Wild Boy of Aveyron." A historical trail of thinking and programmatic innovations dealing with handicapped and disadvantaged children follows Itard's work with Victor (Lane, 1976; Shattuck, 1980). In Scotland at about the same time, Robert Owen, subscribing also to Rousseau and Locke, opened his infant school at his New Lanark Mill. Owen's work stands near the beginning of a 200-year-old sequence of programs, traditions, and policies in early education (White & Buka, 1987). In England, addressing himself to another educational register, James Mill undertook his intensive early educational program for the young John Stuart Mill (1873).

As the reciprocating interchange moves towards the beginnings of the twentieth century, the actors change costumes. The educators go to teachers' colleges, turn professional, and bureaucracies arise around them. The philosophers turn professional. As they do, they spin off behavioral and social scientists, who also turn professional. The *most* professional of the neophilosophers live in universities, but some, only slightly less committed to philosophy for their livelihood, make up a heterogeneous group of intellectuals and policy people living in the bureaucracies.

Where once the writings of philosophers gave rise to experimental training programs and schools, the concepts and theories of developmental psychologists began to play that role at the beginning of the twentieth century. Now, at times the neophilosophers of the bureaucracies, thinking pretty much in the frameworks of the behavioral and social scientists, make their own innovations (Dewey & Dewey, 1915; White & Buka, 1987).

It is possible that the "laboratories" developmental psychologists and social historians ought to study are the practical experiments that stand in a reciprocal relationship to their ideas. In every generation, people create innovative training programs, educational schemes, schools, and utopian communities. Children are favorite targets of such utopian efforts: born innocent into a world that is tarnished, the docile and powerless children can be given a new way of life, given new training, to show the way toward an improved human society. The experiments are at one and the same time explorations of the possibility of social reform and studies of human nature. Could we study the lives children have led in those special environments?

John Dewey is important for our deliberations here. At a time when most developmental psychologists were committing themselves to a naturalistic orientation to child development, Dewey elaborated a social and historical perspective on childhood (Cahan, 1987). While most psychologists were elaborating "normal sciences" based on the experimental method, Dewey's laboratory school, established during his decade at the University of Chicago (1894–1904), *was* his "normal science." Dewey's laboratory school was designed to study the possibilities of educational change in a changing society.

Was Dewey's laboratory school a reasonable vehicle for the study of child development? Not particularly, if we take the position that child development is universal and invariant. Why pursue the subtleties of child psychology amidst the hullabaloo, chaos, and general confusion to be found in a classroom of an experimental school? However, if we adopt Kessen's (1979, 1983) view that the child is a cultural invention, that childhood changes through history, then a laboratory school becomes a useful and, perhaps, a necessary device for exploring what a child (and a teacher, and a classroom, and a curriculum) *might be* in "schools of tomorrow." The expression "schools of tomorrow" might very well reflect Dewey's hopes and intention as it is the title of a book written with his daughter, Evelyn, in 1915.

How *experimental* was the Chicago Laboratory School? We have to proceed slowly here. Dewey knew, and everyone else knew, that the University of Chicago Laboratory School would probably be a pretty safe, reasonable, positive environment for the children within. Otherwise, neither Dewey, the University of Chicago, the teachers, nor the concerned parents of the children would have consented to the placement of small children within the school. The Chicago Laboratory School was in part an expression of hope – an inquiry into the possibilities for the child and ultimately for society of differing pedagogical environments.

Dewey took change to be a fundamental characteristic of all human institutions, and he knew that he was living in a society in the process of transformation. Dewey perceived an American culture struggling to incorporate the new powers and possibilities of scientific understanding into its institutions. He saw the proper role of philosophy – and its descendants in the social and behavioral sciences – as a mediator in a perpetual process of reconstructing social practices. The philosopher extracts the principles, values, and motives regnant in traditional human institutions, articulates them, and in so doing assists in reestablishing them in newer social forms. Dewey was articulating the possibility of a psychology oriented to the study of individuals living in social systems undergoing change. More recent and important advocates of the idea that psychologists should address themselves to reforms as experiments have been D. T. Campbell (1965, 1969) and Bronfenbrenner (1976).

During the 1960s and 1970s, there was a substantial public investment in special educational programs for disadvantaged children at the preschool and elementary education levels. In a dramatic coincidence between research on cognitive development in children, social turbulence, and a declared War on Poverty, experimental programs for young children proliferated. Along with the passage of Head Start legislation, there was a substantial investment on the part of private foundations and government in research and development programs designed to explore various systematic possibilities of early education.

As in Dewey's era, a moment in history meets a moment in the child's life and education. An educational system in transition strained to meet the demands of change through a transformational experiment. Some examples beyond Head Start and Project Follow Through include Bereiter and Engelmann's "Model 1" preschool for the disadvantaged in the 1960s and Papert's computer-rich environment in the Hennigan School in Boston (see White & Buka, 1987). Some large, private, commercial corporations also entered the early learning field during this time, and the records of these projects and enterprises might yield data as rich as those from the public programs.

There have been thousands of "evaluations" of innovative programs such as these, but the innovations have been thought of as akin to laboratory experiments, and the designs of most evaluations have followed experimental methodology. The general results of all this effort have been unsatisfactory, and it is not clear that we know how to extract useful judgments and public information out of these innovations.

These innovative programs might be looked at as species of Vygotsian *transformational experiments* (for a discussion, see Bronfenbrenner, 1979, pp. 40–41). The programs themselves might be looked at as subjects of historical inquiry, rather than as "treatments," and the participation of the children in such programs might be looked at in a microgenetic framework (rather than testing the children for value-added sorts of "treatment effects"). Something about what is changing and unchanging in child development would be revealed by such studies. In an "experimenting society" such study would allow a little preliminary examination and thought dealing with new social arrangements that change the conditions and nature of childhood. Of course, we would need new psychological methods for the study of people immersed in social change. Wapner and his associates have recently begun an interesting new program directed toward the study of people in transition between environments (Wapner, Ciottone, Hornstein, McNeil, & Pacheco, 1983). And, of course, we must keep in mind that ideology colors both the experiments and the evaluations.

Can laboratory-based knowledge be used in efforts to document children's lives? Can we use knowledge constructed with assumptions about ahistorical children and ahistorical mental abilities to build a picture of the historical child and of the historical nature of some of our cognitive abilities and our social experiments? Can we learn something about the stable and the changing child through our social experiments? With a little readjustment of our traditional expectations of the laboratory as well as our social experiments, we think children's lives can be documented in a way that captures both stability and change in childhood and society.

Conclusion

Our aim in this essay has been to encourage our colleagues in history and in developmental psychology to take advantage of this moment in the dynamics of both disciplines and to return to the joint project of building models for understanding the historical practice of childhood. Toward that end, we suggested a typology for the conditions for the social practice of children's lives, including the physical environment, the social environment, the "imperial" practices of adults, and the "native" practices of children themselves. We also recommended a closer look at the dynamics of children's practices in four living contexts – the field, the laboratory, the case study, and the social experiment – for clues to the connections between conditions and practices and between the known and the unknown.

The reader will find elsewhere in this volume case studies that use some of the strategies we have outlined here. We feel we are at only the beginning of the wished-for collaboration between historians and developmental psychologists, and we have not meant to minimize the difficulties of interdisciplinary research.

But we trust we have communicated some of the exciting prospects we see in bringing together two disciplines in what has been for us, already, an enlightening and profitable conversation. The historical child may still elude and resist us, as do the living children in our midst, but our hope is that this interdisciplinary project brings us somewhat closer to understanding children's lives.

10   A paradigm in question: Commentary

> Here were the developmentalists, dealing with the universals of human
> development and human nature. What was their place in a discussion of
> trends and historical changes and shifting norms?
>
> Sheldon White (1984)

The closing moments of the Belmont Conference provided a chance to reflect on
our cross-disciplinary efforts and to question the practicality of inquiry informed
by the knowledge base of only a single discipline on child development. What is
the historical challenge to the study of child development?

Consider the following "what if" speculation. What if the terms in which
children are described at particular chronological ages have changed over time as
well as the processes that govern their movement into adulthood? What does this
say about how child development should be pursued in the present? The probing
commentaries on the Belmont workshop by the developmentalist William Kessen
and the social historian Michael Zuckerman have much in common with these
considerations.

Each analyst praises the participants for having explored at least a promontory
of fresh intellectual ground, and each calls for efforts that move one level deeper.
Kessen suggests that a more solid interpenetration of the two disciplines may be
achieved through the pursuit of evidential issues and, perhaps, by form of argument, a step taken in part by Emily Cahan and her collaborators in chapter 9.
Zuckerman seeks a more thoroughgoing collaboration across disciplines, requiring different research questions. These questions should bring appropriate sensitivity to the assumptions of each discipline as well as to the common ground of
cross-disciplinary study.

In retrospect, it is gratifying that the underlying issues to which the commentators call our attention fit with those being raised in the borderlands of developmental and social-historical thought today, as in the case of Jerome Bruner
(1986), Michael Cole (Cole & Means, 1981), Michael Frisch (1990), Jerome
Kagan (1984), Dominick LaCapra (1985), and Richard Schweder (1990). Per-

224

haps the common ground Kessen and Zuckerman identify is more achievable today than earlier, as the afterglow of psychology's "cognitive revolution" and of the "social history revolution" brings contextual issues to the forefront of objectives in human development and life studies.

The commentaries of Kessen and Zuckerman present the full range of implications that flow from the cross-disciplinary work that we undertook. They are also, we should note, edited versions of oral presentations offered immediately at the conclusion of our workshop discussions around the key papers. They represent the offerings of colleagues who generously and wholeheartedly accepted a difficult assignment. Much like ethnographers, the commentators were challenged not just to describe but to make sense of what we were up to. We are much indebted to their daring and thoughtfulness.

A developmentalist's reflections

William Kessen

At the end of our meeting, I remembered a Lincoln story. An inexperienced rider was wrestling with a particularly trying mount, and the horse, in its agitation, got a hoof tangled in a stirrup. From the rider: "If you're gettin' on, I'm gettin' off." There is no call for such escape feelings from the present meeting. The seriousness, almost always mixed with humor, the politeness, and the scrutiny of us all have been a model for the conduct of a successful conference – especially, one that draws together historians, sociologists, and psychologists. In the first place, then, congratulations!

A number of comments seem appropriate for me to make, all too brief and probably all too dense. The first one – about the epistemological position of the developmental psychologist – I can best introduce with another story. A famed and honored child psychologist of my knowledge once conducted a careful and numerically crowded study on tapping speed as a variable in the growth of children. Data were presented for a wide range of ages of the tapping speeds of thumb, forefinger, middle finger, ring finger, and little finger of right and left hands. The long monograph then ended!

The story can be writ large by asserting that the traditional strategy of my field is to find something (1) that will change with aging (almost anything will do), (2) that is susceptible to reliable counting or measuring, and (3) that no one else has reported on for at least 10 years. Perhaps I jest, but only with a tear, because such a strategy assures that you will be positivistic, public, and scientific. Often, however, the central problem is more subtle; if you are ingenious, you will have staked out a territory that is *yours*. In the most dramatic cases, you will establish a domain small enough or technically demanding enough for you to be its chief.

You will understand that my own domain is the left eye of the human newborn so that my worrisome comments have to be layered with salt. Still, we must be aware of the inherent push to narrowness among developmental psychologists and the belief of most of us that anything that can be quantified is *automatically* better than anything that cannot. The point will return.

But there is another message in my tapping story, one much more in the texture of our culture and, I sometimes fear, almost as much a problem for the historian as for the psychologist – we are all driven, obsessed even, by *the priority of the individual*. The ascent of the solitary and complete being in the Western world

226

has a long history and some parts of it have been well told, but it is revealing to see that, as recently as 1951, Robert Sears stirred the developmentalist community by his new emphasis on the dyad, the twosome of mother and child. The individual (one of the earlier adjectives in English to achieve noundom) remains in the center of our metaphysics, our ethics, our epistemology, and our scholarship.

This scarifying focus has been worked through the radical secularization of the West over the last century. Gone, for most of us, are the *agencies* of God, Satan, chance, kismet, fate, luck, hazard, accident, spirit, and mysterious force. As a consequence, no one (or, better, nothing) can share the responsibility for the world's events – large in weight or small – with the singular person. Only the individual can be held responsible; only the individual is to blame. The profundity of the modern Western commitment to the solitary being can scarcely be overstated; the individual *contains* traits, wishes, characteristics, sins, dispositions, and a warehouse of psychic furniture that cannot be shipped out of the Grand Solitary. The search for cause, nearly as often as the search for responsibility, is a search for the relevant person.

Forgive my leaning on this point; I have worse to fuss about. The way we all typically try to escape the constraints of individualism is by the *building of categories,* the groupings of folks into collections of the similar. Throughout our meeting, a significant categorical move has been made, I believe, by all those who presented papers. Again, you will not be surprised to learn, there is an introductory story about the instability of categories.

It is said that an American reporter, in an interview with old Doc Duvalier, asked the Haitian dictator, "Approximately what proportion of Haiti's population is white?" The reply was immediate. "Oh, about 96 percent." After some confused further questions, the reporter returned to his original query with a request for clarification. Duvalier: "How do you determine in the United States who is black? You see, we use the *same* procedure in Haiti in counting whites."

So much for one of our most cherished categories of people, one that is false and useful. The first and most significant of our categorical moves precedes discussion of such dimensions as race and gender. Most of our data – historical and behavioral – are drawn from the hegemonic middle class. Even when we try to escape bias by using newspaper announcements or advertising or by sending out questionnaires haphazardly, we will, willy-nilly, collect middle-class subjects. And, of course, as historians have long known, most of the records available to our study – the written course of our past – are the product of the educated, the public, the special. The justification that is sometimes used to continue our curious histories or psychologies is that the writers, the great middle class (also often white men), are the people who define the culture, write the books, and talk to us. I cannot propose a solution to this quandary; I can only keep our attention on the facts when we grow grand in our principles. Over the past year or so, I have been working with a fascinating set of documents, the publications of the United States Children's Bureau. The authors are aware of the poor and the excluded; they even write about them but always *at a distance*. The *voice* of the American historian, the *voice* of the American psychologist, is the voice of a very special kind of person – a person like us.

Another boundary condition on our important work is the rapidity of change in American culture over the past hundred years. The list often has been called – depressions, wars, the secularization of America, the appearance of AIDS as a health threat, the collection of all young people into the total institution of schools, the new civil importance of women and of blacks, the remarkable socioeconomic progress from Warren Harding to Ronald Reagan. Our voice and the voice of our children is the voice of the present.

Historians have been struggling with the issue of presentist writing for some time, but the psychologist must complicate their task in a peculiar way. Human children, whatever else we want to say about their being, are remarkably *adaptable,* designed by God or Charles Darwin to accept, to *see,* the world around them as composing their necessary set of problems. We are not essentially presentist because we gather in this place at this time but because we became what we are in the recent present; we adapted, and we learned our prejudices, our morals, and our attitudes in the present. Again, it is the bittersweet joy of the commentator to raise all sorts of difficulties that are beyond the capacity or intention of the meeting, and I am so overwhelmed as you are in facing the problem of dealing with a changing world over time when we know so little about the modes of children facing a new set of problems.

A couple of examples may clarify my agitated confusion. Acrobats in China, as seems to be the case in other national groups, are members of acrobatic families that begin the training of children to perform very early in life and, by and large, to the exclusion of any other formal educational activity. They are the children of acrobats in an acrobatic subculture. The instance is dramatic, but it does not differ in essence from the early musical child of musicians or from the chess prodigy who outdoes adults at the game when he or she is 5 or 6. How shall we fit these children into our historical or psychological modes? My point is microscopically simple – we have not faced the awesome variety of humankind. Rather, our categories serve to *limit* the variety so that we control it in our speaking and writing. You doubtlessly know all this, and I apologize for exercising the obvious, particularly an obvious that we can do so little to exorcise.

Perhaps nowhere is the complexity of our joint task more clearly revealed than in our discussions of *gender*. The historical and psychological explorations of the theme over the past 20 years have been argumentative, tangled, and exciting. It is striking to me that Mary Roth Walsh's 1987 book, *The Psychology of Women,* which contains *14* debates among women about critical issues in the story of gender, does not include many of the vital historical controversies.

Permit me one last short Cassandran yelp of regret, and, then, at wretched long last, I will turn to the happier side of my comments.

A talented teacher of my acquaintance used the 10 minutes it required for him to walk from his office to the lecture hall of his introductory psychology class to ponder the following explicit question: How shall I change their lives today? Put aside the mania of the goal for a moment, and recognize that, deeply carved into our professional intention is a desire to change the lives of our readers, to have them believe something that we believe. In grand nineteenth-century style, we can call this the Unspoken Intention that is hidden by the wonderful devices all of us have learned to speak with the voice of certain authority. I recommend for your skeptical amusement the current debate about the nature and quality of American day-care. It is to blush. Or, if you prefer an example at a greater distance, look at Mark Sullivan's comments (1927) on McGuffey's *Readers* over their 90-year history or, even better, look at the *Readers* themselves. The exercise, in either case, will send us to our prefaces to write something like: "I believe *a* and *b* and *c*; when you come to the end of this article, it is my hope that you will be convinced of *d* and *e* and *f*." Our work is packed with our values, our intentions for our small part of the world; a great deal would be gained by a critical analysis and display of those intentions.

All of the foregoing bears on our central shared responsibility – an examination of the rules of evidence. One principle in that set of rules has shone brightly in our meetings. If you do not want anyone to take serious issue with you, make outrageously grand pronouncements. No wonder now about Hegel's domination of his age. On the other side, when John Modell and Robert Siegler write a paper with exposed assumptions and lots of specific numbers, all hell breaks loose. We clearly cannot indicate *the correct degree* of specificity in a presentation, but we are under some call to think about the issue. *And* about the governing principle for evidence in both psychology and history: We do not seek *proofs;* we do not attempt *demonstrations*. We all want to tell *plausible stories*.

We have begun to see, during the meetings, what plausible argument may look like in our shared domain – the lives of children in Western history – but visible are only the edges of a new method and a new form of expression. The work of these days has made future serious collaboration at least plausible.

History and developmental psychology, a dangerous liaison: A historian's perspective

Michael Zuckerman

One of the best things about a working conference is that it can be so much more than just the collection of essays in which it eventuates. And this was a conference which was all that such a conference can be.

I cannot, I fear, convey adequately our gathering cordiality or our onflowing intensity. As the vernacular has it, you had to have been there. Verbatim transcriptions of our sessions might intimate something of the buoyancy and easy erudition of our encounters as the polished chapters that emerge from such sessions never do. But even if it were possible to impose those transcripts on a publisher, and even if bewildered readers were willing to struggle with scrambled grammar and track interrupted trains of thought, such publication could never catch the full flavor, or power, of the continuing conversations.

To do that, we would have had to record every dinner discussion and every tête-à-tête. We would have had to plant bugs in the bedrooms to follow the course of the controversies. I cannot speak for my colleagues, but I confess that my assigned roommate and I stayed up until outlandish hours of the morning, eerily exhilarated to be excavating each other's assumptions and assailing each other's ideologies. We would have had to set parabolic microphones along the trails to pick up some of the most probing elaboration of our differences.

I recall all this because, for me, one of the most suggestive moments of our meetings occurred during the first day's breakfast. I no longer remember whether that was the one with the waffles, but I do know that I was talking with Robert Cairns. We were probably casting about for common ground. In any case, he told me of a time he had tried his hand at a kind of history. He had taken up the trajectory of American psychology since World War II, or at least of a number of its major movements.

Cairns had been struck by the way every one of them had followed the same developmental dynamic. There was, first, the flush of excitement over the invigorating new notion – the authoritarian personality, social reinforcement, achievement motivation – and the rush to replicate, elaborate, and apply the catalyzing concept empirically. There was, then, the onset of criticism, counterevidence, and ideologically tinged antagonism. And there was, finally, the essential abandonment of the entire enterprise as partisans began repeating themselves and as others wearied of the unsettled and apparently unsettlable state of affairs. But he

230

had been struck even more forcibly by something beyond these intriguing morphological symmetries. Each of these leading lines of inquiry had generated a profusion of research that did not in fact amount to the morass of competing and irresolvable claims that psychologists took to justify dismissal of the entire investigation. Each had led, instead, to a clear answer to the question that had initially instigated the research, a clear resolution of the puzzlement that had prompted the first formulation. The answer had simply not been one that the psychologists wanted to hear.

The answer was, if I understood Bob right, that the promise of the original theory – the promise of straightforward comprehension and control – had been fulfilled. Subsequent research had revealed, in every case, that things were more complicated than that. People were subjects as well as objects and ornery, inconsistent subjects at that. They could be rigid in one realm and open-minded in another. They made meaning out of the forces impinging on them, and they made choices among those forces. Their responses to phenomena were mediated, not direct, and situation-specific, not invariant. In effect, psychologists had learned – and did not want to know – what many historians take for granted and indeed know in their bones: that human behavior is invincibly contingent and that social action is crucially conditioned by context.

I know that I should welcome these affirmations and expressions. I know that it is bizarre to bite one of the few behavioral scientific hands that is feeding us or, at any rate, offering to sit down at the same table with us.

But the invocations of context that I heard often made me queasy. All too commonly, the call for context meant merely an appeal for the provision of a prologue. The historian could moderate the immensity of the issue at hand. He could show, as Ross Parke once put it, that the past was not as bad as we thought, and the present not as good. She could reassure, as others sometimes ask us to reassure, that the present is rotten but the past was rotten too, and we survived that, so maybe we will muddle through this. Or, in a somewhat different vein, the historian could serve a therapeutic function or perhaps a political one. As Ruth Striegel-Moore suggested, awareness of historical context might alleviate aloneness, undo the disconnection from the past that led people to suppose they confronted their dilemmas in terrifying isolation and show them that they could not solve collective problems by individual action.

As a historian, I bristle a bit at being assigned such roles, because I cannot escape the suspicion that, after everyone applauds the provision of context, they then move on to the meat of the matter, the contemporary data, over which the developmentalist – or the economist or clinician or politician – presides. Almost invariably, in interdisciplinary affairs, the historians serve as opening speakers. Almost as invariably thereafter, their contributions recede into insignificance as the debate develops over issues of current consequence.

This eclipse testifies, I think, to the essential triviality of such conceptions of context. History that does not even inform, let alone transform, the colloquy that ensues is history that does not require historians, except for their ritual authority. As Ross Parke conceded of his collaboration with Peter Stearns, he could have pried such background out of the contemporary evidence himself if he had been so inclined. The finding of the historical fragility of the father role is implicit in the very data of our own day, which give rise to the notion of the "new" father role. The discovery of paternal ambivalence is, in Parke's phrase, "data-driven." Stearns specifies the ambivalence over past time with a richness and subtlety that are exemplary, but Parke could have arrived at a rough anticipation of such specification without recourse to any historians or historical evidence at all.

The conventional appreciation of context consigns it to an innocuous bit of the background. Such context neither affects our framing of questions nor alters our expectations of answers. It is continuous with our current understanding of issues and enables us to maintain our present apprehension of our predicaments intact. It establishes the perenniality of contemporary conditions or, at any rate, the irrelevance to action of the ages before things began inexorably to be as they are now. It concedes to others uninformed by historical information or imagination the definition of the situation.

I would implore a historical social science in which considerations of context could challenge our sense of our situation. I would entreat a more active construction of context, in which it actually impinged on our agendas themselves. I would wish a history that was ingredient to our analytic purchase on our problems rather than merely a repository of antecedents and illustrations.

I would not be misunderstood. I am not asking merely that historians collaborate with behavioral scientists, though I would certainly celebrate such collaboration. I am urging an enmeshment of historical study in the social-scientific enterprise that would likely be seriously subversive. I am assuming that, if the historical contribution were authentic, it would endanger the analytic assumptions of the other disciplines and lead to questions and conclusions none had foreseen or even suspected. For history is exactly that inquiry that allows us an intimation of worlds unlike our own, whereas the scientistic premise on which most of the social studies proceed is that social relations today may be safely projected onto the past or extrapolated to other societies.

A history that could truly touch the social and behavioral studies in ways that might matter would be a history far more formative than anything presumed in current conceptions of context. It would be one that might pose persisting queries to haunt the subsequent discourse rather than one that presents comforting prologues to assure colleagues they are on the right track. It would be one that might demand discussion of discontinuities, indicate disconcerting reversals, and illuminate unimagined issues.

The model for family scholars of such a vivifying history is Philippe Ariès's magisterial *Centuries of Childhood* (1962). Ariès may be right and he may be wrong about a myriad of matters large and small – the revisionists have been chipping away at his monumental work for almost a generation now – but empirical adequacy is simply not the salient aspect of his achievement in this regard. His indispensable contribution to the modern study of the family in past time did not depend on his archival range and erudition, remarkable though they were. His energizing influence arose primarily from the power of his transforming perspective. His interpretation allowed us to treat the trajectory of the family over the last half millennium on an estimate other than its own. In an era in which scholars and citizens alike pride themselves on their fond and loving families, Ariès revealed a repressive and surveillant side of bourgeois domesticity that exceeded anything the Middle Ages ever managed. His capacity to reconfigure all the roles in the family constellation and to reconceive those unfamiliar components of that premodern family in an unprecedented wholeness opened intriguing vistas with which we have still to reckon. His ability to redefine the rise of the middle class – his insistence that the family was more nearly a cause than an effect of it, an active element rather than a residual – stimulated a quarter century of research marked by an impressive sense of significance and élan. To this day, Ariès's formulations remain regnant in many realms. But even where they are disputed or discredited, they remain responsible for the realignment of the field within which they are now challenged. An investigation that had previously been in mindless thrall to conventional pieties or to the purely putative imbecilities of Parsonian schema became an exhilarating quest exhibiting the conceptual and empirical ingenuity requisite to meeting the master at his own level of intelligence and insight.

We certainly had no overarching theorizations of Arièstian magnitude in our midst at Belmont, but we did have a host of intimations of the issues that might be illuminated if not reconceived in a more expansive historical perspective. In our consideration of the analysis of fatherhood advanced by Parke and Stearns, for instance, we transposed the terms of their treatment of paternal ambivalence to an array of other patterns. We wondered whether playfulness might be seen as more than just an ambiguous attitude of fathers, expressive of emergent possibilities of engagement and escapism, whose antecedents could be tracked. We saw it also as a behavior with a history in its own right. It did not develop in isolation in the dealings of parents and progeny. In truth, its familial manifestations were mere episodes in much more comprehensive cultural movements that eventuated in a tense acceptance of recreation, leisure, and sensual gratification. On just that account, playfulness was bound to be equivocal when it touched a puritanical tradition, and playful parenting was found to be problematic, conflicted, and richly revealing.

Similarly, we wondered whether the unprecedented remoteness of nineteenth-century fathers from their families might be connected to the unparalleled ascendancy of competitiveness as the mode of male relations in that era. As one study of recollections of boyhood found, successful men of the Victorian age scarcely bothered to muffle their animosity toward their fathers (Murphey, 1965). If such open antagonism strained relations around the hearth, fathers may well have withdrawn from their accustomed participation in the upbringing of the young (and the young could then be seen as agents in the evolution of the nineteenth-century family, not just developmental outcomes of it).

Of course, we simply wondered. Extensive empirical study would be necessary to carry our speculations to any larger consequence. But such substantive study, under such auspices, would seek the sort of context that could condition the design of an endeavor rather than simply sketching its background or providing its introduction. And such an endeavor would be able to take an honest account of Leslie P. Hartley's admonition (1953, p. 9) that "the past is a foreign country: they do things differently there."

But I go on too long in these ruminations and recriminations. It is time to make clear that I mean by them no unique rebuke to the psychologists. It is time to confess that, throughout our sessions, I felt at least a comparable queasiness about my own rhetoric and the rhetoric of my fellow historians. If calls for historical context were crucial to the collaboration for the behavioral scientists, appeals for information on developmental outcomes were equally on our lips. I think that, at one point or another, almost every one of the historians at Belmont begged the assumptive expertise of the psychologists on the probable consequences of particular patterns of socialization. Only Peter Stearns managed to maintain a steady sense that outcomes are only one part of wider processes of change that ought really to constitute our quest.

In any case, I suspect that the historians' eagerness for predictable outcomes of antecedent actions is as fondly foolish and condescending as the developmentalists' avidity for context. Indeed, I suspect that, if the developmentalists could anticipate outcomes as fluently as the historians often seemed to believe they could, they would not even have bothered to meet with the historians as they did at Belmont (see, e.g., Kagan, 1984, and Skolnick, 1975).

I do not wish to dichotomize developmentalists and historians unduly. I do not discount the testimony of John Modell and Robert Siegler that in their research and writing they experienced a pervasive reversal of the stereotypical roles. I certainly do not dismiss the evidence of my own eyes and ears, that again and again in our meetings psychologists were sensitive to the significance of specific settings and historians impetuous to overgeneralize in ways we associate with the theoretical scientific enterprise.

Yet I do think there remain real differences. I do believe that, if we are going to carry through our declared concern for context, there remain real difficulties. And I do feel that, at this point, these dilemmas confront the developmentalists disproportionately.

I would ask the developmentalists the very questions that were implicit in my conversation with Robert Cairns. Do developmentalists really want to know? Are they actually ready to deal with what they say they are? Can they truly abandon the positivist presumption of homogeneity and give up the positivist goal of universality? Can they authentically accept radical contingency and indeterminacy and come to terms with situation-specific particularity? Will they dispense with the control of the data, which is, as William Kessen observes, very nearly definitive of disciplinary propriety? Are they about to quit the quest for unchanging childhood in which their field was founded? Do they suppose they can surrender the conviction that the child is, in the apt image of Sheldon White and Emily Cahan, a natural kind rather than a social and historical kind? What will they tell the governor of North Carolina when he wants indicators, predictions, and early identifications?

Some answers to such questions suggested themselves in the course of the conference, and they were intriguingly at odds with the ones that may suggest themselves in these essays. There is, for example, a tantalizing discrepancy between White and Cahan's sophisticated skepticism here and White's endearingly frank confession during our discussions that he was not about to embrace the postpositivist conclusions toward which his piece seemed to tend. There is an analogous discrepancy between Glen Elder's evident eagerness to dig in the gritty specificities of historical sources and his unabashed determination, explicit in our exchanges, to discover the generic effects of wartime experience on the formation of character. And there were still more symptomatic expressions of Elder's deep commitment to the pursuit of lawlike predications – and of the costs and complications of that pursuit – in comments that emerged in our conversations at Belmont and are not even hinted here.

I recall a couple of remarks on Steven Schlossman's study that noted with satisfaction the link his data demonstrated between delinquency and broken homes. The remarks were revealing because, at least as I read Schlossman's evidence, it exhibits no such nexus. Delinquent males were far more likely than errant females to come from intact homes, yet males were still much more prone to brushes with the law than females. These adolescent offenders did have fathers or father figures, yet still they strayed. Schlossman's findings indicate some fascinating departures from conventional interpretations of the sources of delinquency. But the developmentalists could not credit the possibility that the past might truly be a foreign place. They assumed that they already knew the regularities that would order the data. They relied on those accustomed constancies so implicitly that they simply did not see the discrepant evidence before their eyes. They did not see because they took the historical record as replicative rather than recalcitrant.

I do not mean for a moment to suggest that historians did not similarly succumb to conceits of conventional wisdom. I certainly do not mean to say that historians are not positivists by disposition too. Most of them are, personally. I merely mean to insist that the impersonal, implicit logic of historical study points away from positivism, even if most historians resist that implication.

The inherent logic of historical inquiry – the fire with which developmentalists must play if they would consort seriously with history – is one that revels in relativity, compensation, and contradiction. Its materials are always imperfect, its angles of vision always embattled, and its finding always polyvalent if not perverse. Immersion in its ambiguities has a way of making its students ornery, ironic, or both.

There is a story at once apocryphal and canonical among anthropologists, about a crusty old ethnologist who had spent a lifetime in fieldwork among members of a tribe in Bongo Bongo. Now and then he would return from the field to attend a professional meeting. He would listen to the papers of the most prestigious theorists and absorb their most sophisticated generalizations. Then he would rise diffidently during discussion and gently observe, "Not in Bongo Bongo."

Historians are a lot like that earnest ethnologist. They also rejoice in an intimacy with their subject and glory in an attentiveness to intricate detail that moves them to contest deft designs of imaginative reductionism. Much as their more scientifically ambitious colleagues in the social and behavioral studies know too little, they know too much.

Even when the excess of information seems merely to make them cantankerous, historians of this bent may have their uses. Take their reaction to Joan Jacobs Brumberg's illuminating connection of contemporary anorexia to the many strands of modern American culture that make women chary of food and indeed of carnal appetite more generally. The skeptics conceded the inhibition of sexuality, the unease about hedonic release, the pursuit of a painful thinness, and the equation of morality with minimal eating that Brumberg sees so keenly impinging on young women in our time. They only urged that a ceaseless stimulation of sensuality, a relentless celebration of bosomy beauty, and a veritable obsession with sybaritic eating also afflict adolescent females today. And their insistence on such contrarieties was not meant to discredit Brumberg's substantive reading of our society and its values so much as to suggest another conception of culture itself than the one within which she interpreted anorexia. Their invocation of competing norms and values coexistent in the culture was meant to intimate a more conflicted and less holistic understanding of culture than Brumberg presupposes. On this alternative understanding, modern American culture is simply not sufficiently integrated to allow an investigator to predicate the pattern of the culture from a single strand of evidence.

Infatuation with excessive information may also carry us beyond cantankerousness to curiosities more truly vivifying. It may not only alert us to the hidden assumptions on which inquiry presently proceeds but also push us to pursue entirely different lines of inquiry. Take the essays here that treat questions of success and failure in fathering and family life. Though several of them span a century and more, or range over varied ethnic and class configurations, they still measure success and failure by contemporary cosmopolitan standards. They assess the efficacy of fathers and families in promoting the personal development of children. But few fathers and families in former centuries, or in the working classes, or in most ethnic communities, understood their obligations to their offspring in such terms. Few of them took nurturance of unique individuality in the young as a task at all before the eighteenth century, and few fathers accepted such an assignment even in the nineteenth and indeed well into the twentieth century.

The developmental definition of familial and paternal success and failure is anachronistic for those vast majorities of men and women in the past who conceived their responsibilities to their children in terms of provision for their economic futures. And insistence on such anachronism is more than mere antiquarian punctiliousness. It opens out very different vistas of analysis. It makes problematic rather than inevitable and altogether natural the consignment to mothers of the cultivation of youthful character in the nineteenth century. It makes problematic rather than progressive and altogether commendable the reassignment to fathers of a share of such cultivation in our own time. And it forces us to focus on the very concern for the advancement of their children's careers that contemporary fathers and families now essentially abdicate to schools and other formal institutions.

Once we recognize the career-fostering functions of fathers and families in past time, we realize that they are instances of something more than the mere coexistences and incoherences evident in the cultural context of adolescent eating. We begin to glimpse possibilities of deeper relatedness among apparently disparate behaviors. Once we appreciate the contraction as well as the expansion of parental preoccupations in our own time, we see that they are cases of a closer connectedness than anything apparent in the welter of incompatible injunctions about appetite that engulf young women today. We begin to move beyond simplistic formulations of linear succession to far more tantalizing ones of substitution and complementarity.

But if these richer and more empirically adequate formulations reveal advantages in an extravagant amassment of information, they also betray inconveniences implicit in such particularism. Or at least they betray inconveniences for all who are not, like historians, connoisseurs of contradiction and partisans of paradox.

Because they commit themselves to the comprehension of experience in terms close to its inherent complexity, historians entangle themselves incessantly in Gordian knots of analysis and interpretation. Because they expect erratic if not eccentric behavior, they do not, like the legendary Alexander, cut through such skeins with slashing schematic strokes. Perhaps they lack the bold instinct of the ancient Macedonian. Perhaps they are insufficiently eager for the worldly dominion that the oracle promised. Whatever the explanation, they follow their calling in a manner more Sisyphusian than Alexandrian. They try patiently to encompass the inconstancies and to unravel the perplexities of social action. And increasingly they compound complexity by trying to take into account the experience of those whom their predecessors scarcely considered historical actors at all.

Where historians once confined their concern to men at the pinnacle of the political system, they now listen to the inarticulate, define the personal as political or deny the very primacy of the political, and seek to study their subject from the bottom up. Their ascendant ethos of attention to the entire population has created in the house of history a myriad of new mansions, not least among them the new history of the family. It has occasioned a broad-based and often brilliant effort to reclaim the experience of women and a substantial though still infant endeavor to retrieve the experience of children. And the more that is recovered, the more difficult it becomes to escape skepticism that women and children see the world as men do or even in some significant senses inhabit the same world that men do.

Some striking sociological research of recent years has made unmistakable that, in family interactions, there are no privileged observers or points of observation. As often as not, fathers and mothers maintain divergent views of affairs in which they were both involved. As often as not, though they are less often asked, children hold still other understandings of the same episodes (see, e.g., Bernard, 1972, and Furstenberg, 1988).

During our discussions at Belmont, Sheldon White suggested that we think of six psychologists in search of an authentic subject. He imagined them for us, circling round the child, each with pencil and pad, administering different tests, adducing different data, marking and measuring different realities. And the dilemmas of positivism and perspectivism that he caught in that conceit are real enough. There are more than enough distinct developmental theories to supply six psychologists, and there are historical, anthropological, and sociological theories besides. Each of them registers elements of experience that others of them do not emphasize or acknowledge. Each of them posits priorities of observation and explanation that others of them do not. And each can do so because, as White and Cahan insist, "no one can define one super-authentic milieu for the child." All of them have their partial validities; all of them offer their own particular insights. There are no obvious ways of preferring one to another.

Distinctive as they are, though, all the theories White envisioned still share an overarching attachment to approaches that accord ultimate authority to the psychologists with their clipboards and their theories. Anthropologists call all such approaches *etic,* in contrast to others that they characterize as *emic.* Etic approaches privilege the standpoint of the objectifying outsider and the presumption that the individual is not necessarily the best judge of his own behavior. For all their formidable apparatus of coding and calculating, they still divide but one side of the methodological universe. On the other side, emic outlooks start from the standpoint of the subject and oblige the investigator to accommodate the subject's own apprehension of her conduct and condition.

The new historical scholarship on the family, which "discovers" the salience of women and children and seeks out the diverse definitions of the situation that diverse participants held, relativizes the emic realm as radically as White's Pirandellian figure relativizes the etic. We can no more decide rationally whose views to prefer among the new panoply of subjects –the father's? the mother's? the child's? (which child's?) – than we can determine definitively whose theories to embrace among the six psychologists.

Yet we must make choices if we are to proceed with inquiry at all. When the directives of one theory depart from those of another, we must decide which directives to adopt. When the rendition of one family member flies in the face of that of another, we must decide whom to believe or how to reconcile their discordant renditions. We can hardly do the most elementary empirical work, let alone the more exotic theoretical exercise, if we do not address these questions of competing realities, or at least of competing conceptions of reality and competing claims on reality.

Operating as they have on notions of the child as a natural kind and notions of themselves as natural scientists studying the predictable processes of that natural kind, developmentalists have been disinclined to struggle with portents of the relativity they are nonetheless fated to face. In that aversion, they have been at one with the larger community of psychologists that Robert Cairns found turning away again and again from theories that did not yield unequivocal conceptual consensus. But historians have always endured and indeed accepted acrimonious disputation and irreconcilable antagonism. Our extended experience with such symptoms of the epistemological specter that now haunts all the social sciences doubtless conditions our receptivity to the proliferation of perspectives that attended the emergence of the new social history. Our unfading familiarity with the antecedents and consequences of that ineluctable relativity is what finally draws the developmentalists to us, I suspect, even if they prefer to believe that it is the "historical perspective" we can provide.

Of course, only a few historians have gone so far as to say, with such great historians as Carl Becker (1935, 1955) and Charles Beard (1934, 1935), that objectivity is only a noble dream, that the writing of history is irresistibly affected by the situation of the writer, and that, therefore, every person must be his or her own historian. But most of us wrestle routinely with the patent politicization of our sources and of the secondary literature as well. Most of us strive steadily to situate ourselves amid the incessant revisionism that marks our discipline. Most of us understand, if only dimly, that we deal with competing accounts of the past and that, necessarily, we work politically and imaginatively when we try to fit such accounts together or adjudicate among them. Most of us grasp, if only darkly, in the dire imperatives of our own practice, that much of this colligation must be speculative and all of it, in one way or another, expressive.

We reconcile ourselves to the roles of observers and ironists of the human comedy because we are aware that our speculations are, in the end, flights of our own personally and politically charged fancies. We recognize that we cannot pronounce reliable regularities on which to base predictions because we cannot countermand the inexorable contingency of the human condition. We realize that we cannot, consequently, devote ourselves to the procurement of power or even lend ourselves, conscientiously, to the service of the government. I wonder if the developmentalists can live with us – or live without us.

11   Epilogue: An emerging framework for dialogue between history and developmental psychology

Glen H. Elder, Jr., John Modell, and Ross D. Parke

This volume is a testimonial to cross-disciplinary dialogue as a potentially useful and rewarding intellectual exercise. In this epilogue, we briefly explore the implicit models of collaboration in this initial joint enterprise between social history and developmental psychology. Through omission and demonstration, the models suggest other possible forms of collaborative effort that could prove fruitful in the future.

These final remarks assume that cross-disciplinary dialogue is bi-directional in nature and that successful and sustained collaboration will become a reality only to the extent that the disciplines involved recognize its mutual benefits. If this cross-disciplinary enterprise is to succeed, a deeper understanding of the potential contributions of both disciplines needs to be achieved. Clearly, developmentalists should heed Zuckerman's observation that "the call for context meant merely an appeal for the provision of a prologue" and accept a richer definition of the meaning of historical context.

Redefinition of contextual variation would alter the framing of our questions and our expectations of answers – to paraphrase Zuckerman's astute call. As the positivistic legacy of the social sciences, including developmental psychology, begins to crumble (Sameroff, 1989), the door is open to a redefinition of contextual variation, although we are not sure whether the exploration will or can go as far as Zuckerman might hope. Similarly, receptivity to a wider range of theoretical frameworks beyond psychoanalysis is beginning to gain ground among historians. This development should enlarge the potential role that contemporary human-development models can play in interpreting historical data. In short, changes in both disciplines have increased the feasibility and perceived utility of cross-disciplinary dialogue and collaboration.

241

Central themes

Three central themes or implicit models have emerged in this volume demonstrating how history and developmental psychology connect. The first theme, an *institutional model,* specifies some form of social change and its links to children's lives, behaviors, and belief systems. A second theme takes the form of a *cultural model* that traces cultural change and continuity to children's lives and behavior. In our third guiding theme, a *historical time model* is used in research comparing processes at different points in historical time. Does the process generalize beyond a specific time and place? If so, what are the boundaries?

Institutional model

Changes in institutions across time offer promising collaborative opportunities. Traditionally, these shifts have been the "stuff" of history as well as of sociology. Explorations of the economic, political, and social causes and consequences of these changes in societal institutions have been the main focus of historians.

Much less attention has been given to the impact of these changes on children's lives and developmental course. Nor have developmental psychologists commonly recognized the potential value of unplanned institutional changes for evaluating theories of how children respond to change and thus for gaining a better understanding of developmental processes. Historical shifts in institutions represent important and powerful natural experiments that often permit the testing of theories and models under conditions that are much more dramatic than those that developmental scientists could either engineer or produce, ethically or practically, in the laboratory or in field.

Several essays vividly illustrate the mutual benefits that flow from a collaborative and interdisciplinary focus on the impact of institutional change. Elder and Hareven explore, as does Tuttle, the implications for children and adults of mobilization for war. Tuttle shows us how children's development may be modified by the manifold shifts in family organization associated with wartime, including father absence, maternal employment, and increased use of day-care. And Elder and Hareven demonstrate that institutional shifts, such as those resulting from war mobilization, can affect not only child but also adult developmental trajectories. Their experience of serving in the military had a profound impact on the later lives of young soldiers. Moreover, their earlier childhood experiences were clearly modified by events later in their lives – a reminder that plasticity in development occurs at a variety of points across the life span.

Implicit in these essays is the lingering question of how these same developmental or historical events would be experienced in different eras, with their different institutions. For example, do children experience day-care or father absence differently during peacetime than during wartime? How has the shift toward a voluntary army altered the impact of these experiences for both children and adults? Presumably, the planning that could precede military service in a voluntary army would ameliorate some of the adverse effects that may accrue from conscription. This question could profitably be pursued by historians and developmentalists, and it represents only one instance of how institutional change generates an array of questions of interest to scholars from both disciplines.

Changes across time have occurred in institutions such as the court system as Schlossman and Cairns illustrate. The courts enforced female sexual morality in the 1940s and 1950s, but by the 1980s young women were rarely being arrested for "immoral" behavior. Family, school, and social service agencies play a more prominent role in the current era in regulating female sexual behavior than they did in the 1940s. What do such shifts in responsibility across institutions mean for children's behavior patterns, beliefs, and values, and, more generally, for their developmental trajectories? Would awareness of shifting institutional regulatory roles across time aid our understanding of teenage sexuality or of the presumed epidemic of teenage pregnancy in recent decades (Vinovskis, 1988)? Although the subject of the Schlossman and Cairns essay is deviance, this focus should obscure neither the larger cultural context in which the institutions and children's life courses are set nor the broad implications of their inquiry into the interplay of institutional and developmental change.

Cultural model

From the perspective of the cultural model, historians and developmentalists examine how cultural change and continuity are linked to personal and social interpretations of the self and of others. Although historians often focus on culture, they seldom relate shifts at this level of analysis to individual development. Similarly, developmentalists tend to focus on individual development and generally ignore how culture shapes individual lives. (For recent exceptions to this observation, see Rogoff, 1990, and Valsiner, 1989). Because historians often study culture undergoing change, but lack individual levels for how evolving cultural patterns come to be incorporated in individuals' beliefs and behaviors, collaboration at this point is particularly needed and potentially fruitful.

The value of collaboration on culturally based models is illustrated by Brumberg and Striegel-Moore. For example, they depict how shifts over the last century in the cultural meanings of food and eating shaped the explanations for eating disorders as well as the role played by food in defining female identity in the different eras. Their collaboration reveals the value of a culturally sensitive approach for our understanding of the interplay of biology, identity formation, and medical practice. The cultural shaping of these processes is revealed through cross-time comparison.

Male as well as female roles are culturally defined, as revealed by Parke and Stearns. Each historical period provides a unique cultural expectation or ideal of the level of father involvement with their children and the form that it should take, which, in turn, may distort actual behavior patterns. The value of the collaborative effort is evidenced by the corrective stance of the essay, which suggests that modern conceptions of fatherhood have their roots in the past. By a focus on these historical antecedents, some contemporary views of father behavior as the product of conflicting tendencies toward either greater involvement or withdrawal can be better understood. Together the essays by Brumberg and Striegel-Moore and Parke and Stearns underscore how a cultural level of analysis as revealed in different historical eras can sharpen our insights into how culture shapes individual roles.

Historical time model

Our third model represents another approach to the study of links between history and developmental psychology. This perspective compares the processes operating at different points in historical time to assess the degree of cross-time generalizability. In a sense, it treats historical eras as experimental replications to determine if the same set of explanatory processes is applicable during the different periods.

For example, studies of children and families in the Great Depression (Elder, 1974) yielded insights concerning how parent and children cope with stressful change and are influenced by it. Do these findings have relevance to an understanding of family coping adaptation and individual development in other historical eras? Application of the same model to a contemporary situation that rivals the earlier depression experience, namely, the massive loss of jobs in the farming sector of the economy in the 1980s, has recently permitted a cross-time test of the generality of the underlying processes (Conger et al., 1990). Other replications have been reported by students of the unemployed and family life in urban America in the 1980s (Liem & Liem, 1990). Findings indicate a high degree of similarity across time in terms of the processes that account for familial patterns of coping with this type of upheaval.

Similar comparisons could usefully be made for other types of events in other eras. That social historians and developmentalists will not identify processes as "the same" according to the same criteria – historians being far more reluctant to identify them in these terms than developmentalists – may restrict closure for the collaboration, but it should also ensure fruitful challenge and clarification for both disciplines. Historical comparisons, in short, provide opportunities for testing the boundary conditions of our theories of development. At the same time, developmental science offers new analytic tools for understanding the impact on the individual of important historical events and transformations.

Psychological contributions to historical analyses

A major insight gained from our collaborative enterprise came from greater understanding of the implicit psychological models historians have typically employed in their analyses. To a large extent, classic psychoanalytic theory has served as the guiding framework historians use in their application of psychological principles to historical events and outcomes. Ironically, this same psychoanalytic framework is viewed by contemporary developmental scholars as relatively unimportant. The theory is viewed as an influential *early* contribution to the history of psychological theory, but because of its limited value for generating testable hypotheses and the scant empirical support for its basic tenets, the theory has little value in contemporary psychological inquiry.

In contrast, several alternative current theoretical perspectives are of potential value to historians, including a life-course perspective and an ecological framework. In view of the central interest of historians in the social-contextual features of individuals, families, and groups, these viewpoints would seem to hold the most promise as alternative or complementary frameworks for understanding the psychological aspects of historical times and changes.

According to Elder (1984),

the life course approach sensitizes family research to four temporal themes: (1) the interlocking life courses of family members; (2) the interplay between family units and members on matters of development and life chances, obligations and rights; (3) the interdependence of family, individual and social change; and (4) causal relations between early and later events and roles over the life span. (p. 128)

This framework has been successfully used by several historians (Hareven, 1984; Modell, 1989) and sociologists (Elder, 1984, 1987a) as well as by developmental psychologists (Hetherington & Baltes, 1988).

Bronfenbrenner's ecological approach to human development (1979, 1986, 1989) offers a related framework of potential value to historians. It strengthens the importance of understanding the relationship between the organism and various environmental systems such as the family and the community. According to this perspective, the developing child's environment represents "a set of nested structures." Bronfenbrenner proposes four layers or contexts, ranging from the most immediate settings, such as the family or peer group, to the more remote contexts in which the child is not directly involved, such as local government.

The importance of this ecological scheme stems from Bronfenbrenner's stress on the importance of analyzing relationships between the child and a variety of environmental systems as well as relationships among these systems. In addition, the ecology of the child is never static; instead, development involves the interaction of a changing child with a changing matrix of ecological systems. This framework provides historians a set of tools for describing the impact of shifts in the nature of the environmental organization for children and families in different historical periods.

Other psychological theories that may be of value to historians include ethological (Hinde, 1989), social learning (Bandura, 1989), sociobiological (MacDonald, 1988), and family systems (Belsky & Volling, 1987; Reiss, 1981) approaches. Each of these modern theories offers new analytic tools for understanding the nature of development in different historical periods.

Historical contributions to developmental psychology

In recent years, a variety of subdisciplines within psychology have raised serious questions concerning the extent to which psychological theories are time-bound rather than universal or time independent. The most notable example involves social psychology, where a number of theories (e.g., Gergen 1973; McGuire, 1976) have raised questions concerning the assumed ahistorical nature of our theories of human behavior. In turn, these theorists have called for a serious examination of how our social-psychological theories have themselves been shaped by particular historical conditions.

Recently, child developmental psychologists (e.g., Kessen, 1979, 1983) as well as life-span theorists (e.g., Hetherington & Baltes, 1988) and cross-cultural theorists (Rogoff, 1990) have called for a similar examination of the implicit assumption of universality in our theories of development. Instead of assuming a priori that our theories of development are, in fact, universally applicable and relevant to a range of historical periods, it is suggested that this assumption be submitted to empirical scrutiny. Doing so involves several tasks, including the examination of the adequacy of our *current* theories for explaining human development in earlier historical periods. At the same time, this endeavor provides the opportunity to evaluate the generality of our theories by examining their value for explaining behavior under different historical circumstances. (One of the major obstacles in this area is to discern the level of generality or specificity at which the theoretical accidents operate.)

The process involves a description of the social, economic, and political circumstances that may have conditioned the theoretical accounts of development in different historical periods. Although there have been several accounts of the history of changes in formal developmental theories over the last century (e.g.,

R. B. Cairns, 1983; R. B. Cairns & Ornstein, 1979), these reviews do not seek to explain the interplay between the historical circumstances in social, political, and economic arenas and the emergence of particular theoretical explanations of development. Again, several exceptions can be noted, especially Sulloway's (1978) treatment of Freud. Moreover, few theories explicitly recognize the interdependence between secular conditions and the nature of scientific theory. The theory of Vygotsky (1962) is one example of how theories of development are shaped by the sociopolitical context.

Do our folk theories change across time? Do the common expectations, beliefs, and explanations that lay people hold about development shift across time? Implicit in this question is a recognition that childhood, and beliefs or ideas about the nature of development, is itself a cultural construction or, in Kessen's (1979, 1983) view, a cultural invention. Each historical period, with its unique social, economic, political, and philosophical orientations, is likely in turn to define the era of childhood differently and the attributes associated with this life-style in period-specific fashion. Just as we are increasingly aware of the nonuniversal nature of development and recognize the variability in agenda for children in different contemporary cultures, we recognize the same differences across historical time.

Toward a new interdisciplinary research agenda

Developmentalists are beginning to generate a rich research agenda with methods and vocabulary that is guiding the search for an understanding of adults' "ideas" (Goodnow & Collins, 1990) about childhood and development. At the same time, historians (e.g., Ariès, 1962) have been actively exploring the ways in which our construction of childhood as a stage has evolved across time. Historians can provide the "data" for a dialogue about this issue of how childhood as a stage of development has evolved and how adults conceptualized the goals and values associated with the rearing of children in different historical periods. Developmentalists, on the other hand, have theories that permit a more explicit framing of the issues.

A wide variety of questions that can help frame the historical inquiry is currently posed. One set of issues concerns the boundary conditions of the stage of *childhood* itself. What age periods are covered by the term, and how differentiated in terms of stages or separate periods are childhood and adolescence?

A second set of issues concerns the "norms" or expectations about development. At what ages are different skills or competencies assumed to emerge? This is the agenda of developmental timetables research (e.g., Goodnow, 1984; Miller, 1988). Do these skills emerge in a predetermined order?

A third set of issues concerns the presumed determinants of or relevant influences on development. Different periods have made quite different assumptions about the role of heredity versus the role of environment, the degree of plasticity across development, and the importance of early experience.

A fourth set of concerns focuses on the end goals of development. What kinds of children do different interested groups and parties in different historical periods hope to produce? This inquiry represents the issue of social values and provides a window on how different categories of adults think about the kind of society for which they are preparing their children. It should be recognized, however, that there is often disagreement among different groups in a society, based on political, economic, or social-class interests and ideologies, concerning the correct or desired end goals of child development. To assume that a *single* set of goals will adequately capture any historical period is probably to oversimplify. Instead, the research aim ought to be to describe the multiple goals that reflect the values of competing groups in a society.

A fifth issue focuses on beliefs or ideas about the roles played by different individuals in society in fulfilling the developmental agenda. How do parents function relative to extended kin? What role do institutions such as schools, courts, and churches play in the process? Do within-family roles differ, that is, do mothers and fathers assume responsibility for different aspects of development?

Adult perspectives are not the only vantage point from which to consider construction of childhood and development. Children themselves construct their own versions of development, as illustrated by developmental research on children's theories of mind (Harris, 1989; Wellman, 1988) as well as by social historical accounts (Modell, 1989). Are children's accounts similar to or different from adult conceptualizations? Do they shift across history? Do historical periods differ in their recognition of the role the child takes as a "constructor" of his or her own development?

These questions about adult and child understanding of development are but a sample of the issues that can be examined from a historical perspective. It is important also to note that variations in everyday theories of development across different historical periods merit examination in their own right, independent of formal or scientific theories of development. It is of interest, of course, to assess the degree of overlap between formal theories and naive or folk theories of development. Shifts in technology, such as occurred with the advent of print and, more recently, with radio and television, clearly alter the potential for media influence and, especially, for the influence of formal or expert views of development on folk views (e.g., Clarke-Stewart, 1978).

This research agenda, beginning with historical periods and determining the ways in which childhood and development are constructed, is largely a historian's enterprise. Granted, developmentalists can assist in providing a vocabulary for the research agenda, but their contribution is limited by their discipline's research style and perhaps by its epistemological preferences. To achieve an account that will benefit developmental researchers, a further step is needed, namely, to assess the impact of these constructions on children's developmental outcomes. This step is rarely taken, but it is important to determine the significance of these variations in construction for the developing child.

How do variations in the construction of childhood and development modify the kinds of experiences that adults provide for the developing child? How are the practices of adults shaped by their beliefs about the nature of development? For example, an adult who assumes that heredity is a predominant influence on development might offer a very different form of environmental stimulation or be less optimistic about the modifiability of behavior than might a staunch environmentalist. Similarly, parents who value independence and competitiveness are likely to behave differently than parents who value obedience, deference, and passivity (Kohn, 1977). There is ample historical evidence that the desired values and goals for children have shifted markedly over the last several centuries (Alwin, 1986; Demos, 1970, 1974). In turn, child outcomes are probably different as well. The next step on this research agenda, then, is to begin to assess the impact of parental beliefs on children's development.

To summarize, we propose a three-step research process. First, the nature of the constructions of adults and children will need to be retrieved from the historical record. Second, the contexts provided for children that flow from these constructions require descriptive work. Third, research should focus on the implications of these environments for children's developmental outcomes. In many ways, this process deepens the agenda undertaken by the contributors in their collaboration.

This deepening represents recognition by both groups, and an embrace by each, of the less-than-determinate nature of the inquiry characteristically undertaken by the other. In pursuing this agenda, we not only deepen our understanding of the nature of development in different historical periods but also provide opportunities to examine potential links between cognition and action across historical time. In addition to leads and hunches about new interdisciplinary collaborations that will advance history and developmental psychology, we hope that this volume provides something of the excitement and discovery experience that work at disciplinary boundaries can generate.

Bibliography

Abraham, S. F., & Beumont, P. J. V. (1982). How patients describe bulimia or binge eating. *Psychological Medicine, 12,* 625–635.

Agras, W. S., & Kraemer, H. C. (1983). The treatment of anorexia nervosa: Do different treatments have different outcomes? *Psychiatric Annals, 13,* 928–929, 932–935.

Albutt, T. C., & Rolleston, H. D. (Eds.). [1905]. *A system of medicine.* Vol. 3. *Diseases of obscure origin. Alimentary canal and peritoneum.* New York: Macmillan.

Alwin, D. F. (1986). From obedience to autonomy: Changes in traits desired in children, 1924–1978. *Public Opinion Quarterly, 52,* 33–52.

American Psychiatric Association. (1987). *Diagnostic and statistical manual of mental disorders: DSM-III-R* (3rd ed., rev.). Washington, DC: Author.

Anastasi, A. (1968). *Psychological testing* (3rd ed.). New York: Macmillan.

Anderson, J. E. (1960). The prediction of adjustment over time. In I. Iscoe & H. W. Stevenson (Eds.), *Personality development in children* (pp. 28–72). Austin: University of Texas Press.

Ariès, P. (1962). *Centuries of childhood: A social history of family life* (R. Baldick, Trans.). New York: Random House.

Attie, I., & Brooks-Gunn, J. (1989). Development of eating problems in adolescent girls: A longitudinal study. *Developmental Psychology, 25,* 70–79.

Ayres, L. P. (1909). *Laggards in our schools: A study of retardation and elimination in city school systems.* New York: Charities Publication Committee.

Bach, G. R. (1946, March–June). Father-fantasies and father-typing in father-separated children. *Child Development, 17,* 63–80.

Baldwin, J. M. (1911). *Thought and things: A study of the development and meaning of thought or genetic logic* (Vol. 4). London: Swann, Sonnenschein; New York: Macmillan.

Bandura, A. (1989). Social cognitive theory. In R. Vasta (Ed.), *Annals of child development* (pp. 1–60). Greenwich, CT: JAI Press.

Banks, J. A., & Banks, O. (1964). *Feminism and family planning in Victorian England.* New York: Schocken.

Barker, R. G. (1968). *Ecological psychology: Concepts and methods for studying the environment of human behavior.* Stanford, CA: Stanford University Press.

Barker, R. G., & Gump, P. V. (1964). *Big school, small school: High school size and student behavior.* Stanford, CA: Stanford University Press.

Barker, R. G., & Wright, H. F. [(1954?)]. *Midwest and its children: The psychological ecology of an American town.* Evanston, IL: Row, Peterson.

Barkow, J. H. (1989). *Darwin, sex, and status: Biological approaches to mind and culture.* Toronto: University of Toronto Press.

Barnes, E. (Ed.). (1896–1897). *Studies in education: A series of ten numbers devoted to child-study and the history of education, 1896–97.* Stanford, CA: Stanford University Press.

Barthes, R. (1975). Toward a psychosociology of contemporary food consumption. In E. Forster & R. Forster (Eds.), *European diets from pre-industrial to modern times* (pp. 47–49). New York: Harper & Row.

Bass, A. (1988, July 11). Researchers debate day care's effect on kids. *Boston Globe*, p. 30.

Baynes, K., Bohman, J., & McCarthy, T. (Eds.). (1987). *After philosophy: End or transformation?* Cambridge, MA: MIT Press.

Beard, C.A. (1934). Written history as an act of faith. *American Historical Review, 39*, 219–229.

    (1935). Notes and suggestions. That noble dream. *American Historical Review, 41*, 74–87.

Becker, C. L. (1935). *Everyman his own historian: Essays on history and politics.* New York: Appleton-Century-Crofts.

    (1955). What are historical facts? *Western Political Quarterly, 8*, 327–340.

Behar, L. (1985). Changing patterns of state responsibility: A case study of North Carolina. *Journal of Clinical Child Psychology, 14*, 188–195.

Belsky, J., & Volling, B. L. (1987). Mothering, fathering, and marital interaction in the family triad during infancy: Exploring family system's processes. In P. W. Berman & F. A. Pedersen (Eds.), *Men's transitions to parenthood: Longitudinal studies of early family experience* (pp. 37–63). Hillsdale, NJ: Erlbaum.

Bender, T. (1986). Whole and parts: The need for synthesis in American history. *Journal of American History, 73*, 120–136.

Berlin, I. (1978). The concept of scientific history. In H. Hardy (Ed.), *Concepts and categories: Philosophical essays* (pp. 103–142). London: Hogarth Press.

Bernard, J. S. (1972). *The future of marriage.* New York: World.

Bernstein, R. J. (1971). *Praxis and action: Contemporary philosophies of human activity.* Philadelphia: University of Pennsylvania Press.

    (1976). *The restructuring of social and political theory.* New York: Harcourt Brace Jovanovich.

    (1983). *Beyond objectivism and relativism: Science, hermeneutics, and praxis.* Philadelphia: University of Pennsylvania Press.

Birch, E. E., Gwiazda, J., & Held, R. (1982). Stereoacuity development for crossed and uncrossed disparities in human infants. *Vision Research, 22*, 507–513.

Bloom, B. S. (1964). *Stability and change in human characteristics.* New York: Wiley.

Boas, F. (1892). The growth of children. *Science, 20*, 351–352.

    (1895). On Dr. William Townsend Porter's investigation of the growth of the school children of St. Louis. *Science, n.s. 1*, 225–230.

Boas, F., & Wissler, C. (1905). Statistics of growth. In U.S. Bureau of Education, *Annual reports of the Department of the Interior for the fiscal year ending June 30, 1904. Report of the Commissioner of Education for 1904* (Vol. 1, pp. 25–132). (58th Cong., 3rd Session, H.R. Doc. No. 5). Washington, DC: U.S. Government Printing Office.

Book, W. F. (1922). *The intelligence of high school seniors as revealed by a statewide mental survey of Indiana high schools.* New York: Macmillan.

Borchert, J. (1980). *Alley life in Washington: Family, community, religion, and folklife in the city, 1850–1970.* Urbana: University of Illinois Press.

Boskind-White, M., & White, W. (1983). *Bulimarexia: The binge/purge cycle.* New York: Norton.

Bossard, J. H. S. (1944). Family backgrounds of wartime adolescents. *Annals of the American Academy of Political and Social Science, 236*, 33–42.

Branca, P. (1975). *Silent sisterhood: Middle-class women in the Victorian home.* Pittsburgh: Carnegie-Mellon University Press.

Brennan, T., Huizinga, D., & Elliott, D. S. (1978). *The social psychology of runaways.* Lexington, MA: Lexington Books.

Bronfenbrenner, U. (1958). Socialization and social class through time and space. In E. E. Maccoby, T. M. Newcomb, & E. L. Hartley (Eds.), *Readings in social psychology* (pp. 400–425). (3rd ed.). New York: Holt.

(1974). The origins of alienation. *Scientific American, 231*(3), 53–57, 60–61.

(1976). A theoretical perspective for research on human development. In A. Skolnick (Ed.), *Rethinking childhood. Perspectives on development and society* (pp. 108–127). Boston: Little, Brown.

(1979). *The ecology of human development: Experiments by nature and design.* Cambridge, MA: Harvard University Press.

(1986). Ecology of the family as a context for human development: Research perspectives. *Developmental Psychology, 22,* 723–742.

(1989). Ecological systems theory. *Annals of Child Development, 6,* 187–249.

Bronfenbrenner, U., & Crouter, A. C. (1983). The evolution of environmental models in developmental research. In P. Mussen (Ed.), *Handbook of child psychology.* Vol. 1. *History, theory, and methods* (pp. 357–414). (4th ed.). New York: Wiley.

Bronfenbrenner, U., Kessel, F., Kessen, W., & White, S. (1986). Toward a critical social history of developmental psychology. A propaedeutic discussion. *American Psychologist, 41,* 1218–1230.

Bronner, S. J. (Ed. & Comp.). (1988). *American children's folklore.* Little Rock, AR: August House.

Brotz, H., & Wilson, E. (1946). Characteristics of military society. *American Journal of Sociology, 51,* 371–375.

Broughton, J. M. (Ed.). (1987). *Critical theories of psychological development.* New York: Plenum Press.

Brumberg, J. J. (1982). "Ruined" girls: Changing community responses to illegitimacy in Upstate New York, 1890–1920. *Journal of Social History, 18,* 147–272.

(1988). *Fasting girls: The emergence of anorexia nervosa as a modern disease.* Cambridge, MA: Harvard University Press.

Bruner, J. S. (1986). *Actual minds, possible worlds.* Cambridge, MA: Harvard University Press.

Burk, F. (1898). Growth of children in height and weight. *American Journal of Psychology, 9,* 253–326.

Byrns, R., & Henmon, V. A. C. (1936). Parental occupation and mental ability. *Journal of Educational Psychology, 27,* 284–291.

Cahan, E. D. (1987). *James Mark Baldwin, John Dewey, and the concept of development.* Unpublished doctoral dissertation, Yale University, New Haven, CT.

Cairns, B. D. (1989). Adolescents at risk: A longitudinal perspective. *Society for Research in Child Development Abstracts, 6,* 408.

Cairns, R. B. (1979). *Social development: The origins and plasticity of interchanges.* San Francisco: Freeman.

(1983). The emergence of developmental psychology. In P. Mussen (Ed.), *Handbook of child psychology.* Vol. 1. *History, theory, and methods* (pp. 41–102). (4th ed.). New York: Wiley.

Cairns, R. B., Cairns, B. D., & Neckerman, H. J. (1989a). Early school dropout: Configurations and determinants. *Child Development, 60,* 1437–1452.

Cairns, R. B., Cairns, B. D., Neckerman, H. J., Ferguson, L. L., & Gariépy, J.-L. (1989b). Growth and aggression: I. Childhood to early adolescence. *Developmental Psychology, 25,* 320–330.

Cairns, R. B., Cairns, B. D., Neckerman, H. J., Gest, S. D., & Gariépy, J.-L. (1988). Social networks and aggressive behavior: Peer support or peer rejection? *Developmental Psychology, 24,* 815–823.

Cairns, R. B., & Ornstein, P. A. (1979). Developmental psychology. In E. Hearst (Ed.), *The first century of experimental psychology* (pp. 495–510). Hillsdale, NJ: Erlbaum.

Cairns, R. B., Peterson, G., & Neckerman, H. J. (1988). Suicidal behavior in aggressive adolescents. *Journal of Clinical Child Psychology, 17,* 298–309.

Calhoun, D. H. (1973). *Intelligence of a people.* Princeton, N.J.: Princeton University Press.

Campbell, D. (1984). *Women at war with America: Private lives in a patriotic era.* Cambridge, MA: Harvard University Press.

Campbell, D. T. (1965). Variation and selective retention in socio-cultural evolution. In H. R.

Barringer, G. I. Blanksten, & R. W. Mack (Eds.), *Social change in developing areas. A reinterpretation of evolutionary theory* (pp. 19–49). Cambridge, MA: Schenkman.

(1969). Reforms as experiments. *American Psychologist, 24,* 409–429.

Caplow, T., Bahr, H. M., Chadwick, B. A., Hill, R., & Williamson, M. H. (1982). *Middletown families: Fifty years of change and continuity.* Minneapolis: University of Minnesota Press.

Caplow, T., & Chadwick, B. A. (1979). Inequalities and life-styles in Middletown, 1920–1978. *Social Science Quarterly, 60,* 367–386.

Carlsmith, L. (1964). Effect of early father absence on scholastic aptitude. *Harvard Educational Review, 34,* 3–21.

Carnoy, M., & Levin, H. M. (1985). *Schooling and work in the democratic state.* Stanford, CA: Stanford University Press.

Carter, H., & Glick, P. C. (1976). *Marriage and divorce: A social and economic study* (rev. ed.). Cambridge, MA: Harvard University Press.

Cash, T. F., Winstead, B. A., & Janda, L. H. (1986, April). The great American shape-up. *Psychology Today, 20,* 30–37.

Caspi, A. (1989). *Mate selection, marital relations, and developmental change.* Working paper, Harvard University, Department of Psychology, Cambridge, MA.

Cattell, R. A. (1950). The fate of national intelligence: Test of a thirteen-year prediction. *Eugenics Review, 42,* 136–148.

Caughey, J. L. (1984). *Imaginary social worlds: A cultural approach.* Lincoln: University of Nebraska Press.

Cavallo, D. (1981). *Muscles and morals: Organized playgrounds and urban reform, 1880–1920.* Philadelphia: University of Pennsylvania Press.

Cavan, R. S. (1953). *The American family.* New York: Crowell.

Chafe, W. H. (1972). *The American woman: Her changing social, economic, and political roles, 1920–1970.* New York: Oxford University Press.

Chall, J. S. (1979). The great debate: Ten years later, with a modes proposal for reading stages. In L. B. Resnick & P. A. Weaver (Eds.), *Theory and practice of early reading* (Vol. 1, pp. 29–55). Hillsdale, NJ: Erlbaum.

Chandler, J. (1981). Camping for life: Transmission of values at a girls' summer camp. In R. T. Sieber & A. J. Gordon (Eds.), *Children and their organizations: Investigations in American culture* (pp. 122–137). Boston: Hall.

Chernin, K. (1981). *The obsession: Reflections on the tyranny of slenderness.* New York: Harper & Row.

Chodorow, N. (1978). *The reproduction of mothering: Psychoanalysis and the sociology of gender.* Berkeley: University of California Press.

Chudacoff, H. P. (1989). *How old are you? Age consciousness in American culture.* Princeton, NJ: Princeton University Press.

Clague, E. (1945). Problems of migration. *National Conference of Social Work Proceedings, 72,* 66–67.

Clanchy, M. T. (1979). *From memory to written record, England, 1066–1307.* Cambridge, MA: Harvard University Press.

Clark, C. E., Jr. (1986). *The American family home, 1800–1960.* Chapel Hill: University of North Carolina Press.

Clarke-Stewart, K. A. (1978). Popular primers for parents. *American Psychologist, 33,* 359–369.

Clausen, J. A. (Ed.). (1968). *Socialization and society.* Boston: Little, Brown.

(1986). *The life course: A sociological perspective.* Englewood Cliffs, NJ: Prentice-Hall.

Cleary, T. A., Humphreys, L. G., Kendrick, S. A., & Wesman, A. (1975). Educational uses of tests with disadvantaged students. *American Psychologist, 30,* 15–41.

Clifton, E. (1943). Some psychological effects of the war as seen by the social workers. *The Family, 24,* 123–128.

Cole, M., & Means, B. (1981). *Comparative studies of how people think: An introduction.* Cambridge, MA: Harvard University Press.

Coleman, J. S. (1961). *The adolescent society: The social life of the teenager and its impact on education.* [New York]: Free Press.

Coles, R. (1977). *Children of crisis.* Vol. 5. *Privileged ones: The well-off and the rich in America* Boston: Little, Brown.

(1986a). *The moral life of children.* Boston: Atlantic Monthly Press.

(1986b). *The political life of children.* Boston: Atlantic Monthly Press.

Colvin, S. S., & MacPhail, A. H. (1924). *Intelligence of seniors in the high schools of Massachusetts* (Bureau of Education, Bulletin No. 9). Washington, DC: U.S. Department of the Interior, Bureau of Education.

Conger, R. D., & Elder, G. H., Jr. (forthcoming). *Rural families in a changing society.* New York: Aldine–De Gruyter.

Conger, R. D., Elder, G. H., Jr., Lorenz, F. O., Conger, K. J., Simons, R. L., Whitbeck, L. B., Huck, S., and Melby, J. N. (1990). Linking economic hardship to marital quality and instability. *Journal of Marriage and the Family, 52,* 643–656.

Cook, T. D., Appleton, H., Conner, R. F., Shaffer, A., Tamkin, G., & Weber, S. J. (1975). *"Sesame Street" revisited.* New York: Russell Sage Foundation.

Cooney, J. G. (1968). *Television for preschool children: A proposal.* New York: Children's Television Workshop.

Costanzo, P. R., & Woody, E. Z. (1979). Externality as a function of obesity in children: Persuasive style or eating-specific attribute? *Journal of Personality and Social Psychology, 37,* 2286–2296.

Crimmins, E. M. (1981). The changing pattern of American mortality decline, 1940–77, and its implications for the future. *Population and Development Review, 7,* 229–254.

Csikszentmihalyi, M., & Rochberg-Halton, E. (1981). *The meaning of things: Domestic symbols and the self.* Cambridge, England: Cambridge University Press.

Culin, S. (1891). Street games of boys in Brooklyn, N.Y. *Journal of American Folklore, 4,* 221–237.

Daniels, P., & Weingarten, K. (1983). *Sooner or later: The timing of parenthood in adult lives.* New York: Norton.

Dannefer, D. (1984). The role of the social in life-span developmental psychology, past and future: Rejoinder to Baltes and Nesselroade. *American Sociological Review, 49,* 847–850.

Davenport, C. B., & Love, A. G. (1921). *The medical department of the United States Army in the world war.* Vol. 15, Pt. 1. *Army anthropology based on observations made on draft recruits, 1917–18 and on veterans at demobilization, 1919.* Washington, DC: U.S. War Department, Medical Department.

Deetz, J. F. (1977). *In small things forgotten: The archaeology of American life.* Garden City, NY: Anchor Press/Doubleday.

Degler, C. N. (1980). *At odds: Women and the family in America from the Revolution to the present.* New York: Oxford University Press.

Demos, J. (1970). *A little commonwealth: Family life in Plymouth Colony.* New York: Oxford University Press.

(1971). Developmental perspectives on the history of childhood. *The Journal of Interdisciplinary History, 2,* 315–327.

(1974). The American family in past time. *The American Scholar, 43,* 422–446.

(1982). The changing faces of fatherhood: A new exploration in American family history. In S. H. Cath, A. R. Gurwitt, & J. M. Ross (Eds.), *Father and child: Developmental and clinical perspectives* (pp. 425–445). Boston: Little, Brown.

(1986). *Past, present, and personal: The family and the life course in American history.* New York: Oxford University Press.

Dewey, J. (1900). Psychology and social practice. *Psychological Review, 7,* 105–124.

Dewey, J., & Dewey, E. (1915). *Schools of to-morrow.* New York: Dutton.

Douglas, J. W. B., & Simpson, H. R. (1964). Height in relation to puberty[,] family size and social class. *Milbank Memorial Fund Quarterly, 42*(3, Pt. 1), 20–35.

Douglas, N. (1916). *London street games.* London: St. Catherine Press.

Drewnowski, A., Yee, D. K., & Krahn, D. D. (1988). Bulimia in college women: Incidence and recovery rates. *American Journal of Psychiatry, 145,* 753–755.

Druss, R. G., & Silverman, J. A. (1979). Body image and perfectionism of ballerinas. Comparison and contrast with anorexia nervosa. *General Hospital Psychiatry, 1,* 115–121.

Duncan, G. J., with Coe, R. D., Corcoran, M. E., Hill, M. S., Hoffmann, S. D., & Morgan, J. N. (1984). *Years of poverty, years of plenty: The changing economic fortunes of American workers and families.* Ann Arbor: University of Michigan, Institute of Social Research, Survey Research Center.

Duncan, G. J., & Morgan, J. N. (1985). The Panel Study of Income Dynamics. In G. H. Elder, Jr. (Ed.), *Life course dynamics: Trajectories and transitions, 1968–1980* (pp. 50–71). Ithaca, NY: Cornell University Press.

Easterlin, R. A. (1980). *Birth and fortune: The impact of numbers on personal welfare.* New York: Basic Books.

Educational Testing Service. Center for Statistics. (1986). *Contractor report: Factors associated with decline of test scores of high school seniors, 1972–1980.* Princeton, NJ: Author.

Eells, W. C. (1937). The scholastic ability of secondary school pupils. *Educational Record, 18,* 53–67.

Eichorn, D. H., Clausen, J. A., Haan, N., Honzik, M. P., & Mussen, P. H. (Eds.). (1981). *Present and past in middle life.* New York: Academic Press.

Eifermann, R. R. (1970). Level of children's play as expressed in group size. *British Journal of Educational Psychology, 40,* 161–170.

(1971a). *Determinants of children's game styles: On free play in a "disadvantaged" and in an "advantaged" school.* Jerusalem: Israel Academy of Sciences and Humanities.

(1971b). Social play in childhood. In R. E. Herron & B. Sutton-Smith (Eds.), *Child's play* (pp. 270–297). New York: Wiley.

(1972). Cooperativeness and egalitarianism in kibbutz children's games. *Human Relations, 23,* 579–587.

(1973). Rules in games. In A. Elithorn & D. Jones (Eds.), *Artificial and human thinking* (pp. 147–161). San Francisco: Jossey-Bass.

(1974). It's child's play. In L. M. Shears & E. M. Bower (Eds.), *Games in education and development* (pp. 75–102). Springfield, IL: Thomas.

(1978). Games of physical activity. In F. Landry & W. A. R. Orban (Eds.), *Physical activity and human well being* (Book 2, pp. 741–751). Miami: Symposium Specialists.

Eisenstein, E. L. (1979). *The printing press as an agent of change: Communications and cultural transformations in early modern Europe.* Cambridge, England: Cambridge University Press.

Elder, G. H., Jr. (1973). On linking social structure and personality. *American Behavioral Scientist, 16,* 785–800.

(1974). *Children of the Great Depression: social change in life experience.* Chicago: University of Chicago Press.

(1978). Family history and the life course. In T. K. Hareven (Ed.), *Transitions: The family and the life course in historical perspective* (pp. 17–64). New York: Academic Press.

(1979). Historical changes in life patterns and personality. In P. B. Baltes & O. G. Brim, Jr. (Eds.), *Life-span development and behavior* (Vol. 2, pp. 117–159). New York: Academic Press.

(1980). Adolescence in historical perspective. In J. Adelson (Ed.), *Handbook of adolescent psychology* (pp. 3–46). New York: Wiley.

(1981). Social history and life experience. In D. H. Eichorn, J. A. Clausen, N. Haan, M. P. Honzik, & P. H. Mussen (Eds.), *Present and past in middle life* (pp. 3–31). New York: Academic Press.

(1984). Families, kin, and the life course: A sociological perspective. In R. D. Parke (Ed.), *Review of child development research.* Vol. 7. *The family* (pp. 80–136). Chicago: University of Chicago Press.

(1985). *Life course dynamics: Trajectories and transitions, 1968–1980.* Ithaca, NY: Cornell University Press.

(1986). Military times and turning points in men's lives. *Developmental Psychology, 22,* 233–245.

(1987a). Families and lives: Some developments in life-course studies. *Journal of Family History, 12,* 179–199.

(1987b). War mobilization and the life course: A cohort of World War II veterans. *Sociological Forum, 2,* 449–472.

(1991). Lives and social change. In W. R. Heinz (Ed.), *Theoretical advances in life course research* (Vol. 1, pp. 58–86). Status Passages and the Life Course. Weinheim, Germany: Deutscher Studien.

Elder, G. H., Jr., & Caspi, A. (1988). Human development and social change: An emerging perspective on the life course. In N. Bolger, A. Caspi, G. Downey, & M. Moorehouse (Eds.), *Persons in context: Developmental process* (pp. 77–113). Cambridge, England: Cambridge University Press.

(1990). Studying lives in a changing society: Sociological and personological explorations. Henry R. Murray Lecture Series. In A. I. Rabin, R. A. Zucker, R. Emmons, & S. Frank (Eds.), *Studying persons and lives* (pp. 201–247). New York: Springer.

Elder, G. H., Jr., Caspi, A., & Van Nguyen, T. (1986). Resourceful and vulnerable children: Family influences in hard times. In R. K. Silbereisen, K. Eyferth, & G. Rudinger (Eds.), *Development as action in context: Problem behavior and normal youth development* (pp. 167–186). New York: Springer.

Elder, G. H., Jr., & Clipp, E. (1988). Wartime losses and social bonding: Influences across 40 years in men's lives. *Psychiatry, 51,* 177–198.

Elder, G. H., Jr., Conger, R. D., Foster, E. M., & Ardelt, M. (1992). Families under economic pressure. *Journal of Family Issues, 13,* 5–37.

Elder, G. H., Jr., Downey, G., & Cross, C. E. (1986). Family ties and life chances: Hard times and hard choices in women's lives since the 1930s. In N. Datan, A. L. Greene, & H. W. Reese (Eds.), *Life-span developmental psychology: Intergenerational relations* (pp. 151–183). Hillsdale, NJ: Erlbaum.

Elder, G. H., Jr., & Liker, J. K. (1982). Hard times in women's lives: Historical influences across forty years. *American Journal of Sociology, 88,* 241–269.

Elder, G. H., Jr., Liker, J. K., & Cross, C. (1984). Parent–child behavior in the Great Depression: Life course and intergenerational influences. In P. B. Baltes & O. G. Brim (Eds.), *Life-span development and behavior* (Vol. 6, pp. 109–158). New York: Academic Press.

Elder, G. H., Jr., Van Nguyen, T., & Caspi, A. (1985). Linking family hardship to children's lives. *Child Development, 56,* 361–375.

Elder, R. A. (1949). Traditional and developmental conceptions of fatherhood. *Marriage and Family Living, 11,* 98–100, 106.

Elley, W. B. (1969). Changes in mental ability in New Zealand school children, 1936–1968. *New Zealand Journal of Educational Studies, 4,* 140–155.

Elliott, D. S., Huizinga, D., & Menard, S. (1989). *Multiple problem youth: Delinquency, substance use, and mental health problems.* New York: Springer.

Ellis, B. (1981a). The camp mock-ordeal: Theater as life. *Journal of American Folklore, 94,* 486–505.

(1981b). Majaska: Mythmaking in greater Cleveland. *Kentucky Folklore Record, 27,* 76–96.

(1982). Ralph and Rudy: The audience's role in recreating a camp legend. *Western Folklore, 41,* 169–191.

Erikson, E. H. (1950). *Childhood and society.* New York: Norton.

(1958). *Young man Luther: A study in psychoanalysis and history*. New York: Norton.

(1968). *Identity: Youth and crisis*. New York: Norton.

(1975). *Life history and the historical moment*. New York: Norton.

Eron, L. D., & Huesmann, L. R. (1986). The role of television in the development of prosocial and antisocial behavior. In D. Olweus, J. Block, & M. Radke-Yarrow (Eds.), *Development of antisocial and prosocial behavior: Research, theories, and issues* (pp. 285–314). New York: Academic Press.

Fairburn, C. G., Cooper, Z., & Cooper, P. J. (1986). The clinical features and maintenance of bulimia nervosa. In K. D. Brownell & J. P. Foreyt (Eds.), *Handbook of eating disorders: Physiology, psychology, and treatment of obesity, anorexia, and bulimia* (pp. 389–404). New York: Basic Books.

Fass, P. S. (1980). The IQ: A cultural and historical framework. *American Journal of Education, 88,* 431–458.

Featherman, D. L. (1983). Life-span perspectives in social science research. In P. B. Baltes & O. G. Brim, Jr. (Eds.), *Life-span development and behavior* (Vol. 5, pp. 1–57). New York: Academic Press.

Featherman, D. L., Spenner, K. I., & Tsunematsu, N. (1988). Class and the socialization of children: Constancy, change, or irrelevance? In E. M. Hetherington, R. M. Lerner, & M. Perlmutter (Eds.), *Child development in life-span perspective* (pp. 67–90). Hillsdale, NJ: Erlbaum.

Federal Bureau of Investigation, Uniform Crime Reporting Program. (1990). *Age-specific arrest rates and race-specific arrest rates for selected offenses, 1965–1988*. Washington, DC: Federal Bureau of Investigation.

Feldman, D. H. (1986). *Nature's gambit: Child prodigies and the development of human potential*. New York: Basic Books.

Feldman, S. S., Nash, S. C., & Aschenbrenner, B. (1983). Antecedents of fathering. *Child Development, 54,* 1628–1636.

Filene, P. G. (1986). *Him/her/self: Sex roles in modern America* (2nd ed.). Baltimore, MD: Johns Hopkins University Press.

Fine, G. A. (1987). *With the boys: Little League baseball and preadolescent culture*. Chicago: University of Chicago Press.

Fine, G. A., & Glassner, B. (1979). Participant observation with children. *Urban Life, 8,* 153–174.

Fine, G. A., & Sandsrom, K. L. (1988). *Knowing children: Participant observation with minors* (Qualitative Research Methods, Vol. 15). Newbury Park, CA: Sage.

Fisher, R. A. (1937). *The design of experiments*. (2d ed.). Edinburgh: Oliver & Boyd.

Fishkin, J. S. (1983). *Justice, equal opportunity, and the family*. New Haven, CT: Yale University Press.

Flavell, J. H. (1963). Piaget's contributions to the study of cognitive development. *Merrill-Palmer Quarterly, 9,* 245–252.

Fleming, A., & Orpen, G. (1986). Psychobiology of maternal behavior in rats, selected other species and humans. In A. Fogel & G. F. Melson (Eds.), *Origins of nurturance: Developmental, biological and cultural perspectives on caregiving* (pp. 141–207). Hillsdale, NJ: Erlbaum.

Flynn, J. R. (1983). Now the great augmentation of the American IQ. *Nature, 301,* 655.

(1984a). The mean IQ of Americans: Massive gains 1932 to 1978. *Psychological Bulletin, 95,* 29–51.

(1984b). IQ gains and the Binet decrements. *Journal of Educational Measurement, 21,* 283–290.

(1985). Wechsler intelligence tests: Do we really have a criterion of mental retardation? *American Journal of Mental Deficiency, 90,* 236–244.

(1987). Massive IQ gains in 14 nations: What IQ tests really measure. *Psychological Bulletin, 101,* 171–191.

Fogel, R. W., Engerman, S. L ., Floud, R., Friedman, G., Margo, R. A., Sokoloff, K., Steckel, R.

H., Trussell, T. J., Villaflor, G., & Wachter, K. W. (1983). Secular changes in American and British stature and nutrition. *Journal of Interdisciplinary History, 14,* 445–481.

Fogel, R. W., Engerman, S. L., & Trussell, J. (1982). Exploring the uses of data on height. The analysis of long-term trends in nutrition, labor welfare, and labor productivity. *Social Science History, 6,* 401–421.

Fogelman, K. (1983). *Growing up in Great Britain. Papers from the National Child Development Study.* London: Macmillan for the National Children's Bureau.

Foot, H. C., Chapman, A. J., & Smith, J. R. (Eds.). (1980). *Friendship and social relations in children.* Chichester, England: Wiley.

Freedman, R. J. (1986). *Beauty bound.* Lexington, MA: Lexington Books.

Friedlander, M. L., & Siegel, S. M. (1990). Separation–individuation difficulties and cognitive-behavioral indicators of eating disorders among college women. *Journal of Counseling Psychology, 37,* 74–78.

Friedman, G. C. (1982). The heights of slaves in Trinidad. *Social Science History, 6,* 482–515.

Frisch, M. (1990). *A shared authority: Essays on the craft and meaning of oral and public history.* Albany: State University of New York Press.

Furstenberg, F. F., Jr. (1988). Good dads – bad dads: Two faces of fatherhood. In A. J. Cherlin (Ed.), *The changing American family and public policy.* Washington, DC: The Urban Institute.

Furstenberg, F. F., Jr., Brooks-Gunn, J., & Morgan, S. P. (1987). *Adolescent mothers in later life.* New York: Cambridge University Press.

Furstenberg, F. F., Jr., Hershberg, T., & Modell, J. M. (1975). The origins of the female-headed black family: The impact of the urban experience. *Journal of Interdisciplinary History, 6,* 211–233.

Gardner, G. E., & Spencer, H. (1944). Reactions of children with fathers and brothers in the armed forces. *American Journal of Orthopsychiatry, 14,* 36–43.

Gardner, H. (1980). *Artful scribbles: The significance of children's drawings.* New York: Basic Books.

Garfinkel, P. E., & Gardner, D. M. (1982). *Anorexia nervosa: A multidimensional perspective.* New York: Brunner/Mazel.

Garfinkel, P. E., & Kaplan, A. S. (1985). Starvation based perpetuating mechanisms in anorexia nervosa and bulimia. *International Journal of Eating Disorders, 4,* 651–665.

Garn, S. M., & Clark, D. C. (1975). Nutrition, growth, development, and maturation: Findings from the ten-state nutrition survey of 1968–1970. *Pediatrics, 56,* 306–319.

Garner, D. M., Garfinkel, P. E., & Bemis, K. M. (1982). A multidimensional psychotherapy for anorexia nervosa. *International Journal of Eating Disorders, 1*(2), 3–46.

Gay, P. (1985). *Freud for historians.* New York: Oxford University Press.

Gergen, K. J. (1973). Social psychology as history. *Journal of Personality and Social Psychology, 26,* 309–320.

——.(1982). *Toward transformation in social knowledge.* New York: Springer.

Gillis, J. R. (1974). *Youth and history: Tradition and change in European age relations, 1770–present.* New York: Academic Press.

Giordano, P. C. (1978). Research note: Girls, guys and gangs: The changing social context of female delinquency. *The Journal of Criminal Law and Criminology, 69,* 126–132.

Giordano, P. C., Cernkovich, S. A., & Pugh, M. D. (1986). Friendship and delinquency. *American Journal of Socioloy, 91,* 1170–1202.

Girod, M., & Allaume, G. (1976). L'évolution du niveau intellectuel de la population français pendant le dernier quart de siècle [The evolution of the intellectual level of the French population during the last quarter of the century]. *International Review of Applied Psychology, 25,* 121–123.

Goleman, D. (1988, August 18). Compensations detected for smaller of twins. *New York Times,* p. 25.

Gomme, A. B. M. (1894–98). *The traditional games of England, Scotland, and Ireland with tunes, singing-rhymes, and methods of playing according to the various extant and recorded in different parts of the kingdom. A dictionary of British folklore* (G. L. Gomme, Ed.) (2 vols.). London: D. Nutt.

Gooch, M. (1945, November). Ten years of progress in reducing maternal and infant mortality with figures showing changes in the rates between the 2 years 1942–43. *The Child, 10,* 77–83.

Goodman, C. (1979). *Choosing sides: Playground and street life on the Lower East Side.* New York: Shocken Books.

Goodnow, J. J. (1962). A test of milieu effects with some of Piaget's tasks. *Psychological Monographs: General and Applied, 76* (Whole No. 555).

    (1984). Parents' ideas about parenting and development: A review of issues and recent work. In M. E. Lamb, A. L. Brown, & B. Rogoff (Eds.), *Advances in developmental psychology* (Vol. 3, pp. 193–242). Hillsdale, NJ: Erlbaum.

Goodnow, J. J., & Collins, W. A. (1990). *Development according to parents: The nature, sources, and consequences of parents' ideas.* Hillsdale, NJ: Erlbaum.

Goodwin, M. H. (1985). The serious side of jump rope: Conversational practices and the social organization in the frame of play. *Journal of American Folklore, 98,* 315–330.

Gordon, M. (Ed.). (1983). *The American family in social-historical perspective* (3rd ed.). New York: St. Martin's Press.

Grabill, W. H. (1944). Effects of the war on the birth rate and postwar fertility prospects. *American Journal of Sociology, 50,* 107–111.

Graff, H. J. (Ed.). (1987). *Growing up in America.* Detroit: Wayne State University Press.

Greenfield, P. M. (1980). Toward an operational and logical analysis of intentionality: The use of discourse in early child language. In D. R. Olson (Ed.), *The social foundations of language and thought. Essays in honor of Jerome S. Bruner* (pp. 254–279). New York: Norton.

Greven, P. J., Jr. (1970). *Four generations: Population, land, and family in colonial Andover, Massachusetts.* Ithaca, NY: Cornell University Press.

Grimm, W. (1988). *Dear Mili: An old tale.* (Trans.). New York: Michael di Capua Books/Farrar, Straus & Giroux.

Gull, W. (1874). Anorexia nervosa (Apepsia Hysterica, Anorexia Hysterica). *Transactions of the Clinical Society of London, 7,* 22–28.

Haggerty, M. E., & Nash, H. B. (1924). Mental capacity of children and paternal occupation. *Journal of Educational Psychology, 15,* 559–572.

Halévy, E. (1928). *The growth of philosophic radicalism* (M. Morris, Trans.). London: Faber & Gwyer.

Hall, G. S. (1904). *Adolescence: Its psychology and its relations to physiology, anthropology, sociology, sex, crime, religion and education* (2 vols.). New York: Appleton.

Halsey, A. H., Heath, A. F., & Ridge, J. M. (1980). *Origins and destinations: Family, class, and education in modern Britain.* Oxford, England: Clarendon Press.

Hamill, P. V. V., Johnston, F. E., & Lemeshow, S. (1972). *Height and weight of children, socioeconomic status, United States* (National Center for Health Statistics, Series 11, Data from National Health Survey, No. 119; DHEW Publication [HSM] 73-1601). Washington, DC: Department of Health, Education, and Welfare, National Center for Health Statistics, Division of Health Examination Statistics.

Hareven, T. K. (1971). The history of the family as an interdisciplinary field. *Journal of Interdisciplinary History, 2,* 399–414.

    (1982). *Family time and industrial time: The relationship between the family and work in a New England industrial town.* Cambridge, England: Cambridge University Press.

    (1984). Historical perspectives on the family. In R. D. Parke (Ed.), *Review of child development research. Vol. 7. The family* (pp. 137–178). Chicago: University of Chicago Press.

    (1987). Family history at the crossroads. *Journal of Family History, 12,* ix–xxiii.

Hareven, T. K. (Ed.). (1978). *Transitions: The family and the life course in historical perspective.* New York: Academic Press.

Harlow, H. F. (1958). The nature of love. *American Psychologist, 13,* 673–684.

Harris, P. L. (1989). *Children and emotion: The development of psychological understanding.* Oxford, England: Blackwell.

Hartley, L. P. (1953). *The go-between.* London: Hamilton.

Hartmann, S. M. (1982). *The home front and beyond: American women in the 1940s.* Boston: Twayne.

Hastings, W. W. (1902). *A manual for physical measurements for use in normal schools, public and preparatory schools, boys' clubs, and Young Men's Christian Associations, with anthropometric tables for each height of each age from five to twenty years, and vitality coefficients.* Springfield, MA: [International Young Men's Christian Association Training School].

Hathaway, M. L. (1957). *Heights and weights of children and youth in the United States.* (Institute of Home Economics, Agricultural Research Service, Home Economics Research Report No. 2). Washington, DC: U.S. Department of Agriculture.

Hauser, P. M. (1942). Population and vital phenomena. *American Journal of Sociology, 48,* 309–322.

Havighurst, R. J., Eaton, W. A., Baughman, J. W., & Burgess, E. W. (1951). *The American veteran back home: A study of veteran readjustment.* New York: Longmans, Green.

Hawes, J. M. (1971). *Children in urban society: Juvenile delinquency in nineteenth century America.* New York: Oxford University Press.

Hawes, J. M., & Hiner, N. R. (Eds.). (1985). *American childhood: A research guide and historical handbook.* Westport, CT: Greenwood Press.

Hayes, C. D., Palmer, J. L., & Zaslow, M. J. (Eds.). (1990). *Who cares for America's children: Child care policy for the 1990s.* Washington, DC: National Academy Press.

Hetherington, E. M., & Baltes, P. B. (1988). Child psychology and life-span development. In E. M. Hetherington, R. M. Lerner, & M. Perlmutter (Eds.), *Child development in life span perspective* (pp. 1–19). Hillsdale, NJ: Erlbaum.

Hetherington, E. M., Lerner, R. M., & Perlmutter, M. (Eds.). (1988). *Child development in life-span perspective.* Hillsdale, NJ: Erlbaum.

Hill, D. S. (1911). Comparative study of children's ideals. *Pedagogical Seminary, 18,* 219–231.

Hill, R. (1949). *Families under stress.* New York: Harper.

Hinde, A. (1989). Ethological and relationships approaches. In R. Vasta (Ed.), *Annals of child development* (Vol. 6, pp. 251–285). Greenwich, CT: JAI Press.

Hofferth, S. L. (1985a). Children's life course: Family structure and living arrangements in cohort perspective. In G. H. Elder, Jr. (Ed.), *Life course dynamics: Trajectories and transitions, 1968–1980* (pp. 75–112). Ithaca, NY: Cornell University Press.

(1985b). Updating children's life course. *Journal of Marriage and the Family, 47,* 93–115.

Hogan, D. P. (1981). *Transitions and social change: The early lives of American men.* New York: Academic Press.

Hollingshead, A. de B. (1949). *Elmtown's youth: The impact of social classes on adolescents.* New York: Wiley.

Horn, M. (1984). The moral message of child guidance, 1925–1945. *Journal of Social History, 18,* 25–36.

Horney, K. (1937). *The neurotic personality of our time.* New York: Norton.

Hughes, E. C. (1971). *The sociological eye: Selected papers.* Chicago: Aldine-Atherton.

Hughes, L. A. (1983). Beyond the rules of the game: Why are Rooie Rules nice? In F. E. Manning (Ed.), *The world of play: Proceedings of the 7th annual meeting of the Association of the Anthropological Study of Play* (pp. 188–199). West Point, NY: Leisure Press.

(1989). Foursquare: A glossary and native taxonomy of game rules. *Play and Culture, 2,* 103–136.

Humphreys, L. G., Davey, T. C., & Park, R. K. (1985). Longitudinal correlation analysis of standing height and intelligence. *Child Development, 56,* 1465–1478.

Hunt, D. (1970). *Parents and children in history: The psychology of family life in early modern France.* New York: Basic Books.

Husén, T. (Ed.). (1967). *International study of achievement in mathematics. A comparison of twelve countries.* Stockholm: Almqvist & Wiksell; New York: Wiley.

Igel, A. (1945). The effect of war separation on father–child relations. *The Family, 26,* 3–9.

Jencks, C. (1972). *Inequality: A reassessment of the effect of family and schooling in America.* New York: Basic Books.

Johnson, M. W. (1935). The effect on behavior of variation in the amount of play equipment. *Child Development, 6,* 56–68.

Jones, H. E., & Conrad, H. S. (1933). The growth and decline of intelligence: A study of a homogeneous group between the ages of ten and sixty. *Genetic Psychology Monographs. Child Behavior, Animal Behavior, and Comparative Psychology, 13*(3).

Jones, L. Y. (1980). *Great expectations: America and the baby boom generation.* New York: Coward, McCann, & Geoghegan.

Kadambari, R., Gowers, S., & Crisp, A. (1986). Some correlates of vegetarianism in anorexia nervosa. *International Journal of Eating Disorders, 5,* 539–544.

Kaestle, C. F. (1973). *The evolution of an urban school system: New York City, 1750–1850,* Cambridge, MA: Harvard University Press.

Kagan, J. (1984). *The nature of the child.* New York: Basic Books.

Karpinos, B. D., & Sommers, H. J. (1942). Educational attainment of urban youth in various income classes. I. *The Elementary School Journal, 42,* 677–687.

Katz, M. B. (1975). *The people of Hamilton, Canada West: Family and class in a mid-nineteenth-century city.* Cambridge, MA: Harvard University Press.

Katz, M. B., & Davey, I. F. (1978). Youth and early industrialization in a Canadian city. In J. Demos & S. S. Boocock (Eds.), *Turning points: Historical and sociological essays in the family* (pp. S81–S119). Chicago: University of Chicago Press. (Supplement to *American Journal of Sociology, 84.*)

Kaye, W. H., Gwirtsman, H., George, T., Ebert, M. H., & Petersen, R. (1986). Caloric consumption and activity levels after weight recovery in anorexia nervosa: A prolonged delay in normalization. *International Journal of Eating Disorders, 5,* 489–502.

Kelly-Byrne, D. (1989). *A child's play life: An ethnographic study.* New York: Columbia University, Teachers College.

Kelton, A. (1943, April). A boy needs a man. *Parents' Magazine, 18,* 31, 96.

Kertzer, D. I., & Hogan, D. P. (1989). *Family, political economy, and demographic change: The transformation of life in Casalecchio, Italy, 1861–1921.* Madison: University of Wisconsin Press.

Kessel, F. S., & Siegel, A. W. (Eds.). (1983). *The child and other cultural inventions: Houston Symposium 4.* New York: Praeger.

Kessen, W. (1979). The American child and other cultural inventions. *American Psychologist, 34,* 815–820.

(1983). The child and other cultural inventions. In F. S. Kessel & A. W. Siegel (Eds.), *The child and other cultural inventions: Houston Symposium 4* (pp. 26–39). New York: Praeger.

Kett, J. (1977). *Rites of passage: Adolescence in America 1790 to the present.* New York: Basic Books.

Klein, J. T. (1990). *Interdisciplinarity: History, theory, and practice.* Detroit: Wayne State University Press.

Klesges, R. C., Mizes, J. S., & Klesges, L. M. (1987). Self-help dieting strategies in college males and females. *International Journal of Eating Disorders, 6,* 409–417.

Knapp, M., & Knapp, H. (1976). *One potato, two potato . . . : The secret education of American children*. New York: Norton.

Kohlberg, L. (1981). *The philosophy of moral development: Moral stages and the idea of justice*. San Francisco: Harper & Row.

——— (1984). *The psychology of moral development: The nature and validity of moral stages*. San Francisco: Harper & Row.

Kohn, M. L. (1977). *Class and conformity: A study in values, with a reassessment* (2nd ed.). Chicago: University of Chicago Press.

Kohn, M. L., & Schooler, C. (1983). *Work and personality: An inquiry into the impact of social stratificiation*. Norwood, NJ: Ablex.

Kojima, H. (1986a). Becoming nurturant in Japan: Past and present. In A. Fogel & G. F. Melson (Eds.), *Origins of nurturance. Developmental, biological and cultural perspectives on caregiving* (pp. 123–139). Hillsdale, NJ: Erlbaum.

——— (1986b). Japanese concepts of child development from the mid-17th to mid-19th century. *International Journal of Behavioral Development, 9*, 315–329.

Kornblum, W. (1974). *Blue collar community*. Chicago: University of Chicago Press.

Kotelchuck, M. (1976). The infant's relationship to the father: Experimental evidence. In M. E. Lamb (Ed.), *The role of the father in child development* (pp. 329–344). New York: Wiley.

Krell, R. (1980). At a children's hospital: A folklore survey. *Western Folklore. 39*, 223–231.

Kreppner, K., & Lerner, R. M. (1989). Family systems and life-span development: Issues and perspectives. In K. Kreppner & R. M. Lerner (Eds.), *Family systems and life-span development* (pp. 1–13). Hillsdale, NJ: Erlbaum.

LaCapra, D. (1985). *History and criticism*. Ithaca, NY: Cornell University Press.

Lamb, M. E. (1977). Father–infant and mother–infant interaction in the first year of life. *Child Development, 48*, 167–181.

Lamb, M. E. (Ed.). (1981). *The role of the father in child development* (2nd ed.). New York: Wiley.

——— (1986). *The father's role: Cross-cultural perspectives*. Hillsdale, NJ: Erlbaum.

Lamb, M. E., Frodi, A. M., Hwang, C.-P., & Frodi, M. (1982a). Varying degrees of paternal involvement in infant care: Attitudinal and behavioral correlates. In M. E. Lamb (Ed.), *Nontraditional families: Parenting and child development* (pp. 117–137). Hillsdale, NJ: Erlbaum.

Lamb, M. E., Frodi, A. M., Frodi M., & Hwang, C.-P. (1982b). Characteristics of maternal and paternal behavior in traditional and non-traditional Swedish families. *International Journal of Behavioral Development, 5*, 131–141.

Lane, H. L. (1976). *The wild boy of Aveyron*. Cambridge, MA: Harvard University Press.

Lasch, C. (1977). *Haven in a heartless world: The family besieged*. New York: Basic Books.

Lasègue, C. (1873, 27 September). On hysterical anorexia. *Medical Times and Gazette*, p. 378.

Lazar, I., & Darlington, R. (1982). Lasting effects of early education: A report from the consortium for longitudinal studies. *Monographs of the Society for Research in Child Development, 47*(Serial No. 195), 1–141.

Lears, T. J. J. (1985). The concept of cultural hegemony: Problems and possibilities. *American Historical Review, 90*, 567–593.

Lehman, H. C., & Witty, P. A. (1927). *The psychology of play activities*. New York: Barnes.

Lentz, T. F., Jr. (1929). Sex differences in school marks with achievement scores constant. *School and Society, 29*, 65–68.

Lerner, M. (1975). Social differences in physical health. In J. Kosa and I. K. Zola, (Eds.), *Poverty and health: A sociological analysis* (chapter 3). (rev. ed.) Cambridge, MA: Harvard University Press.

——— (1986). *Concepts and theories of human development* (2nd ed.). New York: Random House.

Lévi-Strauss, C. (1966). The culinary triangle (P. Brooks, Trans.). *Partisan Review, 33*, 586–595.

Levine, D. M., & Bane, M. J. (1975). *The "inequality" controversy: Schooling and distributive justice.* New York: Basic Books.

Levine, J. A. (1976). *Who will raise the children? New options for fathers (and mothers).* Philadelphia: Lippincott.

Levy, D. M. (1945). The war and family life: Report for the War Emergency Committee, 1944. *American Journal of Orthopsychiatry, 15,* 140–152.

Levy, F. (1987). *Dollars and dreams: The changing American income distribution.* New York: Russell Sage Foundation for the National Committee for Research on the 1980 Census.

Lewis, C. (1986). *Becoming a father.* Milton Keynes, England: Open University Press.

Liem, J. H., & Liem, G. R. (1990). Understanding the individual and family effects of unemployment. In J. Eckenrode & S. Gore (Eds.), *Stress between work and family* (pp. 175–204). New York: Plenum.

Luriia, A. R. (1976). *Cognitive development: Its cultural and social foundations* (M. Lopez-Morillas & L. Solotaroff, Trans.; M. Cole, Ed.). Cambridge, MA: Harvard University Press.

Lynd, R. S., & Lynd, H. M. (1929). *Middletown: A study in contemporary American culture.* New York: Harcourt, Brace.

(1937). *Middletown in transition: A study in cultural conflicts.* New York: Harcourt, Brace.

Lynn, D. B. (1959). A note on sex differences in the development of masculine and feminine identification. *Psychological Review, 66,* 126–135.

Lynn, R., & Hampson, S. (1986). The rise of national intelligence: Evidence from Britain, Japan and the U.S.A. *Personality and Individual Differences, 7,* 23–32.

Lystad, M. H. (1979). *From Dr. Mather to Dr. Seuss: 200 years of American books for children.* Boston: Hall.

Maccoby, E. E., & Jacklin, C. N. (1974). *The psychology of sex differences.* Stanford, CA: Stanford University Press.

MacDonald, K. B. (Ed.). (1988). *Sociobiological perspectives on human development.* New York: Springer.

Macfarlane, J. W. (1963). From infancy to adulthood. *Childhood Education, 39,* 336–342.

(1971). Perspectives on personality consistency and change from the Guidance Study. In M. C. Jones, N. Bayley, J. W. Macfarlane, & M. P. Honzik (Eds.), *The course of human development. Selected papers from the longitudinal studies, Institute of Human Development, the University of California, Berkeley* (pp. 410–415). Waltham, MA: Xerox College Publishing.

Macfarlane, J. W., Allen, L., & Honzik, M. P. (1954). *A developmental study of the behavior problems of normal children between twenty-one months and fourteen years.* Berkeley: University of California Press.

Machlowitz, M. (1980). *Workalcoholics: Living with them, working with them.* Reading, MA: Addison-Wesley.

Magnusson, D. (1988). *Individual development from an interactional perspective: A longitudinal study.* Hillsdale, NJ: Erlbaum.

Maller, J. B. (1932). Age versus intelligence as basis for prediction of success in high school. *Teachers College Record, 33,* 402–415.

(1933). Economic and social correlates of school progress in New York City. *Teachers College Record, 34,* 655–760.

Mannheim, K. (1952). *Essays on the sociology of knowledge* (P. Kecskemeti, Ed. & Trans.). London: Routledge & Kegan Paul.

Mare, R. D. (1981). Change and stability in educational stratification. *American Sociological Review, 46,* 72–87.

Margo, R. A., & Steckel, R. H. (1982). The heights of American slaves. New evidence on slave nutrition and health. *Social Science History, 6,* 516–528.

Martin, E. A. (1954). *Roberts' nutrition work with children.* Chicago: University of Chicago Press.

Martin, R. A. (Ed.). (1978). *The theater essays of Arthur Miller.* New York: Viking.

Maxwell, J. (1961). *The level and trend of national intelligence. The contribution of the Scottish mental surveys.* London: University of London Press.

McAdoo, J. L. (1988). Changing perspectives on the role of the black father. In P. Bronstein & C. P. Cowan (Eds.), *Fatherhood today: Men's changing role in the family* (pp. 79–92). New York: Wiley.

McCarthy, D. (1954). Language development in children. In L. Carmichael (Ed.), *Manual of child psychology* (pp. 492–630). (2nd ed.). New York: Wiley.

McClelland, D. C. (1961). *The achieving society.* Princeton, NJ: Van Nostrand.

McClymer, J. F. (1986). Late nineteenth-century American working-class living standards. *Journal of Interdisciplinary History, 17,* 379–398.

McDowell, E. (1983, September 28). A fairy tale by Grimm comes to light. *New York Times,* p. I-1.

McGoldrick, M., Pearce, J. K., & Giordano, J. (Eds.). (1982). *Ethnicity and family therapy.* New York: Guilford Press.

McGovern, J. (1969–70). Anna Howard Shaw: New approaches to feminism. *Journal of Social History, 3,* 135–153.

McGuire, W. J. (1976). Historical comparisons: Testing psychological hypotheses with cross-era data. *International Journal of Psychology, 11,* 161–183.

McLaughlin, S. D., Melber, B. D., Billy, J. O. G., Zimmerle, D. M., Winges, L. D., & Johnson, T. R. (1988). *The changing lives of American women.* Chapel Hill: University of North Carolina Press.

McNeill, W. H. (1982). The care and repair of public myth. *Foreign Affairs, 61,* 1–13.

Mead, M. (1942). *And keep your powder dry.* New York: Morrow.

Mechling, J. (1975). Advice to historians on advice to mothers. *Journal of Social History, 9,* 44–63.

(1980a). The magic of the Boy Scout campfire. *Journal of American Folklore, 93,* 35–56.

(1980b). Sacred and profane play in the Boy Scouts of America. In H. B. Schwartzman (Ed.), *Play and culture: 1978 Proceedings of the Association for the Anthropological Study of Play* (pp. 206–213). West Point, NY: Leisure Press.

(1981). Male gender display at a Boy Scout camp. In R. T. Sieber & A. J. Gordon (Eds.), *Children and their organizations: Investigations in American culture* (pp. 138–160). Boston: Hall.

(1984a). High kybo floater: Food and feces in the speech play at a Boy Scout camp. *Journal of Psychoanalytic Anthropology, 7,* 256–268.

(1984b). Patois and paradox in a Boy Scout treasure hunt. *Journal of American Folklore, 97,* 24–42.

(1986a). Children's folklore. In E. Oring (Ed.), *Folk groups and folklore genres: An introduction* (pp. 91–120). Logan: Utah State University Press.

(1986b). Male border wars as metaphor in Capture the Flag. In K. Blanchard (Ed), *The many faces of play. Proceedings of the 9th Annual Meeting of the Association for the Anthropological Study of Play (TAASP) held February 11–16, 1983, at Baton Rouge, Louisiana* (pp. 218–231). Champaign-Urbana, IL: Human Kinetics Press.

(1987a). Dress right, dress: The Boy Scout uniform as a folk costume. *Semiotica, 64,* 319–333.

(1987b). Oral evidence and the history of American children's lives. *Journal of American History, 74,* 579–586.

(1989). Mediating structures and the significance of university folk. In E. Oring (Ed.), *Folk groups and folklore genres: A reader* (pp. 339–349). Logan: Utah State University Press.

Meredith, H. V. (1978). *Human body growth in the first ten years of life.* Columbia, SC: State Printing.

Meredith, H. V., & Meredith, E. M. (1944). The stature of Toronto children half a century ago and today. *Human Biology 16,* 126–131.

Mergen, B. (1982). *Play and playthings: A reference guide.* Westport, CT: Greenwood Press.

Merton, R. K. (1968). *Social theory and social structure* (enl. ed.). New York: Free Press.

Meyer, A. E. (1943, August). War orphans. U.S.A. *Reader's Digest, 43,* 98–102.

(1944). *Journey through chaos.* New York: Harcourt, Brace.

Migdal, S., Abeles, R. P., & Sherrod, L. R. (1981). *An inventory of longitudinal studies of middle and old age.* New York: Social Science Research Council.

Mill, J. S. (1873). *Autobiography.* London: Longmans, Green, Reader & Dyer.

Miller, D. R., & Swanson, G. E. (1958). *The changing American parent: A study in the Detroit area.* New York: Wiley.

Miller, S. A. (1988). Parents' beliefs about children's cognitive development. *Child Development, 59,* 259–285.

Miner, J. B. (1957). *Intelligence in the United States.* New York: Springer.

Minton, J. H. (1972). *The impact of "Sesame Street" on reading readiness of kindergarten children.* Unpublished doctoral dissertation, Fordham University, Bronx, NY.

Minturn, L., & Lambert, W. W. (1964). *Mothers of six cultures: Antecedents of child rearing.* New York: Wiley.

Mintz, S., & Kellogg, S. (1988). *Domestic revolutions: A social history of American family life.* New York: Free Press.

Minuchin, S. (1974). *Families and family therapy.* Cambridge, MA: Harvard University Press.

Minuchin, S., Baker, L., Rosman, B. L., Liebman, R., Milman, L., & Todd, T. C. (1975). A conceptual model of psychosomatic illness in children. Family organization and family therapy. *Archives of General Psychiatry, 32,* 1031–1038.

Minuchin, S., Rosman, B. L., & Baker, L., with Liebman, R. (1978). *Psychosomatic families: Anorexia nervosa in context.* Cambridge, MA: Harvard University Press.

Modell, J. (1989). *Into one's own: From youth to adulthood in the United States, 1920–1975.* Berkeley: University of California Press.

Modell, J., & Campbell, J. (1984). *Family ideology and family values in the "Baby Boom."* Working paper, Family Study Center, Minneapolis.

Modell, J., Furstenberg, F. F., Jr., & Hershberg, T. (1976). Social change and the transitions to adulthood in historical perspective. *Journal of Family History, 1,* 7–32.

Modell, J., & Steffey, D. (1988). Waging war and marriage: Military service and family formation. *Journal of Family History, 13,* 195–218.

Modell, J. S. (1988). Meanings of love: Adoption literature and Dr. Spock, 1946–1985. In C. Z. Stearns & P. N. Stearns (Eds.), *Emotion and social change: Toward a new psychohistory* (pp. 151–191). New York: Holmes & Meier.

Moen, P. (1989). *Working parents: Transformations in gender roles and public policies in Sweden.* Madison: University of Wisconsin Press; London: Adamtine Press.

Moen, P., Kain, E. L., & Elder, G. H., Jr. (1983). Economic conditions and family life: Contemporary and historical perspectives. In R. R. Nelson & F. Skidmore (Eds.), *American families and the economy. The high costs of living* (pp. 213–259). Washington, DC: National Academy Press.

Mogey, J. M. (1957). A century of declining paternal authority. *Marriage and Family Living, 19,* 234–239.

Mori, D., Chaiken, S., & Pliner, P. (1987). "Eating lightly" and the self-presentation of femininity. *Journal of Personality and Social Psychology, 53,* 693–702.

Murphey, M. G. (1965). An approach to the historical study of national character. In M. E. Spiro (Ed.), *Context and meaning in cultural anthropology* (pp. 144–163). New York: Free Press; London: Collier-Macmillan.

Murray, J. P. (1980). *Television and youth: 25 years of research and controversy.* Boys Town, NE: Boys Town Center for the Study of Youth Development.

Nasaw, D. (1985). *Children of the city: At work and at play.* Garden City, NY: Anchor Press/Doubleday.

Nash, G. D. (1985). *The American West transformed: The impact of the Second World War.* Bloomington: Indiana University Press.

Nelsen, E. A., & Maccoby, E. E. (1966). The relationship between social development and differential abilities on the Scholastic Aptitude Test. *Merrill-Palmer Quarterly, 12,* 269–284.

Neville, B., & Parke, R. D. (1987). *Developmental shifts in father and mother play and recreational activities with children.* University of Illinois, Department of Psychology, Urbana.

Newell, W. W. (1883). *Games and songs of American children.* New York: Harper & Brothers.

Nichols, F. B. (1944). Sons of victory. *Hygeia, 22,* 748–749, 799.

Norton, M. B., Katzman, D. M., Escott, P. D., Chudacoff, H. P., Patterson, T. G., & Tuttle, W. M., Jr. (Eds.). (1986). Global wars: Second, cold, and Korean, 1941–1953. In *A People and a nation: A history of the United States.* Vol. 2. *Since 1865* (pp. 778–839). Boston: Houghton Mifflin.

Odell, C. W. (1925). Conservation of intelligence in Illinois high schools. *University of Illinois Bulletin, 22*(25).

Odem, M. E., & Schlossman, S. L. (1991). Guardians of virtue: The juvenile court and female delinquency in early 20th-century Los Angeles. *Crime and Delinquency, 37,* 186–203.

Oden, M. H. (1968). The fulfillment of promise: 40-year follow-up of the Terman gifted group. *Genetic Psychological Monographs, 77,* 3–93.

Olson, D. R. (1977). From utterance to text: The bias of language in speech and writing. *Harvard Educational Review, 47,* 257–281.

(1980). Some social aspects of meaning in oral and written language. In D. R. Olson (Ed.), *The social foundations of language and thought. Essays in honor of Jerome S. Bruner* (pp. 90–108). New York: Norton.

Olson, K. W. (1974). *The G.I. Bill, the veterans and the colleges.* [Lexington]: University Press of Kentucky.

O'Neill, T. J. (1985). *Bakke and the politics of equality: Friends and foes in the classroom of litigation.* Middletown, CT: Wesleyan University Press.

Opie, I. A., & Opie, P. (1959). *The lore and language of schoolchildren.* Oxford, England: Clarendon Press.

(1969). *Children's games in street and playground: Chasing, catching, seeking, hunting, racing, duelling, exerting, daring, guessing, acting, pretending.* Oxford, England: Clarendon Press.

(1985). *The singing game.* Oxford, England: Oxford University Press.

Ozment, S. E. (1983). *When father rules: Family life in Reformation Europe.* Cambridge, MA: Harvard University Press.

Packard, V. (1945, May). Give the war babies a break. *American Magazine, 139,* 24–25, 112–114.

Palmer, C. E. (1933). Growth and the economic depression. *Public Health Reports,* no. 48, 1277–1292.

(1934). Further studies on growth and the economic depression. A comparison of weight and weight increments of elementary-school children in 1921–27 and in 1933–34. *Public Health Reports,* no. 49, 1453–1469.

Parke, R. D. (1979). Perspectives on father–infant interaction. In J. D. Osofsky (Ed.), *Handbook of infant development* (pp. 549–590). New York: Wiley.

(1981). *Fathers.* Cambridge, MA: Harvard University Press.

Parke, R. D., & Beitel, A. (1986). Hospital based interventions for fathers. In M. E. Lamb (Ed.), *The father's role: Applied perspectives* (pp. 299–323). New York: Wiley.

Parke, R. D., & Bhavnagri, N. P. (1989). Parents as managers of children's peer relationships. In D. Belle (Ed.), *Children's social networks and social supports* (pp. 241–259). New York: Wiley.

Parke, R. D., MacDonald, K. D., Beitel, A., & Bhavnagri, N. (1987). The role of the family in the development of peer relationships. In R. DeV. Peters & R. J. McMahon (Eds.), *Social learning and systems approaches to marriage and the family* (pp. 17–44). New York: Brunner/Mazel.

Parke, R. D., & Sawin, D. B. (1975, April). *Infant characteristics and behavior as elicitors of maternal and paternal responsibility in the newborn period.* Paper presented at the biennial meeting of the Society of Research in Child Development, Denver.

(1976). The father's role in infancy: A re-evaluation. *The Family Coordinator, 25,* 365–371.

(1979). Children's privacy in the home: Developmental, ecological, and child-rearing determinants. *Environment and Behavior, 11,* 87–104.

(1980). The family in early infancy: Social interactional and attitudinal analyses. In F. A. Pedersen (Ed.), *The father–infant relationship. Observational studies in the family setting* (pp. 44–70). New York: Praeger.

Parke, R. D., & Slaby, R. G. (1983). The development of aggression. In P. Mussen (Ed.), *The handbook of child psychology.* Vol. 4. *Socialization, personality, and social development* (pp. 605–641). New York: Wiley.

Parke, R. D., & Tinsley, B. R. (1981). The father's role in infancy: Determinants of involvement in caregiving and play. In M. E. Lamb (Ed.), *The role of the father in child development* (pp. 429–457). New York: Wiley.

(1984). Fatherhood: Historical and contemporary perspectives. In K. A. McCluskey & H. W. Reese (Eds.), *Life-span developmental psychology* (pp. 203–248). Orlando, FL: Academic Press.

(1987). Family interaction in infancy. In J. Osofsky (Ed.), *Handbook of infant development* (pp. 579–641). (2nd ed.). New York: Wiley.

Parsons, T., & Bales, R. F. (1955). *Family, socialization and interaction process.* New York: Free Press.

Pearl, D., Bouthilet, L., & Lazar, J. (Eds.). (1982). *Television and behavior: Ten years of scientific progress and implications for the eighties.* Rockville, MD: U.S. Department of Health and Human Services, Public Health Service, Alcohol, Drug Abuse and Mental Health Administration, National Institutes of Mental Health.

Pervin, L. A. (Ed.). (1990). *Handbook of personality: Theory and research.* New York: Guilford Press.

Piaget, J. (1948). *The moral judgment of the child.* Glencoe, IL: Free Press.

(1954). *The construction of reality in the child.* New York: Basic Books.

(1971). *Biology and knowledge: An essay on the relations between organic regulations and cognitive processes.* Chicago: University of Chicago Press.

(1972). Intellectual evolution from adolescence to adulthood. *Human Development, 15,* 1–12.

(1983). Piaget's theory. In P. Mussen, *Handbook of child psychology.* Vol. 1. *History, theory, and methods* (pp. 103–128). (4th ed.). New York: Wiley.

Pittsburgh Post Gazette (1987, June 27):1, 5. Pupils make little progress.

Pleck, E. H., & Pleck, J. H. (Eds.). (1980). *The American man.* Englewood Cliffs, NJ: Prentice-Hall.

Pleck, J. H. (1981). *Changing patterns of work and family roles.* Working Paper No. 81, Wellesley College Center for Research on Women, Wellesley, MA.

(1983). Husband's paid work and family roles: Current research issues. In H. Z. Lopata & J. H. Pleck (Eds.), *Research in the interweave of social roles.* Vol. 3. *Families and jobs. A research annual* (pp. 251–333). Greenwich, CT: JAI Press.

Pleck, J. H., & Sawyer, J. (Eds.). (1974). *Men and masculinity.* Englewood Cliffs, NJ: Prentice-Hall.

Polanyi, K. (1957). *The great transformation.* Boston: Beacon Press.

Polgar, S. K. (1976). The social context of games: Or when is play not play? *Sociology of Education, 49,* 265–271.

Polivy, J., & Herman, C. P. (1985). Dieting and binging. A causal analysis. *American Psychologist, 40,* 193–201.

Pollock, L. A. (1983). *Forgotten children: Parent–child relations from 1500 to 1900.* Cambridge, England: Cambridge University Press.

Popenoe, P. (1942, July). Now is the time to have children. *Ladies' Home Journal, 59,* 60–61.

Postman, N. (1982). *The disappearance of childhood.* New York: Delacorte Press.

(1985). *Amusing ourselves to death: Public discourse in the age of show business.* New York: Viking.

Potter, D. M. (1954). *People of plenty: Economic abundance and the American character.* [Chicago]: University of Chicago Press.

Power, T. G., & Parke, R. D. (1982). Play as context for early learning: Lab and home analyses. In L. M. Laosa & I. E. Sigel (Eds.), *Families as learning environments for children* (pp. 147–178). New York: Plenum Press.

Pressey, L. W. (1918). Sex differences shown by 2,544 school children on a group scale of intelligence, with special reference to variability. *Journal of Applied Psychology, 2,* 323–340.

Preyer, W. (1888–89). *The mind of the child. Observations concerning the mental development of the human being in the first years of life* (H. W. Brown, Trans.). 2 vols. International Education Series. New York: Appleton-Century-Crofts.

Prince, R. (1985). The concept of culture-bound syndromes: Anorexia nervosa and brain-fag. *Social Science and Medicine, 21,* 197–203.

Radding, C. M. (1985). *A world made by men: Cognition and society, 400–1200.* Chapel Hill: University of North Carolina Press.

Ramey, C. T. (1982). Commentary. *Monographs of the Society for Research in Child Development, 47*(Serial No. 195), 142–151.

Reiss, D. (1981). *The family's construction of reality.* Cambridge, MA: Harvard University Press.

Rheingold, H. L., & Cook, K. V. (1975). The contents of boys' and girls' rooms as an index of parents' behavior. *Child Development, 46,* 459–463.

Rhinehart, J. B. (1947). Sex differences in dispersion at the high school and college levels. *Psychological Monographs: General and Applied, 61*(Whole No. 282).

Riesman, D., with Deney, R., & Glazer, N. (1950). *The lonely crowd: A study of the changing American character.* New Haven, CT: Yale University Press.

Rigg, M. G. (1940). The relative variability in intelligence of boys and girls. *Journal of Genetic Psychology, 56,* 211–214.

Riley, M. W., Johnson, M. E., & Foner, A. (Eds.). (1972). *Aging and society.* Vol. 3. *A sociology of age stratification.* New York: Russell Sage Foundation.

Rinsley, D. B. (1986). The adolescent, the family, and the culture of narcissism: A psychosocial commentary. *Adolescent Psychiatry, 13,* 7–28.

Robbins, P. (1944, April). What shall I tell him? *Parents' Magazine, 19,* 21, 94.

Roberts, J. M., & Sutton-Smith, B. (1962). Child training and game involvement. *Ethnology, 1,* 166–185.

(1966). Cross-cultural correlates of games of chance. *Behavior Science Notes, 1,* 131–144.

Robins, L. N. (1966). *Deviant children grown up: A sociological and psychiatric study of sociopathic personality.* Baltimore, MD: Williams & Wilkins.

Robins, L. N., & Rutter, M. (Eds.). (1990). *Straight and devious pathways from childhood to adulthood.* Cambridge, England: Cambridge University Press.

Rochberg-Halton, E. (1986). *Meaning and modernity: Social theory in the pragmatic attitude.* Chicago: University of Chicago Press.

Rock, D. A. et al. [1985?] *Factors associated with decline of test scores of high school seniors, 1972 to 1980. A study of excellence in high school education: Educational policies, school quality, and student outcomes.* [Washington, DC?]: Center for Statistics.

Rogoff, B. (1990). *Apprenticeship in thinking. Cognitive development in social context.* New York: Oxford University Press.

Rorty, R. (1979). *Philosophy and the mirror of nature.* Princeton, NJ: Princeton University Press.

(1982). *Consequences of pragmatism: Essays, 1972–1980.* Minneapolis: University of Minnesota Press.

(1989). *Contingency, irony, and solidarity*. Cambridge, England: Cambridge University Press.

Rosenblatt, J. S. (1969). The development of maternal responsiveness in the rat. *American Journal of Orthopsychiatry, 39*, 36–56.

Rosenblatt, J. S., & Siegel, H. I. (1981). Factors governing the onset and maintenance of maternal behavior among nonprimate animals: The role of hormonal and nonhormonal factors. In D. J. Gubernick & P. H. Klopfer (Eds.), *Parental care in mammals* (pp. 13–76). New York: Plenum.

Ross, H. L., & Sawhill, I. V. (1975). *Time of transition: The growth of families headed by women*. Washington, DC: Urban Institute.

Rothenberg, A. (1986). Eating disorder as a modern obsessive–compulsive syndrome. *Psychiatry, 49*, 45–53.

Rothstein, M. (1988, October 19). From the very busy Sendak, a book of a rare Grimm tale. *New York Times*, pp. C-19, C-24.

Rotundo, E. A. (1985). American fatherhood. A historical perspective. *American Behavioral Scientist, 29*, 7–23.

Rubinstein, D., & Simon, B. (1973). *The evolution of the comprehensive school, 1926–1972*. London: Routledge & Kegan Paul; New York: Humanities Press.

Rundquist, E. A. (1941). Sex, intelligence, and school marks. *School and Society, 53*, 452–458.

Runyan, W. McK. (Ed.). (1988). *Psychology and historical interpretation*. New York: Oxford University Press.

Russell, G. (1979). Bulimia nervosa: An ominous variant of anorexia nervosa. *Psychological Medicine, 9*, 429–448.

(1982). Shared caregiving families: An Australian study. In M. E. Lamb (Ed.), *Nontraditional families: Parenting and child development*. Hillsdale, NJ: Erlbaum.

(1983). *The changing role of fathers?* St. Lucia, Queensland, Australia: University of Queensland Press.

Rutter, M. (1979). Protective factors in children's responses to stress and disadvantage. In M. W. Kent & J. E. Rolf (Eds.), *Primary prevention of psychopathology*. Vol. 3. *Social competence in children* (pp. 49–74). Hanover, NH: University Press of New England.

(1988). *Studies of psychosocial risk: The power of longitudinal data*. Cambridge, England: Cambridge University Press.

Rutter, M., & Madge, N. (1976). *Cycles of disadvantage: A review of research*. London: Heinemann.

Ryder, N. B. (1965). The cohort as a concept in the study of social change. *American Sociological Review, 30*, 843–861.

Sadowski, L. S., Cairns, R. B., & Earp, J. A. (1989). Firearm ownership among nonurban adolescents. *American Journal of Diseases of Children, 143*, 1410–1413.

Sameroff, A. J. (1989). Commentary: General systems and the regulation of development. In M. R. Gunnar & E. Thelen (Eds.), *Systems and development: The Minnesota Symposia on Child Psychology*, (Vol. 22, pp. 219–235). Hillsdale, NJ: Erlbaum.

Sargent, J., Liebman, R., & Silver, M. (1985). Family therapy for anorexia nervosa. In D. M. Garner & P. E. Garfinkel (Eds.), *Handbook of psychotherapy for anorexia nervosa and bulimia* (pp. 157–279). New York: Guilford Press.

Savin-Williams, R. C. (1980a). Dominance hierarchies in groups of middle to late adolescent males. *Journal of Youth and Adolescence, 9*, 75–85.

(1980b). Social interactions of adolescent females in natural groups. In H. C. Foot, A. J. Chapman, & J. R. Smith (Eds.), *Friendship and social relations in children* (pp. 343–364). New York: Wiley.

Schaffer, H. R., & Emerson, P. E. (1964). The development of social attachments in infancy. *Monographs of the Society for Research in Child Development, 29*(3, Whole No. 94).

Schlossman, S. L. (1977). *Love and the American delinquent: The theory and practice of "progressive" juvenile justice, 1825–1920*. Chicago: University of Chicago Press.

Schlossman, S. L., & Turner, S. (1990). *Race, and delinquency in Los Angeles Juvenile Court, 1950.* Sacramento: California Department of Justice, Bureau of Criminal Statistics and Special Services.

Schlossman, S. L., & Wallach, S. (1978). The crime of precocious sexuality: Female juvenile delinquency in the Progressive Era. *Harvard Educational Review, 48,* 65–94.

Schwebel, M., & Raph, J. (Eds.). (1973). *Piaget in the classroom.* New York: Basic Books.

Schweder, R. A. (1990). Cultural psychology – What is it? In J. W. Stigler, R. A. Schweder, & G. Herdt (Eds.), *Cultural psychology. Essays on comparative human development* (pp. 1–43). Cambridge, England: Cambridge University Press.

Sears, R. R. (1951). A theoretical framework for personality and social behavior. *American Psychologist, 6,* 476–483.

Sears, R. S., Pintler, M. H., & Sears, P. S. (1946). Effect of father separation on preschool children's doll play aggression. *Child Development, 17,* 219–243.

Sennett, R. (1970). *Families against the city: Middle class homes of industrial Chicago, 1872–1890.* Cambridge, MA: Harvard University Press.

Shattuck, R. (1980). *The forbidden experiment: The story of the Wild Boy of Aveyron.* New York: Farrar, Straus & Giroux.

Shaycoft, M. F., Dailey, J. T., Orr, D. B., Neyman, C. A., & Sherman, S. E. (1963). *Studies of a complete age group – age 15* (Tech. Rep. to the U.S. Office of Education, Cooperative Research Project No. 566). Pittsburgh: University of Pittsburgh, Project TALENT Office.

Shinn, M. (1978). Father absence and children's cognitive development. *Psychological Bulletin, 85,* 295–324.

Shorter, E. (1975). *The making of the modern family.* New York: Basic Books.

Shuey, A. M. (1966). *The testing of Negro intelligence.* (2nd ed.). New York: Social Science Press.

Siegel, P. M., & Bruno, R. R. (1986). *School enrollment – social and economic characteristics of students: 1982* (U.S. Bureau of the Census, Current Population Reports, Series P-20, Population Characteristics, No. 408). [Suitland, MD]: U.S. Commerce Department, Bureau of the Census, Population Division.

Silberstein, L. R., Striegel-Moore, R. H., & Rodin, J. (1987). Feeling fat: A woman's shame. In H. B. Lewis (Ed.), *The role of shame in symptom formation* (pp. 89–108). Hillsdale, NJ: Erlbaum.

Silberstein, L. R., Striegel-Moore, R. H., Timko, C., & Rodin, J. (1988). Behavioral and psychological implications of body dissatisfaction: Do men and women differ? *Sex Roles, 19,* 219–232.

Simmons, R. G., & Blyth, D. A. (1987). *Moving into adolescence: The impact of pubertal changes and school context.* New York: de Gruyter.

Simonton, D. K. (1990). *Psychology, science, and history: An introduction to historiometry.* New Haven, CT: Yale University Press.

Skolnick, A. (1975). The family revisited: Themes in recent social science research. *Journal of Interdisciplinary History, 5,* 703–719.

Sluckin, A. (1981). *Growing up in the playground: The social development of children.* London: Routledge & Kegan Paul.

Snyder, R. G., Schneider, L. W., Owings, C. L., Reynolds, H. M., Golomb, D. H., & Schork, M. A. (1977). *Anthropometry of infants, children and youths to age 18 for product safety design* (Final report for U.S. Consumer Product Safety Commission). Ann Arbor: University of Michigan, Highway Safety Research Institute.

Solyom, L., Freeman, R. J., Thomas, C. D., & Miles, J. E. (1983). The comparative psychopathology of anorexia nervosa. Obsessive–compulsive disorder or phobia? *International Journal of Eating Disorders, 3*(1), 3–14.

Sorensen, A. B., Weinert, F. E., & Sherrod, L. R. (Eds.). (1986). *Human development and the life course: Multidisciplinary perspectives.* Hillsdale, NJ: Erlbaum.

Sosna, M. (1982, November 5). *More important than the Civil War? The social impact of World War*

II on the South. Paper presented at the Southern Historical Association meetings, Memphis, TN.

Spencer, E. (1983). *The Spencers of Amberson Avenue: A turn-of-the-century memoir*. Pittsburgh: University of Pittsburgh Press.

Spenner, K. I. (1988). Occupations, work settings and the course of adult development: Tracing the implications of select historical changes. In P. B. Baltes, D. L. Featherman, & R. M. Lerner (Eds.), *Life-span development and behavior* (Vol. 9, pp. 243–285). Hillsdale, NJ: Erlbaum.

Spenner, K. I., & Featherman, D. L. (1978). Achievement ambitions. *Annual Review of Sociology, 4*, 373–420.

Spock, B. M. (1946). *The common sense book of baby and child care*. New York: Duell, Sloane & Pearce.

Stattin, D., Magnusson, D., & Reichel, H. (1989). Criminal activity at different ages: A study based on a Swedish longitudinal research population. *British Journal of Criminology, 29*, 368–385.

Stearns, C. Z., & Stearns, P. N. (1986). *Anger: The struggle for emotional control in America's history*. Chicago: University of Chicago Press.

Stearns, P. N. (1975). *Lives of labor: Working in a maturing industrial society*. New York: Holmes & Meier.

Stedman, L. C., & Kaestle, C. F. (1987). Literacy and reading performance in the United States, from 1880 to the present. *Reading Research Quarterly, 22*, 8–46.

Stevenson, H. W., & Azuma, H. (1983). IQ in Japan and the United States. *Nature, 306*, 291–292.

Stolz, L. H. M., & Dowley, E. M., Chance, E., Stevenson, N. G., Faust, M. S., Johnson, L. C., Faust, W. L., Engvall, A., Ullmann, L., Ryder, J. M., & Gowin, D. B. (1954). *Father relations of war-born children: The effect of postwar adjustment of father on the behavior and personality of first children born while the fathers were at war*. Stanford, CA: Stanford University Press.

Stone, G. P. (1971). The play of little children. In R. E. Herron & B. Sutton-Smith (Eds.), *Child's play* (pp. 4–17). New York: Wiley.

Stone, L. (1977). *Family, sex and marriage in England, 1500–1800*. New York: Harper & Row.

Stouffer, S. A., Lumsdaine, A. A., Lumsdaine, M. H., Williams, R. M., Jr., Smith, M. B., Janis, I. L., Star, S. A., & Cottrell, L. S., Jr. (1949). *The American soldier: Combat and its aftermath* (Vol. 2). Studies in social psychology in World War II. Princeton, NJ: Princeton University Press.

Striegel-Moore, R. H., & Kearney-Cooke, A. (1991). *Exploring the determinants and consequences of parents' attitudes about their children's physical appearance*. Manuscript submitted for publication. (Department of Psychology, Wesleyan University, Middletown, CT.)

Striegel-Moore, R. H., Silberstein, L. R., & Rodin, J. (1986). Toward an understanding of risk factors in bulimia. *American Psychologist, 41*, 246–258.

Strober, M. (1980). Personality and symptomatological features in young, nonchronic anorexia nervosa patients. *Journal of Psychosomatic Research, 24*, 353–359.

(1985). Personality factors in anorexia nervosa. *Pediatrician, 12*, 134–138.

Strober, M., & Humphrey, L. L. (1987). Familial contributions to the etiology and course of anorexia nervosa and bulimia. *Journal of Consulting and Clinical Psychology, 55*, 654–659.

Stroud, J. B., & Lindquist, E. F. (1942). Sex differences in achievement in the elementary and secondary schools. *Journal of Educational Psychology, 33*, 657–667.

Strutt, J. (1801). *Glig-gamena angel-deod; or, the sports and pastimes of the people of England . . . from the earliest period to the present time*. London: J. White.

Sullivan, M. (1927). *Our times: The United States, 1900–1925*. Vol. 2. *America finding herself*. New York: Scribner's.

Sulloway, F. J. (1978). *Freud, biologist of the mind: Beyond the psychoanalytic legend*. New York: Basic Books.

Sutton-Smith, B. (1959a). A formal analysis of game meaning. *Western Folklore, 18*, 13–24.

(1959b). *The games of New Zealand children*. Berkeley: University of California Press.

(1972). *The folkgames of children.* Austin: University of Texas Press for the American Folklore Society.

(1981). *A history of children's play: New Zealand, 1840–1950.* Philadelphia: University of Pennsylvania Press.

(1982). A performance theory of peer relations. In K. M. Borman (Ed.), *The social life of children in a changing society* (pp. 65–77). Hillsdale, NJ: Erlbaum; Norwood, NJ: Ablex.

(1986). *Toys as culture.* New York: Gardner Press.

Taeuber, C. F. (1946). Wartime population changes in the United States. *Milbank Memorial Fund Quarterly, 24,* 235–250.

Taeuber, C. F., & Taeuber, I. B. (1971). *People of the United States in the 20th century.* (A Census monograph; prepared in cooperation with the Social Research Council.) Washington, DC: U.S. Department of Commerce, Bureau of the Census.

Taeuber, I. B. (1965). *Population trends in the United States, 1900–60* (U.S. Bureau of the Census, Tech. Paper No. 10). Suitland, MD: U.S. Department of Commerce, Bureau of the Census.

Tanner, J. M. (1962). *Growth at adolescence, with a general consideration of the effects of heredity and environmental factors upon growth and maturation from birth to maturity* (2nd ed.). Oxford, England: Blackwell Scientific Publications.

(1966). Galtonian eugenics and the study of growth. The relation of body size, intelligence test score, and social circumstances in children and adults. *The Eugenics Review, 58,* 122–135.

(1970). Physical growth. In P. H. Mussen (Ed.), *Carmichael's manual of child psychology* (Vol. 1, 77–155). (3rd ed.). New York: Wiley.

(1979). A concise history of growth studies from Buffon to Boas. In F. Falkner & J. M. Tanner (Eds.), *Human growth.* Vol. 3. *Neurobiology and nutrition* (pp. 515–593). New York: Plenum Press.

(1982). The potential of auxological data for monitoring economic and social well-being. *Social Science History, 6,* 571–581.

Taylor, K. W. (1942). Shall they marry in wartime? *Journal of Home Economics, 34,* 213–219.

Teitelbaum, M. S., & Winter, J. M. (1985). *The fear of population decline.* Orlando, FL: Academic Press.

Tenenbaum, S. (1945). The fate of wartime marriages. *American Mercury, 61,* 530–536.

Terman, L. M., with the assistance of others. (1925). *Genetic studies of genius.* Vol. 1. *Mental and physical traits of a thousand gifted children.* [Stanford, CA]: Stanford University Press.

Thomas, A., Chess, S., Birch, H. G., Hertzig, M. E., & Korn, S. (1963). *Behavioral individuality in early childhood.* New York: New York University Press.

Thomas, W. I. (1909). *Source book for social origins: Ethnological materials, psychological standpoint, classified and annotated bibliographies for the interpretation of savage society* (5th ed.). Boston: Badger.

Thomas, W. I., & Znaniecki, F. (1918–20). *The Polish peasant in Europe and America.* Boston: R. G. Badger, Gorham Press.

Thompson, E. P. (1963). *The making of the English working class.* New York: Pantheon.

Thompson, T. (1981). *Edwardian childhoods.* London: Routledge & Kegan Paul.

Thorndike, R. L., & Gallup, G. H. (1944). Verbal intelligence of the American adult. *The Journal of General Psychology, 30,* 75–85.

Tilly, C. (1987). Family history, social history and social change. *Journal of Family History, 12,* 319–330.

Toews, J. E. (1987). Intellectual history after the linguistic turn: The autonomy of meaning and the irreducibility of experience. *American Historical Review, 92,* 879–907.

Toombs, A. (1944, April). War babies. *Woman's Home Companion, 71,* 32.

Trumbach, R. (1978). *The rise of the egalitarian family: Aristocratic kinship and domestic relations in eighteenth-century England.* New York: Academic Press.

Truxal, A. G., & Merrill, F. E. (1947). *The family in American culture*. New York: Prentice-Hall.

Tuddenham, R. D. (1948). Soldier intelligence in World Wars I and II. *The American Psychologist, 3*, 54–56.

Turner, J. A. (1989, February 15). In math ability, differences between sexes disappearing. *Chronicle of Higher Education, 35*(23), A10.

Turner, R. H. (1960). Sponsored and contest mobility and the school system. *American Sociological Review, 25*, 855–867.

Turner, V. W. (1977). Process, system, and symbol: A new anthropological synthesis. *Daedalus, 106*(3), 61–80.

Turner, V. W., & Bruner, E. M. (Eds.). (1986). *The anthropology of experience*. Urbana: University of Illinois Press.

Tuttle, W. M., Jr. (in press). *Their war, too: America's homefront children during the Second World War*. New York: Oxford University Press.

U.S. Bureau of Economic Analysis. (1973). *Long-term economic growth, 1860–1970*. Washington, DC: U.S. Department of Commerce, Bureau of Economic Analysis.

U.S. Bureau of the Census. (1943). *Sixteenth census of the United States: 1940. Population*. Vol. 4. *Characteristics by age, marital status, relationship, education, and citizenship*. Pt. 1. *United States summary*. Washington, DC: U.S. Government Printing Office.

(1975). *Historical statistics of the United States, colonial times to 1970* (2 parts). (Bicentennial ed.). Washington, DC: U.S. Department of Commerce, Bureau of the Census.

(1984). *1980 census of population*. Vol. 1. *Characteristics of the population*. Chapter D. *Detailed population characteristics*. Pt. 1. *U.S. Summary*. Sections A–C. Washington, DC: U.S. Department of Commerce, Bureau of the Census.

U.S. Department of the Interior, Bureau of Education. (1921). *Biennial survey of education, 1916–18* (Vol. 3; Bulletin, 1919, No. 90). Washington, DC: [U.S.] Government Printing Office.

U.S. Health Services and Mental Health Administration. (1970). *Height and weight of children in the United States, India, and the United Arab Republic*. Vital and Health Statistics Analytical Studies. (Series 3, No. 14). Rockville, MD: U.S. Department of Health, Education, and Welfare, Public Health Service, Health Services and Mental Health Administration.

U.S. National Center for Health Statistics. (1972). *Height and weight of children: Socioeconomic status. United States*. Data from the National Health Survey. (Series 11, No. 119; DHEW Publication [HSM] 73-1601). Rockville, MD: U.S. Department of Health, Education, and Welfare, Public Health Service, Health Resources Administration, National Center for Health Statistics.

U.S. National Center for Health Statistics, Vital and Health Statistics. (1973). *Intellectual development of youths as measured by a short form of the Wechsler Intelligence Scale. United States*. Data from the National Health Survey. (Series 11, No. 128; DHEW Publication No. [HRA] 74-1610). Rockville, MD: U.S. Department of Health, Education, and Welfare, Public Health Service, Health Resources Administration, National Center for Health Statistics.

(1977). *NCHS growth curves for children. Birth–18 years, United States*. Data from the National Health Survey. (Series 11, No. 165; DHEW Publication No. [HRA] 78-1650). Rockville, MD: U.S. Department of Health, Education, and Welfare, Public Health Service, Health Resources Administration, National Center for Health Statistics.

(1981). *Height and weight of adults ages 18–74 years by socioeconomic and geographic variables*. Data from the National Health Survey. (Series 11, No. 224; DHEW Publication No. [PHS] 78-1674). Rockville, MD: U.S. Department of Health, Education, and Welfare, Public Health Service, Health Resources Administration, National Center for Health Statistics.

Valsiner, J. (1987). *Culture and the development of children's action. A cultural-historical theory of developmental psychology*. New York: Wiley.

(1989). *Human development and culture: The social nature of personality and its study*. Lexington, MA: Lexington Books.

Vanek, M. (1981). Division of household work: A decade comparison – 1967–1977. *Home Economics Research Journal, 10,* 175–180.

Verdonik, F., & Sherrod, L. R. (1984). *An inventory of longitudinal research of childhood and adolescence.* New York: Social Science Research Council.

Veroff, J., Douvan, E., & Kulka, R. A. (1981). *The inner American: A self-portrait from 1957 to 1976.* New York: Basic Books.

Vinovskis, M. A. (1986). Young fathers and their children. Some historical and policy perspectives. In A. B. Elster & M. E. Lamb (Eds.), *Adolescent fatherhood* (pp. 171–192). Hillsdale, NJ: Erlbaum.

   (1988). The historian and the life course: Reflections on recent approaches to the study of American family life in the past. In P. B. Baltes, D. L. Featherman, & R. M. Lerner (Eds.), *Life-span development and behavior* (Vol. 8, pp. 33–59). Hillsdale, NJ: Erlbaum.

von Glascoe, C. A. (1980). The work of playing "Redlight." In H. B. Schwartzman (Ed.), *Play and culture. 1978 proceedings of the Asociation for the Anthropological Study of Play* (pp. 228–231). West Point, NY: Leisure Press.

Vygotsky, L. S. (1962). *Thought and language* (E. Hanfmann & G. Vakar, Eds. & Trans.). Cambridge, MA: MIT Press.

Waller, W. W. (1940). *War and the family.* New York: Dryden Press.

Walsh, M. R. (1987). *The psychology of women: Ongoing debates.* New Haven, CT: Yale University Press.

Wapner, S., Ciottone, R. A., Hornstein, G. A., McNeil, O. V., & Pacheco, A. M. (1983). An examination of studies of critical transitions through the life cycle. In S. Wapner & B. Kaplan (Eds.), *Toward a holistic developmental psychology* (pp. 111–132). Hillsdale, NJ: Erlbaum.

Wartofsky, M. (1983). The child's construction of the world and the world's construction of the child: From historical epistemology to historical psychology. In F. S. Kessel & A. W. Siegel (Eds.), *The child and other cultural inventions: Houston Symposium 4* (pp. 188–215). New York: Praeger.

Weiss, R. S. (1979). Growing up a little faster: The experience of growing up in a single-parent household. *Journal of Social Issues, 35*(4), 97–111.

Weitzman, L. J. (1985). *The divorce revolution: The unexpected social and economic consequences for women and children in America.* New York: Free Press; London: Collier Macmillan.

Wellman, H. M. (1988). First steps in the child's theorizing about the mind. In J. W. Astington, P. L. Harris, & D. R. Olson (Eds.), *Developing theories of mind* (pp. 64–92). Cambridge, England: Cambridge University Press.

Werner, H. (1948). *Comparative psychology of mental development* (rev. ed.). Chicago: Follett.

Whipple, G. M. (1927). Sex differences in intelligence-test scores in the elementary school. *Journal of Educational Research, 15,* 111–117.

White, S. H. (1980). Cognitive competence and performance in everyday environments. *Bulletin of the Orton Society, 30,* 29–45.

   (1991). Three visions of educational psychology. In L. Tolchinsky-Landsmann (Ed.), *Culture, schooling, and psychological development* (pp. 1–38). Norwood, NJ: Ablex.

White, S. H., & Buka, S. L. (1987). Early education: Programs, traditions, and policies. In E. Z. Rothkopf (Ed.), *Review of research in education* (Vol. 14, pp. 43–91). Washington, DC: American Educational Research Association.

White, S. H., & Siegel, A. W. (1984). Cognitive development in time and space. In B. Rogoff & J. Lave (Eds.), *Everyday cognition: Its development in social context* (pp. 238–277). Cambridge, MA: Harvard University Press.

Whiting, B. B. (1965). Sex identity conflict and physical violence: A comparative study. *American Anthropologist, 67*(6, Pt. 2), 123–140.

Whiting, B. B., & Edwards, C. P. (1973). A cross-cultural analysis of sex differences in the behavior of children three through 11. *Journal of Social Psychology, 91,* 171–188.

Whiting, B. B., & Whiting, J. W. M. (1975). *Children of six cultures: A psycho-cultural analysis.* Cambridge, MA: Harvard University Press.

Whiting, J. W. M. (1960). *Social structure and child rearing: a theory of identification.* Unpublished lectures presented at Tulane University as part of the Mona Bronsman Scheckman Lectures in Social Psychiatry, March, 1960.

Whiting, J. W. M., & Child, I. L. (1953). *Child training and personality: A cross-cultural study.* New York: Yale University Press.

Whiting, J. W. M., Child, I. L., & Lambert, W. W., Fischer, A. M., Fischer, J. L., Nydegger, C., Nydegger, W., Maretzki, T., Minturn, L., Romney, A. K., & Romney, R. (1966). *Six cultures series.* Vol. 1. *A field guide for the study of socialization.* New York: Wiley.

Williams, J. (1945). *Sixteenth census of the United States: 1940. Population. Education, educational attainment of children by rental value of home.* Washington, DC: U.S. Government Printing Office.

Williams, R. (1973). Base and superstructure in Marxist cultural theory. *New Left Review, 82,* 3–16. (1980). *Problems in materialism and culture: Selected essays.* London: Verso.

Williams, T. M., & Kornblum, W. (1985). *Growing up poor.* Lexington, MA: Lexington Books.

Williamson, J. G., & Lindert, P. H. (1980). *American inequality: A macroeconomic history.* New York: Academic Press.

Winner, E. (1982). *Invented worlds; The psychology of the arts.* Cambridge, MA: Harvard University Press.

Winter, J. M. (1985). The demographic consequences of the Second World War for Britain. In *Measuring socio-demographic change* (pp. 101–114). (University of Sussex, 9–11 September 1985 Conference Papers). London: Office of Population Censuses and Surveys.

Wishy, B. W. (1967). *The child and the Republic: The dawn of modern American child nurture.* Philadelphia: University of Pennsylvania Press.

Wolff, G. (1941). Further results on the trend of weight in white school children. *Child Development, 12,* 183–205.

Yager, J. (1982). Family issues in the pathogenesis of anorexia nervosa. *Psychosomatic Medicine, 44,* 43–60.

Zelizer, V. A. R. (1985). *Pricing the priceless child: The changing value of children.* New York: Basic Books.

Zuckerman, M. (1984). Myth and method: The current crisis in American historical writing. *The HIstory Teacher, 17,* 219–245.

Author index

277

Subject index

abstract thinking, 216
achievement
  developmentalist study of, 184
  laboratory studies of, 214–215
acquaintance ideals, 213–214
adolescent mothers, *see* teenage mothers
Adolescent Society, The (Coleman), 7–8
aesthetic development, 213
age factors
  in life transition impact, 20
  and World War II effects, 31–32
aggressive behavior
  developmentalist study of, 183–184, 186
  girls versus boys, 115
  television effect on, 186
  trends among girls, 117–120
anger, 201
anorexia nervosa, 131–146, 236–237
  and bulimia, 143–145
  contradictory cultural factors in, 236–237
  eating behavior in, 139–141
  and family dynamics, 135–139
  fathers in, 139
  hyperactivity in, 142–143
  language of presentation, 134–135
  obsessive-compulsive features, 141
  socioeconomic factors, 135–136
  symptomatology of, trends, 141–145
  trend in severity, 145
  two-stage conceptualization of, 131–132
  in Victorian period, 135–144
"anthropology of experience," 201
appetite, societal influences on, 139–140
aspirations, 184
assault, in girls, 118–119
attachment relationship
  developmentalist study of, 184
  and fathers, 158–159
  of latchkey children, 39–40
attitudes, and father's role, 165

baby boom
  and fathers, 149
  in World War II, 34–36
Berkeley cohort, 5, 47–72
  and the Great Depression, 14–17, 47–72
  Manchester cohort comparison, 71–72
  military service effect on, 50–72
  and problem behaviors, 19
  and turning point thesis, 54, 58–59
Best Years of Our Lives, The, 41
bingeing behavior, 144
biological constraints
  in child development, 218–219
  and fatherhood, 159, 165
birthrate
  father's role in determining, 148–149
  in World War II, 34–36
black children
  educational attainment of, trends, 87
  IQ differential, 98–102
body weight
  in anorexia nervosa, trends, 145
  trends in United States, 83–84
boys
  educational attainment of, trends, 85
  father absence effects on, 42–44, 152
  versus girls, problem behavior, 114–115,
    235
  height variation in, 91–92
  images of adulthood, 213–214
  IQ differential to girls, 95–98
  violent behavior of, trends, 117–119
British school system, 76–77
bulimia, 143–145; *see also* anorexia ner-
    vosa
"bureaucratic" family style, 198

California Boy Scout troop study, 205
Carolina Longitudinal Study, 115
case study approach, 217–218